T0344367

Technological Advancements in Data Processing for Next Generation Intelligent Systems

Shanu Sharma
ABES Engineering College, Ghaziabad, India

Ayushi Prakash
Ajay Kumar Garg Engineering College, Ghaziabad, India

Vijayan Sugumaran
Oakland University, Rochester, USA

A volume in the Advances in
Systems Analysis, Software
Engineering, and High Performance
Computing (ASASEHPC) Book Series

Published in the United States of America by
    IGI Global
    Engineering Science Reference (an imprint of IGI Global)
    701 E. Chocolate Avenue
    Hershey PA, USA 17033
    Tel: 717-533-8845
    Fax: 717-533-8661
    E-mail: cust@igi-global.com
    Web site: http://www.igi-global.com

Library of Congress Cataloging-in-Publication Data

Names: Sharma, Shanu, 1985- editor. | Prakash, Ayushi, 1987- editor. |
  Sugumaran, Vijayan, 1960- editor.
Title: Technological advancements in data processing for next generation
  intelligent systems / edited by: Shanu Sharma, Ayushi Prakash, Vijayan
  Sugumaran.
Description: Hershey PA : Engineering Science Reference, [2024] | Includes
  bibliographical references. | Summary: "With a focus on the development
  of more efficient next-generation intelligent systems, this book is
  intended to provide a comprehensive overview of novel technologies such
  as Quantum Computing, Edge Computing, Federated Learning, Memory based
  computing, etc"-- Provided by publisher.
Identifiers: LCCN 2023048621 (print) | LCCN 2023048622 (ebook) | ISBN
  9798369309681 (hardcover) | ISBN 9798369309698 (ebook)
Subjects: LCSH: Artificial intelligence--Industrial applications.
Classification: LCC TA347.A78 T43 2024 (print) | LCC TA347.A78 (ebook) |
  DDC 006.3--dc23/eng/20240402
LC record available at https://lccn.loc.gov/2023048621
LC ebook record available at https://lccn.loc.gov/2023048622

This book is published in the IGI Global book series Advances in Systems Analysis, Software Engineering, and High Performance Computing (ASASEHPC) (ISSN: 2327-3453; eISSN: 2327-3461)

British Cataloguing in Publication Data
A Cataloguing in Publication record for this book is available from the British Library.
All work contributed to this book is new, previously-unpublished material.
The views expressed in this book are those of the authors, but not necessarily of the publisher.
For electronic access to this publication, please contact: eresources@igi-global.com.

Advances in Systems Analysis, Software Engineering, and High Performance Computing (ASASEHPC) Book Series

ISSN:2327-3453
EISSN:2327-3461

Editor-in-Chief: Vijayan Sugumaran, Oakland University, USA

MISSION

The theory and practice of computing applications and distributed systems has emerged as one of the key areas of research driving innovations in business, engineering, and science. The fields of software engineering, systems analysis, and high performance computing offer a wide range of applications and solutions in solving computational problems for any modern organization.

The **Advances in Systems Analysis, Software Engineering, and High Performance Computing (ASASEHPC) Book Series** brings together research in the areas of distributed computing, systems and software engineering, high performance computing, and service science. This collection of publications is useful for academics, researchers, and practitioners seeking the latest practices and knowledge in this field.

COVERAGE

- Metadata and Semantic Web
- Performance Modelling
- Enterprise Information Systems
- Distributed Cloud Computing
- Network Management
- Storage Systems
- Virtual Data Systems
- Computer System Analysis
- Engineering Environments
- Computer Networking

IGI Global is currently accepting manuscripts for publication within this series. To submit a proposal for a volume in this series, please contact our Acquisition Editors at Acquisitions@igi-global.com or visit: http://www.igi-global.com/publish/.

Titles in this Series

For a list of additional titles in this series, please visit:
http://www.igi-global.com/book-series/advances-systems-analysis-software-engineering/73689

Advanced Applications in Osmotic Computing
G. Revathy (SASTRA University, India)
Engineering Science Reference • © 2024 • 370pp • H/C (ISBN: 9798369316948) • US $300.00

Omnichannel Approach to Co-Creating Customer Experiences Through Metaverse Platforms
Babita Singla (Chitkara Business School, Chitkara University, Punjab, India) Kumar Shalender (Chitkara Business School, Chitkara University, India) and Nripendra Singh (Pennsylvania Western University, USA)
Engineering Science Reference • © 2024 • 223pp • H/C (ISBN: 9798369318669) • US $270.00

Uncertain Spatiotemporal Data Management for the Semantic Web
Luyi Bai (Northeastern University, China) and Lin Zhu (Northeastern University, China)
Engineering Science Reference • © 2024 • 518pp • H/C (ISBN: 9781668491089) • US $325.00

Bio-Inspired Optimization Techniques in Blockchain Systems
U. Vignesh (Vellore Institute of Technology, Chennai, India) Manikandan M. (Manipal Institute of Technology, India) and Ruchi Doshi (Universidad Azteca, Mexico)
Engineering Science Reference • © 2024 • 288pp • H/C (ISBN: 9798369311318) • US $300.00

Enhancing Performance, Efficiency, and Security Through Complex Systems Control
Idriss Chana (ESTM, Moulay Ismail University of Meknès, Morocco) Aziz Bouazi (ESTM, Moulay Ismail University of Meknès, Morocco) and Hussain Ben-azza (ENSAM, Moulay Ismail University of Meknes, Morocco)
Engineering Science Reference • © 2024 • 371pp • H/C (ISBN: 9798369304976) • US $300.00

701 East Chocolate Avenue, Hershey, PA 17033, USA
Tel: 717-533-8845 x100 • Fax: 717-533-8661
E-Mail: cust@igi-global.com • www.igi-global.com

Table of Contents

Foreword xvii

Preface xix

Acknowledgment xxiii

Chapter 1
Cloud Computing for IoT Sensing Data 1
Deepansh Kumar, ABES Engineering College, Ghaziabad, India
Himanshu Sharma, ABES Engineering College, Ghaziabad, India
Ayushi Prakash, Ajay Kumar Garg Engineering College, India
Mohammad Husain, Islamic University of Madinah, Saudi Arabia

Chapter 2
Comprehensive Analysis of Attacks and Defenses in IoT Sensory Big Data
Analysis 24
Mohammad Ishrat, Koneru Lakshmaiah Education Foundation, India
Wasim Khan, Koneru Lakshmaiah Education Foundation, India
Faheem Ahmad, University of Technology and Applied Science, Al
*   Musanna, Oman*
Monia Mohammed Al Farsi, University of Technology and Applied
*   Science, Al Musanna, Oman*
Shafiqul Abidin, Department of Computer Science, Aligarh Muslim
*   University, India*

Chapter 3
Elevating IoT Sensor Data Management and Security Through Blockchain
Solutions 58
Neha Bhati, AVN Innovations, India
Narayan Vyas, Chandigarh University, India

Chapter 4

Unveiling the Depths of Explainable AI: A Comprehensive Review 78
    Wasim Khan, Koneru Lakshmaiah Education Foundation, India
    Mohammad Ishrat, Koneru Lakshmaiah Education Foundation, India

Chapter 5

Convergence of Artificial Intelligence and Self-Sustainability: Ethical
Considerations and Social Implications 107
    R. Pitchai, Department of Computer Science and Engineering, B.V. Raju
        Institute of Technology, India
    Shiv Kant Tiwari, Institute of Business Management, GLA University,
        India
    R. Krishna Kumari, College of Engineering and Technology, SRM
        Institute of Science and Technology, India
    K. Janaki, Department of Mathematics, Saveetha Engineering College,
        India
    Pramoda Patro, Department of Mathematics, Koneru Lakshmaiah
        Education Foundation, India
    S. Murugan, Nana College of Technology, India

Chapter 6

Integration of Precision Agriculture Technology, IoT Sensors, and System
Efficiency for Sustainable Farming Practices 141
    M. Maravarman, Department of Computer Science Engineering, B.V.
        Raju Institute of Technology, India
    Shahana Gajala Qureshi, Department of Cyber Security and Digital
        Forensics, School of Computing Science and Engineering (SCSE),
        VIT Bhopal University, India
    V. Krishnamoorthy, Department of Management Studies, Kongu
        Engineering College, India
    Gurpreet Singh, Department of Computer Science and Engineering,
        Punjab Institute of Technology, Rajpura (MRSPTU Bathinda), India
    Sreekanth Rallapalli, Department of Master of Computer Application,
        Nitte Meenakshi Institute of Technology, India
    S. B. Boopa, KS Institute of Technology, India

Chapter 7

Quantum Computing-Powered Agricultural Transformation: Optimizing
Performance in Farming 169
    Premendra J. Bansod, Department of Mechanical Engineering, G.H.
        Raisoni College of Engineering and Management, India
    R. Usharani, Department of Computational Intelligence, Faculty of

Engineering and Technology, School of Computing, School of Computing, SRM Institute of Science and Technology, India
A. *Sheryl Oliver, Department of Computational Intelligence, Faculty of Engineering and Technology, School of Computing, SRM Institute of Science and Technology, India*
S. J. *Suji Prasad, Department of Electronics and Instrumentation Engineering, Kongu Engineering College, Erode, India*
Durgesh M. Sharma, Shri Ramdeobaba College of Engineering and Management, India
Sureshkumar Myilsamy, Department of Mechanical Engineering, Bannari Amman Institute of Technology, India

Chapter 8
Fog Computing-Integrated ML-Based Framework and Solutions for
Intelligent Systems: Digital Healthcare Applications 196
R. *Pitchai, Department of Computer Science and Engineering, B.V. Raju Institute of Technology, India*
K. *Venkatesh Guru, Department of Computer Science and Engineering, KSR College of Engineering, India*
J. *Nirmala Gandhi, Department of Computer Science and Engineering, KSR College of Engineering, India*
C. R. *Komala, Department of Information Science and Engineering, HKBK College of Engineering, India*
J. R. *Dinesh Kumar, Department of Electronics and Communication Engineering, Sri Krishna College of Engineering and Technology, India*
Sampath Boopathi, Mechanical Engineering, Muthayammal Engineering College, India

Chapter 9
Artificial Intelligence (AI) and Machine Learning (ML) Technology-Driven
Structural Systems 225
Akash Mohanty, School of Mechanical Engineering, Vellore Institute of Technology, India
G. S. *Raghavendra, Department of Computer Science and Engineering, Koneru Lakshmaiah Education Foundation, India*
J. *Rajini, Department of English, Kongu Engineering College, India*
B. *Sachuthananthan, Department Mechanical Engineering, Sree Vidyanikethan Engineering College, India*
E. *Afreen Banu, Department of Computing Technologies, Saveetha School of Engineering, Saveetha Institute of Medical and Technical Sciences (SIMATS), India*
B. *Subhi, MEC Engineering College (Autonomous), India*

Chapter 10

Additive Manufacturing and 3D Printing Innovations: Revolutionizing
Industry 5.0 255
    M. D. Mohan Gift, Department of Mechanical Engineering, Panimalar
        Engineering College, India
    T. S. Senthil, Department of Marine Engineering, Noorul Islam Centre
        for Higher Education, India
    Dler Salih Hasan, Department of Computer Science and Information
        Technology, College of Science, University of Salahaddin, Iraq
    K. Alagarraja, Department of Mechanical Engineering, New Prince
        Shri Bhavani College of Engineering and Technology, India
    P. Jayaseelan, Department of Mechanical Engineering, Achariya
        College of Engineering and Technology, India
    Sampath Boopathi, Mechanical Engineering, Muthammal Engineering
        College, India

Chapter 11

Smart Grid Fault Detection and Classification Framework Utilizing AIoT in
India 288
    Sandhya Avasthi, ABES Engineering College, Ghaziabad, India
    Tanushree Sanwal, KIET Group of Institutions, Delhi, India
    Shikha Verma, ABES Engineering College, Ghaziabad, India

Compilation of References 309

About the Contributors 350

Index 355

Detailed Table of Contents

Foreword xvii

Preface xix

Acknowledgment xxiii

Chapter 1
Cloud Computing for IoT Sensing Data 1

Deepansh Kumar, ABES Engineering College, Ghaziabad, India
Himanshu Sharma, ABES Engineering College, Ghaziabad, India
Ayushi Prakash, Ajay Kumar Garg Engineering College, India
Mohammad Husain, Islamic University of Madinah, Saudi Arabia

The integration of sensor cloud technology has emerged as a revolutionary force across numerous sectors in the ever-evolving field of intelligent technologies. Born out of the confluence of cloud-based technologies with internet of things (IoT), sensor clouds provide a flexible and scalable framework for a variety of applications, including environmental monitoring, healthcare, and agriculture. This chapter aims to provide a thorough examination of sensor cloud technology, elucidating its potential, drawbacks, and many applications. It delves into the complexities of IoT sensor data and highlights the vital significance that effective processing methods play. In managing the complexity and variety inherent in IoT sensor data, it emphasises the value of techniques like data fusion, denoising, data aggregation, etc. The specifics of certain sensor cloud applications, including iDigi, Xively, Nimbits, ThingSpeak, and healthcare monitoring systems are then explored. The chapter ends by emphasizing how innovation and technological advancements are essential to overcoming these obstacles.

Chapter 2
Comprehensive Analysis of Attacks and Defenses in IoT Sensory Big Data
Analysis..24

    Mohammad Ishrat, Koneru Lakshmaiah Education Foundation, India
    Wasim Khan, Koneru Lakshmaiah Education Foundation, India
    Faheem Ahmad, University of Technology and Applied Science, Al
        Musanna, Oman
    Monia Mohammed Al Farsi, University of Technology and Applied
        Science, Al Musanna, Oman
    Shafiqul Abidin, Department of Computer Science, Aligarh Muslim
        University, India

This chapter takes a deep dive into the security issues surrounding IoT sensory big data analysis, which is becoming increasingly important in today's world of ubiquitous connectivity and big data analysis. Starting with an introduction to this crucial juncture, the chapter proceeds to guide the reader through the complex terrain of IoT systems, with a focus on the far-reaching consequences of security precautions. From simple denial of service (DoS) attacks to complex man-in-the-middle (MitM) incursions, data manipulation, injection exploits, and unauthorised access are all under the microscope. Readers will obtain a sophisticated understanding of the many methods used by bad actors to exploit vulnerabilities in IoT systems as they are systematically explored. In addition, the chapter details a wide variety of defence measures, providing a versatile toolkit for shoring up IoT ecosystems. Intrusion detection systems (IDS), secure communication protocols, secure boot procedures, and strong data encryption are all part of these multi-layered plans of action.

Chapter 3
Elevating IoT Sensor Data Management and Security Through Blockchain
Solutions 58

    Neha Bhati, AVN Innovations, India
    Narayan Vyas, Chandigarh University, India

The internet of things, security, and blockchain all come together to deal with the influx of sensor data. The autonomous vehicle industry, for example, relies heavily on effective data management. IoT applications in supply chains, healthcare, and smart cities can all benefit from the immutability, decentralization, and transparency offered by blockchain technology. The research gives recommendations for optimizing blockchain integration and managing scalability concerns. The methodology is supported by real-world case studies, which highlight the potential of blockchain technology to improve efficiency and security in dynamic environments.

Chapter 4

Unveiling the Depths of Explainable AI: A Comprehensive Review 78

Wasim Khan, Koneru Lakshmaiah Education Foundation, India
Mohammad Ishrat, Koneru Lakshmaiah Education Foundation, India

Explainable AI (XAI) has become increasingly important in the fast-evolving field of AI and ML. The complexity and obscurity of AI, especially in the context of deep learning, provide unique issues that are explored in this chapter. While deep learning has shown impressive performance, it has been criticised for its opaque reasoning. The fundamental motivation behind this research was to compile a comprehensive and cutting-edge survey of XAI methods applicable to a wide variety of fields. This review is achieved through a meticulous examination and analysis of the various methodologies and techniques employed in XAI, along with their ramifications within specific application contexts. In addition to highlighting the existing state of XAI, the authors recognize the imperative for continuous advancement by delving into a meticulous examination of the limitations inherent in current methods. Furthermore, they offer a succinct glimpse into the future trajectory of XAI research, emphasizing emerging avenues and promising directions poised for significant progress.

Chapter 5

Convergence of Artificial Intelligence and Self-Sustainability: Ethical Considerations and Social Implications 107

R. Pitchai, Department of Computer Science and Engineering, B.V. Raju Institute of Technology, India
Shiv Kant Tiwari, Institute of Business Management, GLA University, India
R. Krishna Kumari, College of Engineering and Technology, SRM Institute of Science and Technology, India
K. Janaki, Department of Mathematics, Saveetha Engineering College, India
Pramoda Patro, Department of Mathematics, Koneru Lakshmaiah Education Foundation, India
S. Murugan, Nana College of Technology, India

This chapter explores the convergence of artificial intelligence (AI) and self-sustainability while emphasizing the ethical considerations and social implications inherent in this dynamic intersection. It examines the intricate balance between technological progress and ecological responsibility, the need for equitable access to AI-powered sustainability solutions, and the profound impact of AI automation on traditional industries. The chapter also addresses the importance of reskilling and upskilling for sustainable employment, outlines policies and strategies for a just transition, and delves into responsible AI development and governance. Furthermore, it underscores the significance of inclusivity and stakeholder engagement in shaping AI and sustainability policies that prioritize fairness, equity, and the well-being of all.

Chapter 6
Integration of Precision Agriculture Technology, IoT Sensors, and System Efficiency for Sustainable Farming Practices 141

M. Maravarman, Department of Computer Science Engineering, B.V. Raju Institute of Technology, India
Shahana Gajala Qureshi, Department of Cyber Security and Digital Forensics, School of Computing Science and Engineering (SCSE), VIT Bhopal University, India
V. Krishnamoorthy, Department of Management Studies, Kongu Engineering College, India
Gurpreet Singh, Department of Computer Science and Engineering, Punjab Institute of Technology, Rajpura (MRSPTU Bathinda), India
Sreekanth Rallapalli, Department of Master of Computer Application, Nitte Meenakshi Institute of Technology, India
S. B. Boopa, KS Institute of Technology, India

The chapter explores the transformative impact of precision agricultural technology, focusing on the integration of IoT sensors, GPS technology, and automated systems in farming practices. It introduces the concept, traces its history, and explores its role in agriculture. The chapter discusses IoT sensors, GPS technology, drones, and automated machinery in precision planting, crop monitoring, and operational efficiency. It also discusses resource optimization in precision agriculture, including efficient water management, targeted fertilizer application, and pest control. The chapter addresses technological challenges, adoption challenges, and emerging trends. It concludes with a comprehensive examination of regulatory and ethical considerations, including data privacy, security, and ethical dimensions. The chapter emphasizes the need for collaboration among farmers, technology developers, policymakers, and regulatory bodies to ensure sustainable, efficient, and equitable farming.

Chapter 7

Quantum Computing-Powered Agricultural Transformation: Optimizing
Performance in Farming 169

*Premendra J. Bansod, Department of Mechanical Engineering, G.H.
Raisoni College of Engineering and Management, India*

*R. Usharani, Department of Computational Intelligence, Faculty of
Engineering and Technology, School of Computing, School of
Computing, SRM Institute of Science and Technology, India*

*A. Sheryl Oliver, Department of Computational Intelligence, Faculty of
Engineering and Technology, School of Computing, SRM Institute of
Science and Technology, India*

*S. J. Suji Prasad, Department of Electronics and Instrumentation
Engineering, Kongu Engineering College, Erode, India*

*Durgesh M. Sharma, Shri Ramdeobaba College of Engineering and
Management, India*

*Sureshkumar Myilsamy, Department of Mechanical Engineering,
Bannari Amman Institute of Technology, India*

This chapter explores the potential of quantum computing in agriculture, highlighting its potential to enhance efficiency, sustainability, and environmental stewardship. Quantum computing can process vast datasets, simulate complex systems, and optimize resource allocation. Applications include crop optimization, weather modeling, and precision agriculture. Case studies show quantum-assisted solutions for crop yield prediction, pest and disease management, and soil analysis, demonstrating the benefits of quantum computing in real-world agricultural scenarios. The integration of quantum computing in agriculture faces challenges such as technology accessibility, data management, energy consumption, and privacy concerns. However, the fusion of quantum technology and agriculture holds potential for global food security, environmental sustainability, and resource-efficient farming.

Chapter 8

Fog Computing-Integrated ML-Based Framework and Solutions for
Intelligent Systems: Digital Healthcare Applications 196

    *R. Pitchai, Department of Computer Science and Engineering, B.V. Raju
        Institute of Technology, India*

    *K. Venkatesh Guru, Department of Computer Science and Engineering,
        KSR College of Engineering, India*

    *J. Nirmala Gandhi, Department of Computer Science and Engineering,
        KSR College of Engineering, India*

    *C. R. Komala, Department of Information Science and Engineering,
        HKBK College of Engineering, India*

    *J. R. Dinesh Kumar, Department of Electronics and Communication
        Engineering, Sri Krishna College of Engineering and Technology,
        India*

    *Sampath Boopathi, Mechanical Engineering, Muthayammal
        Engineering College, India*

The integration of fog computing and machine learning (ML) in digital healthcare has revolutionized patient care, operations, and personalized treatment. This chapter explores the potential of fog computing in telemedicine, remote monitoring, and personalized treatment. It highlights its role in addressing data processing challenges, enabling real-time data analytics, and ensuring secure transmission of medical information. Key case studies demonstrate how these integrated solutions are driving innovation in the healthcare industry. The combination of fog computing and ML offers a promising avenue for the future of digital healthcare, focusing on data-driven decision-making and precision medicine.

Chapter 9

Artificial Intelligence (AI) and Machine Learning (ML) Technology-Driven
Structural Systems 225

    *Akash Mohanty, School of Mechanical Engineering, Vellore Institute of
        Technology, India*

    *G. S. Raghavendra, Department of Computer Science and Engineering,
        Koneru Lakshmaiah Education Foundation, India*

    J. Rajini, Department of English, Kongu Engineering College, India

    *B. Suchuthananthan, Department Mechanical Engineering, Sree
        Vidyanikethan Engineering College, India*

    *E. Afreen Banu, Department of Computing Technologies, Saveetha
        School of Engineering, Saveetha Institute of Medical and Technical
        Sciences (SIMATS), India*

    B. Subhi, MEC Engineering College (Autonomous), India

This chapter explores the integration of artificial intelligence (AI) and machine learning (ML) technologies in structural engineering, focusing on their applications in automating design processes, optimizing structural configurations, and assessing performance metrics. It highlights the efficiency of AI-driven algorithms in generating design alternatives, predicting structural behavior, and enhancing sustainability. The chapter also provides a performance comparison framework for evaluating different structural designs, considering safety, cost-effectiveness, and environmental impact. It discusses case studies and practical examples that demonstrate the advantages of AI/ML-driven autonomous design in achieving superior structural performance while minimizing resource utilization. The chapter emphasizes the potential of AI and ML in revolutionizing structural engineering, enabling engineers to create sustainable and high-performing structures, contributing to a more environmentally conscious and economically viable built environment.

Chapter 10

Additive Manufacturing and 3D Printing Innovations: Revolutionizing
Industry 5.0 255

    M. D. Mohan Gift, Department of Mechanical Engineering, Panimalar Engineering College, India

    T. S. Senthil, Department of Marine Engineering, Noorul Islam Centre for Higher Education, India

    Dler Salih Hasan, Department of Computer Science and Information Technology, College of Science, University of Salahaddin, Iraq

    K. Alagarraja, Department of Mechanical Engineering, New Prince Shri Bhavani College of Engineering and Technology, India

    P. Jayaseelan, Department of Mechanical Engineering, Achariya College of Engineering and Technology, India

    Sampath Boopathi, Mechanical Engineering, Muthammal Engineering College, India

Additive manufacturing (AM), commonly known as 3D printing, has emerged as a transformative technology with profound implications for multiple industries. The convergence of AM with Industry 4.0 principles and advanced technologies has given rise to Industry 5.0, a new era of manufacturing characterized by enhanced integration and digitalization. This chapter explores the dynamic landscape of AM within the context of Industry 5.0, highlighting research trends, innovations, and challenges. Key developments include materials advancements, multi-material printing, digital twins, bioprinting, AI-driven design, and sustainability initiatives. Industry 5.0's impact is felt globally, with applications spanning aerospace, healthcare, fashion, and beyond. Collaboration between academia and industry, regulatory frameworks, and the pursuit of sustainable practices are driving forces shaping the future of AM in Industry 5.0.

Chapter 11
Smart Grid Fault Detection and Classification Framework Utilizing AIoT in
India 288
    Sandhya Avasthi, ABES Engineering College, Ghaziabad, India
    Tanushree Sanwal, KIET Group of Institutions, Delhi, India
    Shikha Verma, ABES Engineering College, Ghaziabad, India

The energy sector is facing obstacles such as increased consumption, efficiency, and losses affecting mainly developing countries. One of the major challenges is unauthorized power connections due to which a significant portion of consumed energy is not billed, causing business loss. The misuse of energy indirectly increases the amount of CO_2 emissions because unauthorized users utilize energy irresponsibly. As the third-largest producer and consumer of electricity in the world, India is facing a variety of power-related issues such as distribution losses, electricity fraud, and environmental issues. The artificial internet of things (AIoT) is proving beneficial in energy use optimization, fault detection, and identification. The technological issues and solutions are discussed for fault detection and classification in a smart grid. A case study is provided as a first step towards automated fault detection in smart grids. This chapter aims to identify factors that could assist India in developing its smart infrastructure and evaluate the numerous components of the smart grid.

Compilation of References 309

About the Contributors 350

Index... 355

Foreword

Few years ago, the subject matter of this book, *Technological Advancements in Data Processing for Next Generation Intelligent Systems*, would have been unimaginable. In the framework of the digital transformation era, *Technological Advancements in Data Processing for Next Generation Intelligent Systems* offers a thorough examination of state-of-the-art data processing technologies that propel the creation of next-generation intelligent systems. This extensive book explores the importance of data as a resource for businesses or industry in a variety of sectors and how recent advancements in technology have made it possible to handle enormous amounts of data and conduct real-time analysis.

The idea that one day in-memory computing, AI/ML algorithms, and big data frameworks would revolutionize data processing capabilities and enable the development of intelligent systems that foster creativity, optimize workflows, and deliver personalized experiences would have seemed unthinkable. Nearly every other profession in the twenty-first century depends on these services; priorities include real-time analysis, speedier decision-making, enhanced privacy, and efficient management of large volumes of data. Future trends are analyzed with the aim of achieving ubiquitous and fine-grained intelligence through data sensing using optimized data processing techniques.

This book addresses a need that has emerged at the right time. This book will be very helpful to researchers, academicians, and industry professionals who are interested in developing intelligent systems and intelligent data processing techniques in the future.

Anybody working in this quickly evolving field will find the book to be extremely helpful. The book will also be an excellent text for more specialized graduate or upper undergraduate courses, and it will be a great read for practitioners. Many applaud to the editors and authors for their vision in recognizing the potential of this field and for compiling such an impactful collection. Still, there's a lot of work to be done, as the field is still young. Furthermore, a novice would still find it difficult to navigate the multitude of software options and standards, even with the abundance of technologies available to support various aspects of services. However, we believe that a significant portion of these issues will be resolved shortly.

Mohammad Israr
Maryam Abacha American University of Nigeria, Nigeria

Preface

In the era of digital transformation and rapid technological advancements, data has become a vital asset for organizations across various industries. Technological advancements in data processing have paved the way for next-generation intelligent systems capable of handling massive volumes of data, processing it in real-time, and deriving valuable insights.

In the present era, novel technologies such as Artificial Intelligence, Edge Computing, Federated Learning, Quantum Computing, etc., have unlocked the potential to process continuously generated large volumes of information. The integration of big data frameworks, real-time processing, in-memory computing, AI/ML algorithms, and edge computing has revolutionized data processing capabilities, enabling organizations to build intelligent systems that drive innovation, optimize operations, and deliver personalized experiences. The main objective of combining these technologies is to maximize the computing power of the devices for implementing intelligent decisions to bring autonomy. As technology continues to evolve, we can expect further advancements in data processing, fueling the growth of intelligent systems and shaping the future of various industries.

With a focus on the development of more efficient next-generation intelligent systems, this book provides a comprehensive overview of novel technologies such as Quantum Computing, Edge Computing, Federated Learning, Memory based computing, etc. Architectures of integrated data processing technologies with a focus on real-time analysis, faster decision-making, enhanced privacy, and the ability to process large volumes of data efficiently.

With the aim of developing a range of smart and intelligent applications in diverse domains that can provide a positive impact on our surroundings, this book is intended for researchers, practitioners, engineers, and scientists involved in the design of smart applications, devices and methods contributing towards sustainable agriculture sector using these emerging technologies.

The book received a huge response from academicians, industrialists, and research scholars from different parts of the country. It covers basic concepts to advanced implementation scenarios through the convergence of technologies to solve various tasks in industries.

The book presents a cloud-based solution for processing sensor data in Chapter 1. Here, the sensor cloud architecture, which is nowadays essential in managing data in wireless sensor networks is thoroughly discussed. Various issues that occur during the processing of IoT sensing data are also explored. The chapter also discusses various existing sensor cloud infrastructure services that are used to store and process data based on sensors.

In Chapter 2, the security issues surrounding IoT Sensory Big Data Analysis, which is becoming increasingly important in today's world of ubiquitous connectivity and big data analysis are presented by the authors. The chapter discusses the complex terrain of IoT systems, with a focus on the far-reaching consequences of security precautions. The chapter presents a sophisticated understanding of different approaches to exploit vulnerabilities in IoT systems as well as different defense measures to deal with them.

Furthermore, blockchain-based solutions for elevating the security and management of IoT Sensor data are presented in Chapter 3. The content discussed here gives recommendations for optimizing blockchain integration and managing scalability concerns. Various real-world case studies to highlight the potential of blockchain technology to improve efficiency and security in dynamic environments are also explored.

Nowadays Explainable AI (XAI) has become increasingly important in the fast-evolving field of AI and ML. Today, where deep learning has shown impressive performance in different scenarios, it has been criticized for its opaque reasoning. In Chapter 4, a comprehensive review of XAI methods applicable to a wide variety of fields is presented. In addition to highlighting the existing state of XAI, the imperative for continuous advancement by delving into a meticulous examination of the limitations inherent in current methods is recognized here.

Chapter 5 explores the convergence of AI and self-sustainability while emphasizing the ethical considerations and social implications inherent in this dynamic intersection. It examines the intricate balance between technological progress and ecological responsibility, the need for equitable access to AI-powered sustainability solutions, and the profound impact of AI automation on traditional industries. The chapter also addresses the importance of reskilling and upskilling for sustainable employment, outlines policies and strategies for a just transition, and delves into responsible AI development and governance. Furthermore, it underscores the significance of inclusivity and stakeholder engagement in shaping AI and sustainability policies that prioritize fairness, equity, and the well-being of all.

Precision agriculture, a revolutionary approach to farming, combines cutting-edge technologies like GPS, sensors, and data analytics to optimize resource utilization, minimize environmental impact, and enhance productivity. Chapter 6 explores the transformative impact of precision agricultural technology, focusing on the integration of IoT sensors, GPS technology, and automated systems in farming practices. The chapter discusses IoT sensors, GPS technology, drones, and automated machinery in precision planting, crop monitoring, and operational efficiency. It also discusses resource optimization in precision agriculture, including efficient water management, targeted fertilizer application, and pest control. The chapter addresses technological challenges, adoption challenges, and emerging trends. It emphasizes the need for collaboration among farmers, technology developers, policymakers, and regulatory bodies to ensure sustainable, efficient, and equitable farming.

The potential of quantum computing to enhance efficiency, sustainability, and environmental stewardship in agriculture is explored in Chapter 7. Quantum computing can process vast datasets, simulate complex systems, and optimize resource allocation. Case studies presented in the chapter show quantum-assisted solutions for crop yield prediction, pest and disease management, and soil analysis, demonstrating the benefits of quantum computing in real-world agricultural scenarios.

In digital healthcare, the integration of fog computing and machine learning (ML) can revolutionize patient care, operations, and personalized treatment. Chapter 8 explores the potential of fog computing in telemedicine, remote monitoring, and personalized treatment. It highlights its role in addressing data processing challenges, enabling real-time data analytics, and ensuring secure transmission of medical information. Key case studies presented in this chapter demonstrate how these integrated solutions are driving innovation in the healthcare industry.

Chapter 9 explores the integration of AI and ML technologies in structural engineering, focusing on their applications in automating design processes, optimizing structural configurations, and assessing performance metrics. It highlights the efficiency of AI-driven algorithms in generating design alternatives, predicting structural behavior, and enhancing sustainability. The chapter also provides a performance comparison framework for evaluating different structural designs, considering safety, cost-effectiveness, and environmental impact. It discusses case studies and practical examples that demonstrate the advantages of AI/ML-driven autonomous design in achieving superior structural performance while minimizing resource utilization. The chapter emphasizes the potential of AI and ML in revolutionizing structural engineering, enabling engineers to create sustainable and high-performing structures, contributing to a more environmentally conscious and economically viable built environment.

Additive Manufacturing (AM), commonly known as 3D printing, recently emerged as a transformative technology with profound implications for multiple industries. The convergence of AM with Industry 4.0 principles and advanced technologies has given rise to Industry 5.0, a new era of manufacturing characterized by enhanced integration and digitalization. Chapter 10 explores the dynamic landscape of AM within the context of Industry 5.0, highlighting research trends, innovations, and challenges.

The energy sector is facing obstacles such as increased consumption, efficiency, and losses affecting mainly developing countries. As the third-largest producer and consumer of electricity in the world, India is facing a variety of power-related issues such as distribution losses, electricity fraud, and environmental issues. The artificial Internet of Things (AIoT) is proving beneficial in energy use optimization, fault detection, and identification. Chapter 11 discusses the technological issues and solutions for fault detection and classification in a smart grid. This chapter aims to identify factors that could assist India in developing its smart infrastructure and evaluate the numerous components of the smart grid.

This book is a product of innovations involved in the development of intelligent methods with the contribution of various authors around the globe. We hope that the book provides meaningful insights to its readers.

Shanu Sharma
ABES Engineering College, India

Ayushi Prakash
Ajay Kumar Garg Engineering College, India

Viajayan Sugumaran
Oakland University, USA

Acknowledgment

First and foremost, we are grateful to the publisher for their confidence in us and for giving us the chance to work together on this book. Throughout the entire book processing cycle, your assistance and direction were outstanding.

The book's Technical Review Committee and Editorial Board members, who assisted us at different stages of its completion, have our sincere gratitude. Their insightful remarks were very helpful and improved the book chapters as a whole. We sincerely appreciate your unwavering support.

Without our kind contributors, this book project would not have been able to be finished. We are grateful that they allowed us to use this book as a platform to highlight their contributions and knowledge.

Finally, but just as importantly, we would like to thank ABES Engineering College, Ghaziabad and Ajay Kumar Garg Engineering College Ghaziaba" for helping us and letting us work on this book project.

Chapter 1
Cloud Computing for IoT Sensing Data

Deepansh Kumar
ABES Engineering College, Ghaziabad, India

Himanshu Sharma
ABES Engineering College, Ghaziabad, India

Ayushi Prakash
Ajay Kumar Garg Engineering College, India

Mohammad Husain
Islamic University of Madinah, Saudi Arabia

ABSTRACT

The integration of sensor cloud technology has emerged as a revolutionary force across numerous sectors in the ever-evolving field of intelligent technologies. Born out of the confluence of cloud-based technologies with internet of things (IoT), sensor clouds provide a flexible and scalable framework for a variety of applications, including environmental monitoring, healthcare, and agriculture. This chapter aims to provide a thorough examination of sensor cloud technology, elucidating its potential, drawbacks, and many applications. It delves into the complexities of IoT sensor data and highlights the vital significance that effective processing methods play. In managing the complexity and variety inherent in IoT sensor data, it emphasises the value of techniques like data fusion, denoising, data aggregation, etc. The specifics of certain sensor cloud applications, including iDigi, Xively, Nimbits, ThingSpeak, and healthcare monitoring systems are then explored. The chapter ends by emphasizing how innovation and technological advancements are essential to overcoming these obstacles.

DOI: 10.4018/979-8-3693-0968-1.ch001

INTRODUCTION

Sensors are essential to today's technological environment because they are able to recognise and react to changes in the chemical or physical composition of their environment. These gadgets, which can detect the presence of certain compounds or monitor temperature, are used in a variety of fields, including medical monitoring and industrial automation. Sensor networks, made up of nodes positioned strategically, operate together in a Wireless Sensor Network (WSN) to monitor and analyse the environment as a whole (Raghavendra et al., 2006).

These sensors produce large amounts of data, which present management and storage issues. One way to effectively manage and analyse the large amount of sensor data is via cloud storage. Distributed computing is embodied in cloud computing, which provides on-demand services such as Software as a Service (SaaS), Infrastructure as a Service (IaaS), and Platform as a Service (PaaS) (Dwivedi & Kumar, 2018).

The Sensor-Cloud architecture is a new development in sensor technology that is a modified kind of cloud computing designed to manage sensors in wireless sensor networks (WSNs) (Raghavendra et al., 2006), (Akyildiz & Vuran, 2010). This architecture leverages the cloud's enormous processing and storage capacity to link WSNs to it in an easy-to-use manner via sensor and cloud gateways. Significant amounts of data are produced by sensor nodes, and they are effectively handled via compression and cloud transfer. The flow of data transfer if shown in Figure 1. This data is then decompressed and stored in the cloud, which provides a strong foundation for analysis and storage.

The notion of supplying end users with virtualized sensors on demand and integrating them with their IT resources or systems is presented by the Sensor-Cloud infrastructure concept (Ullah et al., 2019). IT resources, including CPUs, storage, and sensor-capable devices, must be ready and operational for the creation of service instances inside this architecture. Through the Sensor-Cloud, users can effortlessly request and manage service instances, guaranteeing cost-effectiveness by removing fees for wasted resources.

This chapter examines how sensor cloud technology is integrated, demonstrating how it may revolutionise a variety of sectors, including environmental monitoring, healthcare, and agriculture. The sensor cloud architecture, which offers a flexible and scalable environment for advanced data collecting, real-time processing, and analysis from various sensor devices and networks, is the result of the convergence of IoT and cloud-based technologies. Examining the intricacy and variety of IoT sensor data, the chapter highlights effective processing techniques and covers a range of sensor cloud applications, emphasising both advantages and disadvantages. sensor cloud technology is resilient and scalable, but it also has drawbacks, including storage capacity constraints, bandwidth limits, security issues, and the need for efficient

Figure 1. IoT integrated with cloud

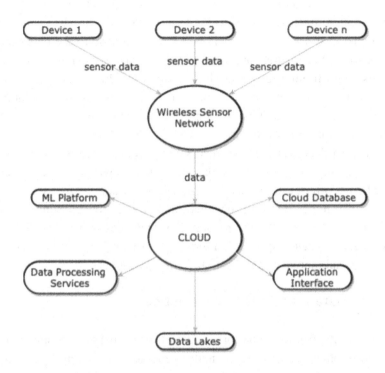

management. The need of innovation is emphasised in the chapter's conclusion in order to fully realise the promise of sensor cloud technology and open the door to a more trustworthy, data-driven, and intelligent global ecosystem.

SENSORS

Sensors are electronic devices that monitor and respond to physical characteristics such as temperature, blood pressure, humidity, and speed. Afterwards, these factors are transformed into measurable electrical impulses. For end users, sensors are an essential component of IT resources like CPU, memory, and disc. Sensors allow for automatic service instance provisioning as well as sensor monitoring and control. With a web browser's user interface, these features are accessible (Doukas & Maglogiannis, 2011). Today, a variety of sensors are utilised for diverse purposes, including body sensors, environmental sensors, and others. Technology advancements have led to the implementation of sensor networks using compact, low-cost, low-power, multipurpose, dispersed sensors with a restricted processing capacity (Chee-

Yee Chong & Kumar, 2003). These sensors are capable of coordinating with other nodes to carry out particular tasks. Traditionally, sensor networks have only had a few wired nodes attached to a centralised processing unit. An extensive number of sensor nodes that are densely positioned inside or close to the event make up a sensor network. Sensor networks and MANETS are two types of wireless Ad hoc networks with limited resources (Bellavista et al., 2013). Yet there are some distinctions between sensor networks and ad hoc networks, such as the number of nodes, communication strategies, memory and power constraints, and particular geographic areas for tracking and monitoring.

A sensor network consists of tiny sensors that can connect to one another directly or via other nodes to form a network. Nodes act as sinks for wired or wireless networks or users. Microcontroller, transceiver, memory, power source, and sensors are all components of a node. Based on detected phenomena, the transducer generates electrical impulses, which the microcontroller processes and stores. Transceiver sends and receives data in response to orders. Nodes run on batteries and may include mobilizer, external memory, and location-finding components.

IoT Sensor Data and Its Characteristics

The IoT sensors either continuously or in response to an outside event start generating the data. In the other process, sensor nodes generate data that must be collected, combined, examined, and displayed in order to produce meaningful insights. Without performing these steps the data remains useless. Following the interpretation of this data, a response to the external trigger and a representable form—that is, deliverable—are produced (Nazari Jahantigh et al., 2020). The data is produced by the networks that are formed by connecting 'n' number of sensors together, and from various other sources too. As a result, in order to analyze historical data, the created data must be combined, stored in an unprecedented way, and transmitted into distant places at a certain network data rate. Nevertheless, this is accompanied by a number of issues and features of sensor data due to variables including data's enormous volume, dynamic, updating it live, data getting old while stored for long term, the fact that data incoming from a variety of sources can be dependent on each other, data shows information complexity (Morais et al., 2019). Often times, the sensors are embedded into various places, things and even bodies of animals and human beings. Important attributes of IoT sensor data are listed below:

- **Technical Restrictions:** Usually, sensors that are used are fairly small which introduces limitations on its ability to process information, use batteries for power, connect to networks, store data, and store memory. These sensors' high susceptibility to malfunction, intrusion, and simple malfunction means that sensor data can be lost and information can be erroneous;

- **Real-Time Processing:** The network made by connecting these sensors would be able to convert raw, unprocessed data incoming from the sensors into useful information after processing and make it insightful by using graphs, charts etc., as well as handle more complicated networking activities;
- **Scalability:** In the real world applications, the sources of data can be several, for a given network of sensors. These sources includes sensors and actuators. Scalable sensor networks are necessary to handle data, support the rapid expansion of sensors and actuators, and fulfil the diverse requirements of IoT applications;
- **Data Representation:** Sensor data is often represented as a tiny tuple of structured data. The several ways that sensor data can be represented include numeric, Boolean, binary, featured values, and continuous data;
- **Heterogeneity:** IoT sensor data are varied in terms of their content. Different data sources exist, such as social network media data streams, embedded systems with sensors, real-time data-generating information networks, rigorously organized data sets, and other participatory sensor networks.

SENSING AS A SERVICE

As part of the IoT, numerous physical devices are networked together in order to collect, manage, analyse, and share real-time data (IoT). This expanding technology encompasses a wide range of devices, including smartphones, tablets, digital cameras, sensors, and many others (Khare & Totaro, 2019). IoT refers to a technological trend towards information exchange as well as data gathering, analysis, and remote device control over the Internet. A significant amount of data and information are generated by the extensive IoT network of linked devices, which also provides a wide range of services. Many sensors included into devices gather data and information. In a sensor network, each sensor is designed to serve a specific function or purpose, by applications that are specific to them, and these apps manage the data from the sensor and the sensor itself too, making it challenging for other applications to use them. This problem is resolved by sensor cloud infrastructure (Gaynor et al., 2004).

The infrastructure of the sensor cloud creates a virtual version of the sensor present as a physical device, on a virtual platform based on cloud computing. This enables the use of the sensors on an IT infrastructure. On these computing platforms, the sensors that have been converted into virtual sensors are dynamic, enabling the autonomous delivery of services as needed by users. Users can monitor these virtual sensors using normal functionalities without having to worry about where different real sensors are physically located or about spaces between physical sensors. The virtual sensors which have been used by the user previously but are longer required, can be destroyed by the user. The sensor cloud infrastructure regularly monitors sensors that are virtual to maintain quality of service (QoS). The Sensor-Cloud system has a user interface that lets you manage virtual sensors, add or remove them, and register or remove physical sensors. You can also monitor and control the virtual sensors, and add or remove users (Swamy & Kota, 2020). Patients may employ wearable computer systems or handheld devices with sensors in a health monitoring environment, for instance, and clinicians may have access to the data the sensors collect. The most rigorous type of monitoring is active continuous monitoring, which requires the patient to wear monitoring equipment in order to have all-encompassing coverage without assistance. The varied monitoring strategy deviates from the following QoS standards, nevertheless.

- **Patient-Centric Healthcare-QoS** is a way of ensuring that healthcare messages are delivered on time and reliably. It involves keeping track of how quickly and how consistently messages are transmitted (Botta et al., 2016).
- **Network-Centric Healthcare-QoS** is related to the healthcare message delivery's efficiency and the total capacity, across the whole network. It involves measuring the amount of data that can be transmitted and the number of patients that can be serviced within a given time frame.
- **Healthcare-QoS** that is focused on healthcare professionals refers to the amount of right medical judgements and the cognitive burden on such professionals. The metadata of a physical sensor refers to information about the sensor, such as what kind of sensor it is, how accurate it is, where it is located, and other related details. This metadata can be represented using the Sensor Modeling Language (SML). The measurement and description of physical sensor processes also use XML encoding. Physical sensors could now be integrated across a variety of hardware, operating systems (OS), apps, and other platforms with comparatively little assistance from humans thanks to this XML encoding (Younas et al., 2023). A connection between the real sensors and their virtual versions is created so that when users send commands to the virtual sensors, they are translated into commands for the actual sensors. This helps to make sure that the sensors can understand and act on the commands properly.

SENSOR CLOUD ARCHITECTURE

Users don't have to worry about the specifics of how the services they receive are implemented thanks to cloud computing services, which offer a framework for offering shared network services to customers. Virtual sensors can be automatically provisioned for customers using cloud computing upon their request. Physical sensors are restricted to their particular applications, but the sensor-cloud architecture can control how these sensor resources might be used for data management.

A publish/subscription approach is used, where sensor networks broadcast their sensor data and metadata, to choose the best physical sensors for an application. In order to access real-time data from physical sensors, applications can then subscribe to one or more sensor networks. Several physical sensors can be utilised to create virtual sensors that can be used by users through the Sensor-Cloud architecture. Users should first verify the availability and calibre of physical sensors before employing virtual ones. The sensor cloud infrastructure delivers the service instances automatically, which is similar to other IT resources including CPU or storage based on disc. These are delivered upon request, to the end user. By choosing an appropriate service template, users can request service instances, which the Sensor-Cloud infrastructure will subsequently deliver for free and automatically. Users can simply delete service instances once they are no longer needed to avoid paying usage fees. Cloud computing services must include automation because it can speed up delivery and increase productivity. Services were previously given manually, which could have a negative impact on performance indicators. Cloud computing, on the other hand, has lowered prices, accelerated delivery times, and improved efficiency and flexibility.

WSN: Wireless Sensor Network is referred to as WSN. It is a particular kind of network made up of several wireless, tiny, low-power sensors. These sensors may wirelessly connect with one another to form a network and are equipped with many sorts of sensors (such as temperature, humidity, light, motion, etc.). WSNs are widely used to monitor and collect data from real world environments, such as buildings, forests, or industrial sites. Many uses for the information gathered include environmental monitoring, traffic management, security monitoring, and healthcare monitoring.

BASIC ARCHITECTURE

IoT is a technological age where connecting physical and virtual items intends to improve human life quality through developing sensor technologies, communication networks, and processing methods, as well as improved applications. Linked smart cities, intelligent transportation networks, intelligent buildings, intelligent healthcare systems, and intelligent grids are a few instances of such cutting-edge applications. By detecting key data from both internal functional systems and external environmental elements, sensor networks play a crucial role in allowing the fast growth of information and communications technology. Since wireless-based sensor networks don't require any infrastructure and can be established on-demand, they are far more common. The wireless sensor network may be randomly distributed and has the ability to self-organize.

The fundamental architecture for the levels of data processing, fusion, and analysis for IoT sensors is shown in Figure 2. The different IoT sensors that are able to monitor the physical surroundings and record changes in the environment in real time make up the IoT sensor data layer. Typical IoT sensors include motion sensors, image, optical, accelerometer, gas, humidity, level, and gyroscopes sensors, Infra-Red (IR) sensors, and Radiofrequency Identification (RFID) sensors. IoT sensors are primarily connected to the power system, Wi-fi, microprocessor, storage, and control units communication channels. IoT sensor devices have limitations with regard to size, processing power, memory, etc. storage capacity and networking capabilities. storage capacity and networking capabilities. Protocols for wireless communication, including memory, networking, storage capacity, Wi-Fi, and Zig Bee. In order to facilitate connection between IoT sensor devices, wireless communication protocols including Bluetooth, Wi-Fi, Zig Bee, Near Frequency connection (NFC), and LTE/4G mobile technologies are frequently utilized (Ateniese et al., 2008).

Most IoT sensor data are processed in real-time for use in scientific, industrial, and healthcare applications. Examples include research endeavours and medical body sensors that track patients' medical conditions. For instance, the medical body sensors used to track patients' vital states would produce enormous amounts of data. Critical situations requiring the processing of these detected data would produce enormous amounts of data. In order to advance knowledge and decision-making, these sensed data must be processed to eliminate ambiguities before being subjected to additional data analysis. eliminate ambiguities before doing more data analysis to advance understanding and decision-making. The data processing layer is responsible for several tasks, including data aggregation, data denoising, data outlier identification, and missing data imputation. To manage the different sensor data issues brought forth by several heterogeneous sensor devices, the data fusion layer is necessary. Integrating authentic sensor data from diverse IoT sensor devices is the goal of the data fusion data. The data analysis layer receives the aggregated data from many sources after which it is used to generate knowledge and make decisions more effectively (Alamri et al., 2013).

Figure 2. A framework for processing, fusing, and analysing data from IoT sensors

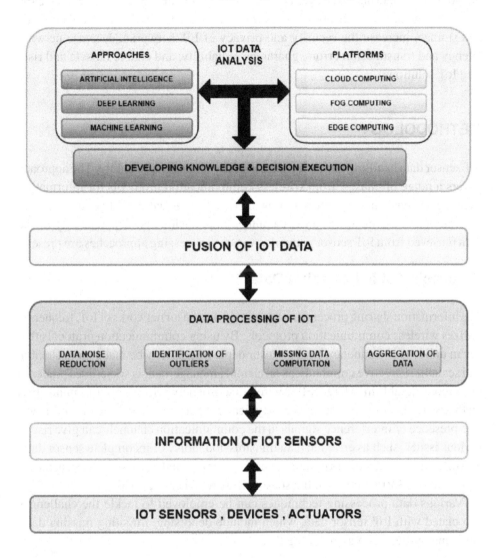

Feature extraction is the first step. After the feature extraction step, the enhanced approach includes data fusion and identity declaration. Sensor data from many sensor devices is combined in the process of data fusion. This approach enables very accurate decision-making and inferences of information. The use of cutting-edge technologies has transformed edge, cloud, and fog computing in recent years, leading to the analysis of IoT sensor data.

These enabling technologies offer a ubiquitous, dependable, and user-friendly platform to manage the dynamic and diverse nature of IoT sensor data. Therefore, the goal of the data analysis layer is to provide intelligent capability that can handle a broad range of IoT applications. These platforms aim to lower the cost of compute and storage, increase the security and privacy of IoT networks, decrease network latency and transmission errors, guarantee scalability, and enable failsafe and risk-free IoT solutions.

METHODOLOGY

IoT sensor data handling and processing is a fairly complex procedure. The approach covers a range of phases, from wireless communication protocols for information exchange in sensor networks to handling interference and data quality issues. In order to overcome these obstacles and guarantee the precision and dependability of the data retrieved from IoT sensor networks, various processing approaches are present.

Processing of IoT Sensing Data

The information sharing process that happens in the sensor networks of IoT, frequently utilizes wireless communication protocols. By using communication protocols that run in unlicensed frequency bands, sensor deployments may be made more flexible and scalable. Effective communication channel management is sometimes hindered by the considerable interference that wireless sensor network (WSN) communication methods in unlicensed frequency bands typically experience, despite their usefulness. The presence of interference signals in the communication channels can give rise to various issues, such as errors in data transmission, noisy or incomplete sensor data, as well as data with outliers or redundancy, making it challenging to obtain accurate and reliable information from the sensors (Sasirekha et al., 2020).

Various data processing techniques can be employed to tackle the challenges associated with IoT sensor data, which include denoising, imputing missing data, detecting outliers, and aggregating data.

- **Denoising:** To make decisions, a large amount of sensor data from the IoT (IoT) network must be quickly processed. High speeds, enormous quantities, and changeable values and kinds make this data difficult. Nevertheless, this data can also be noisy, meaning it contains extraneous information that cannot be used and hence slows down processing and consumes resources.

Wavelet transform techniques can be applied to this problem to describe the signal and efficiently estimate the useable data while reducing the noise. This is accomplished by thresholding the noisy signal coefficient, which aids in maintaining the original signal coefficients (Han et al., 2021). As a result, when employing wavelet transformation to analyse and synthesise continuous-time signal energy, having a precise thresholding strategy is crucial.

- **Data Aggregation:** Data aggregation is a technique for gathering and disseminating information that is valuable for statistical analysis. Data is gathered from various nodes in IoT, however separately transferring data from each node requires huge amount of energy, and the network should have a high bandwidth. But, the life of the network is reduced due to this. These issues are avoided by data aggregation techniques, which summarise data, limit excessive data transfer, lengthen network lifetime, and lower network traffic. There are several methods that can be used for aggregation of data in IoT. This includes the approaches based on tree, approach based on cluster and a centralized approach (Abbasian Dehkordi et al., 2020).

The following categories apply to IoT data aggregation techniques:

- According to the **tree-based strategy**, the network's nodes are deployed in the shape of a tree, with intermediate and hierarchical nodes handling data aggregation and transmission to the root node;
- The **cluster-based method** divides the network into clusters, each of which contains a number of sensor nodes and a cluster head node that performs data aggregation;
- The **centralised method** entails transferring information from each sensor node to a header node that will aggregate the information and send out a single packet (Abbasian Dehkordi et al., 2020).
  - **Data Outlier Detection:** The sensor nodes that are present in the sensor networks of IoT can incur failure and have outside influences, which might produce data outliers. Three well-known spatial correlation-based outlier identification techniques are used to prevent inaccurate data from influencing decision-making: majority voting, classifiers, and principal component analysis (PCA). While classifiers employ machine learning models to identify aberrant data as anomalies, majority voting uses comparisons across sensor nodes to find abnormal sensor nodes. PCA identifies residual values by extracting principle components from the data set, and then T2 score and squared prediction error are used to check for outliers (SPE) (Samara et al., 2022).
  - **Missing Data Imputation:** To deal with incomplete data, imputation is a crucial duty in data analysis. Large amounts of data are produced by the IoT (IoT) in industries including smart cities, healthcare, and

transportation. While it is usual practise to assume complete data, missing or incomplete data can produce incorrect results. To address missing data in IoT, three steps must be completed: determining the causes of missing data, examining the pattern of missing data, and developing a missing value imputation model. Three categories of missing data exist, and two methods can be employed to analyse their patterns. Many strategies can be used to approximate the missing value using the imputation model. With IoT data, conventional imputation strategies might not be appropriate (Krishnamurthi et al., 2020).

IoT Data Fusion

Various applications require data fusion or integration from several sensors to increase accuracy. It can be used, for instance, to track an object in a military or surveillance system, determine the precise location of an off-road vehicle, locate an obstruction in a person's veins, etc. (Krishnamurthi et al., 2020). The following is a quick explanation of the many fields in which data fusion is applied.

- The multi-sensor data fusion technique may be used at microscopic scales up to hundreds of feet away in factories, ships, airplanes, and other environments. For validation and improved accuracy, data from temperature sensors, X-rays, acoustic signals, electromagnetic signals, and other sources can be included into these systems. The system's accuracy will rise as a result of this integration, fostering confidence in the system and facilitating prompt activity maintenance, defect detection, remote repair, and other functions (Alam et al., 2017).
- Medical diagnosis is an essential system that works with the human body and uses NMR, chemical or biological sensors, X-rays, infrared, and other methods to identify disorders, such as tumors, anomalies of the kidneys or lungs, internal ailments, etc.;
- Seismic, electromagnetic radiation, chemical, or biological sensors are used by many satellites, airplanes, subterranean or underwater equipment, and other devices to gather precise data or detect natural events in environment monitoring from extremely great distances;
- This method uses electromagnetic radiation from great distances for military and defence agencies to employ in maritime surveillance, air-to-air or ground-to-air defence, battlefield intelligence, data acquisition, warning, defensive systems, etc.

The process of merging two or more data sources to provide a more reliable, accurate, and consistent assessment of the dynamic system is known as sensor fusion. When compared to using the sensors separately, our estimate yields superior results. The goal of sensor fusion is to increase sensing confidence and precision while reducing costs, device complexity, and component count.

The system state can be things like distance travelled, acceleration, etc., and the data sources can be mathematical models or sensors. Utilizing sensor fusion has benefits such as improvement in data quality, boosting the dependability, measuring unmeasured states and expanding the coverage area.

The data fusion techniques may be broadly classified as knowledge-based, statistical, probabilistic, inference-and reasoning-based techniques. Among the probabilistic techniques are Kalman filtering, inference theory, Bayesian networks, and maximum likelihood estimation techniques. Covariance, cross-variance, and other statistical analyses are examples of statistical procedures. Artificial neural networks, fuzzy logic, genetic algorithms, and other knowledge-based techniques are examples.

RESULTS

The results of data analysis are shown together with a selection of various services and apps that make use of sensor cloud architecture. Notable instances include Nimbits, Xively, ThingSpeak, iDigi, and applications in telematics, agriculture, healthcare, wildlife, and environment surveillance.

Data Analysis

The accuracy and scalability of sensor data are the main issues facing IoT sensor networks. Sensor data mining and analysis approaches, including data collection, data management, data cleansing, knowledge discovery, and data mining, are used to address these problems. In this regard, the results—which involve knowledge creation and decision-making—are mostly dependent on machine learning and deep learning models.

- **IoT Sensor Data Machine Learning Models:** It's hard to effectively extract useful information from IoT sensor data. A method for handling several sensor data characteristics is the Gaussian Mixture Model (GMM). System programs had to be modified for real-time processing in sensor embedded processors, and effective data structures had to be used to handle real-time sensor data analytics.

- **Models of Deep Learning for IoT Sensor Data:** While deep learning algorithms provide reliable feature extraction from IoT sensor data, their high computational overhead on resource-constrained sensor boards presents a problem. Before implementing deep learning models, a suggested pre-processing procedure in the spectrum domain with the goal of addressing these computational limitations.

- **Neural Network for Processing and Analysis of IoT Sensor Data:** When supervised learning techniques are used to pattern recognition issues, Artificial Neural Networks (ANN) are a good fit. Due to their superiority in processing sensor data, Convolutional Neural Networks (CNN) and Recurrent Neural Networks (RNN) are emphasized. CNN is mostly utilized for the analysis of image data, while RNN is better suited for the analysis of time series data.

- **Fog-Based Data Analysis:** In order to categorize signal patterns using neural networks, sensor characteristics must be extracted and processed during IoT sensor data analysis at the fog level. Applications of this categorization include air monitoring, smart home systems, fire alarms, surveillance systems, and fog level event recognition and decision-making.

- **Edge-Based Data Analysis:** In low-level sensor nodes, edge-level analysis encompasses forecasting, time series prediction, and event-based data processing. Many of the models that have been put out strive for effective data analysis at the edge level, guaranteeing low computing costs and resource consumption.

- **Cloud-Based Data Analysis:** For effective data processing, cloud-based data analytics uses a distributed and hierarchical approach. This approach leverages scalability and dynamic data processing using replicated virtual machines located in faraway cloud data centres.

- **Semantic Analysis of IoT Sensor Data:** By using semantic technology to sensor data, one may arrange, structure, and facilitate machine-to-machine communication. Actionable knowledge extraction from raw data is aided by linked open data, real-time processing, rule-based reasoning, machine learning-based techniques, and semantic-based reasoning. Better comprehension and use of IoT data are made possible by the Semantic Sensor Network (SSN) ontology, which aids in representing sensor attributes and observations.

Application and Services

There exist many services that are based on sensor cloud infrastructure that are used to store and process the data based on sensors. Some of these services are provided below.

- **Nimbits:** Sensor data is recorded and shared in the cloud using Nimbit, an open-source IoT platform and cloud-based data processing service for the IoT. By generating a cloud data point, users can supply flexible numerical, text-based, JSON, GPS, or XML values. These data points can be linked to websites, spreadsheets, graphs, Scalable Vector Graphic (SVG) process control, and more. Additionally, data points can be of big use for doing calculations and transmitting data to social networks in the form of alerts. Nimbits also offers a method for managing alerts, a technique for data compression, and a mechanism for calculating data based on sensory data that is being received (Guangzhong, 2020).

- **Xively:** Xively provides services for online databases and enables linking data provided by sensors to the internet. Devices around us provide a large amount of sensor data, which can be used for real-time monitoring. For controlling the sensor data, Xively includes a very interactive webpage and an API, which is easily accessible. The Xively system offers a variety of interfaces for creating applications to control vast amounts of data gathered by sensors in the cloud.

- **ThingSpeak:** ThingSpeak is an IoT application that includes an open API, the purpose of which is to store and retrieve data from devices or objects over LAN or over the Internet through HTTP protocols. This platform helps in developing position tracker software, sensor logger software, and more software. With the help of MATLAB, it can be used for visualizing and analyzing the data.

- **iDigi:** iDigi is a platform that helps in the integration of Machine to Machine (M2M) to application. It helps to avoid obstacles that occur in the development of secure, expandable and affordable solution for companies. iDigi provides features such as information management, storing, and linking. All this can be done throughout the company without worrying about its extent. This also makes it easier for distant asset devices to be connected. It is achieved by using iDigi Dia, which is a connecting software, in use. iDigi Dia helps to make the connection and integration of remote devices easier. iDigi can also be used to control the cross communication between the company's applications and the remote device assets, and this is independent of the location of the network.

- **Healthcare Monitoring:** Collection of patient's data linked to their health, for tracking sleep activity pattern, blood sugar, body temperature, and other respiratory conditions, sensor-clouds can be used for health monitoring. These sensors, which are typically wearable and easily accessible, include accelerometer sensors, proximity sensors, ambient light and temperature sensors, and others. For data streaming, these wearable sensor devices must support BWI (Bluetooth's wireless interface), UWB, and other interfaces.

They connect wirelessly to any smartphone through these interfaces. These smart phone gadgets pretend to act as a gateway connecting the sensor and remote server via the Internet, maybe using GPRS or Wi-Fi (Hassanalieragh et al., 2015).

Smart phone devices link to the server using web-services-based interfaces to convert this system into a services-based structure. The system prototype had to have been designed to be reliable, adaptable, and scalable. When something is robust, it should be able to recover on its own from situations when connectivity may be lost as a result of power (i.e., battery) issues, failure, or gateway shutdown to the patient's wearable devices. Movable in this context indicates that it must be able to track signals into heterogeneous contexts; in other words, it must be able to do so whether the patient left the hospital or building or was still within. It should be scalable in order to be readily deployed for several users at once without having an impact on the performance metrics (Dang et al., 2019).

A prototype system should also be retargetable and extensible, which means it should be able to accommodate different screens with different form factors and screen resolutions and continue to work effectively as new sensing technologies are developed. In order to provide the patient with better emergency care, context awareness can be obtained using data such as recently operating laboratories, missed drug dosages, and number of handicaps. The system shouldn't adhere to modifications made to the operating system or intermediary components of sensing devices, and it shouldn't disrupt services offered to current end users (Verma et al., 2018).

In this case, the patient data are collected by a number of sensors, and the resulting data are sent to a cloud server. If any noisy data is discovered, it is filtered using a server-based filtering technique. After the patient has verified and granted permission, the doctors, nurses, and others can access the patients' cloud-based data using a web service portal.

- **Environment Surveillance to Identify Emergencies or Disasters:** Earthquakes and volcanic eruptions can be detected before they actually happen by making the use of WSNs. This can be achieved by setting up a continuous monitoring system which makes use of various sensors (temperature, image, light, acceleration, barometer, strain etc.). The sensor instances that are involved in monitoring of environment can be used in conjunction with many other sensor instances. This can be achieved by making use of Sensor-Cloud infrastructure. Example: Healthcare department can help in the prevention of casualties, or damage prevention to crops from bad weather (Saleh et al., 2024).

- **Telematics:** In telematics, Sensor-Clouds may be used to provide continuous data flow across large distances from computers or information systems. It permits seamless, intervention-free communication between systems and devices.
- **Google Health:** It's a Google service which offers individual health data and acts as cloud-based health data storage. Users of the Google health system are able to access their accounts to check their records related to health. But, Google recently declared that this health service will no longer be offered.
- **Microsoft HealthVault:** Microsoft created this cloud-based platform to store and manage data about your health and fitness. Users can save, collect, and share health-related information with HealthVault. CSPs, healthcare workers, pharmaceutical companies, dispensaries, lab equipment and users themselves can all provide the data for this.
- **Agriculture and Irrigation Control:** Various sensors, such as cameras, temperature gauges, air quality monitors, and soil moisture sensors, can be employed to achieve this. The sensors continuously transfer field data to the farm owner wirelessly, allowing for real-time monitoring of crop health and enabling timely harvesting.
- **Monitoring of Wildlife.** Data on wildlife refuges, forests, and other locations can be collected using sensor cloud in order to continuously and in-depth monitor the endangered species.

There are currently no secure data access options or interfaces available in sensor-cloud applications to connect to external applications. They don't deal with the problems that heterogeneous data resources in contemporary tracking or healthcare systems cause with data management and interoperability. Infrastructure for cloud computing can aid in resolving these problems.

DISCUSSION

Sensor cloud technology has the potential to revolutionise a number of industries. But because of the innovative combination of cloud-based and IoT technology, it presents both benefits and difficulties.

Advantages of Sensor Cloud

- **More storage capacity for data:** More storage capacity for data: Large volumes of sensor data produced by sensor networks can be stored using the scalable and economical sensor cloud. In order to manage and access historical data for analysis and decision-making, users can do so.

- **More computational power:** Large volumes of sensor data may be instantly and powerfully analysed using the sensor cloud. This makes it possible for consumers to decide quickly and intelligently based on data insights and trends.
- **On-demand services allocation and management:** By dynamically provisioning services based on user demand, sensor cloud enables customers to scale up or down their usage as necessary. Users benefit from increased flexibility and cost savings as a result.
- **Fast response time:** Users can react swiftly to developing situations or occurrences because to the real-time data processing and analysis capabilities offered by sensor clouds. As a result, it takes less time to act on insights from sensor data.
- **Adaptable and versatile:** Users have freedom with sensor clouds since they may create and personalise their sensor networks to suit their own requirements. Users are able to select the sensors and services they require and combine them in ways that best fit their applications thanks to this.
- **Ability to expand to handle larger loads:** Scalability is provided by the sensor cloud by making it simple for users to add and delete sensors and services as required. This facilitates expansion or accommodating new needs while also making it simpler to respond to changing business or environmental conditions.
- **Multiple users sharing resources:** By allowing numerous individuals or organisations to utilise the same sensor network and services, sensor cloud lowers costs and boosts productivity. Users can do this to exchange information and assets while preserving their privacy and security.
- **Ability to quickly adapt to changing requirements:** By allowing customers to swiftly deploy new services or modify existing services to address changing business or environmental situations, sensor clouds offer agility. This enables users to act swiftly in response to fresh possibilities or dangers.
- **Efficient use of resources:** By maximising the effectiveness and efficiency of sensor networks and services, sensor clouds make efficient use of resources possible. Users can use this to lower expenses and boost performance while maintaining the accuracy and dependability of their data.
- **Cooperative working and communication:** By allowing users to exchange data and resources across several organisations and places, sensor clouds facilitate cooperation. Users can cooperate in order to accomplish shared objectives and results thanks to this.

- **Automated processes:** By automating typical processes like data collection, analysis, and reporting, sensor clouds allow users to concentrate on more strategic activities. This boosts effectiveness and lowers mistakes.
- **Use of virtual resources instead of physical ones:** The virtualization features offered by the sensor cloud enable users to build virtual sensors and services that may be shared among numerous individuals or organisations. More efficiency, flexibility, and cost savings are made possible through this (Landaluce et al., 2020).

Issues and Challenges with Sensor Cloud

- **Storage limitations:** Keeping track of sensor data can be difficult due to the rise in data creation. To store the data produced by sensors, the sensor cloud must have adequate storage capacity.
- **Power constraints:** Often, energy for sensor nodes comes from batteries or other sources, which can deplete quickly. To keep the sensor nodes operating, the sensor cloud must make sure that there are sufficient power resources available.
- **Bandwidth limitations:** The amount of data produced by sensors can tax the network's bandwidth. In order to transmit sensor data, there must be enough bandwidth available, according to the sensor cloud.
- **Scalability challenges:** It gets more difficult to manage the network's growing number of sensors. The sensor cloud needs to be built to support large expansion and have the resources required to accommodate more sensors.
- **Sensor Cloud Security and Privacy Concerns**: The paradigm of sensor-cloud computing offers a framework for integrating various sensor networks and makes resource sharing easier. Without concern for conventional constraints, several users can simultaneously develop their sensing applications. Creation of a sensory system which is available on demand and allows multiple users is feasible thorough this. It allows users and applications can share processing, sensing, and network resources. The sensor-cloud architecture has advantages, but because it is so widely accessible, it lacks security and privacy. Due to the infeasibility of current security solutions such as stand-alone sensor networks or cloud architecture, this poses intrinsic issues that demand novel solutions. The cyber security regarding the sensor cloud architecture can be classified into the following elements- the sensors, the channel for communication and the framework of the cloud (Abba Ari et al., 2024).

CONCLUSION

In summary, the incorporation of sensor cloud technology into a wide range of applications has shown that it has the ability to completely transform a number of industries, including healthcare, agriculture, environmental monitoring, and more. The IoT (IoT) and cloud-based technologies have come together to create a framework that offers enormous potential as well as difficulties. A flexible and scalable environment is provided by the sensor cloud architecture, which acts as a catalyst for sophisticated data gathering, real-time processing, and analysis from a wide range of sensor devices and networks. But this system also has to deal with a variety of complex problems, such security worries, storage capacity limitations, bandwidth restrictions, and the requirement for scalable, effective, and affordable administration of a constantly growing sensor network.

The technological limitations, real-time processing, data representation, and data fusion of IoT sensor data highlight the complexity and diversity of sensor-generated information. IoT sensor data processing efficiency depends on methods including data fusion, denoising, data aggregation, outlier identification, and missing data imputation, each of which tackles a different set of issues in the sensor data environment. The wide range of capabilities within the sensor cloud infrastructure, from data processing and storage to machine-to-machine integration and real-time monitoring in healthcare settings, has also been demonstrated by sensor cloud applications like Nimbits, Xively, ThingSpeak, iDigi, and healthcare monitoring systems.

There are difficulties with these programs. They deal with privacy and security concerns, particularly when designing and maintaining safe data access methods and interfaces that guarantee data management and system compatibility. The sensor cloud platform's scalability and resilience show how it can revolutionize data gathering, processing, and use across a wide range of sectors. To solve the current issues and realize the full potential of sensor cloud technology, more innovations and breakthroughs are required to build a more productive, secure, and networked future. sensor cloud architecture might open the door to a more dependable, data-driven, and intelligent global ecosystem through innovation and strategic improvements.

REFERENCES

Abba Ari, A. A., Ngangmo, O. K., Titouna, C., Thiare, O., Mohamadou, A., & Gueroui, A. M. (2024). Enabling privacy and security in Cloud of Things: Architecture, applications, security & privacy challenges. *Applied Computing and Informatics*, *20*(1/2), 119–141. doi:10.1016/j.aci.2019.11.005

Abbasian Dehkordi, S., Farajzadeh, K., Rezazadeh, J., Farahbakhsh, R., Sandrasegaran, K., & Abbasian Dehkordi, M. (2020). A survey on data aggregation techniques in IoT sensor networks. *Wireless Networks*, *26*(2), 1243–1263. doi:10.1007/s11276-019-02142-z

Akyildiz, I. F., & Vuran, M. C. (2010). *Wireless sensor networks*. John Wiley & Sons. doi:10.1002/9780470515181

Alam, F., Mehmood, R., Katib, I., Albogami, N. N., & Albeshri, A. (2017). Data fusion and IoT for smart ubiquitous environments: A survey. *IEEE Access : Practical Innovations, Open Solutions*, *5*, 9533–9554. doi:10.1109/ACCESS.2017.2697839

Alamri, A., Ansari, W. S., Hassan, M. M., Hossain, M. S., Alelaiwi, A., & Hossain, M. A. (2013). A Survey on Sensor-Cloud: Architecture, Applications, and Approaches. *International Journal of Distributed Sensor Networks*, *9*(2), 917923. doi:10.1155/2013/917923

Ateniese, G., Pietro, R. D., Mancini, L., & Tsudik, G. (2008). Scalable and efficient provable data possession. *IACR Cryptol. ePrint Arch.* doi:10.1145/1460877.1460889

Bellavista, P., Cardone, G., Corradi, A., & Foschini, L. (2013). Convergence of MANET and WSN in IoT urban scenarios. *IEEE Sensors Journal*, *13*(10), 3558–3567. doi:10.1109/JSEN.2013.2272099

Botta, A., De Donato, W., Persico, V., & Pescapé, A. (2016). Integration of cloud computing and internet of things: A survey. *Future Generation Computer Systems*, *56*, 684–700. doi:10.1016/j.future.2015.09.021

Chong, C-Y., & Kumar, S. (2003). Sensor networks: Evolution, opportunities, and challenges. *Proceedings of the IEEE, 91*(8), 1247–1256.

Dang, L. M., Piran, M. J., Han, D., Min, K., & Moon, H. (2019). A Survey on Internet of Things and Cloud Computing for Healthcare. *Electronics (Basel)*, *8*(7), 768. doi:10.3390/electronics8070768

de Morais, C. M., Sadok, D., & Kelner, J. (2019). An IoT sensor and scenario survey for data researchers. *Journal of the Brazilian Computer Society*, *25*(1), 1–17. doi:10.1186/s13173-019-0085-7

Doukas, C., & Maglogiannis, I. (2011). Managing Wearable Sensor Data through Cloud Computing. *2011 IEEE Third International Conference on Cloud Computing Technology and Science*, 440–445. 10.1109/CloudCom.2011.65

Gaynor, M., Moulton, S., Welsh, M., LaCombe, E., Rowan, A., & Wynne, J. (2004). Integrating wireless sensor networks with the grid. *IEEE Internet Computing*, *8*(4), 32–39. doi:10.1109/MIC.2004.18

Guangzhong, L. (2020). Application of IoT and Countermeasure in Agriculture of Shandong Province, China. *Internet of Things and Cloud Computing*, *8*(1), 8. doi:10.11648/j.iotcc.20200801.12

Han, G., Tu, J., Liu, L., Martínez-García, M., & Choi, C. (2021). An intelligent signal processing data denoising method for control systems protection in the industrial Internet of Things. *IEEE Transactions on Industrial Informatics*, *18*(4), 2684–2692. doi:10.1109/TII.2021.3096970

Hassanalieragh, M., Page, A., Soyata, T., Sharma, G., Aktas, M., Mateos, G., Kantarci, B., & Andreescu, S. (2015). Health monitoring and management using Internet-of-Things (IoT) sensing with cloud-based processing: Opportunities and challenges. *2015 IEEE International Conference on Services Computing*, 285–292. 10.1109/SCC.2015.47

Khare, S., & Totaro, M. (2019). Big data in IoT. *2019 10th International Conference on Computing, Communication and Networking Technologies (ICCCNT)*, 1–7.

Krishnamurthi, R., Kumar, A., Gopinathan, D., Nayyar, A., & Qureshi, B. (2020). An overview of IoT sensor data processing, fusion, and analysis techniques. *Sensors (Basel)*, *20*(21), 6076. doi:10.3390/s20216076 PMID:33114594

Landaluce, H., Arjona, L., Perallos, A., Falcone, F., Angulo, I., & Muralter, F. (2020). A Review of IoT Sensing Applications and Challenges Using RFID and Wireless Sensor Networks. *Sensors (Basel)*, *20*(9), 2495. doi:10.3390/s20092495 PMID:32354063

Nazari Jahantigh, M., Masoud Rahmani, A., Jafari Navimirour, N., & Rezaee, A. (2020). Integration of Internet of Things and cloud computing: A systematic survey. *IET Communications*, *14*(2), 165–176. doi:10.1049/iet-com.2019.0537

Raghavendra, C. S., Sivalingam, K. M., & Znati, T. (2006). *Wireless sensor networks*. Springer.

Saleh, A., Zulkifley, M. A., Harun, H. H., Gaudreault, F., Davison, I., & Spraggon, M. (2024). Forest fire surveillance systems: A review of deep learning methods. *Heliyon*, *10*(1), e23127. doi:10.1016/j.heliyon.2023.e23127 PMID:38163175

Samara, M. A., Bennis, I., Abouaissa, A., & Lorenz, P. (2022). A survey of outlier detection techniques in IoT: Review and classification. *Journal of Sensor and Actuator Networks, 11*(1), 4. doi:10.3390/jsan11010004

Sasirekha, S., Priya, A., Anita, T., & Sherubha, P. (2020). Data processing and management in IoT and wireless sensor network. *Journal of Physics: Conference Series, 1712*(1), 012002. doi:10.1088/1742-6596/1712/1/012002

Swamy, S. N., & Kota, S. R. (2020). An Empirical Study on System Level Aspects of Internet of Things (IoT). *IEEE Access : Practical Innovations, Open Solutions, 8,* 188082–188134. doi:10.1109/ACCESS.2020.3029847

Ullah, I., Ahmad, S., Mehmood, F., & Kim, D. (2019). Cloud based IoT network virtualization for supporting dynamic connectivity among connected devices. *Electronics (Basel), 8*(7), 742. doi:10.3390/electronics8070742

Verma, P., Sood, S. K., & Kalra, S. (2018). Cloud-centric IoT based student healthcare monitoring framework. *Journal of Ambient Intelligence and Humanized Computing, 9*(5), 1293–1309. doi:10.1007/s12652-017-0520-6

Younas, M. I., Iqbal, M. J., Aziz, A., & Sodhro, A. H. (2023). Toward QoS Monitoring in IoT Edge Devices Driven Healthcare—A Systematic Literature Review. *Sensors (Basel), 23*(21), 8885. doi:10.3390/s23218885 PMID:37960584

Chapter 2
Comprehensive Analysis of Attacks and Defenses in IoT Sensory Big Data Analysis

Mohammad Ishrat
https://orcid.org/0000-0002-9699-4454
Koneru Lakshmaiah Education Foundation, India

Wasim Khan
https://orcid.org/0000-0003-2311-1451
Koneru Lakshmaiah Education Foundation, India

Faheem Ahmad
University of Technology and Applied Science, Al Musanna, Oman

Monia Mohammed Al Farsi
University of Technology and Applied Science, Al Musanna, Oman

Shafiqul Abidin
Department of Computer Science, Aligarh Muslim University, India

ABSTRACT

This chapter takes a deep dive into the security issues surrounding IoT sensory big data analysis, which is becoming increasingly important in today's world of ubiquitous connectivity and big data analysis. Starting with an introduction to this crucial juncture, the chapter proceeds to guide the reader through the complex terrain of IoT systems, with a focus on the far-reaching consequences of security precautions. From simple denial of service (DoS) attacks to complex man-in-the-middle (MitM) incursions, data manipulation, injection exploits, and unauthorised access are all under the microscope. Readers will obtain a sophisticated understanding of the many methods used by bad actors to exploit vulnerabilities in IoT systems as they are systematically explored. In addition, the chapter details a wide variety of defence measures, providing a versatile toolkit for shoring up IoT ecosystems. Intrusion detection systems (IDS), secure communication protocols, secure boot procedures, and strong data encryption are all part of these multi-layered plans of action.

DOI: 10.4018/979-8-3693-0968-1.ch002

1. INTRODUCTION

Processing and analysing massive amounts of data produced by IoT-connected sensors is known as IoT Sensory Big Data Analysis. Sensor data generated by IoT devices, which might range from sensors in industrial machinery to smart home appliances, will be analysed to draw useful insights, patterns, and trends. Data gathering, filtration, and sophisticated analytics are all part of the process (Ambika 2020). This data is crucial for process improvement, better decision making, and the introduction of automation across many fields and uses. Maintaining trust and protecting against potential cyber threats necessitates keeping sensory data secure and private, which highlights the importance of security in IoT devices (Tariq, Khan, and Asim 2021).

Numerous crucial aspects make it impossible to overestimate the significance of security in IoT systems. For starters, due to their ubiquitous connection, these devices are always connected to networks, leaving them vulnerable to cyberattacks (Haddaji, Ayed, and Fourati 2022). They must be protected from hacking and other forms of data breach immediately. Personal information, medical records, and even industrial procedures are just some of the sensitive types of data that many IoT devices deal with. It is critical to maintain the confidentiality and avoid the abuse of such sensitive data. In addition, IoT devices manage and keep tabs on everything from factory equipment to national security networks. Security flaws can result in real and potentially harmful repercussions.

Managing security gets more difficult with the proliferation of IoT devices, as each one is a potential vector for cyberattacks. The limited processing power and memory of many of these devices also makes them more vulnerable to assaults (Tufail et al. 2021). With extended periods of use, security flaws that are discovered later may remain unpatched for a long time if not addressed. In addition, IoT gadgets don't function alone; rather, they're interconnected nodes that exchange data with one another and external resources like the cloud. If one device is compromised, the entire system is at risk. In several fields, there are specialised laws and guidelines that must be followed to ensure the privacy and safety of customer information. A company's legal standing and reputation may be jeopardised if it failed to adhere to these criteria.

In addition, trust must be preserved if the Internet of Things is to see widespread adoption. Both consumers and organisations require reassurance that their data is safe on their respective devices. This includes potentially vulnerable IoT devices that are open to the public. Both online and offline dangers must be countered by security measures. Unauthorised entry, which can lead to misuse of resources, tampering with data, or even physical harm, can be avoided with the use of strong authentication and access restrictions. Finally, resilience in design is essential for Internet of Things systems to survive the ever-changing character of cyber-attacks.

This includes being able to spot threats, counter them, and bounce back swiftly. The sustained confidence and adoption of IoT technology across a wide range of businesses and use cases depends on a high level of security in IoT systems, which is why protecting personal data is so important.

With an emphasis on the crucial relationship between security concerns and disruptive technology, this chapter provides a complete analysis of IoT Sensory Big Data Analysis. It starts with a definition of IoT Sensory Big Data Analysis and several examples of its wide-ranging usefulness. Issues including widespread connectivity vulnerabilities, data sensitivity, and the concrete impact of security breaches are discussed in this chapter to emphasise the critical importance of security in IoT systems. DoS assaults, MitM attacks, data manipulation, unauthorised access, and malware exploits are only some of the attacks that may be encountered, and their attack pathways and weaknesses are discussed in detail. IDS installation, secure communication protocols, robust authentication procedures, firmware updates, and data encryption are just some of the defensive strategies and solutions that are detailed in this chapter. Security audits, user education, incident response strategies, and the creation of safe IoT infrastructures are all highlighted (Yadav et al. 2022). Case studies of major catastrophes and security breaches in the real world might teach us important lessons. Emerging trends in IoT security are also discussed, with a focus on AI-driven threat detection, Blockchain applications, and edge computing. With the information provided in this chapter, stakeholders will be better prepared to deal with the ever-changing world of IoT Sensory Big Data Analysis, all while maintaining a high level of security.

2. TYPES OF ATTACKS IN IOT SENSORY BIG DATA ANALYSIS

In IoT Sensory Big Data Analysis, the security and privacy of personally identifiable information are particularly vulnerable to a wide range of assaults. These assaults consist of:

2.1 Denial of Service (DoS) Attacks

A Denial of Service (DoS) attack is an effort to crash a service or network by flooding it with so much data that it can't handle it. The target audience will have access to the material no longer. DoS attacks take use of flaws in the way that systems process incoming requests, such as capacity issues or other infrastructure flaws. DoS attacks can be especially troublesome in IoT systems because they can disrupt otherwise essential services and equipment like sensors, actuators, and communication lines (Gupta and Dahiya 2021; Mukherjee et al. 2022).

Figure 1. Types of attacks in IoT sensory big data analysis

Vulnerabilities in IoT Systems: There are many flaws in IoT systems that could be used in a denial of service attack. Low-power CPUs, inadequate bandwidth, and limited computational capabilities are just a few examples of the issues that plague IoT devices. Inadequate access controls or authentication processes are only two examples of how lax security measures might leave Internet of Things systems vulnerable to denial-of-service assaults (Blinowski and Piotrowski 2020). The sheer volume of nodes in an Internet of Things network increases the severity of a denial-of-service assault (Srivastava et al. 2020).

Case Studies of DoS Attacks in IoT: DoS attacks have real-world consequences for the Internet of Things, as shown by several case studies. The 2016 Mirai botnet is one example of an attack that took advantage of security flaws in IoT devices like cameras and routers to launch widespread denial-of-service assaults. Major Websites and services were affected by this attack, demonstrating the threat posed by Internet of Things (IoT) devices. Targeted denial-of-service assaults on industrial IoT systems have already disrupted key infrastructure, illustrating the potential impact on life-sustaining industries.

Strong security measures, such as intrusion detection systems, traffic filtering, and load balancing techniques, are necessary to counteract the risk of denial-of-service attacks in the Internet of Things (IoT). DoS attack vulnerabilities must be identified and patched as soon as possible, therefore frequent security audits and timely software updates are essential. The ability to construct safe and resilient IoT ecosystems relies on a firm grasp of DoS attack characteristics, weaknesses, and practical consequences.

2.2 Man-in-the-Middle (MitM) Attacks

Cyberattacks known as "Man-in-the-Middle" (MitM) attacks occur when a malicious third party secretly listens in on, and maybe modifies, a conversation between two parties. This is a widespread problem that can occur in both wired and wireless networks, and it poses a significant security risk. Eavesdropping, data tampering, and unauthorised access are all possible outcomes of Man in the Middle (MitM) attacks in the context of Internet of Things (IoT) networks (Al-Shareeda and Manickam 2022; Al-Shareeda et al. 2020).

2.3 Attack Techniques and Exploitation Vectors

Data sent between IoT devices or between a device and a server is vulnerable to eavesdropping, session hijacking, and DNS spoofing, among other forms of attack. Because of this, sensitive information may be compromised or altered.

2.4 Mitigation Strategies

Mitigation methods are preventative steps taken to lessen the occurrence or severity of a security risk. Security is of the utmost importance in the context of IoT Sensory Big Data Analysis, and several methods can be used to strengthen the ecosystem against threats. Among these methods are:

Figure 2. Mitigation strategies

Intrusion Detection Systems (IDS)	Use IDS to receive instantaneous threat alerts and real-time monitoring.
Secure Communication Protocols	Use TLS or HTTPS encryption to protect sensitive data while it's in transit.
Device Authentication and Access Control	Use tight authentication of users and devices, with predetermined limits on access.
Secure Boot and Firmware Updates	Establish strong access controls and user authentication.
Data Encryption and Integrity Checks	Securely encrypt and periodically verify the integrity of your data.
Designing Secure IoT Architectures	Create an Internet of Things infrastructure with multiple layers of protection.
Regular Security Audits and Assessments	Conduct vulnerability and penetration tests and security audits routinely.
User Education and Training	Security awareness training for users and key stakeholders
Incident Response and Recovery Plans	Plan for security incidents so they can be handled immediately.
AI-Powered Threat Detection in IoT	Make use of ML and AI to examine IoT data for vulnerabilities.
Blockchain for IoT Security	IoT might use Blockchain for reliable record keeping and identity management.
Edge Computing and Security Implications	It's important to think about the efficiency and security of edge processing.

By implementing above mentioned mitigation strategies, organizations can significantly enhance the security posture of their IoT Sensory Big Data Analysis systems, reducing the risk of potential attacks and ensuring the integrity and confidentiality of their data (Jurcut et al. 2020). It is essential to approach security in a holistic and proactive manner, continuously adapting and evolving strategies to counter emerging threats.

2.5 Data Tampering and Injection

Data Tampering and Injection refer to techniques used by attackers to manipulate or modify data in a system, potentially leading to unauthorized access, data loss, or other security breaches. Ensuring data integrity is crucial for maintaining the accuracy and reliability of information (Reda, Anwar, and Mahmood 2022; Liang et al. 2022). Here are some methods related to Data Tampering and Injection:

2.6 Methods of Tampering and Injection

Attackers may manipulate or inject data at various stages, potentially compromising the integrity and reliability of sensory data analysis. This could include altering sensor readings, injecting false data, or tampering with data in transit (Reda, Anwar, and Mahmood 2022; Liang et al. 2022).

SQL Injection: Attackers insert malicious SQL queries into input fields, exploiting vulnerabilities in database query execution.

Example: Inputting SQL code in a vulnerable login form to gain unauthorized access to a database.

Cross-Site Scripting (XSS)

Attackers inject malicious scripts (usually JavaScript) into web pages viewed by other users.

Example: Injecting a script that steals login credentials from other users visiting a compromised web page.

Command Injection

Attackers inject malicious commands into a system to trick it into executing unintended actions.

Example: Injecting operating system commands in a web application's input field to potentially gain unauthorized access to the server.

XML Injection: Attackers inject malicious XML code into an application, potentially disrupting processing or revealing sensitive information.

Example: Injecting XML code into an input field to manipulate the application's behavior in an unintended and insecure way.

Cross-Site Request Forgery (CSRF): Attackers trick users into performing actions on a web application without their knowledge or consent.

Example: Crafting a malicious link that, when clicked by a logged-in user, performs an action on the website on their behalf.

Ensuring Data Integrity: To Ensure Data Integrity and Protect Against Tampering and Injection

Input Validation: Implement strict validation checks on user inputs to prevent the acceptance of malicious code or scripts.

Output Encoding: Encode special characters in output to prevent them from being interpreted as code.

Parameterized Queries: Use parameterized queries or prepared statements to prevent SQL injection attacks.

Content Security Policies (CSP): Implement CSP headers to restrict the sources of executable scripts, mitigating XSS attacks.

Regular Security Audits: Conduct regular security audits and penetration testing to identify and rectify vulnerabilities.

Data Encryption: Encrypt sensitive data both in transit and at rest to prevent unauthorized access or tampering.

Access Controls: Implement strict access controls to ensure that only authorized users have permission to modify or access sensitive data.

By adopting these measures, organizations can significantly reduce the risk of data tampering and injection, thereby safeguarding the integrity of their systems and information.

2.7 Unauthorized Access and Privilege Escalation

Unauthorized Access and Privilege Escalation are critical security concerns that involve unauthorized users gaining access to sensitive information or obtaining higher levels of access than they should have. Here are some aspects related to these concerns:

2.8 Weaknesses in Access Control Mechanisms

Inadequate authentication or authorization processes may lead to unauthorized access to IoT systems. This can occur due to weak passwords, improper configuration, or other vulnerabilities in access controls (A. Khan et al. 2022).

Examples:

1. Insufficient password complexity requirements.
2. Lack of multi-factor authentication.
3. Improperly configured permissions.

2.9 Best Practices for Access Management

These are recommended strategies and measures to ensure secure access control and prevent unauthorized access.

Examples:

Role-Based Access Control (RBAC): Implement RBAC to assign permissions based on roles within an organization. This restricts users to only the permissions they need to perform their job functions (Cruz, Kaji, and Yanai 2018).

Principle of Least Privilege (PoLP): Grant users the minimum level of access required to perform their tasks. This limits potential damage if an account is compromised.

Regular Access Reviews: Conduct periodic reviews of user access rights to ensure they are still appropriate for their roles.

Strong Authentication: Implement multi-factor authentication (MFA) to add an extra layer of security beyond passwords.

By addressing weaknesses in access control mechanisms and following best practices for access management, organizations can significantly reduce the risk of unauthorized access and privilege escalation. This helps maintain the integrity and security of their systems and data.

2.10 Malware and Exploits

Malware and Exploits present significant risks to IoT systems (Rains 2020). Here is an overview of these concerns:

2.11 Types of Malware Targeting IoT

Malicious software aimed at IoT devices manifests in diverse forms, each characterized by unique traits and attack strategies (Humayun et al. 2021). Examples include:

Botnets: These turn IoT devices into a network of bots, frequently employed for DDoS attacks.

Ransomware: This encrypts data or locks users out of their devices, demanding a ransom for restoration.

Spyware: It operates discreetly, gathering information from a device and transmitting it to a third party.

Trojans: Disguised as legitimate software, these can execute malicious activities once installed.

2.12 Preventing and Detecting Malicious Activity

This entails the implementation of measures to thwart malware infiltrations and identify any suspicious behavior on IoT devices. Effective strategies comprise:

Firewalls and Intrusion Detection Systems (IDS): These tools scrutinize network traffic, flagging potentially malicious activity.

Regular Software Updates: Ensuring IoT devices have current firmware and security patches guards against known vulnerabilities.

Behavioral Anomaly Detection: Utilizing AI or machine learning to pinpoint unusual or suspicious behavior on IoT devices.

Network Segmentation: Isolating IoT devices from critical systems curtails the spread of malware in the event of an infection.

By comprehending the varieties of malware targeting IoT devices and enacting robust prevention and detection measures, organizations fortify the security of their IoT networks. This safeguards sensitive data and thwarts potentially catastrophic cyberattacks (Oz et al. 2022; Markkandeyan et al. 2023).

3. ATTACK VECTORS AND VULNERABILITIES:

IoT devices are susceptible to various vulnerabilities, encompassing both hardware and software aspects. These vulnerabilities can be addressed through diligent patch management and regular firmware updates.

- **Hardware Vulnerabilities:** Hardware vulnerabilities in IoT devices pertain to weaknesses in the physical components of the device. These can manifest in various forms, including:

Inadequate Encryption Mechanisms: Some IoT devices may employ weak or outdated encryption methods, making them susceptible to cryptographic attacks. This could potentially lead to unauthorized access or data breaches.

Exposed Ports: Improperly secured ports can serve as entry points for malicious actors. If a port is left open or unprotected, it could be exploited to gain unauthorized access to the device or network.

Insufficient Physical Security Measures: In scenarios where IoT devices are deployed in public or accessible areas, inadequate physical security measures can leave them vulnerable to tampering, theft, or unauthorized manipulation (N.-F. Polychronou et al. 2021).

Lack of Secure Boot and Firmware Verification: Insecure boot processes and verification systems leave devices vulnerable to attacks that substitute safe software with malicious code.

- **Software Vulnerabilities:** Software vulnerabilities, on the other hand, arise from weaknesses in the programming, coding, and overall software architecture of the IoT device. These can include:

Unpatched Software Bugs: If software flaws aren't patched or updated as soon as they're discovered, the device could be exploited. These vulnerabilities could be exploited by adversaries to gain unauthorised entry or control (Torres, Pinto, and Lopes 2021).

Insecure Coding Practices: Vulnerabilities can occur when software has been poorly designed or implemented. This could be due to a lack of sufficient input validation, a buffer overflow, or some other exploitable flaw in the code (N. F. Polychronou et al. 2021).

Insufficient Authentication and Authorization: Unauthorised users may be able to access the device or system if the authentication procedures are insufficient or poorly configured. Because of this, sensitive information could be compromised or stolen.

Lack of Data Integrity Checks: IoT devices could be vulnerable to data tampering if adequate safeguards are not in place to check data integrity, which could result in erroneous or compromised information.

3.1 Addressing Vulnerabilities: We Need a Comprehensive Strategy to Deal With These Weaknesses

Regular Firmware Updates: Maintaining a steady stream of firmware updates and security patches for IoT devices is essential. This aids in patching up previously discovered security flaws and improving protection levels.

1. *Security Audits and Assessments:* Conducting regular security audits and assessments can help identify and rectify vulnerabilities in both hardware and software components.

2.   *Security by Design:* Incorporating security measures from the design phase of IoT devices helps build a more robust foundation against potential vulnerabilities.
3.   *Collaboration with Security Experts:* Engaging with security experts or firms that specialize in IoT security can provide valuable insights and strategies for fortifying devices.

Overall, a comprehensive solution to the problem of IoT device vulnerabilities requires a proactive and multifaceted approach. Organizational IoT networks can benefit immensely from the methodical identification, remediation, and continued monitoring of potential hardware and software vulnerabilities. Inaction on this front would compromise the security of sensitive data and erode the trust of users and other stakeholders (Feng et al. 2022).

3.2 Insecure Communication Channels

Unsafe connections between devices are a major issue for the Internet of Things. This security hole is related to the fact that information could be snatched or altered while in transit. Secure communication practises and strong encryption techniques are necessary to solve this problem.

3.3 Encryption Protocols and Secure Communication

Data security during transit relies heavily on the use of robust encryption techniques. Cryptographic methods are used to encode data so that only authorised users may decode it. Transport Layer Security (TLS) and Secure Sockets Layer (SSL) are two popular encryption techniques used to protect data in transit over networks.

3.4 Securing Data in Transit

Protecting sensitive information from interception or unauthorised access requires maintaining data integrity and confidentiality while in transit. The following procedures are part of this:
    When end-to-end encryption is used, information is encrypted from the sender's end all the way through to the receiver's end, where it can be decrypted only by that person. As a result, there is less chance of being overheard on the road.

3.5 Authentication and Authorization

Authentication systems assist secure data by confirming the identities of communicating parties. This restricts participation in the communication to authorised parties only (Feng et al. 2022; N. F. Polychronou et al. 2021).

3.6 Secure Communication Channels

Protecting sensitive information from eavesdropping and modification is a top priority, which is why many organisations are turning to secure communication frameworks and protocols like Virtual Private Networks (VPNs).

4. REGULAR SECURITY AUDITS

Conducting regular security audits and assessments of communication channels helps identify and rectify vulnerabilities or weaknesses in the encryption and communication protocols.

By prioritizing the use of robust encryption protocols and secure communication practices, organizations can significantly enhance the confidentiality and integrity of data in transit. This proactive approach plays a pivotal role in fortifying the overall security of IoT systems and ensures that sensitive information remains protected throughout its journey across networks.

4.1 Weak Authentication and Authorization Mechanisms

The vulnerability stemming from weak authentication and authorization mechanisms is a critical concern in IoT security. This pertains to the potential for unauthorized access to IoT devices or systems due to inadequate authentication processes and authorization policies.

4.2 Two-Factor Authentication and Strong Password Policies

Implementing two-factor authentication (2FA) and enforcing strong password policies are essential measures to bolster authentication.

Two-Factor Authentication (2FA): This involves using two different methods to verify a user's identity, such as a password or PIN combined with a temporary code sent to their mobile device. As a result, it is more difficult for intruders to get access, thereby increasing security (Ali, Dida, and Elikana Sam 2021; Haq et al. 2022).

Strong Password Policies: Strong authentication is achieved through the use of complicated passwords that include a mix of upper and lower case letters, digits, and special characters. The possibility of credentials being compromised can also be mitigated by requiring frequent password upgrades.

4.3 Role-Based Access Control (RBAC)

To safeguard that users have access to only those features and data that are relevant to their roles, Role-Based Access Control is an effective authorization approach. This helps ensure that no malicious actors gain access to the system's most private data.

Administrator Roles: Administrators have elevated privileges, allowing them to configure settings and manage users. These accounts should be carefully controlled and subject to strong authentication measures.

User Roles: Standard users are granted access to specific functions or data based on their defined roles. This limits their capabilities to only what is necessary for their responsibilities.

By implementing robust authentication methods like 2FA and enforcing strong password policies, coupled with role-based access control, organizations can significantly mitigate the risks associated with weak authentication and authorization mechanisms in IoT systems. These measures collectively contribute to a more secure environment, safeguarding against unauthorized access and potential security breaches.

4.4 Lack of Secure Update Mechanisms

The absence of secure update mechanisms poses a significant security risk in IoT environments. This pertains to the potential for vulnerabilities to persist in devices due to ineffective or non-existent update procedures.

In order to make IoT devices more resistant to new attacks, businesses should implement secure OTA update processes. This aids in keeping the IoT ecosystem safe and sound, even when new vulnerabilities are identified and fixed (Eceiza, Flores, and Iturbe 2021; W. Khan et al. 2023).

4.5 Physical Tampering and Theft

The security of IoT devices is particularly vulnerable to acts of physical tampering and theft. Gaining physical access to a gadget allows an attacker to take control of it, view its data, or even steal it.

Figure 3. Significance of secure OTA updates in IoT security

Ensuring Secure Over-the-Air (OTA) Updates	OTA updates are vital for deploying patches, upgrades, and security enhancements without requiring physical access.
Digital Signatures	Applying digital signatures to updates ensures their authenticity and integrity. This prevents malicious actors from injecting unauthorized or tampered updates into the system.
Encrypted Communication	Using encryption protocols during the update process safeguards the integrity and confidentiality of the transmitted data. This prevents interception or tampering during transit.
Rollback Mechanisms	Implementing rollback protection prevents attackers from reverting a device to a previous, potentially vulnerable state after an update.
Notification and Verification	There is an additional degree of protection provided by alerting users or administrators to available updates and providing ways to check the legitimacy of the update source.
Scheduled and Staged Rollouts	Updates can be tested and validated before being rolled out to the masses if they are first deployed to a small sample of devices. In this way, any problems that may arise will be less severe.

4.5.1 Physical Security Measures for IoT Devices

Safeguarding Internet of Things (IoT) devices from manipulation and theft requires the implementation of effective physical security measures (Yang et al. 2022).

These listed above physical safeguards help businesses greatly lessen the possibility of tampering with or stealing Internet of Things gadgets. This ensures that the hardware and data it stores remain unaltered and safe.

Figure 4. Physical security measures for IoT devices

Tamper-Evident Enclosures	Using enclosures that show visible signs of tampering when opened can deter unauthorized access.
Locks and Seals	Incorporating locks or seals on critical components can prevent unauthorized entry and indicate if tampering attempts have been made.
Access Controls	Restricting physical access to authorized personnel only, such as through secure facilities or locked cabinets, can prevent unauthorized tampering.
Insufficient Physical Security Measures	In scenarios where IoT devices are deployed in public or accessible areas, inadequate physical security measures can leave them vulnerable to tampering, theft, or unauthorized manipulation.
Surveillance and Monitoring	Utilizing security cameras or sensors can help detect and record any suspicious activity around IoT devices.
Geolocation and Tracking	Implementing tracking technologies can aid in locating and recovering stolen or misplaced devices.
Remote Lockdown or Wiping	Having the capability to remotely lock down or wipe a device in the event of theft can protect sensitive data.
Auditing and Logging	Keeping detailed logs of physical access to devices can help track any unauthorized entry.

5. CASE STUDIES OF REAL-WORLD ATTACKS

The vulnerabilities and repercussions of Internet of Things (IoT) systems can be better understood by analysing actual assaults on these devices.

5.1 Notable Incidents and Breaches in IoT Systems

Mirai Botnet Attack (2016): The Mirai botnet exploited infected Internet of Things (IoT) devices like cameras and routers to perform distributed denial of service (DDoS) assaults. Major internet services were interrupted, demonstrating the urgent need for improved security measures in the Internet of Things.

Stuxnet Worm (2010): Stuxnet showed how virus might affect industrial IoT systems in general, not only specifically. It damaged Iran's nuclear program by exploiting vulnerabilities in SCADA systems.

Ring Camera Hacks (2019): Numerous incidents involved hackers gaining access to Ring smart cameras, enabling unauthorized surveillance and harassment of homeowners.

5.2 Lessons Learned From Past Attacks

These attacks underscore the importance of robust authentication and authorization mechanisms, as many breaches result from weak or default passwords.

They emphasize the need for regular firmware updates and security patches to address known vulnerabilities.

Attacks like Mirai highlight the significance of securing IoT devices, even seemingly inconsequential ones, to prevent them from being used as attack vectors (Tariq, Khan, and Asim 2021).

Incidents such as the Ring camera hacks underscore the need for better user education and awareness regarding IoT security.

5.3 Impact on Industry and Consumers

IoT security incidents erode consumer trust and confidence in connected devices, slowing down adoption.

They can result in financial losses for affected individuals or organizations, including costs associated with data breaches and device replacements.

Attacks targeting critical infrastructure can have severe consequences, affecting public safety and national security.

By studying these real-world attacks and their repercussions, organizations and policymakers can make informed decisions to strengthen IoT security and protect against similar threats in the future.

6. DEFENSIVE STRATEGIES AND SOLUTIONS

Defensive Strategies and Solutions in IoT Security encompass a range of measures designed to safeguard Internet of Things (IoT) environments from potential cyber threats and attacks. These strategies are critical in ensuring the integrity, confidentiality, and availability of IoT systems. They include:

6.1 Intrusion Detection Systems (IDS) for IoT

Intrusion Detection Systems (IDS) are crucial components of cybersecurity infrastructure that play a pivotal role in safeguarding IoT environments. They operate by monitoring and analyzing network traffic and system activities for signs of unauthorized access or malicious activities. The IDS will send out alerts to administrators or security teams whenever it detects anything out of the ordinary, giving them time to take appropriate action.

6.2 Types of IDS for IoT Environments

a.   *Signature-Based IDS:* Signature-based In order to detect malicious actions, IDS uses predetermined patterns or signatures of known attacks. It does this by comparing data on potential attacks with patterns seen in actual network traffic or system behaviour (Jasim 2022).

Application: In particular, it excels at identifying assaults and threats with well-established signatures. However, it may struggle to recognise attack routes that are novel or in flux and for which there are no known signatures.

b.   *Anomaly-Based IDS:* Anomaly-based if an IoT device deviates from its learned pattern of behaviour, an IDS system will sound an alarm. Normal patterns are established, and outliers are found.

Application: This category excels at uncovering attacks and threats that have never been seen before because their signatures may not exist. Any variation from the taught baseline is marked as suspicious, however this could lead to false positives.

c.   *Hybrid IDS:* To take use of the benefits of both signature-based and anomaly-based methods, hybrid IDS combines them. It seeks to establish a symmetrical method of detecting threats.

Application: Because it makes use of both predetermined signatures and anomaly detection, Hybrid IDS improves detection accuracy. This has the potential to lessen the occurrence of false positives while still covering all potential dangers.

6.3 Implementing IDS in IoT Networks

a.   *Network Segmentation:* Segmenting a network means breaking it up into smaller, more manageable pieces, known as subnetworks. A breach in one section of the network would not immediately affect the remainder, reducing the severity of any attack.

Application: By dividing the network into separate sections, other parts can stay secure even if one is breached. It's a must-have safety precaution for keeping dangers at bay.

b.   *Traffic Monitoring and Analysis*: Network traffic monitoring entails keeping a watchful eye on the flow of data within the network at all times. This aids in spotting trends that may point to criminal intent or other forms of danger.

Application: Potential security breaches can be quickly identified and dealt with thanks to real-time traffic monitoring. As a result, security teams can respond swiftly and effectively to new threats.

c.   *Behavioral Profiling:* Behavioral profiling establishes baselines for normal device behavior. It triggers alerts when deviations from this established behavior are detected, indicating potential security breaches.

Application: Behavioural profiling is useful for spotting out-of-the-ordinary actions that may point to a security compromise. By changing with the times, it can detect new threats as they emerge.

These preventative measures and answers are important building blocks of an Internet of Things security architecture. Having them in place helps deter hackers from breaching security and safeguards private information. When used together, these parts strengthen the safety of IoT networks in their own special ways (Li et al. 2019).

6.4 Secure Communication Protocols in IoT

If you want to protect the privacy, security, and veracity of information passing over the Internet of Things (IoT), you need to implement secure communication protocols. SSL/TLS and MQTT are two popular technologies for safeguarding communications in the IoT.

SSL/TLS and MQTT for IoT: In order to communicate securely across a network, a cryptographic mechanism known as SSL/TLS (Secure Sockets Layer/Transport Layer Security) is used. It makes sure that any information passed between IoT gadgets and servers is encrypted and safe from prying eyes. SSL/TLS is essential in the IoT for protecting sensitive information like personal details, medical records, and command inputs.

Message Queuing Telemetry Transport, or MQTT, is a popular messaging protocol used in IoT applications because to its small footprint and high efficiency. It allows devices to both create and subscribe to topics, improving IoT network connectivity. When used in conjunction with SSL/TLS, MQTT protects data during transmission to prevent eavesdropping (Chen et al. 2020).

6.4.1 Securing MQTT Communication Channels

Authentication and Authorization: Only authorised devices will be able to publish or subscribe to MQTT topics if strong authentication measures, such as usernames and passwords, are implemented. RBAC is a method of fine-tuning permissions such that only authorised users can perform a certain action.

TLS Encryption: TLS encryption provides an additional safeguard for MQTT exchanges. This prevents any unauthorised parties from gaining access to the sensitive information passed between devices and brokers (Chen et al. 2020; Li et al. 2019).

Certificate-based Authentication: X.509 certificates enable devices to validate each other's identities prior to establishing a network connection. This helps boost confidence in IoT networks.

Secure Broker Configuration: It is essential to configure the MQTT broker with secure settings, such as a robust cypher suite and encrypted protocols. This eliminates the possibility of exploitable flaws or incorrect settings.

Regular Security Audits: Periodic assessments of MQTT implementations and configurations help identify and rectify potential security weaknesses, ensuring ongoing protection against threats.

With these secure communication protocols and practises in place, businesses can lay a solid groundwork for safe Internet of Things (IoT) installations. Protecting sensitive information, user privacy, and the security of Internet of Things networks in the face of constantly increasing cyber threats is aided by this.

6.5 Device Authentication and Access Control in IoT

6.5.1 Implementing Robust Authentication Measures

To do so, robust methods must be used to verify the identities of IoT devices before allowing them access to the network or other system resources.

Techniques required:

Public Key Infrastructure (PKI): Utilizes cryptographic keys for establishing secure connections between devices, ensuring authentication is secure.

Certificate-Based Authentication: Involves the exchange of digital certificates among devices to validate their identities, thereby enhancing the security of the authentication process.

Multi-Factor Authentication (MFA): Requires devices to provide multiple forms of authentication, such as passwords, tokens, or biometrics, thereby enhancing security.

Secure Tokens and Keys: Devices are furnished with unique tokens or cryptographic keys for authentication, which must be stored and managed securely.

6.5.2 Role-Based Access Control (RBAC) in IoT

This technique of security controls who can access the system based on their function inside the business.

Role Assignment: Specific roles are allocated to devices or applications, endowing them with predefined access rights based on their functions.

Example: An IoT sensor might possess read-only access, whereas a control system has read and write privileges.

Advantages:

Precise Control: RBAC enables meticulous control over which devices or applications can execute specific actions within the IoT ecosystem.

Risk Reduction: By constraining access to only essential functions, the potential attack surface is minimized, diminishing the risk of unauthorized or malicious activities.

Regular Review and Updates: To keep access controls relevant to the ever-changing nature of operations, it is crucial to review and revise role assignments on a regular basis.

Organisations may set up a formidable security architecture for their IoT deployments through the use of strong authentication mechanisms and the incorporation of RBAC. This not only protects private information but also reduces the possibility of harm coming from outside the IoT ecosystem.

6.5.3 Secure Boot and Firmware Updates

This involves implementing measures to ensure that the boot process of an IoT device is secure and has not been tampered with.

Ensuring Secure Device Boot Process:

Securing the Device Boot Process involves implementing measures to guarantee the integrity and security of the IoT device's boot sequence, ensuring it hasn't been tampered with (El Jaouhari and Bouvet 2022).

Best Practices:

Employ a Secure Bootloader: Utilize a secure bootloader that verifies the firmware's integrity before execution.

Apply Cryptographic Signatures: Use digital signatures on firmware images to authenticate their validity during the boot process.

Establish a Hardware-Based Root of Trust: Utilize hardware-based methods to establish a root of trust, ensuring the initial executed code is secure.

Utilize Hardware Security Modules (HSMs): Employ HSMs to securely store cryptographic keys and carry out secure boot operations.

6.5.4 Best Practices for Firmware Updates

Best Practices for Firmware Updates involve setting up guidelines and practices to ensure secure application of firmware updates.

Recommendations:

a. *Implement Code Signing:* Digitally sign firmware updates to validate their authenticity and integrity prior to installation.
b. *Utilize Secure Channels:* Use encrypted channels for transmitting firmware updates to devices, preventing interception or tampering.
c. *Incorporate Rollback Protection:* Put in place measures to prevent the installation of older or potentially vulnerable firmware versions.
d. *Ensure Timely Patching:* Guarantee that firmware updates are promptly applied to address known vulnerabilities.

By implementing these practices, organizations can strengthen the boot process of IoT devices and ensure that firmware updates are securely applied, thus reducing the risk of unauthorized access or malicious activities (Moquin et al. 2019).

6.5.5 Data Encryption and Integrity Checks

Securing IoT systems hinges on two critical elements: Data Encryption and Integrity Checks (Cabrera-Gutiérrez et al. 2022).

Implementing End-to-End Encryption

This practice involves leveraging cryptographic techniques to fortify data transmission, guaranteeing that only authorized entities can decipher and access the information. Methods Applicable:

a. *Advanced Encryption Standard (AES):* This employs symmetric-key encryption to ensure secure data transmission.
b. *Transport Layer Security (TLS):* Commonly used in web applications, TLS establishes secure communication over networks.
c. *Secure Sockets Layer (SSL):* SSL is pivotal in securing data transfers over the internet, especially within web browsers.
d. *Public Key Infrastructure (PKI):* PKI employs asymmetric cryptography to facilitate secure key exchange (Cabrera-Gutiérrez et al. 2022).

6.5.6 Data Integrity Verification Methods

These techniques serve the purpose of validating that data remains unaltered during transit or storage, offering a defense against unauthorized alterations (Xie et al. 2021).

Methods Applicable

1. *Hash Functions:* These generate unique cryptographic hash values for data, enabling straightforward verification of integrity.
2. *Message Authentication Codes (MACs):* MACs employ cryptographic algorithms to generate a distinctive tag for data, thereby assuring its integrity.
3. *Cyclic Redundancy Check (CRC):* CRC serves to verify the integrity of data blocks by computing a checksum.
4. *Digital Signatures:* Through cryptographic techniques, digital signatures validate both the authenticity and integrity of data.

By implementing robust end-to-end encryption and utilizing effective data integrity verification methods, organizations can establish a shield around the confidentiality and integrity of their IoT data. This proactive approach safeguards against unauthorized access and tampering (Xie et al. 2021).

7. SECURITY BEST PRACTICES FOR IOT SENSORY BIG DATA ANALYSIS

Security Best Practices for IoT Sensory Big Data Analysis encompass a range of measures to ensure the integrity and confidentiality of sensitive information. Here are some crucial strategies (Dartmann, Song, and Schmeink 2019):

a. Designing Secure IoT Architectures

This involves giving paramount importance to security in the development of IoT infrastructures.

Implementation: This includes integrating security-by-design principles like robust access controls, encryption, and secure communication protocols into the architecture of IoT systems.

b. Segmentation and Network Isolation

This practice involves partitioning IoT networks into isolated segments to confine device communication, thereby minimizing the potential impact of security breaches.

Implementation: Techniques such as virtual LANs (VLANs) and firewalls are employed to separate IoT devices into distinct network segments based on their functions and security requirements.

c. Implementing Zero Trust Security Models

- The assumption is made that any and all devices, users, and processes could be malicious.
- It is important that all transactions within the IoT ecosystem use the same authentication, authorisation, and verification methods.
- This method aids in keeping Internet of Things (IoT) systems safe from potential dangers, such as data corruption or fraudulent analysis results.

d. Vulnerability Scanning and Penetration Testing

Vulnerability Scanning: It's the process of actively looking for and evaluating security holes in a system. Exploitable weak spots can be located with the help of automated tools and methods.

Penetration Testing: In this case, known vulnerabilities are deliberately tried to be exploited to see what effects they might have. To mimic real-life cyberattacks, it often uses both automatic and manual testing methods (Nagpure and Kurkure 2017).

The security posture of a system can be fully understood by an organization if vulnerability scanning and penetration testing are both performed. This data is essential for making well-informed decisions about how to fortify and safeguard their infrastructure.

e. Continuous Monitoring for Anomalies

This method entails keeping a close eye on user activity, system logs, and network traffic for signs of malicious or suspicious activity.

Implementation: Using monitoring technologies like as intrusion detection systems (IDS), security information and event management (SIEM) software, and more to detect and respond to possible security events as they happen in real time.

By adopting these procedures, businesses may take a more preventative approach to security in the face of threats to their IoT sensors and the big data they collect. Taking this method helps keep the IoT ecosystem secure and prevents critical data from ever being compromised.

f. User Education and Training

Users must be given the proper education and training to equip them with the knowledge, abilities, and best practises necessary to connect with IoT systems securely. Several strategies exist for accomplishing this goal which are as follows.

Workshops and Seminars: Educating people by holding seminars or workshops on how to spot phishing scams, create secure passwords, and spot unusual behaviour.

Interactive Modules: Making user-friendly, on-demand resources for IoT security education, such as interactive modules or e-learning courses. *Simulated Exercises:* providing users with simulated exercises or drills to assist them prepare for future security events and practise responding to them.

Feedback Loops: Facilitating user reporting of security issues and giving prompt responses and direction.

g. Raising Security Awareness among IoT Users

To increase security awareness, people must be made aware of the dangers of using Internet of Things (IoT) devices and taught how to protect themselves and their data (Al-Garadi et al. 2020)(M. A. Khan et al. 2023). This can be accomplished by:

Communication Channels: Spreading information about security measures using a variety of channels, including electronic mail, periodicals, posters, and in-house messaging programmes.

Scenario-based Training: Using examples and scenarios from the real world to demonstrate the relevance and utility of security measures in a variety of contexts.

Regular Updates: Notifying users on a frequent basis of new security risks, vulnerabilities, and best practises.

Security Champions: Appointing "security champions" within the company to promote security awareness and communicate useful information is an effective strategy.

h. Providing Resources for Secure Usage

Tools, instructions, and materials that facilitate the effective adoption and implementation of security measures on the part of users are what we mean by "resources for secure usage." This can be achieved by:

Security Portals or Websites: Making specific online hubs where people may go to find information on protecting their IoT devices is also recommended.

Downloadable Materials: Make available to users downloadable resources, such security checklists, infographics, and tip sheets, to help them stay safe when dealing with Internet of Things devices.

Training Materials: Creating in-depth resources for learners of varying skill levels, covering a wide range of topics related to IoT security.

Organisations can encourage user participation in ensuring a safe IoT environment by investing in comprehensive user education and training programmes. This not only helps lessen the likelihood of security problems, but it also helps spread a sense of security consciousness throughout the company.

i. Incident Response and Recovery Plans

Organisations should have a plan in place for how to respond to and recover from security incidents and breaches. These plans define actions to take in order to contain an incident, mitigate its effects, and recover as quickly as possible.

This can be achieved by:

Establishing Response Teams: Assigning people or groups to handle incidents arising from the Internet of Things. The members of these groups need to know their specific tasks.

Creating Playbooks: Creating playbooks for responding to various sorts of IoT-related problems, including how to investigate, contain, eliminate, and recover from them.

Simulated Drills: The effectiveness of response plans can be evaluated, improvement areas can be pinpointed, and response teams can be trained by conducting regular simulated incident response exercises.

Communication Protocols: Instances should be reported both internally and, if necessary, to external stakeholders using well-defined routes and protocols for doing so.

Documentation and Reporting: Making sure that occurrences are properly recorded, including what happened, what was done, and what was learned. After an incident, this data can be used to better understand what went wrong and how to prevent it from happening again.

j. Developing IoT-Specific Incident Response Protocols

To deal with security issues and breaches involving IoT devices and systems, specialised protocols have been developed (Altaş, Dalkiliç and Cabuk 2022). This involves:

IoT Device Identification: Creating a system to instantly detect compromised Internet of Things (IoT) devices, pinpoint their locations, and assess the potential damage to the IoT network as a whole.

Forensic Analysis: Methods are outlined for gathering evidence and determining the cause of an incident involving a compromised Internet of Things device.

IoT-Specific Mitigation Techniques: Defining specialized techniques for mitigating IoT-related threats, which may involve isolating compromised devices, applying patches, or taking other specific actions.

Legal and Regulatory Considerations: Addressing legal and regulatory requirements specific to IoT devices, such as data privacy laws or industry-specific compliance standards.

k. Business Continuity and Disaster Recovery for IoT

Critical Internet of Things (IoT) systems can continue running even if there is a disruption or disaster, thanks to business continuity and disaster recovery plans. This includes:

Redundancy and Failover: In the event of a hardware breakdown or a network outage, continuous service can be maintained through the use of redundant IoT systems and failover techniques.

Data Backups and Recovery: Establishing regular backup methods for IoT data and systems is crucial, as is having a plan in place to quickly restore operations in the event of data loss or system failure.

Alternative Power and Connectivity: Preparing for backup power and communication channels is crucial to ensuring that Internet of Things (IoT) systems can continue functioning in the event of a power outage or network disruption.

Testing and Validation: Regular testing of disaster recovery and business continuity plans is essential to ensuring their efficacy in the event of an emergency.

By developing and regularly testing incident response, IoT-specific incident protocols, and business continuity and disaster recovery plans, organizations can ensure a swift and effective response to security incidents, minimize disruptions, and maintain the integrity and availability of IoT systems.

8. FUTURE TRENDS AND EMERGING THREATS

A future trend is a type of technological advancement or invention that is likely to have a major impact on a certain industry or field in the near future. They help companies and individuals adapt to new environments and maintain a competitive edge. Following are the key points for future trends and Emerging Threats.

8.1 Future Trends

AI-Powered Threat Detection: In the realm of IoT security, the integration of artificial intelligence (AI) and machine learning (ML) marks a significant advancement. This amalgamation equips IoT security systems with the capability to process vast volumes of data in real-time. Through this, systems can discern patterns and anomalies that may signify potential security threats. The practical application of AI in this context goes beyond conventional methods, providing a more agile and anticipatory approach to the identification and mitigation of security risks (El Akrami et al. 2023).

Blockchain for IoT Security: Blockchain technology, renowned for its decentralized and tamper-resistant ledger, finds compelling application in IoT security. When adapted to the IoT landscape, Blockchain introduces a layer of enhanced security. It furnishes a secure and transparent framework for recording device interactions and transactions. By leveraging this technology, trust is established, data integrity is ensured, and unauthorized alterations or tampering are effectively prevented within IoT networks (Andoni et al. 2019).

Figure 5. Future trends and emerging threats

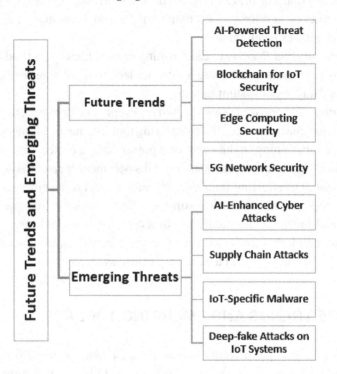

Edge Computing Security: As the significance of processing data closer to its source gains prominence through edge computing, ensuring security at this decentralized level emerges as a critical concern. The shift towards localized critical processes mandates robust security measures at the edge devices themselves. This approach diminishes reliance on centralized servers, thereby safeguarding sensitive data and vital operations.

5G Network Security: The advent of 5G networks promises a new era of possibilities for IoT applications. However, it concurrently introduces fresh security challenges. Safeguarding the augmented volume of data transmitted over these networks necessitates specialized security measures. This includes encryption protocols, authentication frameworks, and stringent access controls tailored to the distinctive attributes of 5G networks (Meena et al. 2022; Jatothu et al. 2022; Abidin et al. 2022).

8.2 Emerging Threats

AI-Enhanced Cyber Attacks: Cybercriminals are progressively harnessing the potential of AI and ML to orchestrate sophisticated and adaptive attacks. These attacks possess the ability to evolve in real-time, rendering conventional security measures less effective (Apostolakis et al. 2021). The implications are substantial; AI-enhanced attacks can potentially breach traditional security barriers, leading to an elevated risk of successful breaches and compromised data.

Supply Chain Attacks: A growing concern lies in the targeting of the supply chain of IoT devices by malicious actors. By compromising devices at various stages of production or distribution, attackers can embed malicious components or software before devices reach end-users. This tactic poses significant risks, potentially resulting in compromised devices with inherent vulnerabilities. Such compromises expose users to the threat of unauthorized access and data breaches.

IoT-Specific Malware: The proliferation of malware tailored explicitly for IoT devices underscores a burgeoning threat. These malicious entities are meticulously crafted to exploit the distinctive characteristics and vulnerabilities of IoT ecosystems. The repercussions are far-reaching, as IoT-specific malware can lead to device compromise. This, in turn, can facilitate unauthorized control, data theft, or even physical harm in critical applications.

Deepfake Attacks on IoT Systems: The advancing capabilities of deepfake technology present a notable threat to IoT systems reliant on voice or image recognition for authentication. Attackers can generate convincingly deceptive audio or video content, potentially deceiving IoT systems. This deception can culminate in unauthorized access to IoT devices or systems, imperiling security and privacy. (Mitra et al. 2021)(Sridevi et al. 2022)

Understanding these future trends and emerging threats is paramount for organizations aiming to proactively mitigate potential security risks in the ever-evolving landscape of IoT technology. It empowers them to implement robust security measures and safeguards, thus ensuring the protection of their IoT ecosystems and sensitive data.

9. CONCLUSION

In this extensive exploration of IoT Sensory Big Data Analysis, we have delved into the intricate domain of securing interconnected systems, underscoring the paramount importance of safeguarding sensitive information. We initiated our journey with a meticulous scrutiny of various threat vectors, spanning from Denial of Service (DoS) attacks to Man-in-the-Middle (MitM) attacks, dissecting their distinct traits and potential ramifications on IoT systems. Subsequently, we provided a comprehensive exposition of mitigation strategies, presenting a panoramic view of how organizations can establish robust defenses against these threats.

As the technological landscape continues its rapid evolution, so too does the security paradigm surrounding IoT Sensory Big Data Analysis. Emerging trends, such as the integration of artificial intelligence (AI) and machine learning (ML) for threat detection, the incorporation of Blockchain for heightened data integrity, and the imperative of securing edge computing, are poised to revolutionize the security posture of IoT ecosystems. The deployment of 5G networks, while promising unprecedented opportunities, introduces a fresh set of security challenges, necessitating tailored measures to safeguard the surge of transmitted data. However, in parallel with these advancements, new threats emerge. AI-augmented cyber-attacks, vulnerabilities within supply chains, IoT-targeted malware, and the spectre of deepfake incursions cast a significant shadow, underscoring the need for heightened vigilance and forward-thinking security protocols.

At its essence, the endeavour to secure IoT Sensory Big Data Analysis transcends the confines of technology; it emerges as a foundational imperative in an era of escalating interconnectivity. By immersing themselves in a comprehensive understanding of the intricacies of IoT security, organizations fortify their systems against latent vulnerabilities and nascent threats. This proactive stance not only fortifies the bastions of sensitive data but also upholds the integrity and reliability of insights gleaned from IoT sensory data.

As we stand on the threshold of what lies ahead, it is abundantly clear that the fusion of technology and security will delineate the contours of the future in IoT. By remaining astutely attuned to emerging trends and the evolving threat landscape, organizations navigate this dynamic terrain with sagacity, ensconcing the sanctity and confidentiality of their IoT ecosystems. In this symphony of progress and security, we chart a course toward an interconnected future fortified by knowledge, vigilance, and an unwavering commitment to safeguarding the digital realms we traverse.

REFERENCES

Abidin, S., & Raghunath, M. P. (2022). Identification of Disease Based on Symptoms by Employing ML. *2022 International Conference on Inventive Computation Technologies (ICICT)*, 1357–62. 10.1109/ICICT54344.2022.9850480

Akrami, N. E., Hanine, M., Flores, E. S., Aray, D. G., & Ashraf, I. (2023). Unleashing the Potential of Blockchain and Machine Learning: Insights and Emerging Trends from Bibliometric Analysis. *IEEE Access : Practical Innovations, Open Solutions*, *11*, 78879–78903. doi:10.1109/ACCESS.2023.3298371

Al-Garadi, M. A., Mohamed, A., Al-Ali, A. K., Du, X., Ali, I., & Guizani, M. (2020). A Survey of Machine and Deep Learning Methods for Internet of Things (IoT) Security. *IEEE Communications Surveys and Tutorials*, *22*(3), 1646–1685. doi:10.1109/COMST.2020.2988293

Al-Shareeda, M. A., Anbar, M., Manickam, S., & Hasbullah, I. H. (2020). Review of Prevention Schemes for Man-in-the-Middle (MITM) Attack in Vehicular Ad Hoc Networks. *International Journal of Engineering and Management Research, 10*(3), 10. doi:10.31033/ijemr.10.3.23

Al-Shareeda, M. A., & Manickam, S. (2022). Man-in-the-Middle Attacks in Mobile Ad Hoc Networks (MANETs): Analysis and Evaluation. *Symmetry, 14*(8), 1543. doi:10.3390/sym14081543

Ali, G., Dida, M. A., & Sam, A. E. (2021). A Secure and Efficient Multi-Factor Authentication Algorithm for Mobile Money Applications. *Future Internet, 13*(12), 299. doi:10.3390/fi13120299

Altaş, H., Dalkiliç, G., & Çabuk, U. C. (2022). Data Immutability and Event Management via Blockchain in the Internet of Things. *Turkish Journal of Electrical Engineering and Computer Sciences, 30*(2), 451–468. doi:10.3906/elk-2103-105

Ambika, P. (2020). Machine Learning and Deep Learning Algorithms on the Industrial Internet of Things (IIoT). *Advances in Computers, 117*(1), 321–338. doi:10.1016/bs.adcom.2019.10.007

Andoni, M., Robu, V., Flynn, D., Abram, S., Geach, D., Jenkins, D., McCallum, P., & Peacock, A. (2019). Blockchain Technology in the Energy Sector: A Systematic Review of Challenges and Opportunities. *Renewable & Sustainable Energy Reviews, 100*, 143–174. doi:10.1016/j.rser.2018.10.014

Apostolakis, K. C., Dimitriou, N., Margetis, G., Ntoa, S., Tzovaras, D., & Stephanidis, C. (2021). DARLENE–Improving Situational Awareness of European Law Enforcement Agents through a Combination of Augmented Reality and Artificial Intelligence Solutions. *Open Research Europe*, 1. PMID:37645167

Blinowski, G. J., & Piotrowski, P. (2020). CVE Based Classification of Vulnerable IoT Systems. *Theory and Applications of Dependable Computer Systems: Proceedings of the Fifteenth International Conference on Dependability of Computer Systems DepCoS-RELCOMEX, June 29–July 3, 2020, Brunów, Poland, 15*, 82–93. 10.1007/978-3-030-48256-5_9

Cabrera-Gutiérrez, A. J., Castillo, E., Escobar-Molero, A., Alvarez-Bermejo, J. A., Morales, D. P., & Parrilla, L. (2022). Integration of Hardware Security Modules and Permissioned Blockchain in Industrial Iot Networks. *IEEE Access : Practical Innovations, Open Solutions, 10*, 114331–114345. doi:10.1109/ACCESS.2022.3217815

Chen, F., Huo, Y., Zhu, J., & Fan, D. (2020). A Review on the Study on MQTT Security Challenge. *2020 IEEE International Conference on Smart Cloud (SmartCloud)*, 128–33. 10.1109/SmartCloud49737.2020.00032

Cruz, J. P., Kaji, Y., & Yanai, N. (2018). RBAC-SC: Role-Based Access Control Using Smart Contract. *IEEE Access : Practical Innovations, Open Solutions*, 6, 12240–12251. doi:10.1109/ACCESS.2018.2812844

Dartmann, G., Song, H., & Schmeink, A. (2019). *Big Data Analytics for Cyber-Physical Systems: Machine Learning for the Internet of Things*. Elsevier.

Eceiza, M., Flores, J. L., & Iturbe, M. (2021). Fuzzing the Internet of Things: A Review on the Techniques and Challenges for Efficient Vulnerability Discovery in Embedded Systems. *IEEE Internet of Things Journal*, 8(13), 10390–10411. doi:10.1109/JIOT.2021.3056179

Feng, Zhu, Han, Zhou, Wen, & Xiang. (2022). Detecting Vulnerability on IoT Device Firmware: A Survey. *IEEE/CAA Journal of Automatica Sinica*, 10(1), 25–41.

Gupta, B. B., & Dahiya, A. (2021). *Distributed Denial of Service (DDoS) Attacks: Classification, Attacks, Challenges and Countermeasures*. CRC Press. doi:10.1201/9781003107354

Haddaji, A., Ayed, S., & Fourati, L. C. (2022). Artificial Intelligence Techniques to Mitigate Cyber-Attacks within Vehicular Networks: Survey. *Computers & Electrical Engineering*, 104, 108460. doi:10.1016/j.compeleceng.2022.108460

Haq, A. U., Ping Li, J., Khan, G. A., Khan, J., Ishrat, M., Guru, A., & Agbley, B. L. Y. (2022). Community Detection Approach Via Graph Regularized Non-Negative Matrix Factorization. *2022 19th International Computer Conference on Wavelet Active Media Technology and Information Processing, ICCWAMTIP 2022*. 10.1109/ICCWAMTIP56608.2022.10016496

Humayun, M., Jhanjhi, N. Z., Alsayat, A., & Ponnusamy, V. (2021). Internet of Things and Ransomware: Evolution, Mitigation and Prevention. *Egyptian Informatics Journal*, 22(1), 105–117. doi:10.1016/j.eij.2020.05.003

Jaouhari, S. E., & Bouvet, E. (2022). Secure Firmware Over-The-Air Updates for IoT: Survey, Challenges, and Discussions. *Internet of Things : Engineering Cyber Physical Human Systems*, 18, 100508. doi:10.1016/j.iot.2022.100508

Jasim, A. D. (2022). A Survey of Intrusion Detection Using Deep Learning in Internet of Things. *Iraqi Journal For Computer Science and Mathematics*, 3(1), 83–93.

Jatothu, R., & Lal, J. D. (2022). End-to-End Latency Analysis for Data Transmission via Optimum Path Allocation in Industrial Sensor Networks. *Wireless Communications and Mobile Computing*.

Jurcut, A., Niculcea, T., Ranaweera, P., & Le-Khac, N.-A. (2020). Security Considerations for Internet of Things: A Survey. *SN Computer Science*, *1*(4), 1–19. doi:10.1007/s42979-020-00201-3

Khan, A., Ahmad, A., Ahmed, M., Sessa, J., & Anisetti, M. (2022). Authorization Schemes for Internet of Things: Requirements, Weaknesses, Future Challenges and Trends. *Complex & Intelligent Systems*, *8*(5), 3919–3941. doi:10.1007/s40747-022-00765-y

Khan, M. A., Khan, G. A., Khan, J., Anwar, T., Ashraf, Z., Atoum, I., Ahmad, N., Shahid, M., Ishrat, M., & Alghamdi, A. A. (2023). Adaptive Weighted Low-Rank Sparse Representation for Multi-View Clustering. *IEEE Access : Practical Innovations, Open Solutions*, *11*, 60681–60692. doi:10.1109/ACCESS.2023.3285662

Khan, W., Ishrat, M., Haleem, M., Khan, A. N., Hasan, M. K., & Farooqui, N. A. (2023). *An Extensive Study and Review on Dark Web Threats and Detection Techniques*. doi:10.4018/978-1-6684-8133-2.ch011

Li, W., Tug, S., Meng, W., & Wang, Y. (2019). Designing Collaborative Blockchained Signature-Based Intrusion Detection in IoT Environments. *Future Generation Computer Systems*, *96*, 481–489. doi:10.1016/j.future.2019.02.064

Liang, H., Zhu, L., Yu, F. R., & Wang, X. (2022). A Cross-Layer Defense Method for Blockchain Empowered CBTC Systems against Data Tampering Attacks. *IEEE Transactions on Intelligent Transportation Systems*, *24*(1), 501–515. doi:10.1109/TITS.2022.3211020

Markkandeyan, & Shivani Gupta, Narayanan, Reddy, Al-Khasawneh, Ishrat, & Kiran. (2023). Deep Learning Based Semantic Segmentation Approach for Automatic Detection of Brain Tumor. *International Journal of Computers, Communications & Control*, *18*(4). Advance online publication. doi:10.15837/ijccc.2023.4.5186

Meena, P., Pal, M. B., Jain, P. K., & Pamula, R. (2022). 6G Communication Networks: Introduction, Vision, Challenges, and Future Directions. *Wireless Personal Communications*, *125*(2), 1097–1123. doi:10.1007/s11277-022-09590-5

Mitra, Mohanty, Corcoran, & Kougianos. (2021). IFace: A Deepfake Resilient Digital Identification Framework for Smart Cities. *2021 IEEE International Symposium on Smart Electronic Systems (ISES)*, 361–66. 10.1109/iSES52644.2021.00090

Moquin, Kim, Blair, Farnell, Di, & Mantooth. (2019). Enhanced Uptime and Firmware Cybersecurity for Grid-Connected Power Electronics. 2019 IEEE CyberPELS (CyberPELS), 1–6.

Mukherjee, S., Gupta, S., Rawlley, O., & Jain, S. (2022). Leveraging Big Data Analytics in 5G-enabled IoT and Industrial IoT for the Development of Sustainable Smart Cities. *Transactions on Emerging Telecommunications Technologies*, *33*(12), e4618. doi:10.1002/ett.4618

Nagpure, S., & Kurkure, S. (2017). Vulnerability Assessment and Penetration Testing of Web Application. *2017 International Conference on Computing, Communication, Control and Automation (ICCUBEA)*, 1–6. 10.1109/ICCUBEA.2017.8463920

Oz, H., Aris, A., Levi, A., & Selcuk Uluagac, A. (2022). A Survey on Ransomware: Evolution, Taxonomy, and Defense Solutions. *ACM Computing Surveys*, *54*(11s), 1–37. doi:10.1145/3514229

Polychronou, N. F., & Thevenon, P.-H. (2021). Securing Iot/Iiot from Software Attacks Targeting Hardware Vulnerabilities. *2021 19th IEEE International New Circuits and Systems Conference (NEWCAS)*, 1–4.

Polychronou, N.-F., Thevenon, P.-H., Puys, M., & Beroulle, V. (2021). A Comprehensive Survey of Attacks without Physical Access Targeting Hardware Vulnerabilities in IoT/IIoT Devices, and Their Detection Mechanisms. *ACM Transactions on Design Automation of Electronic Systems*, *27*(1), 1–35. doi:10.1145/3471936

Rains, T. (2020). *Cybersecurity Threats, Malware Trends, and Strategies: Learn to Mitigate Exploits, Malware, Phishing, and Other Social Engineering Attacks*. Packt Publishing Ltd.

Reda, H. T., Anwar, A., & Mahmood, A. (2022). Comprehensive Survey and Taxonomies of False Data Injection Attacks in Smart Grids: Attack Models, Targets, and Impacts. *Renewable & Sustainable Energy Reviews*, *163*, 112423. doi:10.1016/j.rser.2022.112423

Sridevi, Sameera, Garapati, Krishnamadhuri, & Bethu. (2022). IoT Based Application Designing of Deep Fake Test for Face Animation. *Proceedings of the 2022 6th International Conference on Cloud and Big Data Computing*, 24–30. 10.1145/3555962.3555967

Srivastava, A., Gupta, S., Quamara, M., Chaudhary, P., & Aski, V. J. (2020). Future IoT-enabled Threats and Vulnerabilities: State of the Art, Challenges, and Future Prospects. *International Journal of Communication Systems*, *33*(12), e4443. doi:10.1002/dac.4443

Tariq, N., Khan, F. A., & Asim, M. (2021). Security Challenges and Requirements for Smart Internet of Things Applications: A Comprehensive Analysis. *Procedia Computer Science*, *191*, 425–430. doi:10.1016/j.procs.2021.07.053

Torres, N., Pinto, P., & Lopes, S. I. (2021). Security Vulnerabilities in LPWANs—An Attack Vector Analysis for the IoT Ecosystem. *Applied Sciences (Basel, Switzerland)*, *11*(7), 3176. doi:10.3390/app11073176

Tufail, S., Parvez, I., Batool, S., & Sarwat, A. (2021). A Survey on Cybersecurity Challenges, Detection, and Mitigation Techniques for the Smart Grid. *Energies*, *14*(18), 5894. doi:10.3390/en14185894

Xie, G., Liu, Y., Xin, G., & Yang, Q. (2021). Blockchain-Based Cloud Data Integrity Verification Scheme with High Efficiency. *Security and Communication Networks*, *2021*, 1–15. doi:10.1155/2021/9921209

Yadav, C. S., Singh, J., Yadav, A., Pattanayak, H. S., Kumar, R., Khan, A. A., Haq, M. A., Alhussen, A., & Alharby, S. (2022). Malware Analysis in Iot & Android Systems with Defensive Mechanism. *Electronics (Basel)*, *11*(15), 2354. doi:10.3390/electronics11152354

Yang, X., Shu, L., Liu, Y., Hancke, G. P., Ferrag, M. A., & Huang, K. (2022). Physical Security and Safety of Iot Equipment: A Survey of Recent Advances and Opportunities. *IEEE Transactions on Industrial Informatics*, *18*(7), 4319–4330. doi:10.1109/TII.2022.3141408

Chapter 3
Elevating IoT Sensor Data Management and Security Through Blockchain Solutions

Neha Bhati

(iD) https://orcid.org/0009-0008-0171-2786
AVN Innovations, India

Narayan Vyas
Chandigarh University, India

ABSTRACT

The internet of things, security, and blockchain all come together to deal with the influx of sensor data. The autonomous vehicle industry, for example, relies heavily on effective data management. IoT applications in supply chains, healthcare, and smart cities can all benefit from the immutability, decentralization, and transparency offered by blockchain technology. The research gives recommendations for optimizing blockchain integration and managing scalability concerns. The methodology is supported by real-world case studies, which highlight the potential of blockchain technology to improve efficiency and security in dynamic environments.

1. INTRODUCTION

The convergence of new technologies has ushered in a revolutionary era in the field of managing data from sensors connected to the Internet of Things. This chapter explores the crucial intersection of Internet of Things sensor data, data security, and blockchain implementation. Internet of Things (IoT) sensor data is fundamental

DOI: 10.4018/979-8-3693-0968-1.ch003

to the digital age and powers numerous sectors. Given the inherent weaknesses of this ecosystem, however, there is a pressing need for robust data management and security (Zaabar et al., 2021).

This chapter explains why blockchain technology should be implemented, what it is, how it works, and its significant concepts. IoT data management and security difficulties are broken down to examine blockchain's potential role as a trust-enhancing layer in greater depth. To dig into applications ranging from intelligent city infrastructure to supply chain management. Following fascinating case studies and a look into the future of this dynamic synergy between IoT and blockchain, this article provides practical insights into implementation tactics, scalability, and performance optimization.

1.1 Introduction to Internet of Things Sensor Data

The sheer variety of sensors available in the IoT sensor ecosystem allows it to cover much ground. These can be as simple as a thermometer or a motion detector or as complex as an RFID tag. It is important to note that these sensors have not only permeated our lives but also found applications in various fields, from connected smart homes and the rapidly developing healthcare sector to complex manufacturing procedures and the pioneering landscape of today's agriculture. Realizing the full extent and potential of IoT sensor data requires familiarity with the whole breadth and depth of the sensor ecosystem (B. Sharam et al., 2023).

1.2 Data Management and Security Are Paramount in the Internet of Things (IoT)

Effective data management and robust security measures are crucial as the Internet of Things continues its pervasive expansion (Zheng et al., 2020).

The data produced as an afterthought by the Internet of Things is now a valuable strategic asset in its own right. It is crucial in guiding choices, inspiring creativity, and enhancing efficiency. An in-depth discussion of data's essential function in the IoT ecosystem follows. In addition, it discusses the many difficulties inherent to playing such a crucial part. Among these difficulties are the urgent and ever-evolving security issues and ensuring the data quality being collected and used (Al Sadawi et al., 2021).

1.3 The Benefits of Implementing Blockchain Technology

Integrating blockchain technology is an appealing and innovative answer to the growing and complex problems of IoT data management and security. IoT data can be made more trustworthy by using blockchain, known for its immutable and transparent ledger. Therefore, the framework for understanding how blockchain might significantly improve data integrity and security inside the IoT ecosystem is laid in this section. The combination of blockchain technology and the Internet of Things has tremendous potential, and this paper introduces the notion of intelligent contracts to explore this potential. In addition, the importance of compatibility between blockchain and IoT technologies for facilitating efficient communication and collaboration is discussed (Bhaskar et al., 2020).

2. BLOCKCHAIN TECHNOLOGY: FUNDAMENTALS AND PRINCIPLES

Blockchain technology has evolved beyond its Bitcoin-specific roots to become a disruptive force with far-reaching consequences in many fields. This includes the IoT. Here, This will explore the core ideas behind blockchain, laying the groundwork for how the technology might be used in the Internet of Things (Garg et al., 2021).

2.1 Blockchain: A Brief Overview

Although it was developed to support Bitcoin's monetary system, blockchain technology has since expanded beyond digital currency to become a game-changing innovation across various industries, including IoT (Sheth & Dattani, 2019).

Blockchains are distributed ledgers built to record transactions and data in a safe, transparent, and unchangeable way. Beginning with a look at where blockchain came from, this in-depth exploration demonstrates why this technology is so vital in today's rapidly evolving digital sphere (Tijan et al., 2019).

2.2 Foundational Ideas in Blockchain

Several core ideas provide the foundation for understanding blockchain technology (Erevelles et al., 2022).

- **Decentralization:** Blockchain's basic tenet is decentralization, a radical departure from the centralized authorities of the past. Since no middlemen are involved in a blockchain transaction, the level of trust between users is increased. Because of its lack of central control, this system allows for more private and direct communication between users.
- **Immutability:** This is a crucial feature of blockchain technology. Information recorded securely within a block cannot be altered or removed after it has been

sealed using cryptography. This feature makes blockchain an unbreakable and tamper-proof ledger, guaranteeing the most significant levels of data integrity (Akansha et al., 2023).

- **Transparency:** Blockchain systems are distinguished by their transparency. In this system, everyone can see every transaction because everyone can access the same ledger. All participants in the system can check and double-check the legitimacy of the transactions and data stored on the blockchain, which promotes a culture of trust and responsibility.

Table 1 illustrates fundamental blockchain concepts: Decentralization, Consensus Mechanisms, Cryptographic Hashing, and Distributed Ledger, providing clarity for readers (Xu et al., 2019).

Table 1. Key blockchain concepts

Concept	Description
Decentralization	Explanation of how blockchain eliminates central authorities.
Consensus Mechanisms	Overview of different consensus algorithms like Proof of Work and Proof of Stake.
Cryptographic Hashing	Explanation of how hashing ensures data integrity in the blockchain.
Distributed Ledger	Explanation of how the ledger is distributed across network nodes.

2.3 Different Blockchains and their Architectures

Different blockchain ecosystems exist, each built on a unique foundation and optimized for particular use cases (Xu et al., 2019).

- **Public vs. Private Blockchains**: Differentiating between public and private blockchains highlights a key distinction in how they function. Bitcoin and Ethereum are examples of public blockchains since they are accessible to anybody and may be used on a worldwide scale. On the other hand, private blockchains only provide access to a select set of users and provide greater privacy, security, and flexibility.
- **Blockchain Frameworks:** Various blockchain frameworks and platforms have arisen, each with advantages and disadvantages. Hyperledger Fabric, explicitly designed for enterprise-level use cases, and Ethereum, well-known for its ability to execute smart contracts, are two prominent examples (Lao et al., 2021).

Table 2. Blockchain types and frameworks

Type/Framework	Description
Public Blockchain	Characteristics and examples (e.g., Bitcoin, Ethereum).
Private Blockchain	Key attributes and use cases (e.g., Hyperledger Fabric).
Consortium Blockchain	Explanation and instances of consortium blockchains.
Hybrid Blockchain	Features and practical applications of hybrid blockchains.

Table 2 explains various blockchain types and frameworks, including Public, Private, Consortium, and Hybrid blockchains, providing readers with a comprehensive overview.

2.4 Using IoT Smart Contracts

In the Internet of Things context, incorporating intelligent contracts is a crucial and ground-breaking use of blockchain technology (R. et al..,2023).

- **Introduction to Smart Contracts:** An Overview of Smart Contracts Smart contracts are agreements that can carry out their terms once created. They are exceptional in their ability to automate processes and transactions, carrying out predetermined actions immediately upon detecting that certain conditions have been satisfied.
- **Smart Contracts in IoT:** Incorporating intelligent contracts into the IoT environment brings a revolutionary degree of automation and trust to device interactions. With the help of smart contracts, IoT devices can safely and reliably make purchases, carry out tasks, and set off events on their own. As dive deeper into the synergistic fusion of blockchain technology with the IoT landscape, where secure, transparent, and immutable data management is a cornerstone of progress and innovation, This must have a firm grasp of these fundamental blockchain principles and concepts (Ante, 2021)

3. CHALLENGES IN IOT SENSOR DATA MANAGEMENT AND SECURITY

Numerous serious problems need to be addressed and countered in IoT sensor data management and security. These issues highlight the complexity of the IoT world and the need for solid data management and security.

Table 3. Challenges in IoT sensor data management and security

Challenge	Description
Data Integrity and Authenticity	Discussion on ensuring data accuracy and origin authenticity.
Scalability and Performance	Challenges related to handling large-scale IoT data.
Privacy and Confidentiality	Concerns regarding the privacy of IoT data and user information.
Interoperability	The issue of different IoT devices and platforms communicating effectively.

Table 3 outlines IoT data hurdles: Ensuring Integrity, Managing Scalability, Safeguarding Privacy, and Ensuring Interoperability, offering insight into these critical issues (R.Punugoti et al., 2023).

3.1. Data Integrity and Authenticity

Data Integrity: Maintaining data honesty is still a top priority. Erroneous conclusions and compromised activities may occur from data corruption or unauthorized manipulation in the ever-changing IoT setting (Sun et al., 2023)

- **Authenticity Verification:** Verifying the veracity of information is crucial. When working with data streams from disparate and unreliable IoT devices, determining the authenticity and reliability of those sources is a continuing problem.
- **Blockchain as a Solution:** Blockchain technology shows great promise as a potential answer to these problems. Data integrity and authenticity are bolstered by the system's use of cryptographic techniques and immutable ledger (Zhang et al., 2019).

3.2 Performance and Scalability

- **Exponential Data Growth:** Data created by IoT devices is expected to rise exponentially, creating a significant scaling concern. Data from various IoT devices can be generated quickly, and conventional data management systems may need help keeping up.
- **Real-time Requirements:** In many cases, Internet of Things apps must handle and analyze data in real time. Industries like driverless vehicles and manufacturing processes, where quick decisions are essential, have an exceptionally high demand for this.

- **Scaling Strategies:** Distributed computing, edge computing, and optimized database solutions are just a few of the scalability and performance measures necessary to ensure IoT ecosystems can handle and analyze data effectively.

3.3 Privacy and Confidentiality

- **Privacy Implications**: Accumulating data from various IoT sources might lead to serious privacy risks. Data collected by IoT sensors raises concerns regarding individual privacy and regulatory compliance when the data is pooled and evaluated.
- **Data Encryption:** Strong data encryption at rest and in motion is essential for protecting private information in the Internet of Things. It is crucial to use encryption that complies with industry standards and best practices to reduce the likelihood of privacy and confidentiality breaches.
- **Regulatory Compliance**: Compliance with rules Strict compliance procedures are required due to the ever-changing nature of the regulatory landscape, which includes data protection rules such as GDPR. Compliance with these rules is essential for protecting the privacy of individuals' Internet of Things data.

3.4 Interoperability

- **Fragmented Ecosystem**: Interoperability across the many components of the Internet of Things ecosystem takes time to achieve. Different protocols and standards are used by different IoT devices and platforms, which makes it more challenging to share and exchange data between them.
- **Data Silos**: Data silos form when connected devices fail to share information adequately. IoT data loses some of its value due to the difficulty in analyzing it and making informed decisions based on that analysis.
- **Standardization Initiatives**: Efforts to define and accept IoT standards and protocols, such as MQTT, CoAP, and industry-specific standards, play an essential role in resolving interoperability issues and paving the way for the seamless integration of disparate IoT components (R.Punugoti et al.,2023).

4. IOT DATA MANAGEMENT AND BLOCKCHAIN

Data integrity, security, and efficiency are all boosted within the IoT ecosystem thanks to blockchain technology's essential role in tackling the problems of managing IoT (Azbeg et al., 2022).

4.1 Blockchain as a Trust Layer

- **Foundations of Trust:** Blockchain provides a crucial trust layer for the IoT data management paradigm, laying the groundwork for its use. It eliminates the need for intermediaries because the ledger is distributed and difficult to alter(Chawla, 2020).
- **Trust in Data Sources**: Blockchain protects the reliability of data sources by creating a transparent and immutable record of data transfers. Data from IoT sensors may be trusted because it cannot be altered in transit (Dedeoglu et al., 2019).

Figure 1 depicts IoT data management challenges and how blockchain offers solutions like trust, decentralized storage, immutability, and access control.

Figure 1. Flowchart representing the IoT-blockchain integration process

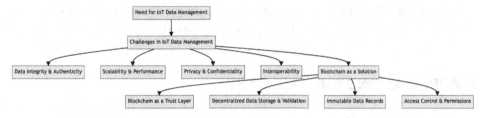

4.2 Dispersed Database Maintenance and Verification

- **Data Decentralization**: Blockchain's distributed ledger technology provides an appealing answer to the problem of storing data from the Internet of Things devices. By spreading it out across multiple nodes, we reduce the risk of data loss and increase data redundancy.
- **Consensus Processes Validation**: Nodes in the blockchain network collaboratively validate and agree on the legitimacy of transactions through consensus processes. This validation procedure improves the data's precision and trustworthiness (Farooq et al., 2020).

4.3 Permanently Stored Information

- **Inviolable Records:** Blockchain's immutability is one of its defining characteristics. Once information is stored in a block, it cannot be changed or removed. This feature guarantees the reliability of IoT data archives (Glaser et al., 2019).

- **Audit Trails:** Immutability also makes it easier to keep detailed audit trails necessary for retrieving past data and meeting legal requirements. The healthcare and supply chain management industries can significantly benefit from having this skill.

4.4 Permissions and Access Management

- **Enhanced Access Control:** Improved Permissions and Access Controls Blockchain technology ushers in novel permissions and access control approaches. With the ability to specify fine-grained access rights, blockchain network participants may guarantee that only authorized parties can view private IoT data.
- **Smart Contracts for Permissions**: By utilizing smart contracts and blockchain-executed computer programs, permissions can be automatically enforced. They regulate data access based on predetermined circumstances, making data breaches less likely to occur (A. et al., 2019).

5. APPLICATIONS AND USE CASES

Because of its adaptability, blockchain technology finds compelling use cases and applications in various industries, changing the nature of data management and security in the IoT (Banerjee, 2019).

Table 4 showcases practical blockchain applications: Supply Chain Transparency, Healthcare Advancements, Smart City Solutions, and Industrial IoT Optimization, highlighting their real-world significance.

Table 4. Use cases and applications

Use Case	Description
Supply Chain Management	Examples of how blockchain enhances supply chain transparency.
Healthcare and Medical Devices	Instances of blockchain usage in healthcare IoT.
Smart Cities and Infrastructure	Applications of blockchain in creating smarter cities.
Industrial IoT (IIoT) and Manufacturing	How blockchain benefits the industrial sector.

5.1 The Management of the Supply Chain

- **Enhanced Traceability:** Blockchain improves supply chain traceability by recording transactions in an immutable distributed ledger. This quality is paramount in sectors where authenticity and traceability are essential, such as the food and pharmaceutical industries.
- **Reduced Risk of Counterfeiting:** Blockchain's decentralized, immutable ledger of goods origins makes counterfeiting much more difficult to pull off. By allowing stakeholders to check the legitimacy of products, the availability of fakes is curtailed (Bumblauskas et al., 2020).
- **Efficient Asset Management:** Blockchain improves asset tracking and management, which in turn cuts down on waste and inefficiency. When Internet of Things (IoT) sensors are combined with blockchain technology, they can track inventory in real-time.

5.2 Medical Care and Related Technologies

- **Secure Health Records**: Blockchain technology makes Electronic health records more secure and easier to handle. Everyone benefits when patients are in charge of their information, and doctors have access to complete medical histories.
- **Medical Device Authentication**: For patient safety, medical equipment must be verified for its validity. Blockchain technology permits medical equipment authentication and lifetime tracking (Ullah et al., 2019).
- **Clinical Trials and Research:** Blockchain makes it possible to conduct clinical trials in a transparent and auditable way by securely capturing data at each stage. Research is accelerated, and data integrity is protected in this way.

5.3 High-Tech Urban Areas and Their Infrastructure

- **Efficient Resource Management:** Smart city resource management is optimized by blockchain-based IoT systems. They permit real-time tracking of resources like water and power, improving utilization and reducing waste.
- **Traffic Management**: Congestion Reduction & Real-Time Data Collection IoT sensors and blockchain revolutionize traffic management by enabling adaptive traffic control systems and offering real-time data collection on traffic conditions.
- **Citizen Services**: Voting, property management, and identity verification are examples of how blockchain technology improves citizen services in today's intelligent cities (Vellido, 2020).

5.4 Internet of Things (IoT) in Manufacturing

- **Predictive Maintenance:** Machine Predictive Maintenance is made possible by integrating IoT devices with blockchain. By recording sensor data in an immutable ledger, preventative maintenance may be performed, resulting in less downtime.
- **Supply Chain Optimization**: In the manufacturing industry, supply chains can be optimized with blockchain technology by increasing transparency, decreasing lead times, and facilitating closer cooperation between suppliers, manufacturers, and distributors.
- **Quality Assurance**: Blockchain technology records data on the production processes of products, guaranteeing their legitimacy and quality. This is of paramount importance in the aerospace and automobile industries (Tang et al., 2019).

These implementations show how blockchain technology can revolutionize the Internet of Things. Improved efficiency, credibility, and creativity in IoT ecosystems result from blockchain's ability to solve pressing problems and inspire user confidence (Perwej et al., 2019).

6. IOT SENSOR DATA MANAGEMENT WITH BLOCKCHAIN

Strategic planning and execution are required for successful blockchain integration with IoT sensor data management. This section will examine the fundamentals of integrating blockchain solutions into the Internet of Things (Zheng et al., 2020).

6.1 Approaches to Integration

- **Evaluating Integration Points**: The first thing to do when incorporating blockchain technology into the Internet of Things is to evaluate the integration points. Figure out where blockchain can be most helpful, whether in collecting, transferring, or storing data.
- **Hybrid Architectures:** Learn more about hybrid architectures, which combine blockchain with preexisting Internet of Things infrastructures. Using this method, the transition can be made gradually, with minimal impact on ongoing operations.
- **IoT Protocols:** Consider how MQTT and CoAP, two popular IoT protocols, can be modified to function with blockchain networks. For effective data transport, various protocols must be compatible (Jiang et al., 2019).

6.2 How to Decide on a Blockchain Service Provider

- **Platform Selection Criteria:** Assess the needs of your IoT application to determine which blockchain solution is most suited to your needs. Consider how well your system scales, how you would reach consensus, and how intelligent contracts would work.
- **Public vs. Private:** Determine whether a public or private blockchain would be better suited to your needs. Regarding blockchain technology, there are two main types: public and private.
- **Open Source vs. Enterprise:** Choose between Hyperledger Fabric and other enterprise-focused solutions or open-source blockchain systems like Ethereum. The requirements and resources of your company's IT department should guide your decision.

6.3 Constructing Internet of Things Smart Contracts

- **Defining Contract Logic:** Define the constraints and logic that intelligent contracts in the IoT ecosystem must impose. Define the steps to be executed if and when certain thresholds are reached.
- **External Data Oracles**: Explain how smart contracts can use "oracles," external data sources. Oracles facilitate the execution of contracts on the blockchain by connecting it to external data, such as that collected by Internet of Things devices (R.Punugoti et al., 2023).
- **Testing and Validation:** Promote the value of rigorously testing and validating intelligent contracts in your organization. If tested thoroughly, contracts are more likely to work as intended and have fewer security flaws or mistakes.

6.4 Strategies for Data Migration and Changeover

- **Data Migration Strategies:** In order to get older IoT data into the blockchain, you'll need to create data migration procedures. Maintain the data's integrity by migrating it accurately and safely.
- **Transition Planning:** Plan the transition so that as little time as possible is lost while the changes are implemented. It is essential to take things slowly when rolling out blockchain-enabled IoT technologies and training the people administering them.
- **Contingency Measures:** Prepare for unexpected problems that may arise during the relocation and transition by putting in place backup plans. The ability to restore previous versions of data is a crucial safety measure.

A well-considered strategy that fits the technology with the application's demands is essential for successful blockchain implementation in IoT sensor data management. Organizations can use the revolutionary potential of blockchain technology in IoT ecosystems through the deliberate selection of integration methods, the selection of the appropriate blockchain platform, the definition of smart contract logic, and the planning for data migration and transition.

7. SCALABILITY AND EFFICIENCY

7.1 Challenges in Scaling Blockchain for IoT

- **Increasing Data Volumes:** The exponential growth of data produced by IoT devices is the primary source of the scalability problem in blockchain-IoT integration. In particular, public blockchains have difficulty keeping up with the volume and speed of data produced by sensors (D. Khan et al., 2021).
- **Latency and Throughput:** Since real-time responsiveness is essential for many Internet of Things (IoT) applications, the transaction processing speed of blockchain networks might be a bottleneck. Critical processes might need to be improved by high latency and low throughput (Lu, 2019).
- **Consensus Overhead:** Consensus methods, while crucial for preserving blockchain integrity, add extra work in computing and communication. Network agreements may become more challenging to achieve as the volume of transactions rises.

7.2 Options for Improvements and Fixes

- **Layered Architectures:** Using a multi-tiered design for the blockchain can help with scalability issues. It is possible to boost performance without compromising security by separating the data and consensus layers.
- **Sharding:** The blockchain network can be broken down into more manageable chunks, or "shards," via a technique called "sharding." Increasing scalability without compromising security, shards process a fraction of transactions.
- **Off-Chain Solutions:** To alleviate the strain on the main blockchain, we can look into off-chain solutions like state channels and sidechains. Congestion can be reduced, and these measures can improve overall performance.

7.3 Optimization and Performance Measurement

- **Monitoring Tools:** The health and efficacy of blockchain-IoT systems can be regularly evaluated with the help of dependable performance monitoring technologies, which should be implemented. When problems with performance are detected in real-time, they can be addressed immediately.
- **Resource Allocation:** Optimize the distribution of available resources across the IoT network. Consider the specialized needs of IoT sensors and intelligent contracts when allocating computing resources, network bandwidth, and storage space.
- **Load Balancing:** Use load balancing strategies to distribute data processing demands fairly among blockchain nodes. Increased resource usage and eliminating any one node acting as a performance bottleneck are benefits of load balancing.

8. CASE STUDIES

8.1 Practical Applications of Blockchain-Internet of Things Integration

- **Supply Chain Transparency:** Look at how businesses have used blockchain to improve supply chain visibility. Blockchain records allow for complete traceability, which helps combat fraud and guarantees genuine goods.
- **Smart Grids:** Explore practical blockchain applications for managing intelligent grids. Blockchain impacts sectors such as decentralized energy trade, grid efficiency, and secure billing.

8.2 Best Practices and Lessons Learned

- **Data Archiving:** Gain insight into the significance of data archiving through reflection on past events. The size of the blockchain needs to be managed to allow for the safe storage of crucial data from the past.
- **Safeguards:** Research cutting-edge procedures for protecting blockchain-based Internet of Things networks. You should use encryption, intrusion detection, and multi-factor authentication to protect yourself from hackers.

9. EMERGING PATTERNS AND NEW DIRECTIONS

9.1 Evolving Blockchain and IoT Technologies

- **Scalable Blockchains:** Look for the development of scalable blockchain platforms that can better meet the data-intensive needs of IoT applications (Menon & Jain, 2021).
- **Integration Standards:** Expect the development of sector-specific integration standards that will make using blockchain in IoT networks easier (Bhaskar et al., 2020).

Figure 2. Evolution of IoT and blockchain technologies

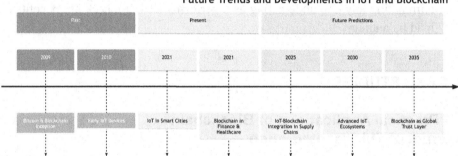

This timeline showcases the past, present, and predicted advancements in IoT and blockchain, highlighting their transformative journey and potential future.

9.2 Factors Related to Regulation and Compliance

- **Data Privacy Regulations:** Be aware of how the ever-changing data privacy standards affect IoT data handling. Avoiding legal trouble requires following rules like GDPR.
- **Blockchain Governance:** As blockchain technology develops, governments may create governance structures to ensure responsible and open implementation.

9.3 Future Prognostication

- **Increased Adoption:** Predict a rise in blockchain-based Internet of Things solutions as businesses learn to appreciate the advantages of increased data security and transparency.
- **Convergence:** Blockchain and IoT technologies will continue to converge, opening the door to novel uses in sectors such as autonomous vehicles, healthcare, and smart cities.

To fully realize the potential of blockchain-IoT integration in the future, it will be essential to overcome scalability and performance obstacles, learn from real-world case studies, adopt best practices, and keep abreast of emerging trends and legislation (Tang et al., 2019).

10. CONCLUSION

In conclusion, this in-depth investigation of IoT sensor data management, security, and blockchain integration revealed the tremendous impact of developing technologies on our digital world. Recognizing the exponential growth of sensor data and the real-time demands of diverse businesses, we have dove into the essential importance of solid data management and security in the IoT ecosystem. Blockchain technology has emerged as a critical component because it adds a layer of trust, permits decentralized data storage and validation, guarantees immutable records with stringent access control, and so on.

The practical benefits and transformative potential of blockchain-IoT integration across various use cases spanning supply chain management, healthcare, smart cities, and industrial IoT. Information migration and integration strategies, brilliant contract creation and development, and blockchain platform selection have all been discussed.

The difficulties of scaling blockchain for the Internet of Things have been recognized, along with several proposed remedies and optimization techniques. Successful implementations have been documented in detail through case studies, and the lessons learned and best practices gleaned from these studies have provided invaluable advice for future efforts. The development of blockchain and IoT technologies and legal and compliance considerations will shape the future landscape of this dynamic synergy. IoT sensor data management is expected to improve efficiency, security, and originality thanks to the foundational principles of blockchain technology.

REFERENCES

Akanksha, K. R., & Vyas, N. (2023). Deep Learning-Based Automatic Face Expression Recognition Framework. *2023 International Conference on Circuit Power and Computing Technologies (ICCPCT)*, 1291–1296. 10.1109/ICCPCT58313.2023.10245885

Al Sadawi, A., Hassan, M. S., & Ndiaye, M. (2021). A survey on integrating blockchain with IoT to enhance performance and eliminate challenges. *IEEE Access : Practical Innovations, Open Solutions*, *9*, 54478–54497. doi:10.1109/ACCESS.2021.3070555

Ante, L. (2021). Smart contracts on the blockchain–A bibliometric analysis and review. *Telematics and Informatics*, *57*, 101519.

Azbeg, K., Ouchetto, O., & Andaloussi, S. J. (2022a). BlockMedCare: A healthcare system based on IoT, Blockchain, and IPFS for data management security. *Egyptian Informatics Journal*, *23*(2), 329–343. doi:10.1016/j.eij.2022.02.004

Banerjee, A. (2019). Blockchain with IoT: Applications and use cases for a new supply chain paradigm driving efficiency and cost. In *Advances in Computers* (Vol. 115, pp. 259–292). Elsevier. https://www.sciencedirect.com/science/article/pii/S0065245819300336

Bhaskar, P., Tiwari, C. K., & Joshi, A. (2020). Blockchain in education management: Present and future applications. *Interactive Technology and Smart Education*, *18*(1), 1–17. doi:10.1108/ITSE-07-2020-0102

Bhaskar, P., Tiwari, C. K., & Joshi, A. (2020). Blockchain in education management: Present and future applications. *Interactive Technology and Smart Education*, *18*(1), 1–17. doi:10.1108/ITSE-07-2020-0102

Bumblauskas, D., Mann, A., Dugan, B., & Rittmer, J. (2020). A blockchain use case in food distribution: Do you know where your food has been? *International Journal of Information Management*, *52*, 102008. doi:10.1016/j.ijinfomgt.2019.09.004

Chawla, C. (2020). Trust in blockchains: Algorithmic and organizational. *Journal of Business Venturing Insights*, *14*, e00203.

Dedeoglu, V., Jurdak, R., Putra, G. D., Dorri, A., & Kanhere, S. S. (2019). A trust architecture for blockchain in IoT. *Proceedings of the 16th EAI International Conference on Mobile and Ubiquitous Systems: Computing, Networking and Services*, 190–199. 10.1145/3360774.3360822

Erevelles, S., Bordia, K., Whelan, B., Canter, J. R., & Guimont-Blackburn, E. (2022). Blockchain and the transformation of customer co-creation. *Journal of Indian Business Research*, *14*(2), 88–107. doi:10.1108/JIBR-03-2021-0085

Farooq, M. S., Khan, M., & Abid, A. (2020). A framework to make charity collection transparent and auditable using blockchain technology. *Computers & Electrical Engineering*, *83*, 106588. doi:10.1016/j.compeleceng.2020.106588

Garg, P., Gupta, B., Chauhan, A. K., Sivarajah, U., Gupta, S., & Modgil, S. (2021). Measuring the perceived benefits of implementing blockchain technology in the banking sector. *Technological Forecasting and Social Change*, *163*, 120407.

Glaser, F., Hawlitschek, F., & Notheisen, B. (2019). Blockchain as a Platform. In H. Treiblmaier & R. Beck (Eds.), *Business Transformation through Blockchain* (pp. 121–143). Springer International Publishing. doi:10.1007/978-3-319-98911-2_4

Jiang, Y., Wang, C., Wang, Y., & Gao, L. (2019). A cross-chain solution to integrating multiple blockchains for IoT data management. *Sensors (Basel)*, *19*(9), 2042. doi:10.3390/s19092042 PMID:31052380

Khan, A. S., Balan, K., Javed, Y., Tarmizi, S., & Abdullah, J. (2019). Secure trust-based blockchain architecture to prevent attacks in VANET. *Sensors (Basel)*, *19*(22), 4954. doi:10.3390/s19224954 PMID:31739437

Khan, D., Jung, L. T., & Hashmani, M. A. (2021). Systematic literature review of challenges in blockchain scalability. *Applied Sciences (Basel, Switzerland)*, *11*(20), 9372. doi:10.3390/app11209372

Lao, L., Li, Z., Hou, S., Xiao, B., Guo, S., & Yang, Y. (2021). A Survey of IoT Applications in Blockchain Systems: Architecture, Consensus, and Traffic Modeling. *ACM Computing Surveys*, *53*(1), 1–32. doi:10.1145/3372136

Lu, Y. (2019). The blockchain: State-of-the-art and research challenges. *Journal of Industrial Information Integration*, *15*, 80–90.

Menon, S., & Jain, K. (2021). Blockchain technology for transparency in agri-food supply chain: Use cases, limitations, and future directions. *IEEE Transactions on Engineering Management*. https://ieeexplore.ieee.org/abstract/document/9578927/

Perwej, Y., Haq, K., Parwej, F., Mumdouh, M., & Hassan, M. (2019). The Internet of Things (IoT) and its application domains. *International Journal of Computer Applications*, *975*(8887), 182. doi:10.5120/ijca2019918763

Punugoti, R., Duggar, R., Dhargalkar, R. R., & Bhati, N. (2023). Intelligent Healthcare: Using NLP and ML to Power Chatbots for Improved Assistance. *2023 International Conference on IoT, Communication and Automation Technology (ICICAT)*, 1–6. 10.1109/ICICAT57735.2023.10263708

Punugoti, R., Dutt, V., Anand, A., & Bhati, N. (2023). Exploring the Impact of Edge Intelligence and IoT on Healthcare: A Comprehensive Survey. *2023 International Conference on Sustainable Computing and Smart Systems (ICSCSS)*, 1108–1114. 10.1109/ICSCSS57650.2023.10169733

Punugoti, R., Dutt, V., Kumar, A., & Bhati, N. (2023). Boosting the Accuracy of Cardiovascular Disease Prediction Through SMOTE. *2023 International Conference on IoT, Communication and Automation Technology (ICICAT)*, 1-6. 10.1109/ICICAT57735.2023.10263703

Punugoti, R., Vyas, N., Siddiqui, A. T., & Basit, A. (2023). The Convergence of Cutting-Edge Technologies: Leveraging AI and Edge Computing to Transform the Internet of Medical Things (IoMT). *4th International Conference on Electronics and Sustainable Communication Systems (ICESC)*, 600–606. 10.1109/ICESC57686.2023.10193047

Sharma, B., & Vyas, N. (2023). Healthcare in the Aftermath of COVID-19: Charting a Course for the Future. *2023 International Conference on Circuit Power and Computing Technologies (ICCPCT)*, 1280–1285. 10.1109/ICCPCT58313.2023.10244828

Sheth, H., & Dattani, J. (2019). Overview of blockchain technology. *Asian Journal For Convergence In Technology (AJCT)*. http://asianssr.org/index.php/ajct/article/view/728

Sun, Z., Luo, X., & Zhang, Y. (2023). Panda: Security analysis of Algorand smart contracts. *32nd USENIX Security Symposium (USENIX Security 23)*, 1811–1828. https://www.usenix.org/conference/usenixsecurity23/presentation/sun

Tang, S., Shelden, D. R., Eastman, C. M., Pishdad-Bozorgi, P., & Gao, X. (2019). A review of building information modeling (BIM) and the Internet of Things (IoT) devices integration: Present status and future trends. *Automation in Construction*, *101*, 127–139. doi:10.1016/j.autcon.2019.01.020

Tijan, E., Aksentijević, S., Ivanić, K., & Jardas, M. (2019). Blockchain technology implementation in logistics. *Sustainability (Basel)*, *11*(4), 1185. doi:10.3390/su11041185

Ullah, H., Nair, N. G., Moore, A., Nugent, C., Muschamp, P., & Cuevas, M. (2019). 5G communication: An overview of vehicle-to-everything, drones, and healthcare use-cases. *IEEE Access : Practical Innovations, Open Solutions*, *7*, 37251–37268. doi:10.1109/ACCESS.2019.2905347

Vellido, A. (2020). The importance of interpretability and visualization in machine learning for applications in medicine and health care. *Neural Computing & Applications*, *32*(24), 18069–18083. doi:10.1007/s00521-019-04051-w

Xu, X., Weber, I., & Staples, M. (2019). *Architecture for Blockchain Applications*. Springer International Publishing. doi:10.1007/978-3-030-03035-3

Zaabar, B., Cheikhrouhou, O., Jamil, F., Ammi, M., & Abid, M. (2021). HealthBlock: A secure blockchain-based healthcare data management system. *Computer Networks*, *200*, 108500. doi:10.1016/j.comnet.2021.108500

Zhang, L., Wang, Y., Li, F., Hu, Y., & Au, M. H. (2019). A game-theoretic method based on Q-learning to invalidate criminal intelligent contracts. *Information Sciences*, *498*, 144–153. doi:10.1016/j.ins.2019.05.061

Zheng, X., Lu, J., Sun, S., & Kiritsis, D. (2020). Decentralized Industrial IoT Data Management Based on Blockchain and IPFS. In B. Lalic, V. Majstorovic, U. Marjanovic, G. Von Cieminski, & D. Romero (Eds.), *Advances in Production Management Systems. Towards Smart and Digital Manufacturing* (Vol. 592, pp. 222–229). Springer International Publishing. doi:10.1007/978-3-030-57997-5_26

Chapter 4

Unveiling the Depths of Explainable AI:
A Comprehensive Review

Wasim Khan
iD https://orcid.org/0000-0003-2311-1451
Koneru Lakshmaiah Education Foundation, India

Mohammad Ishrat
iD https://orcid.org/0000-0002-9699-4454
Koneru Lakshmaiah Education Foundation, India

ABSTRACT

Explainable AI (XAI) has become increasingly important in the fast-evolving field of AI and ML. The complexity and obscurity of AI, especially in the context of deep learning, provide unique issues that are explored in this chapter. While deep learning has shown impressive performance, it has been criticised for its opaque reasoning. The fundamental motivation behind this research was to compile a comprehensive and cutting-edge survey of XAI methods applicable to a wide variety of fields. This review is achieved through a meticulous examination and analysis of the various methodologies and techniques employed in XAI, along with their ramifications within specific application contexts. In addition to highlighting the existing state of XAI, the authors recognize the imperative for continuous advancement by delving into a meticulous examination of the limitations inherent in current methods. Furthermore, they offer a succinct glimpse into the future trajectory of XAI research, emphasizing emerging avenues and promising directions poised for significant progress.

DOI: 10.4018/979-8-3693-0968-1.ch004

1. INTRODUCTION

A substantial portion of the credit for the birth of revolutionary technologies, such as the Internet of Things (IoT), autonomous vehicles, augmented and virtual reality, can be attributed to the advancement of communication systems. Similarly, the concept of intelligent 'objects' has heralded a new era of innovation in the domain of applications and services, which has profoundly and positively impacted our daily lives. These applications generate vast amounts of high-dimensional and heterogeneous data, necessitating effective strategies for data mining and insight extraction (Khan & Haroon, 2022b). Depending on the distance and duration of travel, an autonomous vehicle can generate anywhere from five to twenty terabytes of data daily. Such data, required for monitoring, prediction, decision-making, and control (e.g., for autonomous navigation), often demands real-time or near-real-time processing. In these instances, data analytics tools like Artificial Intelligence (AI), Machine Learning (ML), and Deep Learning (DL) are typically employed (Tien, 2017).

Mathematical models serve as the foundation of machine learning (ML), a subset of artificial intelligence. ML employs these models to make accurate predictions for individual test samples, without the need for explicit programming. These models are constructed and trained on specific datasets. Deep learning, the predominant subfield of ML today, strives to replicate the decision-making process of the human brain by analysing extensive datasets and identifying patterns (Pramod et al., 2021). Deep neural networks, a key component of deep learning, find increasing applications in various domains, including computer vision (CV), natural language processing (NLP), and the Internet of Things (IoT). Despite deep learning's exceptional performance relative to conventional ML algorithms and its industry-leading achievements, it occasionally faces criticism for being opaque and inscrutable. This criticism arises from its inability to articulate the rationale behind a particular decision (Khan & Haroon, 2022c).

Applications based on traditional algorithms often struggle to gain widespread acceptance due to their lack of openness, adaptability, and reliability, particularly when critical decisions are at stake. In many contexts, providing context for an answer is crucial for enhancing credibility and transparency. In fields like medicine, where professionals must have high confidence in their findings, questions may arise about how AI arrived at a diagnosis based on a CT scan (Lebovitz et al., 2022). Even the most advanced AI systems have their limitations, and understanding the reasoning behind a diagnosis is vital for two primary reasons: building trust and reducing the risk of potentially life-threatening errors. In different contexts, such as law and order, answers to other "wh" questions (e.g., "why," "when," "where") may also be necessary. Traditional AI is ill-equipped to handle "wh" queries like these. Hence, there is a growing demand for a new generation of interpretable models that can match the performance of state-of-the-art models (Tennyson, 2013). These interpretable models offer additional transparency, which can enhance the practicality of AI systems in three essential ways:

- Ensuring Fairness: Interpretable models can identify and rectify biases in training data, promoting fairness in the learning process. This helps in eliminating unfair discrimination and ensuring equitable outcomes.
- Enhancing Robustness: By highlighting potential sources of noise that may affect performance, interpretable models improve the system's resilience. This can lead to more reliable and consistent results, even in the presence of uncertainties.
- Feature Selection: Interpretable models enable a clear understanding of the essential features that influence a model's output. This can lead to more efficient and effective decision-making by focusing on the most relevant information.

Some survey studies have summarised the methodologies and essential distinctions among different XAI approaches, and these methods show a wide range of dimensions and descriptions to help with understanding deep learning models. However, there hasn't been much research into the state-of-the-art study of existing methodologies and constraints for various XAI-enabled application domains. The central aim of this study is to provide an elevated perspective on Explainable Artificial Intelligence (XAI) approaches within a broad spectrum of application domains. This is accomplished through a thorough investigation and analysis of the numerous methodologies used in XAI, along with the implications tailored to particular applications. We also acknowledge the need for further improvements by delving into a thorough review of the shortcomings of the currently available methods. Finally, we provide a brief overview of where XAI research is headed, focusing on promising new directions for progress.

2. BACKGROUND AND THE NEED OF XAI

The objective of Explainable Artificial Intelligence (XAI) is to enhance the comprehensibility of AI system outputs. In 2004, (Core et al., 2006) introduced this term to elucidate their system's capacity to furnish justifications for the actions executed by AI-controlled entities, particularly in the domain of simulation games. Despite its relatively recent coinage, researchers have been contending with the challenge of explainability since the mid-1970s, when they commenced investigations into this issue within the context of expert systems. Nevertheless, despite the remarkable advancements in machine learning, progress toward resolving these issues has decelerated as AI has reached a turning point.

In recent times, there has been a marked resurgence of interest within the realm of Explainable Artificial Intelligence (XAI). The widespread proliferation of AI/ML applications across various industries and their substantial impact on decision-making processes have spurred a renewed focus on this area of study. Despite the inherent challenge of providing a detailed explanation for the conclusions reached by AI/ML systems (Ahmed & Zubair, 2022), the growing social, ethical, and legal pressures underscore the necessity for developing new AI techniques capable of rendering conclusions comprehensible and legally defensible. For quite some time, scholars have recognized the imperative of establishing a universally accepted definition of XAI that encompasses all its essential characteristics. Consequently, various theories have emerged in an attempt to provide a comprehensive understanding of the concept of XAI.

Two fundamental challenges lie at the core of our inability to provide a rational explanation for how certain machine learning (ML) systems attain human-level performance. Firstly, there exists a substantial disconnect between the perspectives of the research community and the business sectors regarding ML. This disparity has made it arduous to seamlessly integrate or replace the most recent ML systems within heavily regulated industries (L. Cheng & Yu, 2019). The second challenge revolves around the uncertainty of AI's performance. Numerous applications now employ ML models, and some of these systems are beginning to exhibit performance levels akin to human capabilities (Benbya et al., 2020; Khan et al., 2023). The remarkable capacity of these applications to accurately process vast quantities of data is a direct consequence of their utilization of cutting-edge AI and ML techniques (Rasool & Khan, 2015).

The need for Explainable Artificial Intelligence (XAI) arises from several critical considerations:

- Transparency and Accountability: To increase the credibility of AI and ML models, XAI is needed. It aids in comprehending the decision-making process of AI systems, allowing for responsibility to be placed when things go wrong. The healthcare, autonomous vehicle, and financial sectors are just a few examples where this is crucial.
- Ethical Considerations: When it comes to AI ethics, XAI is indispensable. As a result, decisions made by AI systems can be trusted to be objective and fair. This is especially crucial in fields like recruiting, financing, and the criminal justice system, where the effects of biased judgements can be devastating.

- User Trust: XAI is critical to establishing reliability in AI systems. Users are more inclined to adopt AI-powered technology if they have faith in the decisions made by those systems. In the medical field, for instance, AI recommendations must be trusted by clinicians before they can be included into patient treatment.
- Regulatory Compliance: There are several industries that must adhere to regulations that demand openness and responsibility in their decision-making. By using XAI, businesses are able to follow these rules and avoid potential financial and legal consequences. Financial firms, for instance, have an obligation to justify their loan acceptance or denial decisions.
- Error Detection and Correction: Errors and anomalies in AI systems may be detected with the assistance of XAI. By providing rationales for their actions, AI systems can help ensure that they are operating appropriately and safely.

3. EXPLAINABLE AI TAXONOMY

In contrast to the "black box" quality of some Artificial Intelligence, Machine Learning, and especially Deep Learning models, various terminology has emerged in the literature to describe their opposites. The taxonomies are displayed in Figure 1.

Figure 1. XAI taxonomy

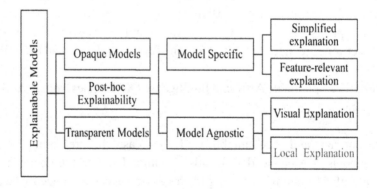

- *Transparency:* a model is deemed transparent if it can be understood from its own terms. As (Adadi & Berrada, 2018) put it, "black-box" is the exact opposite of transparency.
- *Interpretability:* the ability to deliver explanations in language a human can grasp (Tjoa & Guan, 2020).

- *Explainability:* As a means of communication between humans and AI, "explainability" is intrinsically linked to the concept of explanation. Accurate and human-understandable artificial intelligence systems are included (Shin, 2021).

Despite their lexical similarities, these terms imply varying degrees of artificial intelligence (AI) that are acceptable to humans. More specifically, XAI's ontology and taxonomy can be described as follows at a high level:

- *Opaque model:* Random forests, neural networks, support vector machines are examples of these models (Shafiei et al., 2022). These models are typically very accurate, but they lack transparency.
- *Transparent Model:* k-nearest neighbours (kNN), decision trees, rule-based learning, Bayesian networks are instances of transparent models (Arrieta et al., 2020). While these models frequently produce clear decisions, this quality alone is not sufficient to ensure a model's explainability.
- *Model-specific:* These techniques generally leverage prior knowledge to increase the level of model transparency (Khan et al., 2022).
- *Model-independent:* Model-independent XAI methods are built with generalizability in mind (Kangra & Singh, 2022). Hence, they must possess the adaptability to operate solely by aligning the input of a model with its outputs, irrespective of the model's underlying architecture.
- *Simplified explanation:* By approximating a model, we can uncover simpler models that nevertheless explain the prediction of interest. A simpler model can be constructed around the predictions of a more sophisticated model, such as a linear model or a decision tree (Mittelstadt et al., 2019).
- *Feature-relevant explanation:* This XAI strategy is comparable to the idea of simplicity. It aims to evaluate a feature by taking into account all plausible permutations and calculating its average predicted marginal contribution to the decision of the model (Di Martino & Delmastro, 2023; Keshk et al., 2023).
- *Visual Explanation:* This method relies on visual explanations. Therefore, the family of data visualization methods can be used to get insight into the input data for the prediction or decision (Zhou et al., 2018).
- *Local Explanation:* To better understand how the model handles similar inputs to the one we're trying to explain, we can turn to local explanations (Ciravegna et al., 2023), which provide an approximation in a limited region.

4. EXPLAINABLE AI(XAI) METHODS

Several explanation methods and strategies, particularly for ML algorithms, have been recommended in a short amount of time in the effort to make AI systems explainable. We undertake a literature review and categorize the various approaches based on their (i) interpretability complexity, (ii) interpretability scoop, and (iii) degree of ML model dependence. Figure 2 is showing the various types of XAI Methods.

Figure 2. XAI methods

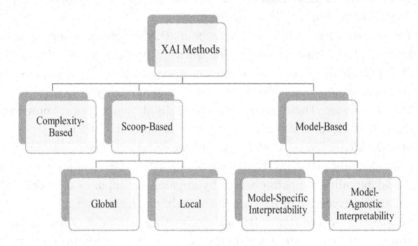

4.1 Complexity-Based Methods

The more sophisticated a machine learning model, the less easily it may be interpreted. Complex models are notoriously difficult to describe and explain. Therefore, the quickest way to interpretable AI/ML would be to use an algorithm that is already naturally and innately interpretable.

The developers of a decision tree-based model presented by (Letham et al., 2015), called Bayesian Rule Lists (BRL), asserted that BRLs provide a simple and persuasive capability to earn domain experts' faith in their preliminary interpretable models. (Bender et al., 2018) detailed the use of a generalized additive model-based learning approach to the pneumonia problem. Using real medical data, they demonstrated that their model was understandable. An attention-based approach for discovering the semantics of images was presented by (Xu et al., 2015). They demonstrated the model's ability to comprehend the findings through visualization.

4.2 Scoop-Based Methods

Understanding an automated model necessitates interpretability, which allows for two flavours of interpretability: grasping the complete model's behaviour and grasping a particular prediction. Both originating and resolving issues are addressed in the canonized works. In light of this, we make a distinction between (i) globally interpretable and (ii) locally interpretable.

The capacity to understand the full logic of a model and trace its reasoning to its various outputs is greatly aided by its global interpretability. When ML models are essential for informing decisions at the population level, such as when analysing patterns in drug use or the effects of climate change (G. Yang et al., 2022), this family of approaches can be useful. A global effect estimate is more useful in these situations than numerous explanations for all the potential anomalies. Additive models for forecasting pneumonia risk and rule sets created from a sparse Bayesian generative model are two examples of works that propose universally interpretable models (Lisboa et al., 2023). However, these models are typically specialized, resulting in restricted predictability so as to maintain interpretability. The objective is to create a global interpretation tree that encompasses various machine learning (ML) models based on their individual local explanations.

By contrast, interpretability at the local level refers to an explanation of the reasoning behind a single decision or forecast. This measure of explainability is used to formulate a unique justification of the model's decision-making process in a given instance. Multiple articles we found provide local explanation strategies. Local Interpretable Model-Agnostic Explanation (LIME) was proposed by (Ribeiro et al., 2016). For any given prediction of interest, this model can provide a close approximation, on a local scale, to a black-box model. Anchors (Ribeiro et al., 2018) is a new, related, and much-anticipated piece of work by the LIME developers that expands LIME with decision rules. Similarly, leave-one-covariate-out (LOCO) (Lei et al., 2018) is a well-known method for developing local explanatory models that provide local variable importance metrics. (Chen et al., 2023) make another effort to generate regional explanations. The authors of this paper introduced a method that utilizes local gradients, which indicate how a data point should be adjusted to alter its predicted label. This approach can elucidate the local decision-making process of arbitrary nonlinear classification algorithms. Following this trail of thought, we come across a group of papers employing comparable techniques for picture classification models (Mankodiya et al., 2022; Varam et al., 2023).

4.3 Model-Based Methods

Model interpretability methods can also be categorized based on whether they are model agnostic, or universally applicable, or model specific, or limited to a specific class of ML algorithms.

Model-Specific Interpretability: The methods for the achievement of model-specific interpretability can only be used with certain types of models. By definition, intrinsic approaches are model-dependent. One potential problem of this method is that it may prevent us from employing a more predictive and representative model when we need a specific kind of interpretation. As a result, model-free interpretability approaches have recently seen a resurgence in popularity.

Model-Agnostic Interpretability: There is no requirement for a specific ML model in order to use model-agnostic techniques. In other words, these techniques create a partition between forecasting and explanatory work. Model-independent interpretations are typically utilized for interpreting ANN and can be either locally or globally based on context. Numerous model-agnostic approaches, drawing on diverse statistical, ML, and DS methods, have been developed in recent years to enhance the interpretability of AI models. These broadly fall into four technique types: (i) Visualization, (ii) Knowledge extraction, and (iii) Influence methods.

Visualization: Visualizing an ML model's representations is a common approach to deciphering its inner workings, and this is especially true with deep neural network models. As may be expected, this line of inquiry has generated a steady amount of work, with researchers employing a wide range of visualization methods to peer into these opaque systems. Supervised learning models are the primary target of visualization methods. It has been found that Surrogate models, and Partial Dependence Plots (PDPs), are the most effective methods of visualizing the evaluated literature.

- Surrogate Models: To better explain a more complicated model, a simpler "surrogate" model is often utilized. An interpretable model, like a linear model or decision tree, is trained with the predictions of a black-box model so that the results can be comprehended by individuals. To construct local surrogate models from a small number of observations, one can use the LIME technique (Ribeiro et al., 2016). Surrogate models are employed by (Yuan et al., 2022), who extracted a decision tree to reflect the model's behaviour.
- Partial Dependence Plot: Using a partial-difference plot (PDP) is a useful way to see how a black-box model's predictions are related to the average

of several input variables. Bayesian Additive Regression Trees (Prado et al., 2021), are used to make predictions, and PDPs are used to understand the relationship between predictors and the conditional average treatment effect for a voter mobilization experiment (Angelini et al., 2023). To learn how various environmental conditions affect the distribution of a certain freshwater (Welchowski et al., 2022), who rely on stochastic gradient boosting, studied PDPs in the ecology literature.

Knowledge Extraction: The goal of explanation extraction is to retrieve, in an understandable form, the information that an ANN has learned during training and stored as an internal representation. Several methods are proposed in the studied literature for decoding the ANN, but two stand out as particularly useful: (i) Rule Extraction and (ii) Model Distillation.

- Rule Extraction: Methods advocated in studies endorse this approach by deriving rules that approximate the decision-making process within artificial neural networks (ANNs) using the ANN's input and output. This results in a symbolic and understandable representation of the knowledge acquired by the network during its training. Interestingly, this type of information aligns with what is typically found in traditional AI expert systems. (Singh et al., 2020) did a review using the categorization of rule extraction methods.
- Model Distillation: It is another strategy for extracting useful information. Distillation is a model compression technique used to teach shallow networks (the ''student'') what deep networks (the ''teacher'') already know. Model distillation was studied by (Tan et al., 2018) to learn how to simplify and clarify complicated models.

Influence Methods: These methods calculate a feature's significance by experimenting with different inputs or internals and keeping track of the impact on the model's accuracy. Many influence strategies have visual representations. (i) Sensitivity analysis, and (ii) Feature Importance are two main approaches to determine input variable's relevance in the examined literature.

- Sensitivity Analysis: By experimenting with different inputs or internal components and keeping track of how they affect model performance, this method provides an estimate of a feature's importance or relevance. It's common to picture influence tactics in one's head. The literature review identified three distinct approaches for determining the relevance of input variables: sensitivity analysis, layer-wise relevance propagation, and feature importance.

- Feature Importance: The variable importance measures the weight of each feature's contribution to a complex ML model's prediction. To determine a feature's significance, we permute it and then assess the increase in the model's prediction error. The model error grows when crucial feature values are switched around. When performing a permutation, the model maintains the same level of error since it disregards the values of irrelevant characteristics. (Fisher et al., 2019) built on this method to propose Model Class Reliance (MCR), a model-independent variant of the feature importance. However, the aforementioned study provided a permutation-based shapley local variant of the feature importance dubbed SFIMP (Casalicchio et al., 2019) .

Our proposed classification of methods is grounded in a thorough analysis of the existing literature. New model-independent methods are developed frequently as a result of the expanding body of study in this area of methodology.

5. APPLICATIONS OF EXPLAINABLE AI

Consequently, there has been a recent explosion of interest in XAI models in different areas. Recently, it has been reported that XAI has been applied in several critical domain applications shown in Figure 3.

Figure 3. XAI applications

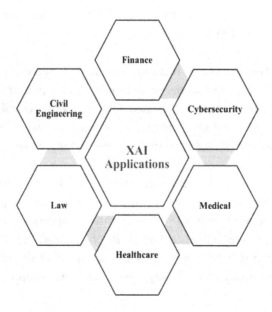

5.1 Finance

Financial forecasting (Chinu & Bansal, 2023) and credit risk management (W. Yang et al., 2023a) are two primary areas of use for XAI in the financial sector. Forecasting financial outcomes like profit, financial health ratios, etc. is known as financial forecasting. How to handle credit risks across different areas is the problem of credit risk management. When a bank's model determines that a customer is at high risk of default, for instance, it must provide an explanation that all relevant parties can comprehend.

In the financial sector, XAI typically takes the form of an explanation of how the AI model prioritizes certain features. To determine the significance of the features, many statistical methods can be applied under this framework. The goal of XAI models in the legal sector is to determine which words in a text are most consequential to a prediction when that text is a natural language text. Most XAI models used in finance are driven by data, intended, and cognitive in nature since they rely on facts and figures rather than human judgement. Those XAI algorithms are cognitively objective in the legal realm because the highlighted words come directly from the input data. In order to describe the AI model trained for legal language (Chaddad et al., 2023), general XAI approaches (e.g., Grad-CAM, LIME, SHAP) for Convolutional Neural Networks were utilized. XAI models, such as LIME, can show the impact of each word in the phrase on the final forecast by highlighting the role the word "awesome" played in producing a positive sentiment prediction.

Institutions such as fund and asset managers are typical consumers of XAI's financial data forecasting services. Financial experts may better understand the rationale behind investment recommendations, risk evaluations, and other decisions with the help of AI models. They can then use this evidence to back up their recommendations and explain their thinking to customers more clearly. When it comes to explaining things that never happened in the past, XAI methods have a problem. The explanations offered by XAI may not be sufficient to account for events in novel and unusual situations, which could lead to incorrect predictions. The specific computing cost of XAI models in finance has received little attention in recent studies.

5.2 Cybersecurity

In order to prevent unauthorized access to or destruction of information, programs, networks, or servers, cyber security measures are put in place (Gopinath & Sethuraman, 2023). The complexity and volume of modern cyberspace make it increasingly difficult to maintain adequate security (Khan & Haroon, 2022a).

Many different artificial intelligence (AI) techniques and technologies have been created to counteract insider and external threats to networked computer systems and applications. Given the absence of explanations and rational justifications in the developed AI-based network security decision-making model (Jo et al., 2023), it becomes challenging for humans to grasp the underlying processes that lead to these outcomes. This is because AI models are opaque, which causes these problems. Because of this security hole, the network's defence mechanism becomes an opaque black box, leaving it open to data loss and AI manipulation (W. Yang et al., 2023b). The developing problem of the black box in AI can be countered with XAI, which is used to protect against cyber security attacks that exploit AI's weaknesses. AI-based models can be comprehensible to both experts and non-experts due to Explainable AI's (XAI) logical interpretation and its ability to provide essential data that demonstrates interoperability.

Both objective and subjective explanations are source-oriented, with the former relying on observed system or network data and the latter drawing on the knowledge and experience of analysts. Contemporary approaches to Explainable Artificial Intelligence (XAI) encompass both these objective and subjective dimensions. For instance, (Sivamohan & Sridhar, 2023) introduced a framework that combines model-generated explanations with the insights of analysts to mitigate false positive errors in AI-generated judgments. One prevalent representation-oriented strategy involves integrating human-readable text directly into the decision-making process. In the context of Explainable Deep Neural Networks (DNNs) for Denial-of-Service (DoS) anomaly detection in process monitoring, as demonstrated by (Amarasinghe et al., 2018), text summaries are employed to elucidate the cause of an anomaly to end-users.

Thus, the current difficulty with systems based on artificial intelligence is that, unlike conventional model-based algorithms, they may make irrational choices (Ucci et al., 2019). This is why XAI is essential for boosting people's faith in security systems powered by AI. The application of XAI in cybersecurity calls for a more methodical approach, one that makes use of a wide range of integrated methodologies from a variety of disciplines under the direction of an engaged research community intent on elevating the level of formalism. In order to improve the analysis and prevention of cyber-attacks, certain areas like malware detection require unified and properly stated methodologies. Furthermore, there is currently no accepted method of determining which XAI systems are the most user-intelligent.

5.3 Medical

One of the most common areas where deep learning techniques are utilised is clinical and medical image analysis, which includes tasks like as image authorization, adaptation, recognising morphological and cell components, tissue segmentation, and computer-aided illness diagnosis. Its influence on medical guidance and therapeutic decision-making is continuously expanding. Given the effectiveness of deep learning in medical image analysis, an ever-growing number of researchers have increasingly adopted these methods in recent years to tackle challenges within the field. Despite significant advancements, deep learning-based medical image analysis continues to struggle with some pressing issues. Incorporating findings from explainable deep learning research into large-scale medical systems is a powerful and engaging strategy to advance medical intelligence. This will improve the capabilities of AI-assisted diagnostics.

A source-oriented perspective distinguishes between objective cogitative explanations, which rely on observable and quantifiable findings from medical examinations, tests, or images, and subjective cogitative explanations, which consider the expertise of medical specialists and the individual circumstances of each patient. Contemporary approaches to Explainable Artificial Intelligence (XAI) encompass both these objective and subjective dimensions. For instance, objective cogitative explanations can be exemplified by the gradient-weighted class activation mapping (Grad-CAM) method introduced in (Selvaraju et al., 2017). Grad-CAM offers explanations by highlighting the relevant regions of an image, grounded in objective data. On the other hand, subjective cogitative explanations, as seen in (Holzinger et al., 2021), involve a combination of time series data, histological images, knowledge databases, and patient histories. These sources can be considered subjective, as they rely on the expertise and context provided by medical specialists and individual patient information.

In the realm of medical image patch classification, explanations are crafted using a technique called locally-interpretable model-agnostic explanations (LIME), as described by (Palatnik de Sousa et al., 2019). Through rule-based segmentation and perturbation-based analysis, these explanations elucidate the significance of each feature visually represented in the image. The concept of attribution (Graziani et al., 2020) is introduced to quantify how traits of interest impact the decision-making of the Convolutional Neural Network (CNN) network. Symbolic techniques in this context focus on representing information symbolically, mirroring a physician's decision-making process in natural language, as well as generating decision outcomes like primary diagnostic reports. For example, (Kim et al., 2018) introduced concept activation vectors (CAVs), which provide a comprehensible depiction of how neural networks operate in terms of familiar concepts. Meanwhile, (M. Cheng et al., 2023) developed computer-aided diagnoses by combining a visual pointing map with diagnostic phrases based on a predefined knowledge base, making the diagnoses more explainable.

5.4 Healthcare

Medical uses of AI-assisted exploration range from disease detection to new drug development (Ezzat et al., 2021; Preuer et al., 2018). Classification challenges, such as determining the progression of dementia from an MRI image, were solved with great success by use of deep learning approaches (Altinkaya et al., 2020). Since these resources aren't always enough on their own to serve the medical community, and doctors and nurses may not have had much experience using AI models for treatment and diagnosis, it's possible that these systems can be difficult to implement.

(Garvin et al., 2020) added to the extensive literature on SARS-CoV-2 mutations by analyzing a mutation matrix using iRF-LOOP (Cliff et al., 2019), a XAI algorithm, and Random Intersection Trees (RIT). A score for a mutation's capacity to foretell the presence or absence of another mutation at a variable site is included in the iRF-LOOP model's output network. The oligonucleotide compositions of SARS-Cov-2 genomes were analyzed by (Ikemura et al., 2020) using the unsupervised XAI approach BLSOM (batch-learning self-organizing map). This technique used a heat map to visually depict the relative contributions of the variables at each node in the tree.

While representation-oriented explanations of AI models are more widely relevant to AI operations, special care must still be taken with individual judgements in the healthcare industry. The two most important characteristics of XAI in healthcare are causality, the ability to recognise accidental correlations among the system's various components, and transferability, the ability to adapt the information produced by the XAI to different issue domains(Loh et al., 2022). When it comes to providing rational explanations, correlation analysis is the norm in the medical field. Hospital admission (Duckworth et al., 2021), quality of life (Antoniadi et al., 2021), surgical complications (Zeng et al., 2021), are only few of the areas where SHAP has been put to use.

Patients and their loved ones, as well as doctors and nurses, are among the many potential recipients of healthcare XAI systems. Due to the gravity of some medical decisions, it is essential that those affected by AI-assisted judgments or diagnoses have confidence in and understanding of them. With the help of XAI, difficult medical decisions may be easier to understand and explain, which could ultimately lead to better patient care. XAI can aid doctors in making better treatment decisions by explaining the reasoning behind AI-driven forecasts, such as the identification of risk factors for a disease. Better communication with their healthcare professionals and a higher sense of agency in their care might benefit patients as well when they are given more information about their health condition and prognosis. These models not only help physicians by emphasizing the most relevant elements for making a diagnosis, but also by providing a visual explanation of the model's logic. The same is true in the pharmaceutical industry, where XAI can help speed up and enhance the precision of drug development by finding novel therapeutic targets and forecasting the efficacy of candidate medications. XAI's involvement in this process has the potential to hasten the regulatory clearance time by increasing trust and confidence in the recommendations.

5.5 Law

The goal of XAI models in the legal sector is to isolate the most consequential words that lead to the final forecast, which is expressed as natural language texts. Those XAI algorithms are cognitively objective in the legal realm because the highlighted words come directly from the input data. In order to describe the AI model trained for legal language (Mardaoui & Garreau, 2021), general XAI approaches (e.g. Grad-CAM, LIME, SHAP) for CNNs were utilized. XAI models, such as LIME, can show the impact of each word in the phrase on the final forecast by highlighting the role the word "awesome" played in producing a positive sentiment prediction.

There aren't many logically-oriented XAI models in the finance sector. The cases, as in the financial sphere, involve the forecasting of a probability or a numerical value, and the inquiries into the rationale behind AI models typically centre on the relative weights of the various inputs. Since the explanation has been formulated as the connection between input words and output predictions, XAI models in the legal area are end-end relationships.

Legal uses of AI need explainability, and in some cases the law mandates explainability (such as the General Data Protection Regulation) for AI applications. By its very nature, the outcomes of legal choices need to be explicable (Eliot, 2021). Justifications are required for all value judgments. Judges need to cite relevant publications or cases to back up their decisions, and lawyers need to explain the situation to their clients (Górski & Ramakrishna, 2021). Why this is meaningful, as opposed to just listing relevant papers or similar instances, is more useful information for AI-powered legal consulting or recommender systems. Explainability is essential for judge outcome prediction to be useful to experts like lawyers.

5.6 Civil Engineering

The decision-making processes of road transportation and electricity systems are profoundly affected by AI systems utilized in civil engineering research. Navigation and path planning, scene recognition, lane and obstacle detection, and planning, monitoring, and controlling the power system are just some of the deep learning techniques used in autonomous driving techniques in road transport and power system analysis and power systems.

By facilitating efficient interaction, XAI can help advance smart civil engineering by enhancing the management of autonomous driving and the power system. Because it is not only influenced by data, but also related to expert knowledge and ethical principles, deep learning interpretation research is a common interpretable deep learning approach in autonomous driving and power systems. Subjective interpretability takes into account the knowledge of automotive or electrical professionals and the ethical standards of respective areas, whereas objective interpretability obtains visible or measurable results from 2D or 3D images or underlying datasets.

XAI concepts as they stand today incorporate both objective and subjective forms of cognition. For instance, the highlighting of crucial portions in 2D or 3D images can be explained with the help of CAM, an objective cognition method. Subject sources used to describe the model include time series, 2D photos, 3D images, Lidar images, knowledge databases, and ethical requirements (Lorente et al., 2021; W. Yang et al., 2023c). The most common kind of XAI applied to self-driving cars is visual interpretation, which uses high-level semantics to determine which portions of an image have an effect on the model by placing special emphasis on the visual structure of the data and the model. Gradient-based and back propagation-based categories exist to classify these XAI techniques. CAM and its improved forms such as Guided Grad-CAM, Grad-CAM, Grad-CAM++, and Smooth Grad CAM++ are all examples of gradient-based interpretation techniques. When used for scene identification, CAM can draw attention to the unique features of an image. Methods such as guided backpropagation, layered relevance propagation, visual backprop, and deep lift are all based on backpropagation.

6. IMPACT OF EXPLAINABLE AI ACROSS SECTORS

The essence of XAI transcends theoretical discourse, manifesting profoundly in sectors where its applications not only innovate but also in still trust, ensure ethical compliance, and democratize AI technologies for broader acceptance. In Healthcare, XAI has emerged as a cornerstone, empowering clinicians with tools that offer not just predictions but explanations, thereby enhancing patient care through transparency and trust. The elucidation of AI-driven diagnostics and treatment recommendations has facilitated a more informed decision-making process, embodying a paradigm where technology and human expertise coalesce for superior outcomes. Within the Financial Sector, the advent of XAI has heralded a new era of transparency, particularly in areas such as credit scoring and risk assessment. By demystifying the decision-making process of AI systems, XAI has enabled financial institutions to provide customers with clear, understandable reasons for decisions, fostering a climate of trust and accountability crucial for the sector's integrity and regulatory compliance.

The Domain of Autonomous Vehicles represents another frontier where XAI is making significant inroads. As these vehicles navigate complex environments, the imperative for explainable decision-making becomes paramount. XAI facilitates this by making the rationale behind navigational and safety decisions transparent, thereby bolstering public trust and paving the way for the societal acceptance of autonomous technologies. Reflections on the Future of XAI underscore the importance of continuing to bridge the gap between AI's capabilities and human understanding. As we venture further into an AI-integrated future, the role of XAI in ensuring that these technologies are not only effective but also equitable, understandable, and ethically responsible becomes increasingly central. It is through deepening our commitment to these principles that we can harness the full potential of AI to benefit society at large.

7. XAI CASE STUDIES

By providing clear explanations of AI processes, XAI facilitates broader acceptance, ethical compliance, and more informed decision-making, bridging the gap between advanced AI technologies and their practical, real-world applications. We explored the specific case studies that illustrate XAI's impact across different domains.

7.1 Enhancing Diagnostic Accuracy in Healthcare With Explainable AI

In the realm of healthcare, Explainable AI (XAI) plays a pivotal role in revolutionizing diagnostic processes, particularly in medical imaging. Techniques like Layer-wise Relevance Propagation (LRP) offer a window into the AI's reasoning by highlighting features in medical images that lead to specific diagnoses. This not only fosters a deeper understanding among clinicians about AI-driven decisions but also boosts their confidence in utilizing these technologies for patient care. The adoption of XAI in diagnosing diseases from medical images, such as detecting tumors in radiology scans, exemplifies its potential to improve accuracy and personalize treatment plans, thereby significantly enhancing patient outcomes.

7.2 Advancing Fairness and Transparency in Finance Through Explainable AI

The finance sector has seen transformative changes with the introduction of AI in credit scoring systems. The application of XAI, particularly through methodologies like SHAP (SHapley Additive exPlanations) values, has made the opaque decision-making processes of AI in credit evaluations more transparent and understandable. This not only ensures adherence to regulatory compliance and fairness but also builds trust among customers by providing clear, understandable reasons for credit decisions. Such advancements highlight the crucial role of explainability in AI applications within finance, paving the way for more ethical and equitable financial services.

7.3 Fostering Trust in Autonomous Vehicles With Explainable AI

Autonomous vehicles represent a cutting-edge application of AI, where safety and trust are paramount. XAI contributes significantly to this field by making the decision-making processes of self-driving cars transparent. Techniques like decision trees and simulation-based explanations demystify the AI's operational logic, providing passengers and the public with a clear understanding of how safety decisions are made. This not only enhances safety but also promotes wider acceptance of autonomous vehicles by alleviating concerns over the unpredictability of AI actions. Through such applications, XAI proves essential in bridging the trust gap between advanced AI technologies and their human users.

Incorporating these detailed case studies not only provides tangible examples of XAI's impact across diverse sectors but also underscore the importance of transparency and explainability in fostering trust, enhancing outcomes, and ensuring fairness in AI-driven decisions.

8. XAI LIMITATIONS AND FUTURE SCOPE

Regulations like the General Data Protection Regulation (GDPR) (Hamon et al., 2022) lay out the transparency criteria around data processing in light of the growing concerns over the lack of explainability in XAI. Since most contemporary AI systems are data-driven AI, these specifications are universally relevant. Not only must anything be explicable, but it must also be explicable in a certain way. Finally, we will highlight future research paths and evaluate the shortcomings of current XAI techniques based on the aforementioned evaluation of each application domain.

8.1 Limitations

Adaptable explanation and integration: Many current approaches deliver explanations in a generic manner, without taking into account the various backgrounds (cultural, context, etc.) and skill levels of users. This universal approach can make it difficult to effectively communicate with both new and experienced users. Technical jargon can be difficult for new users to grasp, while simplistic explanations can feel superficial to seasoned pros.

Interactive explanation: The current state of XAI research acknowledges that a single explanation may not be adequate to address all user concerns and queries in decision-making scenarios; this is where interactive explanation comes in. Thus, efforts are currently directed on creating interactive explanations that promote a fluid and iterative procedure. To successfully develop interactive explanation systems, however, several obstacles must be overcome.

Hybrid explanation consistency: When discussing hybrid explanations in XAI, it is essential to guarantee coherence and consistency between several explanations. To provide robustness and interpretability, hybrid approaches strive to leverage numerous techniques to give users in different domains with distinct application purposes. The potential for conflicts and the need for coordinated integration of different components within these hybrid systems must be addressed, however.

Predictive accuracy against model interpretability: Researchers are currently working on hybrid approaches, such as using post-hoc interpretability techniques with complex models or designing new model architectures, that aim to strike a better balance between interpretability and accuracy in model predictions.

8.2 Future Scope

Prototype-based models offer a potential route for future study, as opposed to abstract and heavily embedded systems. Prototype-based models, from the simplest (and very efficient) example of kNN to RBF types of ANNs and IF...THEN rules, have been around for some time (Khan et al., 2015). Tibshirani recognized the utility of prototype-based models in (Bien & Tibshirani, 2011), but they have not yet been developed in the context of DL. Such models might combine a more robust architecture with an easily explicable representation. Although it's effective, the kNN approach is not a learning technique because it needs access to all the data in advance. Sparsity is required and can be achieved using either straightforward unsupervised learning techniques like clustering or more involved methods like end-to-end auto-encoders. Parametric learning by optimization (minimization) of a cost (or loss) function is widely believed to be the only form of learning. Humans learn by constructing mental models based on similarities amongst data samples. Instead of focusing on the parameters/weights like the standard method does, prototype-based models shift the focus to the location and characteristics of the prototypes in the feature/data space (Khan et al., n.d.).

9. CONCLUSION

In conclusion, this review paper has delved into the pivotal role of Explainable Artificial Intelligence (XAI) in the evolving landscape of artificial intelligence and machine learning. We have explored how XAI serves as a critical bridge between the remarkable capabilities of AI systems and the need for transparency, fairness, accountability, and practicality in their application across diverse domains. Our exploration began by acknowledging the transformative impact of communication systems on revolutionary technologies like IoT, autonomous vehicles, and augmented and virtual reality. These technologies generate vast amounts of complex data, necessitating the use of AI, ML, and DL for real-time processing and decision-making. However, issues of accountability and transparency have been raised due to the lack of detail in many AI models. Despite its impressive results, deep learning has been criticised for being incomprehensible because it lacks an explanation for its choices.

Fairness, robustness, and feature selection can all be attained through the use of interpretable models, a cornerstone of XAI. They help people recognise and correct their own biases, become more resilient in the face of uncertainty, and get insight into what factors have the most impact on their decisions. XAI promotes trust and lessens the likelihood of significant errors in fields as diverse as medical and law enforcement by responding to "wh" questions and providing understandable explanations. Our conversation has shown how XAI is becoming increasingly popular in many different industries and how crucial it is to have interpretable models that can compete with cutting-edge AI in terms of efficiency. We have emphasised the importance of XAI in ensuring regulatory compliance, developing ethical AI, and gaining user approval. Future predictions show that ethical concerns and legal frameworks are just as important as technology developments in shaping the future of XAI. As an illustration of the growing concern for ethics, reason, trustworthiness, and bias in AI, consider the European General Data Protection Regulation (GDPR). Finally, the significance of XAI in today's AI-driven world is demonstrated by this review. It has shed light on the need of AI systems being transparent and interpretable, and how XAI may help with that. As AI becomes increasingly embedded in our daily lives, XAI will become an essential tool for making sure these technologies are not only effective, but also trustworthy, ethical, and transparent.

REFERENCES

Adadi, A., & Berrada, M. (2018). Peeking inside the black-box: A survey on explainable artificial intelligence (XAI). *IEEE Access : Practical Innovations, Open Solutions, 6,* 52138–52160. doi:10.1109/ACCESS.2018.2870052

Ahmed, M., & Zubair, S. (2022). Explainable artificial intelligence in sustainable smart healthcare. In Explainable Artificial Intelligence for Cyber Security: Next Generation Artificial Intelligence (pp. 265–280). Springer. doi:10.1007/978-3-030-96630-0_12

Altinkaya, E., Polat, K., & Barakli, B. (2020). Detection of Alzheimer's disease and dementia states based on deep learning from MRI images: A comprehensive review. *Journal of the Institute of Electronics and Computer, 1*(1), 39–53.

Angelini, M., Blasilli, G., Lenti, S., & Santucci, G. (2023). A Visual Analytics Conceptual Framework for Explorable and Steerable Partial Dependence Analysis. *IEEE Transactions on Visualization and Computer Graphics.* PMID:37027262

Antoniadi, A. M., Galvin, M., Heverin, M., Hardiman, O., & Mooney, C. (2021). Prediction of caregiver quality of life in amyotrophic lateral sclerosis using explainable machine learning. *Scientific Reports, 11*(1), 12237. doi:10.1038/s41598-021-91632-2 PMID:34112871

Arrieta, A. B., Díaz-Rodríguez, N., Del Ser, J., Bennetot, A., Tabik, S., Barbado, A., García, S., Gil-López, S., Molina, D., & Benjamins, R. (2020). Explainable Artificial Intelligence (XAI): Concepts, taxonomies, opportunities and challenges toward responsible AI. *Information Fusion, 58,* 82–115. doi:10.1016/j.inffus.2019.12.012

Benbya, H., Davenport, T. H., & Pachidi, S. (2020). Artificial intelligence in organizations: Current state and future opportunities. *MIS Quarterly Executive, 19*(4).

Bender, A., Groll, A., & Scheipl, F. (2018). A generalized additive model approach to time-to-event analysis. *Statistical Modelling, 18*(3–4), 299–321. doi:10.1177/1471082X17748083

Bien, J., & Tibshirani, R. J. (2011). Sparse estimation of a covariance matrix. *Biometrika, 98*(4), 807–820. doi:10.1093/biomet/asr054 PMID:23049130

Casalicchio, G., Molnar, C., & Bischl, B. (2019). Visualizing the feature importance for black box models. *Machine Learning and Knowledge Discovery in Databases: European Conference, ECML PKDD 2018, Dublin, Ireland, September 10–14, 2018. Proceedings, 18*(Part I), 655–670.

Chaddad, A., Peng, J., Xu, J., & Bouridane, A. (2023). Survey of explainable AI techniques in healthcare. *Sensors (Basel)*, *23*(2), 634. doi:10.3390/s23020634 PMID:36679430

Chen, R. J., Wang, J. J., Williamson, D. F. K., Chen, T. Y., Lipkova, J., Lu, M. Y., Sahai, S., & Mahmood, F. (2023). Algorithmic fairness in artificial intelligence for medicine and healthcare. *Nature Biomedical Engineering*, *7*(6), 719–742. doi:10.1038/s41551-023-01056-8 PMID:37380750

Cheng, L., & Yu, T. (2019). A new generation of AI: A review and perspective on machine learning technologies applied to smart energy and electric power systems. *International Journal of Energy Research*, *43*(6), 1928–1973. doi:10.1002/er.4333

Cheng, M., Zhang, Y., Xie, Y., Pan, Y., Li, X., Liu, W., Yu, C., Zhang, D., Xing, Y., Huang, X., Wang, F., You, C., Zou, Y., Liu, Y., Liang, F., Zhu, H., Tang, C., Deng, H., Zou, X., & Li, M. (2023). Computer-Aided Autism Spectrum Disorder Diagnosis With Behavior Signal Processing. *IEEE Transactions on Affective Computing*, *14*(4), 2982–3000. doi:10.1109/TAFFC.2023.3238712

Chinu & Bansal, U. (2023). Explainable AI: To Reveal the Logic of Black-Box Models. *New Generation Computing*, 1–35.

Ciravegna, G., Barbiero, P., Giannini, F., Gori, M., Lió, P., Maggini, M., & Melacci, S. (2023). Logic explained networks. *Artificial Intelligence*, *314*, 103822. doi:10.1016/j.artint.2022.103822

Cliff, A., Romero, J., Kainer, D., Walker, A., Furches, A., & Jacobson, D. (2019). A high-performance computing implementation of iterative random forest for the creation of predictive expression networks. *Genes*, *10*(12), 996. doi:10.3390/genes10120996 PMID:31810264

Core, M. G., Lane, H. C., Van Lent, M., Gomboc, D., Solomon, S., & Rosenberg, M. (2006). Building explainable artificial intelligence systems. AAAI, 1766–1773.

Di Martino, F., & Delmastro, F. (2023). Explainable AI for clinical and remote health applications: A survey on tabular and time series data. *Artificial Intelligence Review*, *56*(6), 5261–5315. doi:10.1007/s10462-022-10304-3 PMID:36320613

Duckworth, C., Chmiel, F. P., Burns, D. K., Zlatev, Z. D., White, N. M., Daniels, T. W. V., Kiuber, M., & Boniface, M. J. (2021). Using explainable machine learning to characterise data drift and detect emergent health risks for emergency department admissions during COVID-19. *Scientific Reports*, *11*(1), 23017. doi:10.1038/s41598-021-02481-y PMID:34837021

EliotD. L. B. (2021). The Need For Explainable AI (XAI) Is Especially Crucial In The Law. *Available at* SSRN 3975778. doi:10.2139/ssrn.3975778

Ezzat, D., Hassanien, A. E., & Ella, H. A. (2021). An optimized deep learning architecture for the diagnosis of COVID-19 disease based on gravitational search optimization. *Applied Soft Computing*, *98*, 106742. doi:10.1016/j.asoc.2020.106742 PMID:32982615

Fisher, A., Rudin, C., & Dominici, F. (2019). All Models are Wrong, but Many are Useful: Learning a Variable's Importance by Studying an Entire Class of Prediction Models Simultaneously. *Journal of Machine Learning Research*, *20*(177), 1–81. PMID:34335110

Garvin, M. R., & Prates, E., Pavicic, M., Jones, P., Amos, B. K., Geiger, A., Shah, M. B., Streich, J., Felipe Machado Gazolla, J. G., & Kainer, D. (2020). Potentially adaptive SARS-CoV-2 mutations discovered with novel spatiotemporal and explainable AI models. *Genome Biology*, *21*, 1–26. doi:10.1186/s13059-020-02191-0 PMID:33357233

Gopinath, M., & Sethuraman, S. C. (2023). A comprehensive survey on deep learning based malware detection techniques. *Computer Science Review*, *47*, 100529. doi:10.1016/j.cosrev.2022.100529

Górski, Ł., & Ramakrishna, S. (2021). Explainable artificial intelligence, lawyer's perspective. *Proceedings of the Eighteenth International Conference on Artificial Intelligence and Law*, 60–68.

Graziani, M., Andrearczyk, V., Marchand-Maillet, S., & Müller, H. (2020). Concept attribution: Explaining CNN decisions to physicians. *Computers in Biology and Medicine*, *123*, 103865. doi:10.1016/j.compbiomed.2020.103865 PMID:32658785

Hamon, R., Junklewitz, H., Sanchez, I., Malgieri, G., & De Hert, P. (2022). Bridging the gap between AI and explainability in the GDPR: Towards trustworthiness-by-design in automated decision-making. *IEEE Computational Intelligence Magazine*, *17*(1), 72–85. doi:10.1109/MCI.2021.3129960

Holzinger, A., Malle, B., Saranti, A., & Pfeifer, B. (2021). Towards multi-modal causability with graph neural networks enabling information fusion for explainable AI. *Information Fusion*, *71*, 28–37. doi:10.1016/j.inffus.2021.01.008

Ikemura, T., Wada, K., Wada, Y., Iwasaki, Y., & Abe, T. (2020). Unsupervised explainable AI for simultaneous molecular evolutionary study of forty thousand SARS-CoV-2 genomes. Biorxiv, 2010–2020. doi:10.1101/2020.10.11.335406

Jo, J., Cho, J., & Moon, J. (2023). A Malware Detection and Extraction Method for the Related Information Using the ViT Attention Mechanism on Android Operating System. *Applied Sciences (Basel, Switzerland)*, *13*(11), 6839. doi:10.3390/app13116839

Kangra, K., & Singh, J. (2022). Explainable Artificial Intelligence: Concepts and Current Progression. In Explainable Edge AI: A Futuristic Computing Perspective (pp. 1–17). Springer.

Keshk, M., Koroniotis, N., Pham, N., Moustafa, N., Turnbull, B., & Zomaya, A. Y. (2023). An explainable deep learning-enabled intrusion detection framework in IoT networks. *Information Sciences*, *639*, 119000. doi:10.1016/j.ins.2023.119000

Khan, W., Bitm, L., & Awasthi, M. S. (n.d.). *MATLAB based implementation and comparative analysis of de-blocking algorithms*. Academic Press.

Khan, W., Ansari, H., & Shaikh, A. A. (2015). Log files utility for software maintenance. *International Journal of Advanced Research in Computer Engineering and Technology*, *4*(9).

Khan, W., & Haroon, M. (2022a). A Pilot Study and Survey on Methods for Anomaly Detection in Online Social Networks. *Human-Centric Smart Computing Proceedings of ICHCSC*, *2022*, 119–128.

Khan, W., & Haroon, M. (2022b). An efficient framework for anomaly detection in attributed social networks. *International Journal of Information Technology : an Official Journal of Bharati Vidyapeeth's Institute of Computer Applications and Management*, *14*(6), 3069–3076. Advance online publication. doi:10.1007/s41870-022-01044-2

Khan, W., & Haroon, M. (2022c). An unsupervised deep learning ensemble model for anomaly detection in static attributed social networks. *International Journal of Cognitive Computing in Engineering*, *3*, 153–160. doi:10.1016/j.ijcce.2022.08.002

Khan, W., Haroon, M., Khan, A. N., Hasan, M. K., Khan, A., Mokhtar, U. A., & Islam, S. (2022). DVAEGMM: Dual Variational Autoencoder With Gaussian Mixture Model for Anomaly Detection on Attributed Networks. *IEEE Access : Practical Innovations, Open Solutions*, *10*, 91160–91176. doi:10.1109/ACCESS.2022.3201332

Khan, W., Ishrat, M., Haleem, M., Khan, A. N., Hasan, M. K., & Farooqui, N. A. (2023). An Extensive Study and Review on Dark Web Threats and Detection Techniques. In *Advances in Cyberology and the Advent of the Next-Gen Information Revolution* (pp. 202–219). IGI Global. doi:10.4018/978-1-6684-8133-2.ch011

Kim, B., Wattenberg, M., Gilmer, J., Cai, C., Wexler, J., & Viegas, F. (2018). Interpretability beyond feature attribution: Quantitative testing with concept activation vectors (tcav). *International Conference on Machine Learning*, 2668–2677.

Lebovitz, S., Lifshitz-Assaf, H., & Levina, N. (2022). To engage or not to engage with AI for critical judgments: How professionals deal with opacity when using AI for medical diagnosis. *Organization Science*, *33*(1), 126–148. doi:10.1287/orsc.2021.1549

Lei, J., G'Sell, M., Rinaldo, A., Tibshirani, R. J., & Wasserman, L. (2018). Distribution-free predictive inference for regression. *Journal of the American Statistical Association*, *113*(523), 1094–1111. doi:10.1080/01621459.2017.1307116

Letham, B., Rudin, C., McCormick, T. H., & Madigan, D. (2015). *Interpretable classifiers using rules and bayesian analysis: Building a better stroke prediction model*. Academic Press.

Lisboa, P. J. G., Saralajew, S., Vellido, A., Fernández-Domenech, R., & Villmann, T. (2023). The coming of age of interpretable and explainable machine learning models. *Neurocomputing*, *535*, 25–39. doi:10.1016/j.neucom.2023.02.040

Loh, H. W., Ooi, C. P., Seoni, S., Barua, P. D., Molinari, F., & Acharya, U. R. (2022). Application of explainable artificial intelligence for healthcare: A systematic review of the last decade (2011–2022). *Computer Methods and Programs in Biomedicine*, *226*, 107161. doi:10.1016/j.cmpb.2022.107161 PMID:36228495

Lorente, M. P. S., Lopez, E. M., Florez, L. A., Espino, A. L., Martínez, J. A. I., & de Miguel, A. S. (2021). Explaining deep learning-based driver models. *Applied Sciences (Basel, Switzerland)*, *11*(8), 3321. doi:10.3390/app11083321

Mankodiya, H., Jadav, D., Gupta, R., Tanwar, S., Hong, W.-C., & Sharma, R. (2022). Od-xai: Explainable ai-based semantic object detection for autonomous vehicles. *Applied Sciences (Basel, Switzerland)*, *12*(11), 5310. doi:10.3390/app12115310

Mardaoui, D., & Garreau, D. (2021). An analysis of lime for text data. *International Conference on Artificial Intelligence and Statistics*, 3493–3501.

Mittelstadt, B., Russell, C., & Wachter, S. (2019). Explaining explanations in AI. *Proceedings of the Conference on Fairness, Accountability, and Transparency*, 279–288. 10.1145/3287560.3287574

Palatnik de Sousa, I., Maria Bernardes Rebuzzi Vellasco, M., & Costa da Silva, E. (2019). Local interpretable model-agnostic explanations for classification of lymph node metastases. *Sensors (Basel), 19*(13), 2969. doi:10.3390/s19132969 PMID:31284419

Prado, E. B., Moral, R. A., & Parnell, A. C. (2021). Bayesian additive regression trees with model trees. *Statistics and Computing, 31*(3), 1–13. doi:10.1007/s11222-021-09997-3

Pramod, A., Naicker, H. S., & Tyagi, A. K. (2021). Machine learning and deep learning: Open issues and future research directions for the next 10 years. *Computational Analysis and Deep Learning for Medical Care: Principles, Methods, and Applications*, 463–490.

Preuer, K., Renz, P., Unterthiner, T., Hochreiter, S., & Klambauer, G. (2018). Fréchet ChemNet distance: A metric for generative models for molecules in drug discovery. *Journal of Chemical Information and Modeling, 58*(9), 1736–1741. doi:10.1021/acs.jcim.8b00234 PMID:30118593

Rasool, M., & Khan, W. (2015). Big data: Study in structured and unstructured data. *HCTL Open International Journal of Technology Innovations and Research, 14*, 1–6.

Ribeiro, M. T., Singh, S., & Guestrin, C. (2016). "Why should i trust you?" Explaining the predictions of any classifier. *Proceedings of the 22nd ACM SIGKDD International Conference on Knowledge Discovery and Data Mining*, 1135–1144. 10.1145/2939672.2939778

Ribeiro, M. T., Singh, S., & Guestrin, C. (2018). Anchors: High-precision model-agnostic explanations. *Proceedings of the AAAI Conference on Artificial Intelligence, 32*(1). Advance online publication. doi:10.1609/aaai.v32i1.11491

Selvaraju, R. R., Cogswell, M., Das, A., Vedantam, R., Parikh, D., & Batra, D. (2017). Grad-cam: Visual explanations from deep networks via gradient-based localization. *Proceedings of the IEEE International Conference on Computer Vision*, 618–626. 10.1109/ICCV.2017.74

Shafiei, A., Tatar, A., Rayhani, M., Kairat, M., & Askarova, I. (2022). Artificial neural network, support vector machine, decision tree, random forest, and committee machine intelligent system help to improve performance prediction of low salinity water injection in carbonate oil reservoirs. *Journal of Petroleum Science Engineering, 219*, 111046. doi:10.1016/j.petrol.2022.111046

Shin, D. (2021). The effects of explainability and causability on perception, trust, and acceptance: Implications for explainable AI. *International Journal of Human-Computer Studies*, *146*, 102551. doi:10.1016/j.ijhcs.2020.102551

Singh, A., Sengupta, S., & Lakshminarayanan, V. (2020). Explainable deep learning models in medical image analysis. *Journal of Imaging*, *6*(6), 52. doi:10.3390/jimaging6060052 PMID:34460598

Sivamohan, S., & Sridhar, S. S. (2023). An optimized model for network intrusion detection systems in industry 4.0 using XAI based Bi-LSTM framework. *Neural Computing & Applications*, *35*(15), 11459–11475. doi:10.1007/s00521-023-08319-0 PMID:37155462

Speith, T. (2022). A review of taxonomies of explainable artificial intelligence (XAI) methods. *Proceedings of the 2022 ACM Conference on Fairness, Accountability, and Transparency*, 2239–2250. 10.1145/3531146.3534639

Sudmann, A. (2019). The Democratization of Artificial Intelligence: Net Politics in the Era of Learning Algorithms. Transcript Verlag.

Tan, S., Caruana, R., Hooker, G., & Lou, Y. (2018). Distill-and-compare: Auditing black-box models using transparent model distillation. *Proceedings of the 2018 AAAI/ACM Conference on AI, Ethics, and Society*, 303–310. 10.1145/3278721.3278725

Tennyson, R. D. (2013). Artificial intelligence and computer-based learning. *Instructional Technology: Foundations*, 319.

Tien, J. M. (2017). Internet of things, real-time decision making, and artificial intelligence. *Annals of Data Science*, *4*(2), 149–178. doi:10.1007/s40745-017-0112-5

Tjoa, E., & Guan, C. (2020). A survey on explainable artificial intelligence (xai): Toward medical xai. *IEEE Transactions on Neural Networks and Learning Systems*, *32*(11), 4793–4813. doi:10.1109/TNNLS.2020.3027314 PMID:33079674

Ucci, D., Aniello, L., & Baldoni, R. (2019). Survey of machine learning techniques for malware analysis. *Computers & Security*, *81*, 123–147. doi:10.1016/j.cose.2018.11.001

Varam, D., Mitra, R., Mkadmi, M., Riyas, R., Abuhani, D. A., Dhou, S., & Alzaatreh, A. (2023). Wireless Capsule Endoscopy image classification: An Explainable AI approach. *IEEE Access: Practical Innovations, Open Solutions*, *11*, 105262–105280. doi:10.1109/ACCESS.2023.3319068

Welchowski, T., Maloney, K. O., Mitchell, R., & Schmid, M. (2022). Techniques to Improve Ecological Interpretability of Black-Box Machine Learning Models: Case Study on Biological Health of Streams in the United States with Gradient Boosted Trees. *Journal of Agricultural Biological & Environmental Statistics*, *27*(1), 175–197. doi:10.1007/s13253-021-00479-7 PMID:37608853

Xu, K., Ba, J., Kiros, R., Cho, K., Courville, A., Salakhudinov, R., Zemel, R., & Bengio, Y. (2015). Show, attend and tell: Neural image caption generation with visual attention. *International Conference on Machine Learning*, 2048–2057.

Yang, G., Ye, Q., & Xia, J. (2022). Unbox the black-box for the medical explainable AI via multi-modal and multi-centre data fusion: A mini-review, two showcases and beyond. *Information Fusion*, *77*, 29–52. doi:10.1016/j.inffus.2021.07.016 PMID:34980946

Yang, W., Wei, Y., Wei, H., Chen, Y., Huang, G., Li, X., Li, R., Yao, N., Wang, X., & Gu, X. (2023). Survey on Explainable AI: From Approaches, Limitations and Applications Aspects. *Human-Centric Intelligent Systems*, 1–28.

Yuan, J., Barr, B., Overton, K., & Bertini, E. (2022). Visual exploration of machine learning model behavior with hierarchical surrogate rule sets. *IEEE Transactions on Visualization and Computer Graphics*. PMID:36327192

Zeng, X., Hu, Y., Shu, L., Li, J., Duan, H., Shu, Q., & Li, H. (2021). Explainable machine-learning predictions for complications after pediatric congenital heart surgery. *Scientific Reports*, *11*(1), 17244. doi:10.1038/s41598-021-96721-w PMID:34446783

Zhou, B., Sun, Y., Bau, D., & Torralba, A. (2018). Interpretable basis decomposition for visual explanation. *Proceedings of the European Conference on Computer Vision (ECCV)*, 119–134.

Chapter 5
Convergence of Artificial Intelligence and Self-Sustainability:
Ethical Considerations and Social Implications

R. Pitchai
ⓘ https://orcid.org/0000-0002-3759-6915
Department of Computer Science and Engineering, B.V. Raju Institute of Technology, India

Shiv Kant Tiwari
Institute of Business Management, GLA University, India

R. Krishna Kumari
ⓘ https://orcid.org/0000-0002-1802-628X
College of Engineering and Technology, SRM Institute of Science and Technology, India

K. Janaki
Department of Mathematics, Saveetha Engineering College, India

Pramoda Patro
Department of Mathematics, Koneru Lakshmaiah Education Foundation, India

S. Murugan
Nana College of Technology, India

ABSTRACT

This chapter explores the convergence of artificial intelligence (AI) and self-sustainability while emphasizing the ethical considerations and social implications inherent in this dynamic intersection. It examines the intricate balance between technological progress and ecological responsibility, the need for equitable access to AI-powered sustainability solutions, and the profound impact of AI automation on traditional industries. The chapter also addresses the importance of reskilling and upskilling for sustainable employment, outlines policies and strategies for a just transition, and delves into responsible AI development and governance. Furthermore, it underscores the significance of inclusivity and stakeholder engagement in shaping AI and sustainability policies that prioritize fairness, equity, and the well-being of all.

DOI: 10.4018/979-8-3693-0968-1.ch005

INTRODUCTION

The 21st century has seen a convergence of artificial intelligence (AI) and self-sustainability, offering innovative solutions to pressing human challenges. AI's ability to solve complex problems, analyze data, and make autonomous decisions has made it a powerful tool for driving sustainability initiatives based on resource conservation, environmental responsibility, and social equity, crucial in addressing global crises like climate change, resource depletion, and social inequality (Pastor-Escuredo et al., 2022). The integration of AI and self-sustainability holds significant potential for various applications, including energy optimization, environmental prediction, and precision agriculture. However, these advancements also present ethical and societal challenges that require careful examination, highlighting the need for a comprehensive understanding of the complexities involved (Bayley & Phipps, 2019).

The chapter highlights the importance of understanding the ethical dimensions of AI's fusion with sustainability, focusing on environmental ethics, AI-driven sustainability solutions, data privacy, job displacement, and delegation of critical decisions to AI systems. It emphasizes the need for responsible development and ethics in AI and self-sustainability initiatives(Dsouli et al., 2018). This chapter explores the ethical dilemmas and social repercussions of integrating AI and self-sustainability, aiming to guide responsible development and implementation for environmental and human benefit. It focuses on AI's role in climate change mitigation and ecological preservation (Price et al., 2020). The chapter emphasizes the need for equitable access to AI-powered self-sustainability solutions, irrespective of socioeconomic status. It also addresses data privacy, job displacement, and autonomous decision-making in the context of AI's sustainability efforts, aiming to improve human well-being and societal flourishing (Jha et al., 2016).

This chapter offers guidance on the ethical implications of AI's potential for self-sustainability, emphasizing the need for a thoughtful and inclusive approach to protect human values while harnessing AI's potential. Artificial Intelligence (AI) is a technology that mimics human cognitive functions like learning, reasoning, problem-solving, and decision-making. It has become a ubiquitous presence in our daily lives, with technologies like machine learning algorithms, deep neural networks, natural language processing, and computer vision (R. I. Hussain et al., 2020). AI's applications span healthcare, finance, transportation, and entertainment, enabling virtual personal assistants, industrial automation, autonomous vehicles, and medical diagnosis. Its potential to enhance efficiency, optimize resource allocation, and accelerate innovation has made it a transformative force in various industries.

The rise of AI has led to a growing awareness of the need for self-sustainability, which aims to meet human needs while minimizing environmental impact and conserving resources for future generations. This includes initiatives aiming to achieve ecological balance, reduce carbon footprints, and ensure social equity (Jha et al., 2016; Price et al., 2020). Self-sustainability initiatives, such as renewable energy, biodiversity conservation, responsible land use, sustainable agriculture, and circular economies, are gaining momentum due to climate change, resource depletion, pollution, and social disparities. Governments, organizations, and individuals are integrating sustainability principles into their operations and lifestyles.

The Convergence of AI and Self-Sustainability

The integration of AI and self-sustainability offers a promising solution to complex environmental and societal challenges. AI's capacity to process vast data, optimize systems, and make real-time decisions aligns with self-sustainability goals, enhancing resource efficiency, predicting environmental disasters, and promoting sustainable urban planning (Bayley & Phipps, 2019; Pastor-Escuredo et al., 2022). AI-powered smart grids, machine learning models, and precision agriculture are all contributing to self-sustainability. These technologies optimize energy distribution, reduce waste and carbon emissions, and aid in disaster preparedness. However, the integration of AI into these initiatives raises ethical and social challenges. This chapter aims to explore these ethical dilemmas and societal implications, providing a roadmap for responsible development and implementation in this crucial field. The focus is on minimizing pesticide and water use while optimizing crop yields.

Significance of the Convergence of AI and Self-Sustainability

The convergence of AI and self-sustainability is crucial for addressing global challenges, as it offers numerous benefits (Pachiappan et al., 2024; Rebecca et al., 2024; Sundaramoorthy et al., 2024).

- **Climate Change Mitigation**: Climate change is one of the most urgent global challenges, and AI can play a pivotal role in addressing it. AI-powered climate models can analyze vast datasets to make more accurate predictions, helping policymakers and scientists better understand the climate system. AI can also optimize energy usage, reduce emissions, and support the development of renewable energy sources, all essential components of mitigating climate change.
- **Resource Efficiency**: Self-sustainability requires the efficient use of natural resources. AI can optimize resource allocation in agriculture, water management, and industrial processes, reducing waste and minimizing

environmental impact. This efficiency is crucial for ensuring that resources are available for future generations.

- **Resilience to Environmental Disasters**: AI can enhance our ability to prepare for and respond to environmental disasters such as hurricanes, floods, and wildfires. Machine learning models can analyze historical data to predict the likelihood and impact of such events, enabling better disaster planning and resource allocation for emergency responses.

- **Conservation of Biodiversity**: AI can aid in monitoring and protecting endangered species and ecosystems. AI-powered drones and cameras can track wildlife populations and identify illegal activities like poaching. This helps in the conservation of biodiversity, which is vital for ecological balance (Boopathi & Kumar, 2024; Venkateswaran, Kumar, et al., 2023).

- **Urban Planning and Sustainable Cities**: As the world's population increasingly resides in urban areas, AI can help design and manage sustainable cities. AI-driven traffic management, waste reduction, and energy optimization can make cities more livable and environmentally friendly (Boopathi, 2024a).

- **Equitable Access to Sustainable Solutions**: AI can bridge the income gap between affluent and underserved communities by creating accessible, affordable solutions for self-sustainability, ensuring equitable distribution of benefits.

- **Job Creation and Economic Growth**: While there are concerns about job displacement due to automation, the convergence of AI and self-sustainability can also create new job opportunities. Green technology industries, sustainable agriculture, and renewable energy sectors are areas where AI-driven innovations can spur economic growth and employment (Babu et al., 2022; Dhanya et al., 2023a; Z. Hussain et al., 2023; Vijayakumar et al., 2024).

- **Scientific Discovery**: AI can accelerate scientific research in various fields, including medicine, materials science, and climate science. It can analyze vast datasets, identify patterns, and assist researchers in making breakthrough discoveries that contribute to self-sustainability and human well-being.

- **Ethical and Responsible Development**: The convergence of AI and self-sustainability brings to the forefront ethical considerations related to data privacy, decision-making, and equitable access. This significance lies in the need to develop these technologies responsibly and ensure that they align with ethical principles and societal values (Boopathi & Khang, 2023).

- **Global Collaboration**: Solving self-sustainability challenges requires international cooperation. AI can facilitate data sharing and collaboration among countries, organizations, and researchers, making it easier to address global issues collectively.

The integration of AI and self-sustainability is crucial for addressing global issues like climate change, resource depletion, and social inequality, paving the way for a sustainable, resilient, and equitable future for our planet.

AI AND SELF-SUSTAINABILITY: A NEXUS

The integration of artificial intelligence and self-sustainability is a combination of two transformative concepts, each with its unique characteristics and significance as shown in Figure 1.

Figure 1. AI and self-sustainability: A nexus

Interplay Between AI and Self-Sustainability	Promises and Potential Benefits
Data-Driven Decision-Making	Environmental Stewardship
Energy Efficiency	Resource Conservation
Predictive Analytics	Climate Change Mitigation
Precision Agriculture	Economic Growth
Renewable Energy	Human Well-Being
Environmental Monitoring	Resilience
Urban Planning	

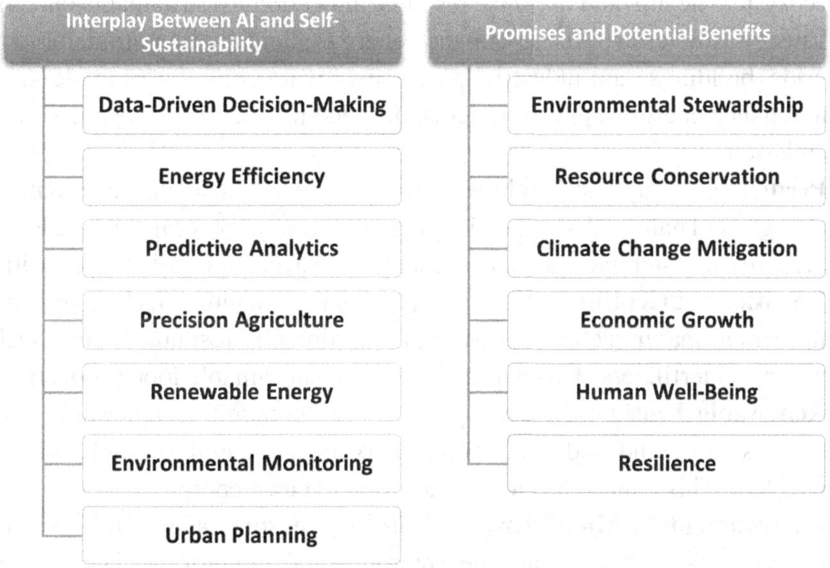

AI is a branch of computer science that focuses on creating machines and software capable of intelligent behavior. It encompasses various subfields, including machine learning, natural language processing, computer vision, and robotics. AI systems can process large volumes of data, learn from experience, make decisions, and perform tasks typically requiring human intelligence (Boopathi & Kumar, 2024; Koshariya, Kalaiyarasi, et al., 2023a; Vanitha et al., 2023a).

Self-sustainability, on the other hand, refers to the practice of meeting human needs while minimizing environmental impact and conserving resources for future generations. Self-sustainability encompasses ecological responsibility, resource conservation, and social equity. It involves initiatives aimed at reducing carbon footprints, conserving biodiversity, promoting renewable energy sources, and ensuring that essential resources are accessible to all.

The Interplay Between AI and Self-Sustainability

AI and self-sustainability are interconnected due to the recognition that AI technologies can enhance sustainability goals across various sectors, facilitated by various factors (Boopathi, 2024c, 2024b; Das et al., 2024; Rahamathunnisa et al., 2024).

- **Data-Driven Decision-Making**: AI's capacity to process vast datasets and extract meaningful insights is instrumental in monitoring and managing environmental resources. AI algorithms can analyze climate data, assess ecosystem health, and optimize resource allocation for sustainable outcomes.
- **Energy Efficiency**: AI can enhance energy efficiency by optimizing power grids, buildings, and industrial processes. Smart grids, for example, use AI to balance energy supply and demand, reducing energy wastage and carbon emissions.
- **Predictive Analytics**: Machine learning models can predict environmental changes and natural disasters with greater accuracy. This capability allows for proactive disaster management and adaptation to changing climate conditions.
- **Precision Agriculture**: AI-driven precision agriculture techniques enable farmers to maximize crop yields while minimizing resource inputs, such as water and fertilizers. This approach supports sustainable food production.
- **Renewable Energy**: AI can optimize the operation of renewable energy sources like wind and solar farms, making them more reliable and cost-effective. This contributes to the transition to clean energy.
- **Environmental Monitoring**: AI-driven sensors and remote sensing technologies facilitate real-time environmental monitoring. These systems track air and water quality, deforestation, and wildlife conservation efforts.
- **Urban Planning**: AI aids in sustainable urban planning by optimizing transportation systems, reducing traffic congestion, and improving energy-efficient infrastructure.

Promises and Potential Benefits

The integration of AI and self-sustainability holds significant potential for tackling global issues and providing numerous advantages (Agrawal, Shashibhushan, et al., 2023; Boopathi, 2023a; Boopathi, Pandey, et al., 2023a; Dhanya et al., 2023a; Gunasekaran & Boopathi, 2023a). The integration of AI in self-sustainability is expected to revolutionize our approach to environmental, economic, and social challenges, potentially leading to a more sustainable future for our planet and its inhabitants, but also raising ethical and social concerns.

- **Environmental Stewardship**: AI can assist in preserving the natural environment by minimizing pollution, conserving resources, and mitigating the effects of climate change.
- **Resource Conservation**: AI's ability to optimize resource use can extend the availability of essential resources, such as clean water and arable land, ensuring their availability for future generations.
- **Climate Change Mitigation**: AI-driven strategies contribute to the reduction of greenhouse gas emissions, helping combat global warming and its associated impacts.
- **Economic Growth**: The development of AI technologies for self-sustainability can stimulate economic growth by creating new industries and employment opportunities.
- **Human Well-Being**: Sustainable practices, facilitated by AI, can enhance the quality of life by ensuring access to clean energy, clean air, and safe environments.
- **Resilience**: AI can enhance society's resilience to environmental disasters, reducing their social and economic impacts.

ENVIRONMENTAL ETHICS IN AI-DRIVEN SUSTAINABILITY

Moral Implications of AI for Environmental Conservation

The integration of AI into environmental conservation efforts has significant moral implications, as AI technologies can significantly impact the natural world, necessitating ethical considerations in this context (Öhman, 2016):

- **Conservation vs. Intervention**: Ethical dilemmas arise when AI is used to intervene in natural ecosystems. Questions about when and how it is morally justified to intervene, such as through the use of AI-controlled drones to combat poaching or AI-guided habitat restoration, must be addressed.
- **Unintended Consequences**: AI-driven conservation interventions may have unintended consequences for ecosystems. Ethical frameworks should account for potential ecological disruptions that could result from well-intentioned AI applications.

Figure 2. Environmental ethics in AI-driven sustainability

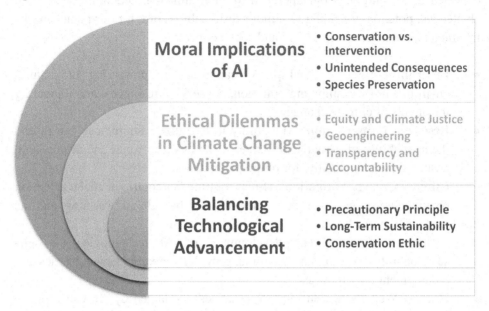

- **Species Preservation**: AI can assist in species monitoring and preservation, but ethical questions emerge concerning whether AI interventions should prioritize charismatic or economically valuable species over less visible ones with intrinsic value.

Ethical Dilemmas in Climate Change Mitigation

AI is crucial in addressing climate change, but its ethical considerations are multifaceted and pressing (Glazebrook, 2012):

- **Equity and Climate Justice**: AI can aid in assessing and mitigating the effects of climate change. However, ethical dilemmas emerge regarding how AI should be used to address the disproportionate impact of climate change on vulnerable communities and nations.
- **Geoengineering**: AI-driven climate solutions may involve controversial geoengineering techniques. Ethical discussions should center on the potential consequences, uncertainties, and risks associated with AI-driven geoengineering initiatives.
- **Transparency and Accountability**: Ethical frameworks must ensure transparency in AI models and decisions related to climate policy.

Accountability mechanisms are needed to address biases, errors, and unintended consequences in AI-driven climate actions.

Balancing Technological Advancement With Ecological Responsibility

Balancing technological advancement with ecological responsibility is a central ethical challenge in AI-driven sustainability (Kronlid & Öhman, 2013). The section emphasizes the need for a comprehensive understanding of environmental ethics in the context of AI-driven sustainability, climate change mitigation, and responsible technology use (Rayhan, 2023). The integration of AI into environmental conservation and sustainability requires a delicate balance between technological advancement and ecological responsibility.

- **Precautionary Principle**: Ethical guidelines should incorporate the precautionary principle, which suggests that, in the absence of scientific consensus, the burden of proof falls on those advocating for new technologies. This principle encourages careful consideration of potential environmental harms before deploying AI solutions.
- **Long-Term Sustainability**: Ethical frameworks must prioritize long-term sustainability over short-term gains. This includes considering the ecological and ethical implications of AI-driven practices that may lead to resource depletion, pollution, or habitat destruction.
- **Conservation Ethics**: Ethical considerations should align with a conservation ethic that values the intrinsic worth of ecosystems and species, recognizing that nature has inherent value beyond its utility to humans. AI applications should respect this ethic and aim to protect and conserve ecosystems rather than solely exploiting them.

EQUITABLE ACCESS AND SOCIOECONOMIC CONSIDERATIONS

Ensuring Fair and Inclusive Access to AI-Powered Sustainability Solutions

The integration of AI and self-sustainability has the potential to yield substantial advantages, as illustrated in Figure 3. Equitable access to AI-powered solutions is crucial to prevent the exacerbation of existing disparities (Rui & Lu, 2021):

Figure 3. Equitable access and socioeconomic considerations

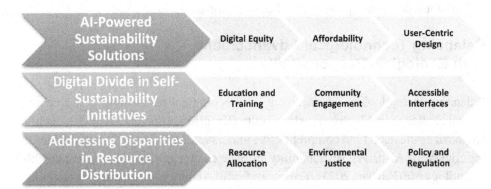

- **Digital Equity**: Ethical considerations demand that AI-driven self-sustainability solutions be accessible to all, irrespective of socioeconomic status. This includes ensuring access to necessary hardware, software, and digital infrastructure, as well as digital literacy and skills development programs.
- **Affordability**: The cost of implementing AI technologies can be a barrier to entry. Ethical frameworks should prioritize affordability, whether through subsidies, public funding, or cost-effective solutions that cater to underserved communities.
- **User-Centric Design**: Developers must prioritize user-centric design that takes into account the diverse needs and abilities of different populations. This approach ensures that AI solutions are usable and accessible to everyone, regardless of age, disability, or technological familiarity.

Bridging the Digital Divide in Self-Sustainability Initiatives

The digital divide, characterized by disparities in access to information and communication technologies, poses significant ethical challenges in the context of AI-driven self-sustainability (Rui & Lu, 2021):

- **Education and Training**: Initiatives to bridge the digital divide must encompass educational programs that provide individuals and communities with the skills and knowledge required to engage with AI technologies effectively.
- **Community Engagement**: Ethical considerations emphasize the importance of involving local communities in the design and deployment of AI-powered

self-sustainability solutions. Community engagement ensures that solutions align with the unique needs and values of each community.
- **Accessible Interfaces**: User interfaces and communication channels must be designed to accommodate individuals with varying levels of technological proficiency and disabilities, ensuring that AI applications are usable by a diverse range of users.

Addressing Disparities in Resource Distribution

The disparities in resource distribution can exacerbate socioeconomic disparities, especially in the realm of AI and self-sustainability (Dougherty, 2017). The convergence of AI and self-sustainability requires ethical frameworks that prioritize inclusive access, digital equity, and resource distribution to ensure that AI-powered sustainability solutions benefit all members of society, regardless of their socioeconomic status or background (Bayley & Phipps, 2019). The aforementioned factors are crucial for promoting a fair and sustainable future for all (Boopathi, 2024b; Rebecca et al., 2024; Venkateswaran, Kumar, et al., 2023).

- **Resource Allocation**: Ethical frameworks should address questions of resource allocation. AI can assist in optimizing resource use, but it must do so in a way that ensures fairness and equitable distribution, avoiding concentration of resources in the hands of a few.
- **Environmental Justice**: AI-driven self-sustainability initiatives should prioritize environmental justice, which entails addressing environmental burdens and benefits equitably across communities, particularly marginalized and vulnerable populations.
- **Policy and Regulation**: Governments and organizations must implement policies and regulations that encourage fair resource distribution. These regulations can include tax incentives, subsidies, and support for disadvantaged communities.

DATA PRIVACY AND SECURITY

Privacy Challenges in AI Applications for Self-Sustainability

The integration of artificial intelligence (AI) into self-sustainability initiatives raises important privacy considerations (Salomon, 2003):

- **Data Sensitivity**: AI applications often require access to sensitive environmental and personal data. Ethical concerns arise regarding the collection, storage, and use of this data, especially when it involves personally identifiable information (PII).
- **Invasive Monitoring**: Some AI-driven environmental monitoring systems may intrude upon individuals' privacy, such as when sensors are used to track air quality, noise pollution, or energy consumption in homes or workplaces.
- **Consent and Transparency**: Ethical data collection necessitates clear and informed consent from individuals or entities whose data is being collected. Transparency about how data will be used and shared is essential to maintain trust.

Ethical Data Collection and Use in Environmental Contexts

Ethical considerations surrounding data collection and usage in environmental contexts are multifaceted (Verginadis et al., 2017):

- **Balancing Public and Private Interests**: Ethical frameworks must strike a balance between the public interest in environmental protection and the privacy rights of individuals. Collecting data for environmental research should not infringe on individuals' privacy rights.
- **Anonymous Data**: Whenever possible, AI applications should use anonymized data to protect individual privacy. Aggregating and anonymizing data can allow for meaningful insights while minimizing privacy risks.
- **Consent in Environmental Data Collection**: Ethical data collection in environmental contexts should involve obtaining consent when personal data is involved. However, obtaining consent for data collected from public spaces or via sensors in the environment presents unique challenges.

Regulatory Frameworks and Data Protection

To address these privacy challenges, regulatory frameworks and data protection measures play a crucial role (Dhanya et al., 2023b; Pramila et al., 2023; Ramudu et al., 2023). The integration of AI into self-sustainability initiatives requires careful consideration of data privacy and security. Ethical data collection, usage, and protection are crucial to maintain trust, respect privacy rights, and ensure the benefits of AI-driven self-sustainability are realized without compromising personal or environmental data (Z. Hussain et al., 2023; Kumar et al., 2023).

- **Data Privacy Laws**: Governments should enact and enforce data privacy laws that apply to AI-driven self-sustainability initiatives. These laws should specify how personal and environmental data can be collected, used, and shared, and they should establish penalties for violations.

- **Ethical Guidelines**: Organizations developing AI solutions for self-sustainability should adhere to ethical guidelines that prioritize data privacy and security. These guidelines should incorporate principles like data minimization, purpose limitation, and data retention policies.
- **Data Encryption and Security**: Robust data encryption and security measures are essential to protect sensitive data. Organizations should invest in cybersecurity practices to safeguard data from breaches and unauthorized access.
- **Data Impact Assessments**: Ethical considerations should involve conducting data impact assessments to evaluate the potential risks and benefits of AI-driven data collection and usage. These assessments can guide responsible data practices.

JOB DISPLACEMENT AND WORKFORCE TRANSFORMATION

The Impact of AI Automation on Traditional Industries

Advancements in AI and automation technologies are poised to significantly impact traditional industries, posing ethical and social challenges (Anitha et al., 2023; Boopathi, 2023c; Karthik et al., 2023). The impact of AI automation on traditional industries raises ethical concerns like job displacement, income inequality, and workforce transformation. A balance between technological advancement and worker well-being is crucial for a just and ethical approach to AI-driven automation in these sectors (Gnanaprakasam et al., 2023).

- **Job Displacement**: One of the primary ethical concerns is the potential for AI automation to displace human workers in traditional industries. AI-powered machines and robots can perform repetitive and routine tasks more efficiently, which can lead to job losses, particularly in sectors like manufacturing, logistics, and customer service.
- **Skill Mismatch**: Job displacement often results in a mismatch between the skills of displaced workers and the requirements of emerging AI-driven job opportunities. This can lead to unemployment and the need for reskilling or upskilling.
- **Income Inequality**: The impact of AI automation on traditional industries can exacerbate income inequality, as those with the skills to work alongside

AI technologies may see increased job opportunities and wages, while others are left with fewer job prospects and lower incomes.

- **Social Disruption**: Communities that rely heavily on traditional industries may experience social disruption due to job loss and economic instability. Ethical considerations include the responsibility to support affected communities in transitioning to new forms of employment.

- **Work-Life Balance**: AI automation can change work dynamics, potentially leading to longer working hours or blurred boundaries between work and personal life, as people interact with AI technologies in various contexts.

- **Ethical AI Design**: Developers and organizations must ensure that AI automation is designed ethically, with a focus on augmenting human capabilities rather than simply replacing human workers. Human-AI collaboration can be optimized to preserve jobs and enhance productivity (Boopathi & Khang, 2023; Reddy et al., 2023a).

- **Reskilling and Lifelong Learning**: Ethical responsibility lies in providing opportunities for reskilling and lifelong learning to help workers adapt to changing job requirements. Governments, educational institutions, and businesses should collaborate to provide accessible training programs.

- **Job Quality**: Beyond mere job preservation, ethical considerations extend to the quality of jobs created by AI automation. Ensuring that these jobs offer fair wages, benefits, and job security is crucial.

- **Safety and Well-Being**: AI automation should prioritize worker safety and well-being. Dangerous or strenuous tasks that are automated can lead to improvements in workplace safety but must be done in a way that maintains worker dignity and rights.

- **Government Policies**: Policymakers play a significant role in addressing the ethical implications of job displacement. Governments may need to implement policies that provide a safety net for displaced workers, support workforce transition, and encourage responsible AI deployment.

Reskilling and Upskilling for Sustainable Employment

The rapid advancement of technology, such as artificial intelligence and automation, is significantly altering the job landscape and necessitating the acquisition of new skills (Bjørnsen et al., 2019; Hellfeldt et al., 2020; Rasmussen et al., 2020a). Reskilling and upskilling are crucial for individuals to prepare for sustainable employment in the evolving job market (Agrawal, Pitchai, et al., 2023; Durairaj et al., 2023):

Reskilling vs. Upskilling

- *Reskilling* involves learning new skills or acquiring entirely different skill sets to transition into a new career or job role. It is often necessary when an individual's current skills become obsolete due to automation or changes in industry demands (Di Fabio & Saklofske, 2021; Djourova et al., 2020).
- *Upskilling*, on the other hand, focuses on improving and expanding existing skills to meet the requirements of more advanced or specialized job roles within the same career field or industry.

Importance of Reskilling and Upskilling

- **Adaptability**: As technology evolves and industries change, workers must be adaptable. Reskilling and upskilling enable individuals to remain relevant in the job market by acquiring skills that are in demand.
- **Employability**: Employers seek individuals who can contribute to their organization's success. Those who continually reskill and upskill are more likely to be considered valuable assets.
- **Job Security**: As automation and AI increasingly handle routine tasks, individuals who possess unique or high-demand skills are less susceptible to job displacement.
- **Economic Growth**: A workforce equipped with up-to-date skills can drive economic growth by fostering innovation and competitiveness on a global scale.

Strategies for Reskilling and Upskilling

- **Identify In-Demand Skills**: Individuals should research and identify the skills that are currently in demand in their industry or the industry they aspire to enter(Figure 4).
- **Online Courses and MOOCs**: Many online platforms offer courses on a wide range of topics. Platforms like Coursera, edX, and LinkedIn Learning provide access to courses from top universities and industry experts.
- **Certifications**: Earning industry-recognized certifications can validate skills and make individuals more appealing to employers.
- **On-the-Job Training**: Many employers offer opportunities for on-the-job training and development. Seeking out these opportunities can be a valuable way to acquire new skills.

Figure 4. Strategies for reskilling and upskilling

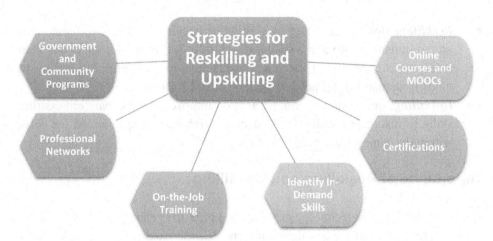

- **Professional Networks**: Joining professional organizations and networks can provide access to resources, mentors, and learning opportunities.
- **Government and Community Programs**: Some governments and community organizations offer reskilling and upskilling programs and funding. These resources can be especially valuable for individuals facing significant career transitions.

Lifelong Learning Culture: Encouraging a culture of lifelong learning within organizations and society at large is crucial. This promotes continuous skill development and helps individuals stay competitive throughout their careers (Bjørnsen et al., 2019; Rasmussen et al., 2020b).

Inclusivity and Accessibility: Efforts should be made to ensure that reskilling and upskilling opportunities are accessible to all individuals, regardless of their background, age, or socioeconomic status.

Monitoring Industry Trends: Staying informed about emerging trends and technologies in one's industry is essential for knowing which skills are likely to be in demand in the future. Reskilling and upskilling are crucial for individuals to secure sustainable employment in a constantly evolving job market. A continuous learning mindset and resource utilization are essential to staying competitive and adaptable, contributing to personal growth and societal economic prosperity (Boopathi, 2023a; Maguluri et al., 2023; Sankar et al., 2023). A just transition is the transition from a heavily carbon-intensive economy to a sustainable, inclusive, and equitable one. The policies and strategies are crucial for promoting fairness, minimizing negative impacts on workers, communities, and the environment, and promoting sustainability and inclusivity in the economy as shown in Figure 4. A just transition is a multifaceted process necessitating comprehensive policies and strategies to ensure equitable and sustainable outcomes. Addressing economic, social, and environmental dimensions, governments and stakeholders can collaborate to create a more equitable and sustainable future.

- **Social Safety Nets:** Provide robust unemployment benefits and financial support to workers who lose their jobs due to the transition. Invest in comprehensive job training and education programs to help workers acquire new skills and transition to new employment opportunities.
- **Economic Diversification:** Promote investment in clean energy, green infrastructure, and sustainable industries to create new job opportunities. Develop regional strategies that focus on diversifying local economies to reduce dependence on declining industries.
- **Worker Rights and Labour Protections:** Protect workers' rights to organize, bargain collectively, and ensure safe working conditions throughout the transition process. Enforce minimum wage laws and advocate for fair wages in emerging industries.
- **Environmental and Health Protections:** Strengthen environmental regulations to ensure that the transition results in cleaner, healthier communities. Invest in public health initiatives to address health disparities and environmental justice concerns in affected communities.
- **Community Engagement:** Involve affected communities in decision-making processes to ensure that their needs and concerns are addressed. Promote community ownership of renewable energy projects and other sustainable initiatives to ensure economic benefits stay within the community.
- **Just Transition Funds:** Establish dedicated funds or grants to support communities and workers in transition. These funds can provide financial assistance for job training, economic development, and infrastructure projects.
- **Regulatory Measures:** Implement carbon pricing mechanisms to incentivize the shift away from carbon-intensive industries. Enforce stricter environmental standards and emissions reductions targets.
- **Public-Private Partnerships:** Encourage collaboration between government, industry, and civil society to develop and implement just transition strategies.
- **Data and Monitoring:** Collect and analyze data on the impacts of the transition on workers, communities, and the environment. Use this information to refine policies and strategies.
- **International Cooperation:** Collaborate with other nations and organizations to address global challenges associated with a just transition, such as climate change and trade considerations.

- **Education and Communication:** Conduct public education campaigns to inform communities and workers about the benefits and necessity of the transition.
- **Legal Protections:** Establish legal protections to prevent discrimination and exploitation of workers and communities during the transition.
- **Equity and Inclusivity:** Prioritize equity and inclusivity in all aspects of the transition, ensuring that marginalized and vulnerable populations are not disproportionately affected.

AUTONOMOUS DECISION-MAKING AND ETHICAL BOUNDARIES

Ethical Considerations in Delegating Critical Decisions to AI Systems

The increasing autonomy of AI systems in making critical decisions raises profound ethical considerations (Reddy et al., 2023b):

- **Accountability**: When AI systems make decisions that have significant consequences, determining accountability becomes challenging. Ethical frameworks must define clear lines of responsibility and accountability, especially when things go wrong.
- **Transparency**: It's essential that the decision-making processes of AI systems are transparent and understandable to humans. Lack of transparency can lead to distrust and hinder ethical evaluation.
- **Bias and Fairness**: AI systems can inherit biases from their training data, potentially leading to unfair or discriminatory decisions. Addressing these biases and ensuring fairness is an ethical imperative.
- **Rights and Values**: Ethical boundaries must be set to ensure that AI systems respect fundamental rights and values, such as privacy, equality, and human dignity.

Ensuring Transparency, Accountability, and Human Oversight

The ethical challenges related to autonomous decision-making by AI systems can be addressed through various principles and strategies (Boopathi et al., 2021; Boopathi, Kumar, et al., 2023; Domakonda et al., 2022a):

- **Transparency**: AI systems should be designed to provide clear explanations of their decision-making processes. This includes disclosing the data used, the algorithms employed, and the factors influencing decisions.
- **Human Oversight**: Critical decisions made by AI should be subject to human oversight. Humans should have the ability to intervene, review, and challenge AI decisions, especially in situations with ethical or legal implications.
- **Algorithmic Auditing**: Conduct regular audits of AI systems to identify biases, errors, and unintended consequences. These audits should be independent and transparent.
- **Ethical Frameworks**: Develop and adhere to ethical frameworks that guide the design, deployment, and use of AI systems, with a focus on respecting human rights and ethical principles.
- **Data Governance**: Establish robust data governance practices to ensure that the data used to train and operate AI systems is unbiased, accurate, and representative.
- **Accountability Mechanisms**: Implement mechanisms to hold organizations and individuals accountable for the decisions made by AI systems under their control. This includes legal and regulatory frameworks.
- **Ethics Boards**: Employ ethics advisory boards or committees to provide guidance on ethical AI development and deployment, particularly in sensitive domains.

Managing AI Biases and Unintended Consequences

Addressing biases and unintended consequences is crucial in ensuring ethical AI decision-making (Anitha et al., 2023; Boopathi et al., 2022; Koshariya, Khatoon, et al., 2023; Vanitha et al., 2023b). As AI systems gain more autonomy in decision-making, ethical boundaries must be established to ensure transparency, accountability, fairness, and respect for human rights and values. Managing biases and unintended consequences is an ongoing ethical responsibility in AI system development and deployment.

- **Bias Mitigation**: Implement bias mitigation strategies during the design and training phases of AI systems. This includes data preprocessing, algorithmic fairness techniques, and diverse data representation.
- **Continuous Monitoring**: Continuously monitor AI systems in real-world scenarios to detect and correct biases and unintended consequences as they arise.
- **Feedback Loops**: Establish feedback loops that allow AI systems to learn and adapt based on user feedback, helping to improve fairness and decision quality over time.

- **Ethics Impact Assessments**: Conduct ethics impact assessments before deploying AI systems, evaluating potential biases and ethical implications in various contexts.
- **Public Engagement**: Engage with the public and stakeholders to gather input and feedback on the ethical boundaries of AI systems, particularly in areas like autonomous vehicles, healthcare, and criminal justice.

RESPONSIBLE AI DEVELOPMENT IN SELF-SUSTAINABILITY

Responsible AI development in self-sustainability involves designing, deploying, and using AI technologies in ways that promote sustainability and align with ethical principles (Boopathi & Kanike, 2023; Koshariya, Kalaiyarasi, et al., 2023b; Ramudu et al., 2023; Sengeni et al., 2023). Here are important aspects of responsible AI development in the context of self-sustainability.

Frameworks for Ethical AI Design and Development

- **Ethical Guidelines**: Develop comprehensive ethical guidelines that outline principles for AI design and deployment. These guidelines should address issues such as transparency, fairness, accountability, and data privacy.
- **AI Ethics Impact Assessment**: Conduct thorough ethics impact assessments before deploying AI systems in self-sustainability initiatives. These assessments should evaluate potential ethical implications, including biases, privacy concerns, and unintended consequences.
- **Ethics Review Boards**: Establish ethics review boards or committees to evaluate the ethical aspects of AI projects and provide guidance on responsible development practices.
- **Interdisciplinary Collaboration**: Encourage collaboration between AI researchers, ethicists, environmental scientists, and domain experts in self-sustainability to ensure that AI technologies are aligned with environmental and ethical goals.
- **Transparency and Explainability**: Prioritize transparency and explainability in AI systems to ensure that their decision-making processes are understandable and accountable. Develop techniques to make AI systems more interpretable.

The Role of Corporate Social Responsibility

- **Ethical AI Policies**: Companies engaged in AI development for self-sustainability should adopt explicit ethical AI policies that guide their practices. These policies should reflect commitments to responsible AI development.
- **Sustainable Business Practices**: Implement sustainable business practices that go beyond profit and consider the environmental and social impact of AI technologies. This may include reducing the carbon footprint of AI infrastructure and ensuring that AI projects align with environmental sustainability goals.
- **Stakeholder Engagement**: Engage with stakeholders, including employees, customers, and the communities affected by AI initiatives, to incorporate their perspectives and concerns into decision-making processes.
- **Transparency and Reporting**: Practice transparency by openly disclosing information about AI projects, their environmental impact, and the ethical considerations taken into account. Regularly report on progress toward ethical and sustainability goals.
- **Ethical Supply Chains**: Ensure that the supply chains for AI hardware and data sources align with ethical and environmental standards, including fair labor practices and responsible sourcing of materials.

Collaborative Efforts for Responsible Innovation

Responsible AI development is crucial for achieving environmental and ethical goals. This involves establishing ethical frameworks, corporate social responsibility practices, and collaborative efforts that prioritize sustainability, transparency, fairness, and accountability in AI system development and deployment (Boopathi, Pandey, et al., 2023b; Dhanya et al., 2023b; Gunasekaran & Boopathi, 2023b; Venkateswaran, Vidhya, et al., 2023; Zekrifa et al., 2023).

- **Multi-Stakeholder Initiatives**: Encourage collaborative efforts involving governments, businesses, academia, civil society, and international organizations to establish standards and guidelines for responsible AI development in self-sustainability.
- **Data Sharing**: Facilitate data sharing and collaboration among different stakeholders to address global self-sustainability challenges. Data sharing can support AI-driven solutions and research.

- **Regulatory Engagement**: Work with regulators and policymakers to develop appropriate regulations and standards that promote ethical AI development in self-sustainability while allowing for innovation.
- **Global Partnerships**: Form global partnerships to address cross-border sustainability challenges with AI-driven solutions. Collaborative efforts can amplify the impact of responsible AI technologies.

PRIORITIZING HUMAN WELL-BEING

The ethical and thoughtful approach is necessary to ensure that AI advancements improve human quality of life while also monitoring and evaluating their societal impacts as shown in Figure 5. The article provides significant factors to consider when prioritizing human well-being in the context of AI (Ahmadi, 2019; Meyer et al., 2021; Puri & Gochhait, 2023; Tharini & Vijayarani, 2020):

Enhance Human Quality of Life

- **Human-Centered Design**: Prioritize human-centered design principles when developing AI technologies. Focus on creating solutions that improve people's lives, enhance their capabilities, and address societal needs.

Figure 5. Prioritizing human well-being

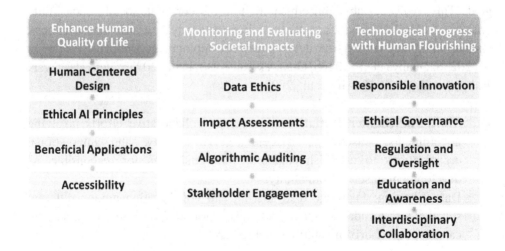

- **Ethical AI Principles**: Embed ethical AI principles, such as fairness, transparency, accountability, and privacy, into the design and deployment of AI systems to ensure that they align with human values and well-being.
- **Beneficial Applications**: Encourage the development of AI applications that have clear and demonstrable benefits for human well-being, such as healthcare innovations, environmental conservation, and disaster response systems.
- **Accessibility**: Ensure that AI technologies are accessible to all, regardless of age, ability, socioeconomic status, or location. Avoid creating AI-driven solutions that exclude or discriminate against vulnerable populations.

Monitoring and Evaluating Societal Impacts

- **Impact Assessments**: Conduct thorough impact assessments to evaluate the societal, economic, and environmental consequences of AI advancements. This includes considering both short-term and long-term effects (Ahmadi, 2019; Meyer et al., 2021; Rasmussen et al., 2020b).
- **Data Ethics**: Implement data ethics practices to ensure that data collection, usage, and sharing align with human well-being and do not lead to unintended harm or privacy violations.
- **Algorithmic Auditing**: Regularly audit algorithms and AI systems for biases, errors, and adverse impacts on individuals or communities. Correct any identified issues promptly.
- **Stakeholder Engagement**: Engage with diverse stakeholders, including affected communities, advocacy groups, and experts, to gather input and feedback on the societal impacts of AI technologies.

Technological Progress With Human Flourishing

The integration of ethical principles, responsible innovation, impact assessments, and inclusive governance is crucial for prioritizing human well-being in the context of AI. This involves multiple stakeholders working together to ensure that AI advancements positively contribute to society and individual well-being (Domakonda et al., 2022b; Revathi et al., 2024).

- **Responsible Innovation**: Promote responsible AI innovation that values human well-being and environmental sustainability over unchecked technological advancement. Develop technologies with a long-term perspective on their impact (Ahmadi-Assalemi et al., 2020; Meyer et al., 2021; Rasmussen et al., 2020b).

- **Ethical Governance**: Establish ethical governance frameworks that guide the development, deployment, and use of AI. These frameworks should prioritize human flourishing and minimize harm.
- **Regulation and Oversight**: Implement regulations and oversight mechanisms that hold organizations and individuals accountable for the societal consequences of their AI technologies. Encourage compliance with ethical standards.
- **Education and Awareness**: Promote public education and awareness about AI technologies, their potential benefits, and the ethical considerations associated with them. Empower individuals to make informed decisions.
- **Interdisciplinary Collaboration**: Encourage collaboration between AI researchers, ethicists, social scientists, and policymakers to ensure that AI advancements are aligned with human well-being and societal values.

INCLUSIVITY AND STAKEHOLDER ENGAGEMENT

The article emphasizes the importance of inclusivity and stakeholder engagement in shaping AI and sustainability policies that prioritize fairness, equity, and the well-being of all (Andreas et al., 2021; Puri & Gochhait, 2023; Tharini & Vijayarani, 2020). Inclusivity and stakeholder engagement are crucial for creating fair, equitable AI and sustainability policies. By involving diverse voices, marginalized groups, and addressing inequalities, policymakers can create initiatives that promote social justice and environmental sustainability, ensuring a responsive and equitable society (Bjørnsen et al., 2019; Hellfeldt et al., 2020; Rasmussen et al., 2020b).

The Importance of Diverse Voices in Shaping AI and Sustainability Policies

- **Comprehensive Perspectives**: Diverse voices bring a wide range of perspectives and experiences to the policymaking process. This diversity ensures that policies consider a broader set of factors and potential impacts.
- **Avoiding Bias and Blind Spots**: Inclusivity helps identify and mitigate biases and blind spots that might otherwise be overlooked in the development of AI and sustainability initiatives.
- **Legitimacy and Trust**: Policies that involve input from various stakeholders are more likely to gain public trust and legitimacy. Inclusivity fosters a sense of ownership among those affected by the policies.

- **Better Outcomes**: Inclusive policymaking is more likely to result in effective, equitable, and sustainable solutions that address the needs and concerns of all stakeholders.

Engaging Communities and Marginalized Groups

- **Community Outreach**: Actively engage with local communities, especially those directly affected by AI and sustainability initiatives. Conduct community outreach to solicit their input, concerns, and priorities.
- **Marginalized Groups**: Pay special attention to engaging marginalized groups, including racial and ethnic minorities, low-income communities, people with disabilities, and indigenous populations. Ensure that their voices are heard and their needs are addressed.
- **Cultural Competence**: Develop cultural competence within policymaking teams to understand and respect the cultural values and practices of diverse communities.
- **Accessible Communication**: Use accessible and culturally sensitive communication methods to reach a wider audience, including those with limited access to technology or language barriers.

Avoiding the Exacerbation of Existing Inequalities

- **Equity Impact Assessments**: Conduct equity impact assessments as part of policy development to identify potential negative consequences on marginalized or vulnerable populations. Mitigate these impacts through targeted interventions.
- **Proactive Mitigation**: Proactively design policies and initiatives to reduce inequalities and address historical injustices. Ensure that AI and sustainability projects benefit those who have been historically marginalized.
- **Resource Allocation**: Allocate resources in a way that prioritizes underserved communities and regions, providing them with the support needed to participate in AI and sustainability efforts.
- **Transparency and Accountability**: Maintain transparency in decision-making processes and hold organizations and policymakers accountable for ensuring inclusivity and addressing inequalities.
- **Legal Protections**: Implement legal protections and anti-discrimination measures to prevent the exacerbation of existing inequalities in AI and sustainability initiatives.

- **Community Benefits**: Ensure that communities impacted by AI projects receive tangible benefits, such as job opportunities, educational resources, and improved infrastructure.

CONCLUSION

This chapter explores the intersection of AI and self-sustainability, highlighting the ethical considerations and social implications. It emphasizes the need for a strong ethical foundation and commitment to the well-being of individuals and the planet when harnessing AI's potential for sustainability. It highlights several main themes and factors.

- The use of AI in self-sustainability requires rigorous ethical scrutiny, prioritizing human well-being, fairness, transparency, and accountability.
- AI's moral implications in environmental conservation and climate change mitigation involve balancing technological advancement with ecological responsibility to prevent unintended harm to the environment.
- AI-powered sustainability solutions must be accessible to all, addressing the digital divide, promoting fair resource distribution, and prioritizing inclusivity as fundamental ethical imperatives.
- AI automation in traditional industries requires reskilling and upskilling to prevent job displacement and ensure sustainable employment, while also considering ethical aspects like job quality and worker well-being.
- Transitioning from unsustainable practices to sustainable alternatives necessitates policies, strategies, and a commitment to social and environmental justice, requiring careful planning and stakeholder engagement.
- Responsible AI development in self-sustainability involves ethical design, transparency, accountability, bias mitigation, corporate social responsibility, and collaborative innovation efforts.
- To ensure fairness and equity in AI and sustainability policies, it's crucial to involve diverse voices, including marginalized communities, and address historical injustices proactively.

The integration of AI and self-sustainability presents ethical and social challenges, necessitating a commitment to ethical principles, inclusivity, and environmental well-being. Responsible AI development and policymaking are vital for a sustainable future.

ABBREVIATIONS

AI - Artificial Intelligence
PII - Personally Identifiable Information
MOOCs - Massive Open Online Courses

REFERENCES

Agrawal, A. V., Pitchai, R., Senthamaraikannan, C., Balaji, N. A., Sajithra, S., & Boopathi, S. (2023). Digital Education System During the COVID-19 Pandemic. In Using Assistive Technology for Inclusive Learning in K-12 Classrooms (pp. 104–126). IGI Global. doi:10.4018/978-1-6684-6424-3.ch005

Agrawal, A. V., Shashibhushan, G., Pradeep, S., Padhi, S., Sugumar, D., & Boopathi, S. (2023). Synergizing Artificial Intelligence, 5G, and Cloud Computing for Efficient Energy Conversion Using Agricultural Waste. In Sustainable Science and Intelligent Technologies for Societal Development (pp. 475–497). IGI Global.

Ahmadi, S. A. A. (2019). Relationship between emotional intelligence and psychological well being. In *Relationship Between Emotional Intelligence and Psychological Well Being*. Academic Press.

Ahmadi-Assalemi, G., Al-Khateeb, H., Maple, C., Epiphaniou, G., Alhaboby, Z. A., Alkaabi, S., & Alhaboby, D. (2020). Digital twins for precision healthcare. *Cyber Defence in the Age of AI, Smart Societies and Augmented Humanity*, 133–158.

Andreas, A., Mavromoustakis, C. X., Mastorakis, G., Batalla, J. M., Sahalos, J. N., Pallis, E., & Markakis, E. (2021). Robust encryption to enhance IoT confidentiality for healthcare ecosystems. *2021 IEEE 26th International Workshop on Computer Aided Modeling and Design of Communication Links and Networks (CAMAD)*, 1–6.

Anitha, C., Komala, C., Vivekanand, C. V., Lalitha, S., & Boopathi, S. (2023). Artificial Intelligence driven security model for Internet of Medical Things (IoMT). *IEEE Explore*, 1–7.

Babu, B. S., Kamalakannan, J., Meenatchi, N., Karthik, S., & Boopathi, S. (2022). Economic impacts and reliability evaluation of battery by adopting Electric Vehicle. *IEEE Explore*, 1–6.

Bayley, J., & Phipps, D. (2019). Extending the concept of research impact literacy: Levels of literacy, institutional role and ethical considerations. *Emerald Open Research*, *1*(3), 14. doi:10.1108/EOR-03-2023-0005

Bjørnsen, H. N., Espnes, G. A., Eilertsen, M.-E. B., Ringdal, R., & Moksnes, U. K. (2019). The relationship between positive mental health literacy and mental well-being among adolescents: Implications for school health services. *The Journal of School Nursing: the Official Publication of the National Association of School Nurses*, *35*(2), 107–116. doi:10.1177/1059840517732125 PMID:28950750

Boopathi, S. (2023a). Internet of Things-Integrated Remote Patient Monitoring System: Healthcare Application. In *Dynamics of Swarm Intelligence Health Analysis for the Next Generation* (pp. 137–161). IGI Global. doi:10.4018/978-1-6684-6894-4.ch008

Boopathi, S. (2023b). Securing Healthcare Systems Integrated With IoT: Fundamentals, Applications, and Future Trends. In Dynamics of Swarm Intelligence Health Analysis for the Next Generation (pp. 186–209). IGI Global.

Boopathi, S. (2024a). Advancements in Machine Learning and AI for Intelligent Systems in Drone Applications for Smart City Developments. In *Futuristic e-Governance Security With Deep Learning Applications* (pp. 15–45). IGI Global. doi:10.4018/978-1-6684-9596-4.ch002

Boopathi, S. (2024b). Energy Cascade Conversion System and Energy-Efficient Infrastructure. In Sustainable Development in AI, Blockchain, and E-Governance Applications (pp. 47–71). IGI Global.

Boopathi, S. (2024c). Sustainable Development Using IoT and AI Techniques for Water Utilization in Agriculture. In Sustainable Development in AI, Blockchain, and E-Governance Applications (pp. 204–228). IGI Global.

Boopathi, S., Balasubramani, V., Kumar, R. S., & Singh, G. R. (2021). The influence of human hair on kenaf and Grewia fiber-based hybrid natural composite material: An experimental study. *Functional Composites and Structures*, *3*(4), 045011. doi:10.1088/2631-6331/ac3afc

Boopathi, S., & Kanike, U. K. (2023). Applications of Artificial Intelligent and Machine Learning Techniques in Image Processing. In *Handbook of Research on Thrust Technologies' Effect on Image Processing* (pp. 151–173). IGI Global. doi:10.4018/978-1-6684-8618-4.ch010

Boopathi, S., & Khang, A. (2023). AI-Integrated Technology for a Secure and Ethical Healthcare Ecosystem. In *AI and IoT-Based Technologies for Precision Medicine* (pp. 36–59). IGI Global. doi:10.4018/979-8-3693-0876-9.ch003

Boopathi, S., & Kumar, P. (2024). Advanced bioprinting processes using additive manufacturing technologies: Revolutionizing tissue engineering. *3D Printing Technologies: Digital Manufacturing, Artificial Intelligence, Industry 4.0*, 95.

Boopathi, S., Kumar, P. K. S., Meena, R. S., Sudhakar, M., & Associates. (2023). Sustainable Developments of Modern Soil-Less Agro-Cultivation Systems: Aquaponic Culture. In Human Agro-Energy Optimization for Business and Industry (pp. 69–87). IGI Global.

Boopathi, S., Pandey, B. K., & Pandey, D. (2023). Advances in Artificial Intelligence for Image Processing: Techniques, Applications, and Optimization. In Handbook of Research on Thrust Technologies' Effect on Image Processing (pp. 73–95). IGI Global.

Boopathi, S., Sureshkumar, M., & Sathiskumar, S. (2022). Parametric Optimization of LPG Refrigeration System Using Artificial Bee Colony Algorithm. *International Conference on Recent Advances in Mechanical Engineering Research and Development*, 97–105.

Das, P., Ramapraba, P., Seethalakshmi, K., Mary, M. A., Karthick, S., & Sampath, B. (2024). Sustainable Advanced Techniques for Enhancing the Image Process. In *Fostering Cross-Industry Sustainability With Intelligent Technologies* (pp. 350–374). IGI Global.

Dhanya, D., Kumar, S. S., Thilagavathy, A., Prasad, D., & Boopathi, S. (2023). Data Analytics and Artificial Intelligence in the Circular Economy: Case Studies. In Intelligent Engineering Applications and Applied Sciences for Sustainability (pp. 40–58). IGI Global.

Di Fabio, A., & Saklofske, D. H. (2021). The relationship of compassion and self-compassion with personality and emotional intelligence. *Personality and Individual Differences*, *169*, 110109. doi:10.1016/j.paid.2020.110109 PMID:32394994

Djourova, N. P., Rodríguez Molina, I., Tordera Santamatilde, N., & Abate, G. (2020). Self-efficacy and resilience: Mediating mechanisms in the relationship between the transformational leadership dimensions and well-being. *Journal of Leadership & Organizational Studies*, *27*(3), 256–270. doi:10.1177/1548051819849002

Domakonda, V. K., Farooq, S., Chinthamreddy, S., Puviarasi, R., Sudhakar, M., & Boopathi, S. (2022a). Sustainable Developments of Hybrid Floating Solar Power Plants: Photovoltaic System. In Human Agro-Energy Optimization for Business and Industry (pp. 148–167). IGI Global.

Domakonda, V. K., Farooq, S., Chinthamreddy, S., Puviarasi, R., Sudhakar, M., & Boopathi, S. (2022b). Sustainable Developments of Hybrid Floating Solar Power Plants: Photovoltaic System. In Human Agro-Energy Optimization for Business and Industry (pp. 148–167). IGI Global.

Dougherty, N. (2017). The Altruistic Self. *Dialogue & Nexus*, 4(1), 5.

Dsouli, O., Khan, N., Kakabadse, N. K., & Skouloudis, A. (2018). Mitigating the Davos dilemma: Towards a global self-sustainability index. *International Journal of Sustainable Development and World Ecology*, 25(1), 81–98. doi:10.1080/1350 4509.2016.1278565

Durairaj, M., Jayakumar, S., Karpagavalli, V., Maheswari, B. U., Boopathi, S., & ... (2023). Utilization of Digital Tools in the Indian Higher Education System During Health Crises. In *Multidisciplinary Approaches to Organizational Governance During Health Crises* (pp. 1–21). IGI Global. doi:10.4018/978-1-7998-9213-7.ch001

Glazebrook, P. (2012). *The agrarian vision: Sustainability and environmental ethics*. Taylor & Francis.

Gnanaprakasam, C., Vankara, J., Sastry, A. S., Prajval, V., Gireesh, N., & Boopathi, S. (2023). Long-Range and Low-Power Automated Soil Irrigation System Using Internet of Things: An Experimental Study. In Contemporary Developments in Agricultural Cyber-Physical Systems (pp. 87–104). IGI Global.

Gunasekaran, K., & Boopathi, S. (2023). Artificial Intelligence in Water Treatments and Water Resource Assessments. In *Artificial Intelligence Applications in Water Treatment and Water Resource Management* (pp. 71–98). IGI Global. doi:10.4018/978-1-6684-6791-6.ch004

Hellfeldt, K., López-Romero, L., & Andershed, H. (2020). Cyberbullying and psychological well-being in young adolescence: The potential protective mediation effects of social support from family, friends, and teachers. *International Journal of Environmental Research and Public Health*, 17(1), 45. doi:10.3390/ijerph17010045 PMID:31861641

Hussain, R. I., Bashir, S., & Hussain, S. (2020). Financial sustainability and corporate social responsibility under mediating effect of operational self-sustainability. *Frontiers in Psychology*, 11, 550029. doi:10.3389/fpsyg.2020.550029 PMID:33424672

Hussain, Z., Babe, M., Saravanan, S., Srimathy, G., Roopa, H., & Boopathi, S. (2023). Optimizing Biomass-to-Biofuel Conversion: IoT and AI Integration for Enhanced Efficiency and Sustainability. In Circular Economy Implementation for Sustainability in the Built Environment (pp. 191–214). IGI Global.

Jha, S. K., Pinsonneault, A., & Dubé, L. (2016). The evolution of an ict platform-enabled ecosystem for poverty alleviation. *Management Information Systems Quarterly*, *40*(2), 431–446. doi:10.25300/MISQ/2016/40.2.08

Karthik, S., Hemalatha, R., Aruna, R., Deivakani, M., Reddy, R. V. K., & Boopathi, S. (2023). Study on Healthcare Security System-Integrated Internet of Things (IoT). In Perspectives and Considerations on the Evolution of Smart Systems (pp. 342–362). IGI Global.

Koshariya, A. K., Kalaiyarasi, D., Jovith, A. A., Sivakami, T., Hasan, D. S., & Boopathi, S. (2023). AI-Enabled IoT and WSN-Integrated Smart Agriculture System. In *Artificial Intelligence Tools and Technologies for Smart Farming and Agriculture Practices* (pp. 200–218). IGI Global. doi:10.4018/978-1-6684-8516-3.ch011

Koshariya, A. K., Khatoon, S., Marathe, A. M., Suba, G. M., Baral, D., & Boopathi, S. (2023). Agricultural Waste Management Systems Using Artificial Intelligence Techniques. In *AI-Enabled Social Robotics in Human Care Services* (pp. 236–258). IGI Global. doi:10.4018/978-1-6684-8171-4.ch009

Kronlid, D. O., & Öhman, J. (2013). An environmental ethical conceptual framework for research on sustainability and environmental education. *Environmental Education Research*, *19*(1), 21–44. doi:10.1080/13504622.2012.687043

Kumar, M., Kumar, K., Sasikala, P., Sampath, B., Gopi, B., & Sundaram, S. (2023). Sustainable Green Energy Generation From Waste Water: IoT and ML Integration. In Sustainable Science and Intelligent Technologies for Societal Development (pp. 440–463). IGI Global.

Maguluri, L. P., Ananth, J., Hariram, S., Geetha, C., Bhaskar, A., & Boopathi, S. (2023). Smart Vehicle-Emissions Monitoring System Using Internet of Things (IoT). In Handbook of Research on Safe Disposal Methods of Municipal Solid Wastes for a Sustainable Environment (pp. 191–211). IGI Global.

Meyer, B., Zill, A., Dilba, D., Gerlach, R., & Schumann, S. (2021). Employee psychological well-being during the COVID-19 pandemic in Germany: A longitudinal study of demands, resources, and exhaustion. *International Journal of Psychology*, *56*(4), 532–550. doi:10.1002/ijop.12743 PMID:33615477

Öhman, J. (2016). New ethical challenges within environmental and sustainability education. *Environmental Education Research*, *22*(6), 765–770. doi:10.1080/135 04622.2016.1165800

Pachiappan, K., Anitha, K., Pitchai, R., Sangeetha, S., Satyanarayana, T., & Boopathi, S. (2024). Intelligent Machines, IoT, and AI in Revolutionizing Agriculture for Water Processing. In *Handbook of Research on AI and ML for Intelligent Machines and Systems* (pp. 374–399). IGI Global.

Pastor-Escuredo, D., Treleaven, P., & Vinuesa, R. (2022). An Ethical Framework for Artificial Intelligence and Sustainable Cities. *AI, 3*(4), 961–974. doi:10.3390/ai3040057

Pramila, P., Amudha, S., Saravanan, T., Sankar, S. R., Poongothai, E., & Boopathi, S. (2023). Design and Development of Robots for Medical Assistance: An Architectural Approach. In Contemporary Applications of Data Fusion for Advanced Healthcare Informatics (pp. 260–282). IGI Global.

Price, O. M., Ville, S., Heffernan, E., Gibbons, B., & Johnsson, M. (2020). Finding convergence: Economic perspectives and the economic practices of an Australian ecovillage. *Environmental Innovation and Societal Transitions, 34*, 209–220. doi:10.1016/j.eist.2019.12.007

Puri, M., & Gochhait, S. (2023). Data Security in Healthcare: Enhancing the Safety of Data with CyberSecurity. *2023 8th International Conference on Communication and Electronics Systems (ICCES)*, 1779–1783.

Rahamathunnisa, U., Sudhakar, K., Padhi, S., Bhattacharya, S., Shashibhushan, G., & Boopathi, S. (2024). Sustainable Energy Generation From Waste Water: IoT Integrated Technologies. In Adoption and Use of Technology Tools and Services by Economically Disadvantaged Communities: Implications for Growth and Sustainability (pp. 225–256). IGI Global.

Ramudu, K., Mohan, V. M., Jyothirmai, D., Prasad, D., Agrawal, R., & Boopathi, S. (2023). Machine Learning and Artificial Intelligence in Disease Prediction: Applications, Challenges, Limitations, Case Studies, and Future Directions. In Contemporary Applications of Data Fusion for Advanced Healthcare Informatics (pp. 297–318). IGI Global.

Rasmussen, E. E., Punyanunt-Carter, N., LaFreniere, J. R., Norman, M. S., & Kimball, T. G. (2020a). The serially mediated relationship between emerging adults' social media use and mental well-being. *Computers in Human Behavior, 102*, 206–213. doi:10.1016/j.chb.2019.08.019

Rasmussen, E. E., Punyanunt-Carter, N., LaFreniere, J. R., Norman, M. S., & Kimball, T. G. (2020b). The serially mediated relationship between emerging adults' social media use and mental well-being. *Computers in Human Behavior, 102*, 206–213. doi:10.1016/j.chb.2019.08.019

Rayhan, A. (2023). *AI and the environment: toward sustainable development and conservation*. Academic Press.

Rebecca, B., Kumar, K. P. M., Padmini, S., Srivastava, B. K., Halder, S., & Boopathi, S. (2024). Convergence of Data Science-AI-Green Chemistry-Affordable Medicine: Transforming Drug Discovery. In *Handbook of Research on AI and ML for Intelligent Machines and Systems* (pp. 348–373). IGI Global.

Reddy, M. A., Reddy, B. M., Mukund, C., Venneti, K., Preethi, D., & Boopathi, S. (2023). Social Health Protection During the COVID-Pandemic Using IoT. In *The COVID-19 Pandemic and the Digitalization of Diplomacy* (pp. 204–235). IGI Global. doi:10.4018/978-1-7998-8394-4.ch009

Revathi, S., Babu, M., Rajkumar, N., Meti, V. K. V., Kandavalli, S. R., & Boopathi, S. (2024). Unleashing the Future Potential of 4D Printing: Exploring Applications in Wearable Technology, Robotics, Energy, Transportation, and Fashion. In *Human-Centered Approaches in Industry 5.0: Human-Machine Interaction, Virtual Reality Training, and Customer Sentiment Analysis* (pp. 131–153). IGI Global.

Rui, Z., & Lu, Y. (2021). Stakeholder pressure, corporate environmental ethics and green innovation. *Asian Journal of Technology Innovation*, *29*(1), 70–86. doi:10.1080/19761597.2020.1783563

Salomon, D. (2003). *Data privacy and security: Encryption and information hiding*. Springer Science & Business Media. doi:10.1007/978-0-387-21707-9

Sankar, K. M., Booba, B., & Boopathi, S. (2023). Smart Agriculture Irrigation Monitoring System Using Internet of Things. In *Contemporary Developments in Agricultural Cyber-Physical Systems* (pp. 105–121). IGI Global. doi:10.4018/978-1-6684-7879-0.ch006

Sengeni, D., Padmapriya, G., Imambi, S. S., Suganthi, D., Suri, A., & Boopathi, S. (2023). Biomedical Waste Handling Method Using Artificial Intelligence Techniques. In *Handbook of Research on Safe Disposal Methods of Municipal Solid Wastes for a Sustainable Environment* (pp. 306–323). IGI Global. doi:10.4018/978-1-6684-8117-2.ch022

Sundaramoorthy, K., Singh, A., Sumathy, G., Maheshwari, A., Arunarani, A., & Boopathi, S. (2024). A Study on AI and Blockchain-Powered Smart Parking Models for Urban Mobility. In *Handbook of Research on AI and ML for Intelligent Machines and Systems* (pp. 223–250). IGI Global.

Tharini, V. J., & Vijayarani, S. (2020). IoT in healthcare: Ecosystem, pillars, design challenges, applications, vulnerabilities, privacy, and security concerns. In *Incorporating the Internet of Things in healthcare applications and wearable devices* (pp. 1–22). IGI Global. doi:10.4018/978-1-7998-1090-2.ch001

Vanitha, S., Radhika, K., & Boopathi, S. (2023). Artificial Intelligence Techniques in Water Purification and Utilization. In *Human Agro-Energy Optimization for Business and Industry* (pp. 202–218). IGI Global. doi:10.4018/978-1-6684-4118-3.ch010

Venkateswaran, N., Kumar, S. S., Diwakar, G., Gnanasangeetha, D., & Boopathi, S. (2023). Synthetic Biology for Waste Water to Energy Conversion: IoT and AI Approaches. *Applications of Synthetic Biology in Health. Energy & Environment*, 360–384.

Venkateswaran, N., Vidhya, K., Ayyannan, M., Chavan, S. M., Sekar, K., & Boopathi, S. (2023). A Study on Smart Energy Management Framework Using Cloud Computing. In 5G, Artificial Intelligence, and Next Generation Internet of Things: Digital Innovation for Green and Sustainable Economies (pp. 189–212). IGI Global. doi:10.4018/978-1-6684-8634-4.ch009

Verginadis, Y., Michalas, A., Gouvas, P., Schiefer, G., Hübsch, G., & Paraskakis, I. (2017). Paasword: A holistic data privacy and security by design framework for cloud services. *Journal of Grid Computing*, *15*(2), 219–234. doi:10.1007/s10723-017-9394-2

Vijayakumar, G. N. S., Domakonda, V. K., Farooq, S., Kumar, B. S., Pradeep, N., & Boopathi, S. (2024). Sustainable Developments in Nano-Fluid Synthesis for Various Industrial Applications. In Adoption and Use of Technology Tools and Services by Economically Disadvantaged Communities: Implications for Growth and Sustainability (pp. 48–81). IGI Global.

Zekrifa, D. M. S., Kulkarni, M., Bhagyalakshmi, A., Devireddy, N., Gupta, S., & Boopathi, S. (2023). Integrating Machine Learning and AI for Improved Hydrological Modeling and Water Resource Management. In *Artificial Intelligence Applications in Water Treatment and Water Resource Management* (pp. 46–70). IGI Global. doi:10.4018/978-1-6684-6791-6.ch003

Chapter 6
Integration of Precision Agriculture Technology, IoT Sensors, and System Efficiency for Sustainable Farming Practices

M. Maravarman
Department of Computer Science Engineering, B.V. Raju Institute of Technology, India

Shahana Gajala Qureshi
Department of Cyber Security and Digital Forensics, School of Computing Science and Engineering (SCSE), VIT Bhopal University, India

V. Krishnamoorthy
Department of Management Studies, Kongu Engineering College, India

Gurpreet Singh
Department of Computer Science and Engineering, Punjab Institute of Technology, Rajpura (MRSPTU Bathinda), India

Sreekanth Rallapalli
iD https://orcid.org/0000-0002-1626-0320
Department of Master of Computer Application, Nitte Meenakshi Institute of Technology, India

S. B. Boopa
KS Institute of Technology, India

ABSTRACT

The chapter explores the transformative impact of precision agricultural technology, focusing on the integration of IoT sensors, GPS technology, and automated systems in farming practices. It introduces the concept, traces its history, and explores its role in agriculture. The chapter discusses IoT sensors, GPS technology, drones, and automated machinery in precision planting, crop monitoring, and operational efficiency. It also discusses resource optimization in precision agriculture, including efficient water management, targeted fertilizer application, and pest control. The chapter addresses technological challenges, adoption challenges, and emerging trends. It concludes with a comprehensive examination of regulatory and ethical considerations, including data privacy, security, and ethical dimensions. The chapter emphasizes the need for collaboration among farmers, technology developers, policymakers, and regulatory bodies to ensure sustainable, efficient, and equitable farming.

DOI: 10.4018/979-8-3693-0968-1.ch006

INTRODUCTION

Precision agriculture, a revolutionary approach to farming, combines cutting-edge technologies like GPS, sensors, and data analytics to optimize resource utilization, minimize environmental impact, and enhance productivity. This departure from traditional farming methods allows for more targeted and efficient use of resources like water, fertilizers, and pesticides. The integration of agriculture with technology can increase yields, reduce waste, and contribute to sustainability by mitigating environmental impacts. This innovative approach has the potential to revolutionize the agricultural landscape and contribute to overall productivity (Sharma et al., 2020).

Precision agriculture, initially known as "precision farming," emerged in the late 20th century as a response to the variability in agricultural fields. The advent of GPS technology allowed farmers to precisely map and monitor their fields, laying the foundation for the development of precision agriculture as we know it today. Advancements in satellite imagery, sensors, and data analytics have made precision agriculture mainstream, allowing farmers to collect and analyze real-time data for informed resource allocation, crop management, and harvesting. This continuous journey of technological integration and adaptation aims to optimize agricultural practices for increased efficiency and sustainability (Bhakta et al., 2019).

Precision agriculture focuses on treating fields as dynamic, variable environments, moving away from a one-size-fits-all approach. It uses data-driven decision-making, spatial variability recognition, and precision technologies to tailor farming practices to specific needs within a field, recognizing the heterogeneity within agricultural landscapes. Precision agriculture is a method that uses precise, repeatable, and efficient methods to optimize input use, maximize crop yields, and reduce environmental impact. It relies on reliable data collection through sensors, consistent application of successful practices across seasons, and targeted resource application to minimize waste and environmental impact (Lowenberg-DeBoer & Erickson, 2019).

The integration of technology in agriculture is a significant shift from traditional labor-intensive methods to data-driven, automated processes. Technologies like GPS, sensors, drones, and automated machinery are essential components of modern farming operations. GPS technology allows for precise mapping and navigation, enabling farmers to monitor and manage their land with unprecedented accuracy (Shafi et al., 2019). Sensors collect real-time data, enabling farmers to make informed decisions. Drones provide a bird's-eye view of fields, identifying areas of concern and facilitating targeted interventions. The integration of technology in agriculture is not just about adopting individual tools; it's about creating interconnected systems that work in harmony. Automated machinery guided by GPS coordinates can perform tasks with unparalleled accuracy. This holistic approach forms the backbone of precision agriculture, enabling farmers to achieve unprecedented levels of efficiency and sustainability (Cisternas et al., 2020).

Precision agriculture is a strategic approach that optimizes agricultural practices by tailoring inputs to specific needs within a field, enhancing economic viability and environmental stewardship. This approach addresses global challenges such as population growth, climate change, and sustainable practices. With a growing world population, the demand for food is increasing, but arable land and essential resources like water are becoming limited. Precision agriculture maximizes efficiency while minimizing ecological footprint, aligning with the goals of achieving food security, environmental sustainability, and economic resilience in a rapidly changing world (Singh et al., 2020).

Purpose and Scope of the Chapter

This chapter explores precision agricultural technology, focusing on IoT sensors and their role in improving agricultural systems. It delves into the transformative potential of precision agriculture, its components, types, applications, and overall efficiency. The chapter also addresses challenges faced by precision agriculture, potential future trends, and ethical considerations surrounding advanced technologies (Agrawal et al., 2024a; Pachiappan et al., 2023; Sankar et al., 2023a). It aims to contribute to a deeper understanding of the paradigm shift in agriculture and its implications for sustainable and efficient food production. The chapter covers the role of IoT sensors in collecting data for informed decision-making and the integration of these technologies into precision agricultural systems.

IOT SENSORS IN AGRICULTURE

The Internet of Things (IoT) has revolutionized agriculture by embedding intelligence into everyday objects. It involves a network of interconnected devices and sensors that collect, transmit, and receive data, providing valuable insights to farmers and agribusinesses, enabling precision agriculture through real-time monitoring, data analysis, and informed decision-making (Mekonnen et al., 2019a). The integration of IoT in agriculture offers numerous advantages, including remote monitoring of crop conditions, soil health, and weather patterns, enabling timely interventions and optimized resource management. The seamless data flow between devices enhances farm efficiency, increasing productivity and sustainability. This overview focuses on the specific types of IoT sensors that are crucial in transforming agriculture into a data-driven, precision industry (Torky & Hassanein, 2020).

Types of IoT Sensors

- *Soil Sensors:* One of the foundational elements of precision agriculture is the monitoring of soil conditions. Soil sensors embedded with IoT technology provide real-time data on moisture levels, nutrient content, and temperature. This information allows farmers to tailor irrigation and fertilization practices to the specific needs of different soil zones within a field, optimizing resource usage and promoting crop health (Boopathi, Siva Kumar, et al., 2023; Gnanaprakasam et al., 2023a; P. R. Kumar et al., 2023a).

- *Weather and Climate Sensors:* Weather variability significantly influences agricultural outcomes. IoT-enabled weather and climate sensors gather data on temperature, humidity, wind speed, and precipitation. This real-time weather information aids farmers in making informed decisions regarding planting, harvesting, and pest control. By integrating this data into precision agriculture systems, farmers can mitigate the impact of adverse weather conditions on crop yields.

- *Crop Health Sensors:* Monitoring the health of crops is vital for early detection of diseases and pests. Crop health sensors equipped with IoT capabilities can detect subtle changes in plant conditions, such as leaf moisture, chlorophyll levels, and temperature. This allows farmers to identify potential threats and implement targeted interventions, reducing the need for broad-spectrum pesticides and minimizing environmental impact (Boopathi, 2023; Reddy et al., 2023; Satav et al., 2024).

- *Livestock Monitoring Sensors:* IoT sensors are not limited to crop monitoring; they also play a crucial role in livestock management. Sensors attached to animals can track health indicators, location, and behavior. Livestock monitoring sensors contribute to efficient herd management, enabling farmers to identify health issues early, optimize feeding schedules, and enhance overall animal welfare.

- *Pest Detection Sensors:* Pests can pose a significant threat to crops, and early detection is crucial for effective pest management. IoT-enabled pest detection sensors utilize various technologies, such as cameras, infrared sensors, and pheromone traps, to monitor and identify potential pest infestations. This proactive approach allows farmers to implement targeted pest control measures, reducing the reliance on chemical pesticides and minimizing environmental impact.

- *Water Quality Sensors:* Water quality is paramount for both crop irrigation and livestock consumption. IoT sensors designed for water quality monitoring assess parameters such as pH levels, salinity, and nutrient content. By continuously monitoring water quality, farmers can ensure that irrigation water meets the specific requirements of crops and that livestock have access to clean and safe drinking water (Gunasekaran & Boopathi, 2023a; Kumar B et al., 2024; Rahamathunnisa et al., 2023; Vanitha, K., et al., 2023).

- *Nutrient Management Sensors:* Optimal nutrient levels are essential for crop growth and yield. Nutrient management sensors equipped with IoT capabilities analyze soil nutrient levels and provide real-time feedback. This information assists farmers in making precise decisions regarding fertilizer application, preventing overuse and minimizing nutrient runoff, which can have detrimental effects on the environment (Boopathi, Siva Kumar, et al., 2023; S. et al., 2022; Samikannu et al., 2023).

- *Crop Growth and Phenology Sensors:* Understanding the growth stages of crops is fundamental to effective management. IoT sensors focused on crop growth and phenology monitor parameters such as plant height, leaf area, and flowering stages. This data aids farmers in predicting harvest times, optimizing the timing of agricultural operations, and ensuring that crops receive the necessary care at each growth stage (Domakonda et al., 2023; Vijayakumar et al., 2023).

- *Air Quality Sensors:* Air quality directly impacts both crops and livestock. IoT-enabled air quality sensors measure parameters such as air pollution, particulate matter, and gases. Monitoring air quality provides insights into potential environmental stressors that may affect agricultural productivity and animal health, allowing farmers to take preventive measures (Durairaj et al., 2023; Kumara, Mohanaprakash, Fairooz, Jamal, Babu, & B., 2023).

- *Energy Consumption Sensors:* In the context of precision agriculture, monitoring energy consumption is crucial, especially in the operation of automated machinery and irrigation systems. Energy consumption sensors with IoT capabilities help farmers track and optimize energy usage, contributing to overall farm efficiency and sustainability (Rahamathunnisa et al., 2023; Syamala et al., 2023; Venkateswaran et al., 2023a).

The integration of diverse IoT sensors in precision agriculture enhances data collection, providing farmers with a holistic understanding of their agricultural ecosystems. This leads to more informed decisions and sustainable farming practices. The technology's versatility in capturing a wide range of data points allows farmers to make precise, data-driven decisions, improving crop yields, resource efficiency, and sustainability in agricultural practices (Puppala et al., 2023).

Implementation

The integration of various IoT sensors into a precision agriculture system involves a cohesive framework for data collection, analysis, and informed decision-making, as illustrated in the following outline (Bhakta et al., 2019; Shafi et al., 2019; Sharma et al., 2020). The implementation of advanced sensors in the precise agricultural system is depicted in Figure 1.

Figure 1. Activities for implementation advanced sensor to the precise agricultural system

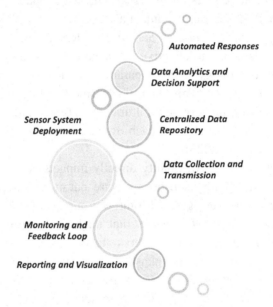

- ***Sensor System Deployment:*** Soil sensors monitor soil moisture, temperature, and nutrient levels, while weather and climate sensors capture real-time data. Crop health sensors track leaf moisture, chlorophyll levels, and temperature. Livestock monitoring sensors track health indicators, pest detection, water quality, nutrient management, crop growth, air quality, and energy consumption sensors. These devices are strategically placed across the farm.
- ***Data Collection and Transmission:*** Sensors collect real-time data, which is transmitted wirelessly to a centralized data repository. Data transmission occurs continuously, providing a steady stream of information from various points across the farm.

- *Centralized Data Repository:* A cloud-based or on-premises data repository stores the collected sensor data. The repository organizes and categorizes data for easy access and analysis.
- *Data Analytics and Decision Support:* Data analytics algorithms process the collected information to derive meaningful insights. Decision support systems analyze the data and provide actionable recommendations to farmers. Farmers can access the insights through a user-friendly interface, such as a web or mobile application.
- *Automated Responses:* Based on the analysis, the system can trigger automated responses, such as adjusting irrigation levels, activating pest control measures, or sending alerts for animal health issues. Automated machinery can be directed to specific areas for targeted interventions based on the sensor data.
- *Monitoring and Feedback Loop:* Continuous monitoring ensures that the system adapts to changing conditions. Farmers receive feedback on the effectiveness of implemented measures, allowing for continuous improvement.
- *Reporting and Visualization:* The system generates comprehensive reports and visualizations, offering farmers a clear overview of farm conditions and performance. Historical data can be analyzed for trends and patterns, aiding in long-term decision-making.

The integrated system optimizes precision agriculture by utilizing IoT sensors to enhance resource management, productivity, and sustainability in farming practices.

COMPONENTS OF PRECISION AGRICULTURE SYSTEMS

Precision agriculture systems are advanced technologies that optimize farming practices by collecting, analyzing, and acting upon data, facilitating data-driven decision-making for farmers, and consist of various components (Koshariya, Kalaiyarasi, et al., 2023). The Figure 2 depicts the key components of advanced precision agriculture systems.

GPS Technology

GPS technology is a crucial element in precision agriculture, providing precise location data for farmers to map and navigate their fields, enabling the creation of detailed field maps that form the foundation for various farming practices (Gnanaprakasam et al., 2023b).

Figure 2. Important components of advanced precision agriculture systems

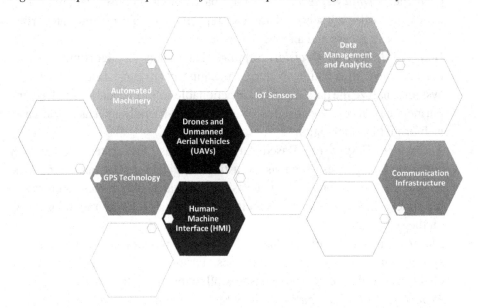

Applications of GPS in Precision Agriculture

- **Precision Navigation:** Farmers can navigate tractors and other machinery with high accuracy, reducing overlap and optimizing field coverage.
- **Variable Rate Technology (VRT):** GPS enables the application of inputs (such as fertilizers, pesticides, and water) at variable rates based on the specific needs of different areas within a field.
- **Mapping and Monitoring:** Field mapping using GPS aids in monitoring soil variations, crop health, and other spatial data, facilitating data-driven decision-making.

Drones and Unmanned Aerial Vehicles (UAVs)

Drones have become invaluable tools in precision agriculture, providing farmers with a bird's-eye view of their fields. Equipped with various sensors and cameras, drones capture high-resolution imagery and data, offering insights into crop conditions, pest infestations, and overall field health (Koshariya, Khatoon, et al., 2023).

Applications of Drones in Precision Agriculture

- **Crop Monitoring:** Drones capture detailed imagery, allowing farmers to monitor crop health, identify diseases, and assess overall vegetation vigor.
- **Field Mapping:** Drones can create accurate and up-to-date field maps, assisting in the identification of variations in soil types and crop performance.
- **Pest and Disease Detection:** Thermal and multispectral cameras on drones enable early detection of pest infestations and diseases, facilitating targeted interventions.
- **Water Management:** Drones assess soil moisture levels and help optimize irrigation practices by identifying areas with varying water needs.

Automated Machinery

Automated machinery, equipped with advanced technologies and GPS guidance systems, plays a pivotal role in precision agriculture. These machines perform tasks with precision, reducing human error, and optimizing the use of inputs (Sankar et al., 2023b).

Applications of Automated Machinery in Precision Agriculture

- **Precision Planting:** Automated planters use GPS technology to precisely place seeds, optimizing plant spacing and enhancing crop yields.
- **Precision Harvesting:** Automated harvesters can selectively harvest crops based on ripeness, reducing waste and improving overall efficiency.
- **Weed Control:** Automated machinery equipped with sensors can identify and selectively apply herbicides to control weeds, minimizing the use of chemicals.
- **Data Collection:** Automated machinery often comes with onboard sensors that collect data on soil conditions, crop yield, and other relevant parameters, contributing to real-time decision-making.

The integration of GPS technology, drones, and automated machinery forms a comprehensive precision agriculture system, empowering farmers with the tools needed to enhance efficiency, reduce resource use, and promote sustainable farming practices.

IoT Sensors

- **Soil Sensors:** Monitor soil moisture, temperature, and nutrient levels to optimize irrigation and fertilization (Gnanaprakasam et al., 2023b).
- **Weather and Climate Sensors:** Provide real-time data on temperature, humidity, wind speed, and precipitation to guide decision-making.
- **Crop Health Sensors:** Monitor leaf moisture, chlorophyll levels, and temperature for early detection of diseases and stress.
- **Livestock Monitoring Sensors:** Track health indicators, location, and behavior of livestock for better management.
- **Pest Detection Sensors:** Identify and monitor potential pest threats, enabling targeted pest control measures.
- **Water Quality Sensors:** Assess water quality parameters for irrigation and livestock consumption.
- **Nutrient Management Sensors:** Analyze soil nutrient levels to optimize fertilizer application.
- **Crop Growth and Phenology Sensors:** Monitor plant height, leaf area, and flowering stages for precise management.

Data Management and Analytics

- **Centralized Data Repository:** Stores data collected from sensors and other sources for analysis.
- **Data Analytics:** Utilizes algorithms to process data and derive meaningful insights.
- **Decision Support Systems:** Analyze data and provide actionable recommendations to farmers.

Communication Infrastructure

- **Wireless Networks:** Enable real-time communication between sensors, machinery, and centralized systems.
- **Internet Connectivity:** Facilitates data transfer to cloud-based platforms and enables remote monitoring and control.

Human-Machine Interface (HMI)

- **User Interface (UI):** Provides farmers with a user-friendly interface for accessing data, monitoring field conditions, and receiving recommendations.

- **Mobile Applications:** Allow farmers to access information and control systems remotely via smartphones or tablets.

The integration of these components creates a comprehensive precision agriculture system, providing farmers with tools to optimize efficiency, reduce environmental impact, and enhance sustainability in agriculture.

SYSTEM EFFICIENCY IN AGRICULTURE

Resource Optimization

This section discusses the importance of resource optimization in agriculture, specifically in water management, fertilizer application, and pest and disease control, highlighting the role of precision agriculture technologies in ensuring efficient and sustainable use of resources (Agrawal et al., 2023, 2024b).

Water Management

Water scarcity is a global issue, necessitating efficient water management for sustainable agriculture. Precision agriculture systems utilize technologies to optimize water usage, ensuring crops receive the right amount at the right time (B et al., 2024; Gunasekaran & Boopathi, 2023b; Vanitha, Radhika, et al., 2023).

Technological Interventions

- **Soil Moisture Sensors:** These sensors provide real-time data on soil moisture levels, enabling farmers to implement precise irrigation practices.
- **Drones with Thermal Imaging:** Drones equipped with thermal cameras can identify variations in crop water stress, allowing for targeted irrigation in specific areas.
- **Weather Stations:** Integration of weather data helps farmers anticipate rainfall and adjust irrigation schedules accordingly.

Benefits

- **Reduced Water Waste:** Precision irrigation minimizes water runoff and ensures that water is delivered directly to the root zones where it's needed.
- **Improved Crop Yields:** Providing the right amount of water at critical growth stages enhances crop health and productivity.

- **Conservation of Water Resources:** Efficient water management contributes to the conservation of water resources, promoting long-term sustainability.

Fertilizer Application

Precision agriculture technologies enable farmers to optimize fertilizer application to meet specific nutrient needs, maximizing crop yields and minimizing environmental impact (Agrawal et al., 2023).

Technological Interventions

- **Variable Rate Technology (VRT):** VRT utilizes GPS and sensor data to adjust fertilizer application rates based on soil nutrient levels, creating a spatially precise nutrient management plan.
- **Nutrient Management Sensors:** These sensors analyze soil nutrient levels in real-time, providing data for informed decision-making.
- **Remote Sensing:** Satellite or drone-based remote sensing technologies help monitor crop health, allowing farmers to adjust fertilizer applications as needed.

Benefits

- **Increased Efficiency:** Targeted fertilizer application reduces overuse and minimizes nutrient runoff, promoting environmental sustainability.
- **Cost Savings:** Precision nutrient management ensures that fertilizers are applied where they are needed most, reducing overall fertilizer costs.
- **Enhanced Soil Health:** Balanced nutrient application contributes to improved soil health and long-term fertility.

Pest and Disease Control

Precision agriculture technologies aid in early detection and targeted control of pest and disease, reducing the need for broad-spectrum treatments in sustainable agriculture.

Technological Interventions

- **Pest Detection Sensors:** These sensors, along with drones and cameras, monitor fields for signs of pest infestations.

- **Data Analytics:** Analyzing historical data helps predict pest and disease outbreaks, allowing for proactive interventions.
- **Integrated Pest Management (IPM) Systems:** These systems combine data from various sources to implement a holistic approach to pest and disease control.

Benefits

- **Reduced Chemical Usage:** Targeted interventions based on real-time data minimize the need for excessive pesticide applications.
- **Preservation of Beneficial Organisms:** Precision pest control methods help preserve natural predators, contributing to ecosystem balance.
- **Early Intervention:** Early detection allows farmers to respond promptly to pest and disease threats, preventing widespread damage.

The integration of resource optimization strategies into precision agriculture systems can improve efficiency, minimize environmental impact, and promote sustainable farming practices.

ADVANCED TECHNOLOGIES AND IMPLEMENTATION: HYDROPONICS, AEROPONICS, AND AQUAPONICS SYSTEMS

The Figure 3 showcases the implementation of advanced technologies such as hydroponics, aeroponics, and aquaponics systems.

Figure 3. Advanced technologies and implementation: Hydroponics, aeroponics, and aquaponics systems

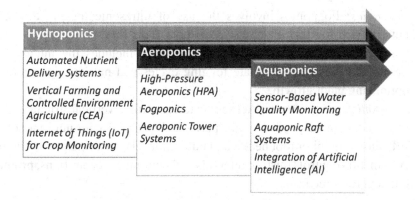

Hydroponics

- *Automated Nutrient Delivery Systems:* Utilizing automated nutrient delivery systems in hydroponics involves the precise control and monitoring of nutrient solutions. IoT sensors measure nutrient levels, pH, and temperature, allowing for real-time adjustments. Automation ensures that plants receive optimal nutrition, leading to increased yields and resource efficiency (P. Kumar et al., 2023; Kumara, Mohanaprakash, Fairooz, Jamal, Babu, & Sampath, 2023; Zekrifa et al., 2023).
- *Vertical Farming and Controlled Environment Agriculture (CEA):* Vertical farming involves stacking layers of hydroponic systems vertically, maximizing space utilization. CEA employs advanced climate control technologies such as artificial lighting, temperature, and humidity regulation. Implementation of these technologies enables year-round, controlled cultivation, independent of external environmental conditions.
- *Internet of Things (IoT) for Crop Monitoring:* IoT devices, including sensors and actuators, are deployed to monitor environmental variables like light intensity, humidity, and temperature. This real-time data is then analyzed to optimize growing conditions. Automated adjustments are made to create an ideal environment, promoting plant growth and health.

Aeroponics

- *High-Pressure Aeroponics (HPA):* HPA systems use high-pressure pumps to create a fine mist of nutrient solution, delivering it directly to plant roots. Advanced pressure regulation and sensor technologies ensure precise nutrient delivery. This method enhances nutrient absorption and promotes faster plant growth (Boopathi et al., 2022; Koshariya, Kalaiyarasi, et al., 2023; P. R. Kumar et al., 2023b).
- *Fogponics:* Fogponics involves the use of ultrasonic foggers to create a nutrient-rich fog that envelops plant roots. This fine mist provides optimal nutrient absorption. Automation in fogponics includes the integration of timers and sensors to regulate fogging cycles and nutrient concentrations, optimizing plant growth.
- *Aeroponic Tower Systems:* Aeroponic towers utilize vertical structures where plant roots are suspended in air, periodically misted with nutrient solution. IoT sensors monitor root health and nutrient levels, ensuring precise delivery. Automation controls misting intervals and nutrient concentrations, promoting efficient resource use.

Aquaponics

- *Sensor-Based Water Quality Monitoring:* Aquaponics combines aquaculture (fish farming) and hydroponics. Advanced sensors monitor water quality parameters such as pH, ammonia, nitrate, and dissolved oxygen. Automated systems regulate water conditions, ensuring a symbiotic relationship between fish and plants (B et al., 2024; Gunasekaran & Boopathi, 2023b; Venkateswaran et al., 2023b; Zekrifa et al., 2023).

- *Aquaponic Raft Systems:* Raft systems in aquaponics involve floating platforms where plants are suspended in water containing fish waste. IoT sensors monitor nutrient levels and fish health, while automated controls adjust water flow and nutrient delivery. This integration optimizes nutrient cycling and minimizes waste.

- *Integration of Artificial Intelligence (AI):* AI algorithms analyze data from sensors and actuators in aquaponics systems. Machine learning models predict optimal conditions for both fish and plants based on historical data, allowing for proactive adjustments. AI-driven automation enhances system efficiency and sustainability.

The integration of these advanced technologies in hydroponics, aeroponics, and aquaponics represents a significant leap forward in sustainable and efficient agriculture. Through precision control, automation, and data-driven decision-making, these systems aim to redefine modern farming practices, ensuring a reliable and environmentally friendly food production system for the future.

CHALLENGES AND FUTURE DIRECTIONS

The Figure 4 outlines the challenges, future trends, and innovations in precision agriculture and explained below.

Technological Challenges

Precision agriculture is promising but faces numerous technological challenges that need to be addressed to fully realize its potential (Gnanaprakasam et al., 2023b; Koshariya, Khatoon, et al., 2023; P. R. Kumar et al., 2023b).

- **Interoperability:** Integrating diverse technologies and systems from different manufacturers can be challenging due to compatibility issues. Standardization

Figure 4. Challenges, future trends, and innovations in precision agriculture

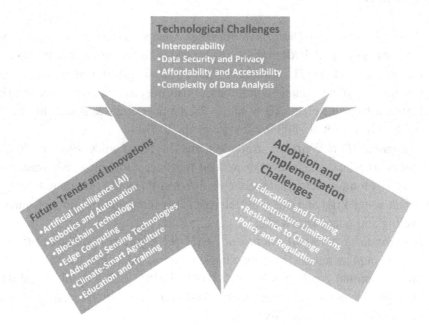

efforts are crucial to ensure seamless communication between various components of precision agriculture systems.

- **Data Security and Privacy:** The collection and sharing of sensitive agricultural data raise concerns about security and privacy. Ensuring robust cybersecurity measures and establishing clear data ownership and consent frameworks are essential.
- **Affordability and Accessibility:** High upfront costs and limited accessibility to advanced technologies pose barriers for smaller farmers. Efforts to make precision agriculture technologies more affordable and user-friendly will be critical for widespread adoption.
- **Complexity of Data Analysis:** The sheer volume of data generated by precision agriculture systems can be overwhelming. Developing advanced analytics tools that can process and interpret data effectively is essential for informed decision-making.

Adoption and Implementation Challenges

The implementation of precision agriculture practices is impeded by issues related to farmer education, infrastructure, and policy support (Boopathi et al., 2022; Koshariya, Kalaiyarasi, et al., 2023; P. R. Kumar et al., 2023b).

- **Education and Training:** Farmers may lack the necessary knowledge and training to effectively implement precision agriculture technologies. Educational programs and training initiatives are needed to bridge this knowledge gap and promote adoption.
- **Infrastructure Limitations:** Precision agriculture often relies on robust internet connectivity and infrastructure. In regions with poor connectivity or outdated infrastructure, the adoption of these technologies may be hindered.
- **Resistance to Change:** Traditional farming practices and a reluctance to embrace new technologies can impede the adoption of precision agriculture. Outreach programs and demonstrating the tangible benefits of these technologies are crucial for overcoming resistance.
- **Policy and Regulation:** The absence of supportive policies and regulations can hinder the widespread adoption of precision agriculture. Governments need to establish clear guidelines, incentives, and regulatory frameworks that encourage the integration of these technologies.

Future Trends and Innovations in Precision Agriculture

The future of precision agriculture is expected to be shaped by various trends and innovations as it continues to evolve (Boopathi et al., 2022; Koshariya, Kalaiyarasi, et al., 2023, 2023; P. R. Kumar et al., 2023b).

- **Artificial Intelligence (AI) and Machine Learning:** AI and machine learning algorithms will play a more significant role in analyzing vast amounts of data to provide actionable insights. These technologies will enhance decision-making processes and contribute to more precise and adaptive farming practices.
- **Robotics and Automation:** The integration of robotics and automation in agriculture will increase, leading to the development of autonomous vehicles, robotic harvesters, and other technologies that reduce labor requirements and improve efficiency.
- **Blockchain Technology:** Blockchain can enhance traceability and transparency in the agricultural supply chain. Implementing blockchain can help track the origin of products, verify authenticity, and improve overall food safety.
- **Edge Computing:** Edge computing involves processing data closer to its source rather than relying solely on cloud-based solutions. This approach can reduce latency and enhance real-time decision-making in precision agriculture applications.

- **Advanced Sensing Technologies:** Ongoing advancements in sensing technologies, such as hyperspectral imaging and advanced drones, will provide more detailed and accurate data for monitoring crops, soil conditions, and overall farm health.
- **Climate-Smart Agriculture:** Precision agriculture will increasingly align with climate-smart practices, emphasizing resilience to climate change, sustainable resource use, and adaptation to varying environmental conditions.

The growth and success of precision agriculture depend on addressing current challenges and embracing future trends, paving the way for a sustainable and efficient global farming practice.

CASE STUDY: PRECISION AGRICULTURE TRANSFORMATION IN FARM

The Farm, a generational farm in the heartland, tackled modern agriculture challenges like fluctuating yields and resource inefficiencies. They embraced precision agriculture, using advanced technologies to optimize their farming operations (Klerkx et al., 2019; Mekonnen et al., 2019b; Tsouros et al., 2019).

Objectives

- **Enhance Crop Yields:** Improve overall crop yields through precise resource management and targeted interventions.
- **Optimize Resource Utilization:** Minimize resource wastage, including water and fertilizers, by adopting variable rate technologies.
- **Mitigate Pest and Disease Impact:** Implement early detection systems and targeted control measures to reduce the impact of pests and diseases.
- **Integrate Automation for Efficiency:** Incorporate automated machinery guided by GPS for precision planting, harvesting, and other farm operations.

Implementation

Deployment of IoT Sensors

- Soil sensors were strategically placed across the fields to monitor soil moisture, temperature, and nutrient levels.
- Weather and climate sensors were installed to provide real-time data on temperature, humidity, wind speed, and precipitation.

- Pest detection sensors were implemented to identify and monitor potential pest threats.
- Livestock monitoring sensors were utilized to track the health indicators, location, and behavior of the farm's cattle.

Precision Planting With GPS Technology

- Automated planters equipped with GPS technology were employed for precise seed placement, optimizing plant spacing and promoting even crop growth.
- Variable rate technology (VRT) was implemented to adjust seeding rates based on the specific needs of different areas within each field.

Drones for Crop Monitoring

- Drones equipped with high-resolution cameras and multispectral sensors were deployed for comprehensive crop monitoring.
- These drones provided detailed imagery for assessing crop health, identifying stress factors, and detecting early signs of diseases.

Automated Machinery for Harvesting

- Precision agriculture systems integrated automated machinery, such as GPS-guided harvesters, to selectively harvest crops based on ripeness.
- Harvesters were equipped with onboard sensors to collect data on crop yield, contributing to overall farm analytics.

Results and Discussions

- **Improved Crop Yields:** The precision planting approach led to more uniform crop growth, resulting in a significant increase in overall crop yields. GPS-guided planting reduced overlaps and gaps, ensuring optimal use of available land.
- **Resource Efficiency:** Utilizing soil sensors and VRT for fertilization led to a reduction in fertilizer usage by 15%, minimizing environmental impact and lowering input costs. Precision irrigation practices based on soil moisture data resulted in a 20% reduction in water consumption.
- **Pest and Disease Control:** Early detection systems using pest detection sensors and drone imagery allowed for timely interventions, reducing the

impact of pests and diseases on crops. Targeted control measures minimized the need for broad-spectrum pesticides.

- **Operational Efficiency:** Automated machinery guided by GPS technology streamlined farming operations. Precision harvesting led to a 25% reduction in labor requirements, allowing the Smiths to reallocate resources to other essential tasks.

Soil sensors monitor soil moisture, temperature, and nutrient levels, while weather and climate sensors capture real-time data. Crop health sensors track leaf moisture, chlorophyll levels, and temperature. Livestock monitoring sensors track health indicators, pest detection, water quality, nutrient management, crop growth, air quality, and energy consumption sensors. These devices are strategically placed across the farm (Boopathi, Kumar, et al., 2023; Gnanaprakasam et al., 2023b; Jeevanantham et al., 2022; P. R. Kumar et al., 2023b).

REGULATORY AND ETHICAL CONSIDERATIONS

Data Privacy and Security

- *Data Ownership and Consent:* Precision agriculture relies heavily on data collection and analysis, including sensitive information about crop yields, soil conditions, and farm operations. Clear guidelines are needed to determine data ownership and obtain informed consent from farmers, ensuring clear ownership and usage of precision agriculture systems (Kavitha et al., 2023; Maguluri et al., 2023).
- *Secure Data Transmission and Storage:* The transmission and storage of agricultural data pose significant challenges in terms of privacy and security. Ensuring the secure transfer of data between devices and centralized systems, as well as implementing robust cybersecurity measures for data storage, is paramount. Encryption, secure cloud platforms, and adherence to industry standards are crucial elements in safeguarding agricultural data.
- *Anonymization and Aggregation:* To protect individual farmers' privacy, precision agriculture systems should employ techniques such as data anonymization and aggregation. Aggregating data at a broader level while removing personally identifiable information helps balance the need for data-driven insights with individual privacy concerns.

Regulatory Frameworks

- *Standardization and Interoperability:* Regulatory bodies play a crucial role in establishing standards for precision agriculture technologies to ensure interoperability and seamless integration. Standardization promotes consistency in data formats, communication protocols, and technology interfaces, fostering a more cohesive and efficient precision agriculture ecosystem.
- *Compliance with Environmental Regulations:* Precision agriculture practices, including the use of fertilizers, pesticides, and water, should comply with environmental regulations to mitigate potential adverse effects. Regulatory frameworks need to evolve to address the dynamic nature of precision agriculture while maintaining a balance between innovation and environmental stewardship.
- *Privacy Regulations:* Data privacy regulations, such as the General Data Protection Regulation (GDPR) in Europe, play a critical role in protecting farmers' personal information. Policymakers must consider the unique challenges posed by agricultural data and ensure that privacy regulations are adapted to the specific needs of the precision agriculture sector.

Ethical Considerations in Precision Agriculture

- *Informed Decision-Making:* Farmers should be well-informed about the capabilities and limitations of precision agriculture technologies. Transparency in how data is collected, processed, and used allows farmers to make informed decisions about adopting these technologies and understanding the potential implications for their operations (Maguluri et al., 2023; Ugandar et al., 2023).
- *Environmental Impact and Sustainability:* Ethical considerations extend to the environmental impact of precision agriculture practices. Balancing increased productivity with sustainability is crucial. Farmers, policymakers, and technology developers should collaborate to ensure that precision agriculture contributes to long-term environmental resilience and biodiversity.
- *Addressing Social Equity:* There is a need to address social equity concerns related to the adoption of precision agriculture. Smaller farmers with limited resources may face challenges in accessing and implementing these technologies. Ethical considerations involve promoting inclusivity and ensuring that the benefits of precision agriculture are accessible to farmers of all scales.

- *Responsible Use of Automation:* As automation becomes more prevalent in precision agriculture, ethical considerations arise concerning the responsible use of technology. Ensuring that automated systems prioritize safety, minimize environmental impact, and adhere to ethical farming practices is essential.

The integration of precision agriculture technologies necessitates a balance between innovation, regulatory compliance, and ethical considerations. Addressing data privacy, establishing regulatory frameworks for innovation, and promoting ethical practices are crucial for the long-term success and sustainability of this farming approach. Collaborative efforts among farmers, technology developers, policymakers, and regulatory bodies are essential for navigating these considerations.

CONCLUSION

The chapter explores the role of technology in precision agriculture, highlighting the integration of IoT sensors, GPS technology, drones, and automated machinery. These technologies contribute to resource optimization, increased efficiency, and sustainable farming practices. IoT sensors collect real-time data, providing farmers with insights into soil health, weather patterns, and crop conditions. GPS technology enables precision navigation, variable rate technology, and precise mapping, promoting accurate and efficient farming operations.

Drones are revolutionizing crop monitoring by providing a comprehensive view of fields, enabling early detection of pests and diseases. Automated machinery, guided by GPS coordinates, enhances operational efficiency and reduces labor. However, challenges like interoperability and data security necessitate standardized solutions. The chapter emphasizes the need for regulatory frameworks to guide responsible implementation of precision agriculture technologies, ensuring environmental compliance and data privacy.

The technological revolution in agriculture is transforming farming practices, but ethical considerations are crucial. Farmers need knowledge and responsible automation to address social equity and environmental sustainability. Artificial intelligence, machine learning, and advanced sensing technologies are expected to enhance precision and efficiency, while robotics and automation will reduce manual labor and increase productivity.

Precision agriculture requires collaboration between farmers, technology developers, policymakers, and regulatory bodies to navigate the technological landscape, address challenges, and uphold ethical considerations. This innovative approach promotes environmental stewardship and social responsibility, paving the way for a sustainable, efficient, and equitable future in agriculture, catering to a growing global population.

ABBREVIATIONS

IoT: Internet of Things
GPS: Global Positioning System
VRT: Variable Rate Technology
AI: Artificial Intelligence
IPM: Integrated Pest Management
GDPR: General Data Protection Regulation
HMI: Human-Machine Interface

REFERENCES

Agrawal, A. V., Magulur, L. P., Priya, S. G., Kaur, A., Singh, G., & Boopathi, S. (2023). Smart Precision Agriculture Using IoT and WSN. In *Handbook of Research on Data Science and Cybersecurity Innovations in Industry 4.0 Technologies* (pp. 524–541). IGI Global. doi:10.4018/978-1-6684-8145-5.ch026

Agrawal, A. V., Shashibhushan, G., Pradeep, S., Padhi, S. N., Sugumar, D., & Boopathi, S. (2024a). Synergizing Artificial Intelligence, 5G, and Cloud Computing for Efficient Energy Conversion Using Agricultural Waste. In B. K. Mishra (Ed.), Practice, Progress, and Proficiency in Sustainability. IGI Global. doi:10.4018/979-8-3693-1186-8.ch026

Agrawal, A. V., Shashibhushan, G., Pradeep, S., Padhi, S. N., Sugumar, D., & Boopathi, S. (2024b). Synergizing Artificial Intelligence, 5G, and Cloud Computing for Efficient Energy Conversion Using Agricultural Waste. In Practice, Progress, and Proficiency in Sustainability (pp. 475–497). IGI Global. doi:10.4018/979-8-3693-1186-8.ch026

B, M. K., K, K. K., Sasikala, P., Sampath, B., Gopi, B., & Sundaram, S. (2024). Sustainable Green Energy Generation From Waste Water. In *Practice, Progress, and Proficiency in Sustainability* (pp. 440–463). IGI Global. doi:10.4018/979-8-3693-1186-8.ch024

Bhakta, I., Phadikar, S., & Majumder, K. (2019). State-of-the-art technologies in precision agriculture: A systematic review. *Journal of the Science of Food and Agriculture*, *99*(11), 4878–4888. doi:10.1002/jsfa.9693 PMID:30883757

Boopathi, S. (2023). Securing Healthcare Systems Integrated With IoT: Fundamentals, Applications, and Future Trends. In A. Suresh Kumar, U. Kose, S. Sharma, & S. Jerald Nirmal Kumar (Eds.), Advances in Healthcare Information Systems and Administration. IGI Global. doi:10.4018/978-1-6684-6894-4.ch010

Boopathi, S., Arigela, S. H., Raman, R., Indhumathi, C., Kavitha, V., & Bhatt, B. C. (2022). Prominent Rule Control-based Internet of Things: Poultry Farm Management System. *IEEE Explore*, 1–6.

Boopathi, S., Kumar, P. K. S., Meena, R. S., Sudhakar, M., & Associates. (2023). Sustainable Developments of Modern Soil-Less Agro-Cultivation Systems: Aquaponic Culture. In Human Agro-Energy Optimization for Business and Industry (pp. 69–87). IGI Global.

Boopathi, S., Siva Kumar, P. K., Meena, R. S. J., S. I., P., S. K., & Sudhakar, M. (2023). Sustainable Developments of Modern Soil-Less Agro-Cultivation Systems: Aquaponic Culture. In P. Vasant, R. Rodríguez-Aguilar, I. Litvinchev, & J. A. Marmolejo-Saucedo (Eds.), Advances in Environmental Engineering and Green Technologies (pp. 69–87). IGI Global. doi:10.4018/978-1-6684-4118-3.ch004

Cisternas, I., Velásquez, I., Caro, A., & Rodríguez, A. (2020). Systematic literature review of implementations of precision agriculture. *Computers and Electronics in Agriculture, 176*, 105626. doi:10.1016/j.compag.2020.105626

Domakonda, V. K., Farooq, S., Chinthamreddy, S., Puviarasi, R., Sudhakar, M., & Boopathi, S. (2023). Sustainable Developments of Hybrid Floating Solar Power Plants: Photovoltaic System. In P. Vasant, R. Rodríguez-Aguilar, I. Litvinchev, & J. A. Marmolejo-Saucedo (Eds.), Advances in Environmental Engineering and Green Technologies. IGI Global. doi:10.4018/978-1-6684-4118-3.ch008

Durairaj, M., Jayakumar, S., Karpagavalli, V. S., Maheswari, B. U., & Boopathi, S. (2023). Utilization of Digital Tools in the Indian Higher Education System During Health Crises: In C. S. V. Negrão, I. G. P. Maia, & J. A. F. Brito (Eds.), Advances in Logistics, Operations, and Management Science (pp. 1–21). IGI Global. doi:10.4018/978-1-7998-9213-7.ch001

Gnanaprakasam, C., Vankara, J., Sastry, A. S., Prajval, V., Gireesh, N., & Boopathi, S. (2023). Long-Range and Low-Power Automated Soil Irrigation System Using Internet of Things: An Experimental Study. In G. S. Karthick (Ed.), Advances in Environmental Engineering and Green Technologies. IGI Global. doi:10.4018/978-1-6684-7879-0.ch005

Gunasekaran, K., & Boopathi, S. (2023a). Artificial Intelligence in Water Treatments and Water Resource Assessments. In V. Shikuku (Ed.), Advances in Environmental Engineering and Green Technologies. IGI Global. doi:10.4018/978-1-6684-6791-6.ch004

Gunasekaran, K., & Boopathi, S. (2023b). Artificial Intelligence in Water Treatments and Water Resource Assessments. In *Artificial Intelligence Applications in Water Treatment and Water Resource Management* (pp. 71–98). IGI Global. doi:10.4018/978-1-6684-6791-6.ch004

Jeevanantham, Y. A., Saravanan, A., Vanitha, V., Boopathi, S., & Kumar, D. P. (2022). Implementation of Internet-of Things (IoT) in Soil Irrigation System. *IEEE Explore*, 1–5.

Kavitha, C. R., Varalatchoumy, M., Mithuna, H. R., Bharathi, K., Geethalakshmi, N. M., & Boopathi, S. (2023). Energy Monitoring and Control in the Smart Grid: Integrated Intelligent IoT and ANFIS. In M. Arshad (Ed.), Advances in Bioinformatics and Biomedical Engineering. IGI Global. doi:10.4018/978-1-6684-6577-6.ch014

Klerkx, L., Jakku, E., & Labarthe, P. (2019). A review of social science on digital agriculture, smart farming and agriculture 4.0: New contributions and a future research agenda. *NJAS Wageningen Journal of Life Sciences*, *90*(1), 100315. doi:10.1016/j.njas.2019.100315

Koshariya, A. K., Kalaiyarasi, D., Jovith, A. A., Sivakami, T., Hasan, D. S., & Boopathi, S. (2023). AI-Enabled IoT and WSN-Integrated Smart Agriculture System. In *Artificial Intelligence Tools and Technologies for Smart Farming and Agriculture Practices* (pp. 200–218). IGI Global. doi:10.4018/978-1-6684-8516-3.ch011

Koshariya, A. K., Khatoon, S., Marathe, A. M., Suba, G. M., Baral, D., & Boopathi, S. (2023). Agricultural Waste Management Systems Using Artificial Intelligence Techniques. In *AI-Enabled Social Robotics in Human Care Services* (pp. 236–258). IGI Global. doi:10.4018/978-1-6684-8171-4.ch009

Kumar, B. M., Kumar, K. K., Sasikala, P., Sampath, B., Gopi, B., & Sundaram, S. (2024). Sustainable Green Energy Generation From Waste Water: IoT and ML Integration. In B. K. Mishra (Ed.), Practice, Progress, and Proficiency in Sustainability. IGI Global. doi:10.4018/979-8-3693-1186-8.ch024

Kumar, P., Sampath, B., Kumar, S., Babu, B. H., & Ahalya, N. (2023). Hydroponics, Aeroponics, and Aquaponics Technologies in Modern Agricultural Cultivation. In IGI: Trends, Paradigms, and Advances in Mechatronics Engineering (pp. 223–241). IGI Global.

Kumar, P. R., Meenakshi, S., Shalini, S., Devi, S. R., & Boopathi, S. (2023). Soil Quality Prediction in Context Learning Approaches Using Deep Learning and Blockchain for Smart Agriculture. In R. Kumar, A. B. Abdul Hamid, & N. I. Binti Ya'akub (Eds.), Advances in Computational Intelligence and Robotics. IGI Global. doi:10.4018/978-1-6684-9151-5.ch001

Kumara, V., Mohanaprakash, T., Fairooz, S., Jamal, K., Babu, T., & Sampath, B. (2023). Experimental Study on a Reliable Smart Hydroponics System. In *Human Agro-Energy Optimization for Business and Industry* (pp. 27–45). IGI Global. doi:10.4018/978-1-6684-4118-3.ch002

Kumara, V., Mohanaprakash, T. A., Fairooz, S., Jamal, K., Babu, T., & B., S. (2023). Experimental Study on a Reliable Smart Hydroponics System. In P. Vasant, R. Rodríguez-Aguilar, I. Litvinchev, & J. A. Marmolejo-Saucedo (Eds.), *Advances in Environmental Engineering and Green Technologies* (pp. 27–45). IGI Global. doi:10.4018/978-1-6684-4118-3.ch002

Lowenberg-DeBoer, J., & Erickson, B. (2019). Setting the record straight on precision agriculture adoption. *Agronomy Journal*, *111*(4), 1552–1569. doi:10.2134/agronj2018.12.0779

Maguluri, L. P., Arularasan, A. N., & Boopathi, S. (2023). Assessing Security Concerns for AI-Based Drones in Smart Cities. In R. Kumar, A. B. Abdul Hamid, & N. I. Binti Ya'akub (Eds.), Advances in Computational Intelligence and Robotics. IGI Global. doi:10.4018/978-1-6684-9151-5.ch002

Mekonnen, Y., Namuduri, S., Burton, L., Sarwat, A., & Bhansali, S. (2019). Machine learning techniques in wireless sensor network based precision agriculture. *Journal of the Electrochemical Society*, *167*(3), 037522. doi:10.1149/2.0222003JES

Pachiappan, K., Anitha, K., Pitchai, R., Sangeetha, S., Satyanarayana, T. V. V., & Boopathi, S. (2023). Intelligent Machines, IoT, and AI in Revolutionizing Agriculture for Water Processing. In B. B. Gupta & F. Colace (Eds.), Advances in Computational Intelligence and Robotics. IGI Global. doi:10.4018/978-1-6684-9999-3.ch015

Puppala, H., Peddinti, P. R., Tamvada, J. P., Ahuja, J., & Kim, B. (2023). Barriers to the adoption of new technologies in rural areas: The case of unmanned aerial vehicles for precision agriculture in India. *Technology in Society*, *74*, 102335. doi:10.1016/j.techsoc.2023.102335

Rahamathunnisa, U., Sudhakar, K., Padhi, S. N., Bhattacharya, S., Shashibhushan, G., & Boopathi, S. (2023). Sustainable Energy Generation From Waste Water: IoT Integrated Technologies. In A. S. Etim (Ed.), Advances in Human and Social Aspects of Technology. IGI Global. doi:10.4018/978-1-6684-5347-6.ch010

Reddy, M. A., Reddy, B. M., Mukund, C. S., Venneti, K., Preethi, D. M. D., & Boopathi, S. (2023). Social Health Protection During the COVID-Pandemic Using IoT. In F. P. C. Endong (Ed.), Advances in Electronic Government, Digital Divide, and Regional Development. IGI Global. doi:10.4018/978-1-7998-8394-4.ch009

S., P. K., Sampath, B., R., S. K., Babu, B. H., & N., A. (2022). Hydroponics, Aeroponics, and Aquaponics Technologies in Modern Agricultural Cultivation: In M. A. Mellal (Ed.), *Advances in Mechatronics and Mechanical Engineering* (pp. 223–241). IGI Global. doi:10.4018/978-1-6684-5887-7.ch012

Samikannu, R., Koshariya, A. K., Poornima, E., Ramesh, S., Kumar, A., & Boopathi, S. (2023). Sustainable Development in Modern Aquaponics Cultivation Systems Using IoT Technologies. In P. Vasant, R. Rodríguez-Aguilar, I. Litvinchev, & J. A. Marmolejo-Saucedo (Eds.), Advances in Environmental Engineering and Green Technologies. IGI Global. doi:10.4018/978-1-6684-4118-3.ch006

Sankar, K. M., Booba, B., & Boopathi, S. (2023a). Smart Agriculture Irrigation Monitoring System Using Internet of Things. In G. S. Karthick (Ed.), Advances in Environmental Engineering and Green Technologies. IGI Global. doi:10.4018/978-1-6684-7879-0.ch006

Sankar, K. M., Booba, B., & Boopathi, S. (2023b). Smart Agriculture Irrigation Monitoring System Using Internet of Things. In *Contemporary Developments in Agricultural Cyber-Physical Systems* (pp. 105–121). IGI Global. doi:10.4018/978-1-6684-7879-0.ch006

Satav, S. D., Hasan, D. S., Pitchai, R., Mohanaprakash, T. A., Sultanuddin, S. J., & Boopathi, S. (2024). Next Generation of Internet of Things (NGIoT) in Healthcare Systems. In B. K. Mishra (Ed.), Practice, Progress, and Proficiency in Sustainability. IGI Global. doi:10.4018/979-8-3693-1186-8.ch017

Shafi, U., Mumtaz, R., García-Nieto, J., Hassan, S. A., Zaidi, S. A. R., & Iqbal, N. (2019). Precision agriculture techniques and practices: From considerations to applications. *Sensors (Basel)*, *19*(17), 3796. doi:10.3390/s19173796 PMID:31480709

Sharma, A., Jain, A., Gupta, P., & Chowdary, V. (2020). Machine learning applications for precision agriculture: A comprehensive review. *IEEE Access : Practical Innovations, Open Solutions*, *9*, 4843–4873. doi:10.1109/ACCESS.2020.3048415

Singh, R. K., Aernouts, M., De Meyer, M., Weyn, M., & Berkvens, R. (2020). Leveraging LoRaWAN technology for precision agriculture in greenhouses. *Sensors (Basel)*, *20*(7), 1827. doi:10.3390/s20071827 PMID:32218353

Syamala, M. C. R., K., Pramila, P. V., Dash, S., Meenakshi, S., & Boopathi, S. (2023). Machine Learning-Integrated IoT-Based Smart Home Energy Management System. In P. Swarnalatha & S. Prabu (Eds.), Advances in Computational Intelligence and Robotics (pp. 219–235). IGI Global. doi:10.4018/978-1-6684-8098-4.ch013

Torky, M., & Hassanein, A. E. (2020). Integrating blockchain and the internet of things in precision agriculture: Analysis, opportunities, and challenges. *Computers and Electronics in Agriculture, 178,* 105476. doi:10.1016/j.compag.2020.105476

Tsouros, D. C., Bibi, S., & Sarigiannidis, P. G. (2019). A review on UAV-based applications for precision agriculture. *Information (Basel), 10*(11), 349. doi:10.3390/info10110349

Ugandar, R. E., Rahamathunnisa, U., Sajithra, S., Christiana, M. B. V., Palai, B. K., & Boopathi, S. (2023). Hospital Waste Management Using Internet of Things and Deep Learning: Enhanced Efficiency and Sustainability. In M. Arshad (Ed.), Advances in Bioinformatics and Biomedical Engineering. IGI Global. doi:10.4018/978-1-6684-6577-6.ch015

Vanitha, S., Radhika, K., & Boopathi, S. (2023). Artificial Intelligence Techniques in Water Purification and Utilization. In *Human Agro-Energy Optimization for Business and Industry* (pp. 202–218). IGI Global. doi:10.4018/978-1-6684-4118-3.ch010

Vanitha, S. K. R., & Boopathi, S. (2023). Artificial Intelligence Techniques in Water Purification and Utilization. In P. Vasant, R. Rodríguez-Aguilar, I. Litvinchev, & J. A. Marmolejo-Saucedo (Eds.), Advances in Environmental Engineering and Green Technologies. IGI Global. doi:10.4018/978-1-6684-4118-3.ch010

Venkateswaran, N., Kumar, S. S., Diwakar, G., Gnanasangeetha, D., & Boopathi, S. (2023). Synthetic Biology for Waste Water to Energy Conversion: IoT and AI Approaches. In M. Arshad (Ed.), Advances in Bioinformatics and Biomedical Engineering. IGI Global. doi:10.4018/978-1-6684-6577-6.ch017

Vijayakumar, G. N. S., Domakonda, V. K., Farooq, S., Kumar, B. S., Pradeep, N., & Boopathi, S. (2023). Sustainable Developments in Nano-Fluid Synthesis for Various Industrial Applications. In A. S. Etim (Ed.), Advances in Human and Social Aspects of Technology. IGI Global. doi:10.4018/978-1-6684-5347-6.ch003

Zekrifa, D. M. S., Kulkarni, M., Bhagyalakshmi, A., Devireddy, N., Gupta, S., & Boopathi, S. (2023). Integrating Machine Learning and AI for Improved Hydrological Modeling and Water Resource Management. In *Artificial Intelligence Applications in Water Treatment and Water Resource Management* (pp. 46–70). IGI Global. doi:10.4018/978-1-6684-6791-6.ch003

Chapter 7

Quantum Computing–Powered Agricultural Transformation:
Optimizing Performance in Farming

Premendra J. Bansod
Department of Mechanical Engineering, G.H. Raisoni College of Engineering and Management, India

R. Usharani
Department of Computational Intelligence, Faculty of Engineering and Technology, School of Computing, School of Computing, SRM Institute of Science and Technology, India

A. Sheryl Oliver
Department of Computational Intelligence, Faculty of Engineering and Technology, School of Computing, SRM Institute of Science and Technology, India

S. J. Suji Prasad
Department of Electronics and Instrumentation Engineering, Kongu Engineering College, Erode, India

Durgesh M. Sharma
ⓘ https://orcid.org/0000-0002-9378-3061
Shri Ramdeobaba College of Engineering and Management, India

Sureshkumar Myilsamy
Department of Mechanical Engineering, Bannari Amman Institute of Technology, India

ABSTRACT

This chapter explores the potential of quantum computing in agriculture, highlighting its potential to enhance efficiency, sustainability, and environmental stewardship. Quantum computing can process vast datasets, simulate complex systems, and optimize resource allocation. Applications include crop optimization, weather modeling, and precision agriculture. Case studies show quantum-assisted solutions for crop yield prediction, pest and disease management, and soil analysis, demonstrating the benefits of quantum computing in real-world agricultural scenarios. The integration of quantum computing in agriculture faces challenges such as technology accessibility, data management, energy consumption, and privacy concerns. However, the fusion of quantum technology and agriculture holds potential for global food security, environmental sustainability, and resource-efficient farming.

DOI: 10.4018/979-8-3693-0968-1.ch007

INTRODUCTION

The growing global population and increasing demands on agriculture for food, fiber, and fuel have led to a technological revolution that could transform farming practices. The integration of quantum computing and agriculture presents a promising solution to these challenges. This chapter explores the application of quantum computing in agriculture, highlighting its potential to revolutionize farming practices for performance optimization. The combination of quantum computing and agriculture could lead to a new era of agricultural innovation. Quantum computing, based on quantum mechanics, offers significant computational power over classical computers. It uses the properties of quantum bits, which can exist in multiple states and be entangled, to create quantum algorithms that outperform classical ones in specific problem domains. This technology has the potential to tackle complex agricultural challenges, including crop yield optimization, weather prediction, precision agriculture, and resource-efficient farming practices (Wei & Zhang, 2019).

Quantum computing can help modern agriculture tackle challenges such as increased productivity, resource conservation, and climate mitigation. By using quantum algorithms, stakeholders can make informed decisions faster and more accurately, leading to more sustainable and profitable farming operations. This chapter will explore the fundamental concepts of quantum computing, its application in agriculture, and real-world case studies to demonstrate its transformative potential (Chan et al., 2023). This text explains the significance and capabilities of quantum computing in agriculture, focusing on its practical applications in crop management, pest control, and soil analysis. It discusses the challenges faced by modern agriculture and how quantum computing can provide solutions. The text also explores the ethical, environmental, and technical aspects of integrating quantum computing into agriculture, highlighting the potential for profound changes. The future prospects of quantum computing in agriculture are also discussed, speculating on the transformational journey ahead (Albataineh & Nijim, 2021).

The integration of quantum technology and agriculture is transforming the world's food systems and promoting a sustainable future. As the global population continues to grow, the agricultural sector faces increasing pressure to provide for the growing population. This era of interconnectedness and data-driven decision-making is leading to a rapid transformation in the agricultural landscape (Gill, 2021). The fusion of agriculture with quantum computing has the potential to revolutionize the way we cultivate, harvest, and sustain our world, making it a pivotal moment in our civilization's history. Quantum computing, a field that combines physics and computer science, uses quantum mechanics principles to perform calculations and process information. It uses quantum bits to explore multiple states simultaneously through superposition, enabling the development of quantum algorithms that transcend classical computational limitations. This intersection of quantum computing and agriculture presents an opportunity to address pressing challenges such as crop production optimization, resource utilization, climate change mitigation, and sustainability enhancement (Aithal, 2023).

This chapter embarks on a journey through the innovative realm of agriculture with quantum computing, where classical paradigms are redefined, and possibilities seem boundless. The pages ahead will introduce you to the fundamental principles of quantum computing, ensuring that both newcomers and seasoned professionals can grasp the profound implications of this transformative technology (Ganapathy, 2021). The real-world issues confronting modern agriculture, from the necessity of feeding a burgeoning global population to the imperative of reducing the industry's environmental footprint are illustrated. Quantum computing offers a powerful toolset to address these issues, revolutionizing crop management, forecasting, and resource allocation. It also explores the use of quantum computing in agriculture, focusing on practical case studies and ethical considerations. It discusses its potential to optimize crop yields, predict weather patterns, manage pests and diseases, and improve soil health (Singh & Khan, 2023). The text highlights the potential for a productive, sustainable, and resilient future, promising a bountiful and ecologically harmonious world where quantum computing plays a pivotal role in securing the future of agriculture.

Objectives

- To provide an in-depth introduction to quantum computing's principles and its application in agriculture, addressing key challenges such as increased food production, resource conservation, and climate adaptation in the modern agricultural sector.
- To explore the potential applications of quantum computing in agriculture, including crop yield optimization, weather modeling, precision agriculture, and data analysis, showcasing real-world case studies and successful implementations of these technologies in farming practices.
- To explain the potential of integrating quantum computing into agriculture, highlighting its benefits such as increased efficiency, sustainability, and productivity, while also addressing ethical, technical, and environmental challenges and highlighting its potential for sustainable farming practices.
- To explain the future of agriculture using quantum computing, focusing on emerging trends, potential breakthroughs, startups' role, and ethical considerations like data privacy, security, and responsible technology adoption in the industry.

- To provide a comprehensive overview of the potential and challenges of quantum computing in agriculture, aiming to engage researchers, farmers, policymakers, and technology enthusiasts, and promote collaboration between the sectors for positive industry change.

MODERN AGRICULTURE CHALLENGES

Modern agriculture faces complex challenges such as food security for a growing global population, climate change effects, and environmental degradation, necessitating innovative solutions for productivity and sustainability (Figure 1).

Figure 1. Modern agriculture facing complex challenges

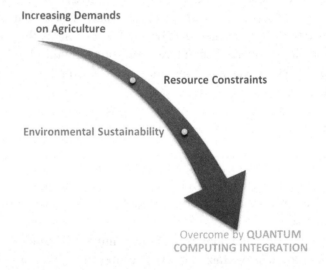

Increasing Demands on Agriculture: As the world's population continues to grow, the demand for food, fiber, and other agricultural products rises. To meet these increasing demands, agriculture must find ways to boost production while maintaining or even improving product quality. Technology plays a pivotal role in increasing agricultural productivity (Agrawal et al., 2023a; Sankar et al., 2023a). Precision agriculture technologies, such as GPS-guided tractors and drones, help optimize planting and harvesting. Biotechnology, like genetically modified crops, can enhance crop yields and resistance to pests and diseases. Advanced data analytics and artificial intelligence enable data-driven decision-making in farming practices (Koshariya, Kalaiyarasi, et al., 2023a; Koshariya, Khatoon, et al., 2023; P. Kumar et al., 2023).

Resource Constraints: Agriculture depends on finite resources such as arable land, water, and energy. The efficient use of these resources is critical to prevent depletion and environmental degradation. Technology can help maximize resource efficiency. For example, smart irrigation systems use sensors and data analysis to deliver the right amount of water to crops, reducing waste. Sustainable energy sources, like solar and wind power, can be integrated into farming operations, reducing reliance on fossil fuels (Agrawal et al., 2024; Gnanaprakasam et al., 2023; Sankar et al., 2023b).

Environmental Sustainability: The environmental impact of agriculture, including deforestation, greenhouse gas emissions, soil degradation, and chemical runoff, is a growing concern. Sustainable and environmentally friendly practices are essential. Technology offers solutions for more sustainable agriculture. Precision agriculture minimizes the use of chemicals and fertilizers by applying them only where needed, reducing environmental pollution. Innovations like vertical farming and hydroponics can produce food with less land and water, and thus reduce the environmental footprint (Boopathi, Alqahtani, et al., 2023a; Gowri et al., 2023a). Technology is a driving force behind agricultural innovation. It provides tools for monitoring, automation, data analysis, and decision support, all of which can enhance productivity and sustainability (Agrawal et al., 2023b; P. R. Kumar et al., 2023a). Emerging technologies like blockchain can improve supply chain transparency and traceability, helping consumers make more informed choices about the food they buy. Additionally, biotechnology, including genetic engineering and CRISPR, can create crops with improved traits, like drought resistance, which are essential in adapting to changing climate conditions.

Technology is crucial in modern agriculture for increasing productivity, optimizing resource use, promoting environmental sustainability, and meeting increasing demands for agricultural products. Its full potential is essential for a resilient and sustainable agricultural sector.

QUANTUM COMPUTING PRIMER

Quantum computing is a rapidly evolving field that uses quantum mechanics principles to perform computational tasks differently from classical computing. This primer provides an overview of important concepts and principles (de Lima Marquezino et al., 2019).

Quantum Bits (Qubits): The fundamental unit of information in quantum computing is the qubit, analogous to the classical bit. However, unlike classical bits that can only exist in one of two states (0 or 1), qubits can exist in multiple states simultaneously, a phenomenon called superposition. This property allows quantum computers to process a vast amount of information in parallel.

Superposition: Superposition is a unique property of qubits. It enables them to exist in a linear combination of both 0 and 1 states at the same time. This property is leveraged in quantum algorithms to explore multiple solutions to a problem simultaneously.

Entanglement: Entanglement is another crucial property of qubits. When qubits become entangled, the state of one qubit is dependent on the state of another, even when separated by large distances. This property allows for highly correlated and coordinated quantum operations.

Quantum Gates: Quantum gates are analogous to classical logic gates but operate on qubits in superposition. These gates can manipulate qubits to perform operations like changing their states, entangling them, or performing mathematical transformations.

Quantum Circuits: Quantum circuits are composed of a series of quantum gates that manipulate qubits to perform specific tasks or calculations. Quantum algorithms are designed using these circuits to solve problems more efficiently than classical algorithms.

Quantum Parallelism: Quantum computers take advantage of superposition to explore multiple solutions simultaneously, making them highly effective for specific types of problems. This capability is referred to as quantum parallelism and is a key advantage of quantum computing.

Quantum Interference: Quantum interference occurs when the possible outcomes of quantum operations are combined to amplify the correct solution and cancel out incorrect ones. This property is essential for quantum algorithms to produce meaningful results.

Quantum Algorithms: Quantum algorithms are specialized algorithms designed to harness the unique properties of quantum computers to solve certain problems more efficiently. Notable examples include Shor's algorithm for factorization and Grover's algorithm for database search.

No-Cloning Theorem: One of the fundamental principles in quantum computing is the no-cloning theorem, which states that an arbitrary quantum state cannot be copied exactly. This property has implications for quantum cryptography and the security of quantum communication.

Quantum Supremacy: Quantum supremacy refers to the point at which a quantum computer can perform a specific task faster than the best classical supercomputers. Achieving quantum supremacy is a milestone in the development of quantum computing.

Quantum computing, a groundbreaking advancement in computation, has potential applications in cryptography, optimization, and simulation. Despite its early stages, it is being researched for practical, scalable quantum computers, capable of solving complex problems.

QUANTUM COMPUTING IN AGRICULTURE

Quantum computing, a quantum mechanics-based technology, has the potential to revolutionize the agriculture sector (Figure 2) by addressing challenges and improving agricultural practices, as it can be applied in various ways (Ali et al., 2022).

Figure 2. Improving agricultural practices through quantum computing

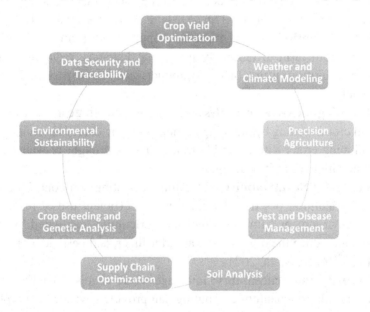

Crop Yield Optimization: Quantum computing can process vast amounts of data to optimize crop yield. By analyzing factors such as weather conditions, soil quality, and plant genetics, quantum algorithms can provide valuable insights into planting strategies, irrigation, and nutrient management. This optimization leads to increased agricultural productivity.

Weather and Climate Modeling: Quantum computing's immense computational power can significantly enhance weather and climate modeling. More accurate predictions of weather patterns and climate changes are crucial for farmers to make informed decisions about planting, harvesting, and adapting to changing conditions.

Precision Agriculture: Precision agriculture relies on data-driven decision-making. Quantum computing can process and analyze data from various sources, such as drones, sensors, and satellites, to create precise agricultural strategies. This results in efficient resource utilization and reduced environmental impact.

Pest and Disease Management: Quantum algorithms can assist in pest and disease management by analyzing vast datasets related to pest behavior, disease patterns, and crop genetics. This enables farmers to implement targeted and timely interventions, reducing the need for chemical treatments.

Soil Analysis: Quantum computing can enhance soil analysis by quickly processing and interpreting soil data. This helps in determining soil composition, nutrient levels, and pH, allowing farmers to make better-informed decisions regarding soil health and treatment (Boopathi, Kumar, et al., 2023a; P. R. Kumar et al., 2023b).

Supply Chain Optimization: Quantum computing can optimize the agricultural supply chain, from farm to table. By improving logistics, reducing waste, and enhancing traceability, it ensures that food products reach consumers more efficiently and sustainably.

Crop Breeding and Genetic Analysis: Quantum computing can accelerate genetic analysis and crop breeding by handling complex genetic data. This technology can aid in developing crops with desirable traits, such as drought resistance, disease resistance, and higher nutritional content.

Environmental Sustainability: Quantum computing can contribute to more sustainable agricultural practices by enabling the efficient use of resources and minimizing environmental impact. Precision agriculture, facilitated by quantum computing, can reduce the overuse of water, fertilizer, and pesticides (Dass james & Boopathi, 2016; Sampath, 2021).

Data Security and Traceability: In an age where data is crucial for decision-making in agriculture, quantum computing can provide advanced encryption and data security solutions. This is particularly important for ensuring the privacy and integrity of sensitive agricultural data.

Challenges and Limitations: Despite its potential, quantum computing in agriculture also faces challenges such as cost, accessibility, and the need for specialized expertise. These limitations need to be addressed as the technology develops.

Quantum computing has the potential to revolutionize agriculture by offering innovative solutions, enhancing productivity, sustainability, and environmental stewardship, contributing to a more resilient global food system.

QUANTUM ALGORITHMS

Quantum algorithms utilize quantum computers' unique properties like superposition and entanglement to efficiently solve specific problems, with the design process varying depending on the problem, and the steps can vary depending on the specific problem (de Lima Marquezino et al., 2019; Khan & Robles-Kelly, 2020).

Problem Formulation: Clearly define the problem you want to solve using a quantum algorithm. Determine the input and desired output. Understand the classical approaches to solving this problem.

Quantum Oracle Design: Create a quantum oracle, which is a quantum subroutine that encodes the classical problem into a quantum state. The oracle is responsible for evaluating the problem's function in a quantum context.

Quantum Circuit Design: Develop a quantum circuit that employs quantum gates to manipulate the qubits. Design the circuit to include the quantum oracle and other gates necessary to solve the problem.

Quantum Algorithm Implementation: Implement the quantum algorithm on a quantum computer or quantum simulator. Ensure that the quantum gates and oracle are correctly configured.

Initialization and Superposition: Prepare the qubits in an initial state. Exploit superposition to represent multiple potential solutions simultaneously.

Quantum Oracle Query: Apply the quantum oracle to the qubits. This step involves querying the problem's function and encoding the result in the qubits.

Quantum Parallelism: Leverage the quantum algorithm's ability to explore multiple states simultaneously to gather information about potential solutions.

Quantum Interference: Design the algorithm in such a way that quantum interference amplifies the correct solutions while diminishing incorrect ones. This is a critical step in quantum algorithms to enhance the probability of measuring the correct result.

Measurement and Output: Perform a measurement on the qubits. The outcome represents the solution to the problem. The quantum algorithm may need to be run multiple times to obtain a reliable result.

Analysis and Optimization: Analyze the results and assess the algorithm's performance. Identify any bottlenecks or areas for improvement. Iteratively optimize the algorithm to enhance its efficiency.

Testing and Verification: Validate the quantum algorithm on various inputs and under different conditions to ensure its correctness and robustness.

Scaling and Realization: If the algorithm proves effective, explore possibilities for scaling it up to larger problem sizes and consider the practical realization of the algorithm on available quantum hardware.

Figure 3. Quantum computing in crop management

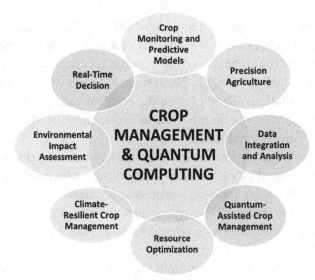

Quantum algorithms require expertise in quantum computing, programming languages like Qiskit or Cirq, and access to quantum hardware or simulators. They may not solve all problems efficiently, so problem suitability assessment is crucial.

CROP MANAGEMENT AND QUANTUM COMPUTING

Quantum computing is revolutionizing crop management by improving crop monitoring (Figure 3), predictive models, precision agriculture, and overall strategies, thereby enhancing the vital role of quantum computing in modern agriculture (Bhatia & Sood, 2020; Gill et al., 2022).

Crop Monitoring and Predictive Models: Quantum computing can process vast amounts of data from various sources, including remote sensing, weather stations, and soil sensors. This data can be used to create predictive models for crop health, disease outbreaks, and yield forecasts. Quantum algorithms can identify intricate patterns and correlations in large datasets, enabling more accurate predictions.

Precision Agriculture: Quantum computing enables precise decision-making in agriculture. It can process real-time data on weather conditions, soil moisture, and crop health, allowing for targeted interventions, such as optimizing irrigation, adjusting nutrient application, and managing pests with pinpoint accuracy. This reduces resource wastage and improves crop health (Agrawal et al., 2023a, 2023a).

Quantum-Assisted Crop Management: Quantum-assisted crop management combines quantum algorithms with classical machine learning to develop more efficient strategies for crop health. This approach enhances the capacity to handle big data, assess the environmental impact of farming practices, and optimize crop management operations.

Data Integration and Analysis: Quantum computing facilitates the integration of diverse data sources. It can simultaneously analyze vast datasets, taking into account multiple variables affecting crop growth, including climate, soil conditions, pest infestations, and historical data. This holistic approach enhances the accuracy of crop monitoring and predictive models (Dhanya et al., 2023; Srinivas et al., 2023).

Quantum-Based Crop Disease Identification: Quantum algorithms can process images and sensor data to identify signs of crop diseases and pest infestations. By leveraging quantum machine learning, it's possible to quickly detect these issues and respond proactively, minimizing crop damage and yield loss.

Resource Optimization: Quantum computing can determine optimal resource allocation for each section of a field based on soil conditions, topography, and weather forecasts. This resource optimization ensures that water, fertilizers, and other resources are used efficiently, reducing waste and environmental impact.

Climate-Resilient Crop Management: Quantum computing can model and predict the effects of climate change on crop growth and adapt crop management strategies accordingly. This is crucial for ensuring food security in the face of shifting weather patterns.

Environmental Impact Assessment: Quantum computing can help assess the environmental impact of various agricultural practices, providing data-driven insights into the sustainability of different methods. This supports the adoption of eco-friendly farming practices.

Real-Time Decision Support: Quantum-assisted crop management provides real-time decision support to farmers. It offers recommendations based on current conditions, allowing for rapid responses to changing circumstances.

Quantum-assisted crop management is still an emerging field with challenges related to quantum hardware accessibility and algorithm development. However, it holds enormous potential for transforming agriculture and addressing the increasing demands on global food production.

Quantum computing's integration into crop management practices holds the potential for a more efficient, sustainable, and environmentally friendly agricultural industry. As technology advances, its application in agriculture will significantly meet the world's growing food needs while minimizing environmental impact.

RESOURCE ALLOCATION AND EFFICIENCY

Quantum computing can significantly optimize resource allocation in agriculture, enhancing productivity and minimizing waste and environmental impact (Figure 4). It can be applied to water and energy management, fertilizer and pesticide optimization, and other areas (B et al., 2024; Gunasekaran & Boopathi, 2023; Venkateswaran et al., 2023; Zekrifa et al., 2023).

Figure 4. Agricultural resources allocation using quantum computing

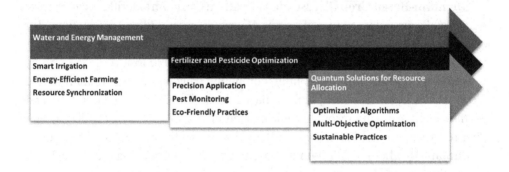

Water and Energy Management: Quantum computing can help optimize water and energy use in agriculture through:

- **Smart Irrigation:** Quantum algorithms can analyze real-time weather data, soil conditions, and crop needs to determine when and how much to irrigate, reducing water wastage.
- **Energy-Efficient Farming:** Quantum-assisted simulations can model energy consumption, aiding in the development of energy-efficient farming practices, including the use of renewable energy sources.
- **Resource Synchronization:** Quantum algorithms can optimize the timing of irrigation and energy use to align with the most critical growth stages of crops, conserving resources.

Fertilizer and Pesticide Optimization: Efficient management of fertilizers and pesticides is vital for crop health and environmental sustainability, and quantum computing can assist by:

- **Precision Application:** Quantum algorithms can analyze soil nutrient data and crop health indicators to precisely apply fertilizers, minimizing excess usage.
- **Pest Monitoring:** Quantum-based sensors can detect pest infestations, enabling targeted pesticide applications and reducing chemical use.
- **Eco-Friendly Practices:** Quantum-aided research can lead to the development of eco-friendly fertilizers and pesticides with reduced environmental impact.

Quantum Solutions for Resource Allocation: Quantum computing offers several solutions for resource allocation and efficiency in agriculture, including:

- **Optimization Algorithms:** Quantum algorithms can find optimal resource allocation strategies, considering various factors, including crop type, location, and environmental conditions.
- **Multi-Objective Optimization:** Quantum-assisted multi-objective optimization can balance conflicting goals, such as maximizing yield while minimizing resource usage and environmental impact.
- **Sustainable Practices:** Quantum-based research can guide the adoption of sustainable agricultural practices that optimize resource allocation while preserving the ecosystem.

Quantum computing can optimize resource allocation in agriculture, leading to higher productivity and sustainable farming practices. By optimizing water, energy, fertilizers, and pesticides, agriculture can reduce its environmental footprint, conserve resources, and contribute to food security while minimizing ecological effects. This integration represents a promising step towards a more sustainable and efficient food production system.

OPTIMIZE THE MODERN AGRICULTURAL SYSTEM USING QUANTUM COMPUTING

The study discusses strategies for optimizing the modern agricultural system using quantum computing, highlighting its potential to enhance various farming aspects (Boopathi, Kumar, et al., 2023b; Gnanaprakasam et al., 2023; Jeevanantham et al., 2022; P. R. Kumar et al., 2023a).

- Quantum algorithms utilize various data sources like soil quality, weather patterns, and crop genetics to optimize planting strategies, irrigation schedules, and nutrient management, thereby increasing crop yields and enhancing agricultural efficiency.

- Quantum simulations enhance weather and climate models, enabling farmers to make informed decisions about planting, harvesting, and adapting to changing conditions, thus improving agricultural efficiency.
- Quantum computing utilizes data from various sources like drones, sensors, and satellites to develop precise agricultural strategies, resulting in efficient resource utilization, reduced environmental impact, and a more sustainable agricultural system.
- Quantum algorithms analyze vast datasets for pest behavior, disease patterns, and crop genetics, enabling farmers to implement targeted interventions, reduce chemical treatments, and ensure healthier crops.
- Quantum computing improves soil analysis by processing and interpreting data, aiding in determining soil composition, nutrient levels, and pH, enabling farmers to make informed decisions about soil health and treatment.
- Quantum computing enhances agricultural supply chain efficiency by improving logistics, reducing waste, and improving traceability, ensuring food products reach consumers sustainably.
- Quantum computing can expedite genetic analysis and crop breeding by handling complex genetic data, enabling the development of desirable traits like drought and disease resistance, thereby optimizing the agricultural system.
- Quantum computing can enhance sustainable agricultural practices by optimizing resource use and minimizing environmental impact, promoting precision agriculture that minimizes overuse of water, fertilizer, and pesticides, thus promoting an eco-friendlier system.
- Quantum computing offers advanced encryption and data security solutions for agriculture, ensuring privacy and integrity of sensitive data in a crucial decision-making age.

Quantum computing has the potential to revolutionize agriculture by offering innovative solutions, enhancing productivity, sustainability, and environmental stewardship (Domakonda et al., 2022; Haribalaji et al., 2021; Ingle et al., 2023; Paul et al., 2024; Sampath et al., 2023). However, challenges such as cost, accessibility, and specialized expertise need to be addressed as the technology evolves. This will contribute to a more resilient and efficient global food system.

ENVIRONMENTAL SUSTAINABILITY AND CLIMATE CHANGE MITIGATION

Modern agriculture is increasingly recognizing its environmental impact and its role in mitigating climate change (Figure 5). Quantum computing can help achieve

Figure 5. Quantum computing in environmental sustainability and climate change mitigation

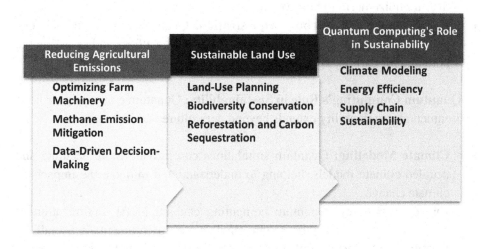

sustainability by reducing agricultural emissions, promoting sustainable land use, and supporting broader sustainability efforts, thereby enhancing the sector's sustainability (Boopathi, 2022a, 2022b; Boopathi, Alqahtani, et al., 2023b; Gowri et al., 2023b).

Reducing Agricultural Emissions: Quantum computing can contribute to emissions reduction in agriculture by:

- **Optimizing Farm Machinery:** Quantum algorithms can improve the efficiency of farming equipment and vehicles, reducing fuel consumption and emissions.
- **Methane Emission Mitigation:** Quantum simulations can model and assess strategies for minimizing methane emissions from livestock, which is a potent greenhouse gas.
- **Data-Driven Decision-Making:** Quantum computing's ability to analyze vast datasets can inform decisions that lead to more sustainable agricultural practices, thereby reducing emissions.

Sustainable Land Use: Quantum computing can help address the challenge of sustainable land use by:

- **Land-Use Planning:** Quantum algorithms can assist in optimal land-use planning by considering factors such as soil quality, ecosystem health, and water resources. This minimizes habitat destruction and soil degradation.

- **Biodiversity Conservation:** Quantum simulations can model the impact of agricultural practices on local ecosystems, facilitating the design of strategies that minimize harm to biodiversity.
- **Reforestation and Carbon Sequestration:** Quantum-assisted models can aid in identifying suitable locations for reforestation efforts and assessing the potential for carbon sequestration in agricultural and forestry systems.

Quantum Computing's Role in Sustainability: Quantum computing's role in environmental sustainability extends beyond agriculture and includes:

- **Climate Modeling:** Quantum simulations can provide more accurate and detailed climate models, helping to understand and mitigate the impacts of climate change.
- **Energy Efficiency:** Quantum computing can aid in the optimization of energy systems, making them more efficient and environmentally friendly.
- **Supply Chain Sustainability:** Quantum-assisted data analytics can enhance transparency and traceability in supply chains, supporting sustainable sourcing and distribution of agricultural products.

Quantum computing's capacity to handle large amounts of data and simulate complex systems can significantly contribute to environmental sustainability and climate change mitigation. It can optimize resource usage, reduce emissions, and guide sustainable practices in agriculture, facilitating a more environmentally conscious food system.

QUANTUM COMPUTING SOLUTIONS IN AGRICULTURE

Quantum computing offers innovative solutions to tackle agricultural challenges, with specific applications in the agricultural sector (Boopathi, 2022c; Gowri et al., 2023b; P. R. Kumar et al., 2023a; Venkateswaran et al., 2023).

Quantum Algorithms for Crop Optimization: Quantum algorithms can revolutionize crop optimization by:

- **Yield Maximization:** Quantum algorithms can analyze vast datasets related to soil quality, weather patterns, and crop genetics to determine optimal planting strategies, irrigation schedules, and nutrient management, leading to increased crop yield.

- **Resource Efficiency:** Quantum computing can help optimize resource allocation, ensuring that water, fertilizers, and pesticides are used more efficiently, thereby reducing waste and environmental impact.
- **Disease and Pest Management:** Quantum algorithms can analyze real-time data to predict and manage the spread of crop diseases and pests more effectively, minimizing crop damage.

Quantum Simulations for Weather and Climate Modeling: Quantum simulations are instrumental in improving weather and climate modeling by:

- **Higher Resolution Models:** Quantum simulations can process complex climate models at higher resolutions, resulting in more accurate and detailed weather forecasts.
- **Rapid Scenario Testing:** Quantum computing can perform rapid scenario testing to assess the impact of climate change on agriculture, enabling more informed adaptation strategies.
- **Disaster Preparedness:** Quantum simulations can predict extreme weather events and provide early warnings, allowing farmers to take preventive measures to safeguard their crops.

Quantum Machine Learning for Precision Agriculture: Quantum machine learning enhances precision agriculture by:

- **Data Analysis:** Quantum machine learning can process and analyze vast datasets from sensors, drones, and satellites to make data-driven decisions for precise resource allocation.
- **Predictive Models:** Quantum machine learning models can predict crop health, pest outbreaks, and yield with higher accuracy, enabling early interventions and more efficient farm management.
- **Optimizing Crop Management:** Quantum machine learning can optimize planting schedules, irrigation, and nutrient application, reducing resource waste and environmental impact.

Quantum computing solutions in agriculture can improve crop management, resource usage, environmental sustainability, and productivity. As technology advances, they can meet global food production demands while minimizing environmental impact, thereby enhancing global food production.

CASE STUDIES

Three case studies highlight the practical applications and benefits of incorporating quantum computing in agriculture (Boopathi, Kumar, et al., 2023b; Dalal et al., 2021; Jeevanantham et al., 2022; Kirubakaran & Midhunchakkaravarthy, 2023; P. R. Kumar et al., 2023a).

Quantum-Assisted Crop Yield Prediction

- **Problem:** A farm faces the challenge of accurately predicting crop yields to optimize resource allocation and plan harvest and distribution. Traditional methods have limitations in handling the complexity of factors affecting yield.
- **Solution:** Quantum computing is employed to process extensive datasets encompassing weather patterns, soil conditions, historical yield data, and other variables. Quantum algorithms analyze this data to generate highly accurate crop yield predictions.
- **Results:** The farm experiences a significant improvement in yield predictions, resulting in optimized resource use, reduced waste, and more efficient distribution. Quantum-assisted predictions allow the farm to adapt quickly to changing conditions and enhance overall crop management.

Quantum-Based Pest and Disease Management

- **Problem:** A farming operation faces ongoing challenges in managing pests and diseases that affect crop health. Traditional methods often involve the indiscriminate use of chemicals, which can harm the environment and lead to resistance issues.
- **Solution:** Quantum computing is utilized to create a sophisticated quantum machine learning model. This model processes real-time data from various sensors and image analysis, identifying early signs of pests or diseases. Quantum algorithms enable precise, targeted interventions.
- **Results:** The farm achieves more efficient and eco-friendlier pest and disease management. Chemical usage is significantly reduced, saving costs and minimizing environmental impact. The early detection and response facilitated by quantum-based solutions lead to healthier crops and higher yields.

Quantum-Simulated Soil Analysis

- **Problem:** A large agricultural estate is seeking to optimize soil management practices to improve crop health and yield. Traditional soil analysis methods are time-consuming and may not provide comprehensive insights.
- **Solution:** Quantum simulations are used to model and analyze soil conditions with a high level of detail. These simulations consider factors like nutrient content, pH levels, and moisture distribution. Quantum computing enables rapid and precise soil analysis.
- **Results:** The estate gains a thorough understanding of soil characteristics, leading to more effective nutrient management and irrigation strategies. The quantum-simulated soil analysis provides actionable insights for improving soil health and crop productivity. It allows for targeted soil treatments, reducing the need for excessive fertilizer use and enhancing sustainability.

Case studies demonstrate the practical applications of quantum computing in agriculture, addressing challenges in crop yield prediction, pest and disease management, and soil analysis, contributing to more efficient and sustainable agricultural practices.

BENEFITS AND CHALLENGES

The integration of quantum computing into agriculture presents both potential benefits and significant challenges, requiring careful consideration of key aspects (Bhatia & Sood, 2020; Dalal et al., 2021; Gill et al., 2022).

Improved Agricultural Efficiency and Productivity

Benefits

- **Enhanced Yield:** Quantum computing enables more accurate crop yield predictions and optimized resource allocation, leading to increased agricultural productivity.
- **Resource Efficiency:** Improved resource management through quantum computing results in reduced waste of water, energy, fertilizers, and pesticides, contributing to greater resource efficiency.
- **Precision Agriculture:** Quantum-assisted precision agriculture allows for more targeted interventions, reducing the environmental impact of farming practices.

Challenges

- **Technological Maturity:** Quantum computing technology is still evolving and may not be readily accessible to all agricultural stakeholders, limiting its widespread adoption.
- **Data Requirements:** Quantum algorithms rely on vast datasets, and collecting and managing such data can be challenging for some farmers, particularly smaller operations.

Environmental and Sustainability Implications

Benefits

- **Sustainable Practices:** Quantum computing can guide the adoption of more sustainable agricultural practices, reducing the environmental impact of farming.
- **Emissions Reduction:** Quantum algorithms and simulations can assist in reducing greenhouse gas emissions from agriculture by optimizing equipment and resource use.
- **Resource Conservation:** Precise resource allocation, supported by quantum computing, helps conserve resources like water and arable land.

Challenges

- **Energy Consumption:** Quantum computers themselves have energy consumption considerations, and ensuring they run on sustainable energy sources is a challenge.
- **Data Privacy:** The vast amount of data involved in quantum-assisted agriculture raises concerns about data privacy and security.

Adoption Challenges and Technical Limitations

Benefits

- **Potential for Innovation:** The adoption of quantum computing in agriculture has the potential to drive innovation and collaboration between the agricultural and tech sectors.
- **Improved Decision-Making:** Quantum-assisted decision support systems can lead to more informed and timely decision-making for farmers.

Challenges

- **Accessibility:** Quantum computing is not yet universally accessible, and adoption can be constrained by cost and the need for specialized expertise.
- **Quantum Hardware:** Technical limitations, such as quantum hardware errors and decoherence, can impact the reliability and scalability of quantum algorithms.
- **Data Integration:** Aggregating and integrating diverse data sources for quantum analysis can be complex, requiring robust data management infrastructure.

The successful integration of quantum computing in agriculture requires balancing its benefits and challenges, as it has the potential to significantly transform the sector, making it more efficient, sustainable, and environmentally conscious as it becomes more accessible.

FUTURE PROSPECTS

The future of quantum computing in agriculture presents both opportunities and challenges, with key areas to monitor (Ali et al., 2022; Bhatia & Sood, 2020; Dalal et al., 2021; Gill et al., 2022).

Quantum Computing in Startups: As quantum computing technology matures, startups specializing in quantum-assisted solutions for agriculture are expected to surge, driving innovation and bringing quantum solutions to a wider range of stakeholders.

Collaboration with Traditional Agriculture: Collaboration between traditional agriculture and quantum technology experts will be crucial. This collaboration will involve the integration of quantum solutions into existing farming practices, ensuring that the benefits of quantum computing are accessible to all farmers, regardless of the scale of their operations (Koshariya, Kalaiyarasi, et al., 2023b; Sankar et al., 2023a).

Policy and Ethical Considerations: As quantum computing becomes more prominent in agriculture, policymakers and regulators will need to establish guidelines and standards for its use. Issues related to data privacy, security, and the ethical implications of quantum-assisted agriculture will require careful consideration.

Global Food Security: Quantum computing's contribution to improving crop yield predictions and resource management will be instrumental in addressing global food security challenges. More accurate predictions and sustainable practices can help meet the increasing demand for food production.

Environmental Stewardship: Quantum-assisted agriculture can play a significant role in mitigating the environmental impact of farming practices. Sustainable resource management and precision agriculture enabled by quantum computing can contribute to reducing greenhouse gas emissions, conserving water, and promoting biodiversity.

Quantum Computing Accessibility: The accessibility of quantum computing technology will be a critical factor in its adoption. Advancements in quantum hardware and the development of user-friendly interfaces will determine how quickly and widely quantum solutions can be integrated into agriculture.

Ongoing Research and Development: Ongoing research and development in quantum computing and quantum algorithms will continue to expand the potential applications of this technology in agriculture. Innovations and breakthroughs are likely to emerge, further advancing the field.

The future of quantum computing in agriculture holds significant potential for transformative change, offering solutions to long-standing challenges. Collaboration, policy development, and responsible technology integration are crucial for its benefits to the agricultural industry and the global community.

CONCLUSION

Quantum computing's potential to process large datasets, simulate complex systems, and optimize resource allocation in agriculture presents a promising avenue for improving efficiency, sustainability, and environmental stewardship, thereby overcoming industry challenges. Quantum computing has the potential to revolutionize agriculture by improving crop optimization, providing accurate weather forecasts, and transforming precision agriculture practices. It can also aid in disaster preparedness and climate adaptation. However, the adoption of quantum computing faces challenges such as technology accessibility, data management, energy consumption, and data privacy. Addressing these issues is crucial for the widespread and effective integration of quantum solutions into farming practices. Case studies demonstrate the tangible benefits of quantum computing in real-world agricultural scenarios, but further research is needed to fully realize its potential.

Quantum computing is poised to revolutionize agriculture, with AgTech startups leading innovation. Collaboration between traditional agriculture and quantum technology experts is crucial for making quantum solutions accessible. Policymakers and regulators will establish guidelines for responsible use, addressing ethical and privacy concerns. The fusion of quantum computing and agriculture could significantly contribute to global food security, environmental sustainability, and resource efficiency. As technology advances, its impact on agriculture will be transformative, offering a more resilient and sustainable food production system.

TERMINOLOGY

pH- potential of hydrogen

REFERENCES

Agrawal, A. V., Magulur, L. P., Priya, S. G., Kaur, A., Singh, G., & Boopathi, S. (2023a). Smart Precision Agriculture Using IoT and WSN. In *Handbook of Research on Data Science and Cybersecurity Innovations in Industry 4.0 Technologies* (pp. 524–541). IGI Global. doi:10.4018/978-1-6684-8145-5.ch026

Agrawal, A. V., Magulur, L. P., Priya, S. G., Kaur, A., Singh, G., & Boopathi, S. (2023b). Smart Precision Agriculture Using IoT and WSN. In *Handbook of Research on Data Science and Cybersecurity Innovations in Industry 4.0 Technologies* (pp. 524–541). IGI Global. doi:10.4018/978-1-6684-8145-5.ch026

Agrawal, A. V., Shashibhushan, G., Pradeep, S., Padhi, S. N., Sugumar, D., & Boopathi, S. (2024). Synergizing Artificial Intelligence, 5G, and Cloud Computing for Efficient Energy Conversion Using Agricultural Waste. In Practice, Progress, and Proficiency in Sustainability (pp. 475–497). IGI Global. doi:10.4018/979-8-3693-1186-8.ch026

Aithal, P. (2023). Advances and New Research Opportunities in Quantum Computing Technology by Integrating it with Other ICCT Underlying Technologies. *International Journal of Case Studies in Business IT and Education, 7*(3), 314–358.

Albataineh, H., & Nijim, M. (2021). Enhancing the cybersecurity education curricula through quantum computation. *Advances in Security, Networks, and Internet of Things: Proceedings from SAM'20, ICWN'20, ICOMP'20, and ESCS'20,* 223–231.

Ali, S., Yue, T., & Abreu, R. (2022). When software engineering meets quantum computing. *Communications of the ACM, 65*(4), 84–88. doi:10.1145/3512340

B, M. K., K, K. K., Sasikala, P., Sampath, B., Gopi, B., & Sundaram, S. (2024). Sustainable Green Energy Generation From Waste Water. In *Practice, Progress, and Proficiency in Sustainability* (pp. 440–463). IGI Global. doi:10.4018/979-8-3693-1186-8.ch024

Bhatia, M., & Sood, S. K. (2020). Quantum computing-inspired network optimization for IoT applications. *IEEE Internet of Things Journal, 7*(6), 5590–5598. doi:10.1109/JIOT.2020.2979887

Boopathi, S. (2022a). An investigation on gas emission concentration and relative emission rate of the near-dry wire-cut electrical discharge machining process. *Environmental Science and Pollution Research International, 29*(57), 86237–86246. doi:10.1007/s11356-021-17658-1 PMID:34837614

Boopathi, S. (2022b). Cryogenically treated and untreated stainless steel grade 317 in sustainable wire electrical discharge machining process: A comparative study. *Springer :Environmental Science and Pollution Research*, 1–10.

Boopathi, S. (2022c). Experimental investigation and multi-objective optimization of cryogenic Friction-stir-welding of AA2014 and AZ31B alloys using MOORA technique. *Materials Today. Communications, 33*, 104937. doi:10.1016/j. mtcomm.2022.104937

Boopathi, S., Alqahtani, A. S., Mubarakali, A., & Panchatcharam, P. (2023). Sustainable developments in near-dry electrical discharge machining process using sunflower oil-mist dielectric fluid. *Environmental Science and Pollution Research International*, 1–20. doi:10.1007/s11356-023-27494-0 PMID:37199846

Boopathi, S., Kumar, P. K. S., Meena, R. S., & Sudhakar, M. (2023). Sustainable Developments of Modern Soil-Less Agro-Cultivation Systems: Aquaponic Culture. In Human Agro-Energy Optimization for Business and Industry (pp. 69–87). IGI Global.

Chan, H. H. S., Meister, R., Jones, T., Tew, D. P., & Benjamin, S. C. (2023). Grid-based methods for chemistry simulations on a quantum computer. *Science Advances, 9*(9), eabo7484. doi:10.1126/sciadv.abo7484 PMID:36857445

Dalal, A., Bagherimehrab, M., & Sanders, B. C. (2021). Quantum-assisted support vector regression for detecting facial landmarks. *arXiv Preprint arXiv:2111.09304*.

Dass James, A., & Boopathi, S. (2016). Experimental Study of Eco-friendly Wire-Cut Electrical Discharge Machining Processes. *International Journal of Innovative Research in Science, Engineering and Technology, 5*.

de Lima Marquezino, F., Portugal, R., & Lavor, C. (2019). *A primer on quantum computing*. Springer. doi:10.1007/978-3-030-19066-8

Dhanya, D., Kumar, S. S., Thilagavathy, A., Prasad, D., & Boopathi, S. (2023). Data Analytics and Artificial Intelligence in the Circular Economy: Case Studies. In Intelligent Engineering Applications and Applied Sciences for Sustainability (pp. 40–58). IGI Global.

Domakonda, V. K., Farooq, S., Chinthamreddy, S., Puviarasi, R., Sudhakar, M., & Boopathi, S. (2022). Sustainable Developments of Hybrid Floating Solar Power Plants: Photovoltaic System. In Human Agro-Energy Optimization for Business and Industry (pp. 148–167). IGI Global.

Ganapathy, A. (2021). Quantum computing in high frequency trading and fraud detection. *Engineering International*, *9*(2), 61–72. doi:10.18034/ei.v9i2.549

Gill, S. S. (2021). A manifesto for modern fog and edge computing: Vision, new paradigms, opportunities, and future directions. In Operationalizing Multi-Cloud Environments: Technologies, Tools and Use Cases (pp. 237–253). Springer.

Gill, S. S., Kumar, A., Singh, H., Singh, M., Kaur, K., Usman, M., & Buyya, R. (2022). Quantum computing: A taxonomy, systematic review and future directions. *Software, Practice & Experience*, *52*(1), 66–114. doi:10.1002/spe.3039

Gnanaprakasam, C., Vankara, J., Sastry, A. S., Prajval, V., Gireesh, N., & Boopathi, S. (2023). Long-Range and Low-Power Automated Soil Irrigation System Using Internet of Things: An Experimental Study. In Contemporary Developments in Agricultural Cyber-Physical Systems (pp. 87–104). IGI Global.

Gowri, N. V., Dwivedi, J. N., Krishnaveni, K., Boopathi, S., Palaniappan, M., & Medikondu, N. R. (2023). Experimental investigation and multi-objective optimization of eco-friendly near-dry electrical discharge machining of shape memory alloy using Cu/SiC/Gr composite electrode. *Environmental Science and Pollution Research International*, *30*(49), 1–19. doi:10.1007/s11356-023-26983-6 PMID:37126160

Gunasekaran, K., & Boopathi, S. (2023). Artificial Intelligence in Water Treatments and Water Resource Assessments. In *Artificial Intelligence Applications in Water Treatment and Water Resource Management* (pp. 71–98). IGI Global. doi:10.4018/978-1-6684-6791-6.ch004

Haribalaji, V., Boopathi, S., & Asif, M. M. (2021). Optimization of friction stir welding process to join dissimilar AA2014 and AA7075 aluminum alloys. *Materials Today: Proceedings*, *50*, 2227–2234. doi:10.1016/j.matpr.2021.09.499

Ingle, R. B., Swathi, S., Mahendran, G., Senthil, T., Muralidharan, N., & Boopathi, S. (2023). Sustainability and Optimization of Green and Lean Manufacturing Processes Using Machine Learning Techniques. In *Circular Economy Implementation for Sustainability in the Built Environment* (pp. 261–285). IGI Global. doi:10.4018/978-1-6684-8238-4.ch012

Jeevanantham, Y. A., Saravanan, A., Vanitha, V., Boopathi, S., & Kumar, D. P. (2022). Implementation of Internet-of Things (IoT) in Soil Irrigation System. *IEEE Explore*, 1–5.

Khan, T. M., & Robles-Kelly, A. (2020). Machine learning: Quantum vs classical. *IEEE Access: Practical Innovations, Open Solutions, 8*, 219275–219294. doi:10.1109/ACCESS.2020.3041719

Kirubakaran, A. P., & Midhunchakkaravarthy, J. (2023). A Hybrid Application of Quantum Computing Methodologies to AI Techniques for Paddy Crop Leaf Disease Identification. In *Integrating Blockchain and Artificial Intelligence for Industry 4.0 Innovations* (pp. 69–83). Springer.

Koshariya, A. K., Kalaiyarasi, D., Jovith, A. A., Sivakami, T., Hasan, D. S., & Boopathi, S. (2023). AI-Enabled IoT and WSN-Integrated Smart Agriculture System. In *Artificial Intelligence Tools and Technologies for Smart Farming and Agriculture Practices* (pp. 200–218). IGI Global. doi:10.4018/978-1-6684-8516-3.ch011

Koshariya, A. K., Khatoon, S., Marathe, A. M., Suba, G. M., Baral, D., & Boopathi, S. (2023). Agricultural Waste Management Systems Using Artificial Intelligence Techniques. In *AI-Enabled Social Robotics in Human Care Services* (pp. 236–258). IGI Global. doi:10.4018/978-1-6684-8171-4.ch009

Kumar, P., Sampath, B., Kumar, S., Babu, B. H., & Ahalya, N. (2023). Hydroponics, Aeroponics, and Aquaponics Technologies in Modern Agricultural Cultivation. In IGI: Trends, Paradigms, and Advances in Mechatronics Engineering (pp. 223–241). IGI Global.

Kumar, P. R., Meenakshi, S., Shalini, S., Devi, S. R., & Boopathi, S. (2023). Soil Quality Prediction in Context Learning Approaches Using Deep Learning and Blockchain for Smart Agriculture. In R. Kumar, A. B. Abdul Hamid, & N. I. Binti Ya'akub (Eds.), Advances in Computational Intelligence and Robotics. IGI Global. doi:10.4018/978-1-6684-9151-5.ch001

Paul, A., Thilagham, K. KG, J., Reddy, P. R., Sathyamurthy, R., & Boopathi, S. (2024). Multi-criteria Optimization on Friction Stir Welding of Aluminum Composite (AA5052-H32/B4C) using Titanium Nitride Coated Tool. Engineering Research Express.

Sampath, B. (2021). *Sustainable Eco-Friendly Wire-Cut Electrical Discharge Machining: Gas Emission Analysis*. Academic Press.

Sampath, B., Sasikumar, C., & Myilsamy, S. (2023). Application of TOPSIS Optimization Technique in the Micro-Machining Process. In IGI: Trends, Paradigms, and Advances in Mechatronics Engineering (pp. 162–187). IGI Global.

Sankar, K. M., Booba, B., & Boopathi, S. (2023). Smart Agriculture Irrigation Monitoring System Using Internet of Things. In *Contemporary Developments in Agricultural Cyber-Physical Systems* (pp. 105–121). IGI Global. doi:10.4018/978-1-6684-7879-0.ch006

Singh, R. K., & Khan, A. (2023). A Comparative Study of Quantum and Classical Deep Learning for Intelligent Agriculture. *Journal of Information and Computational Science*, 13.

Srinivas, B., Maguluri, L. P., Naidu, K. V., Reddy, L. C. S., Deivakani, M., & Boopathi, S. (2023). Architecture and Framework for Interfacing Cloud-Enabled Robots. In *Handbook of Research on Data Science and Cybersecurity Innovations in Industry 4.0 Technologies* (pp. 542–560). IGI Global. doi:10.4018/978-1-6684-8145-5.ch027

Venkateswaran, N., Kumar, S. S., Diwakar, G., Gnanasangeetha, D., & Boopathi, S. (2023). Synthetic Biology for Waste Water to Energy Conversion: IoT and AI Approaches. In M. Arshad (Ed.), Advances in Bioinformatics and Biomedical Engineering. IGI Global. doi:10.4018/978-1-6684-6577-6.ch017

Wei, Q., & Zhang, F. (2019). Mining New Scientific Research Ideas from Quantum Computers and Quantum Communications. *2019 14th International Conference on Computer Science & Education (ICCSE)*, 1069–1074.

Zekrifa, D. M. S., Kulkarni, M., Bhagyalakshmi, A., Devireddy, N., Gupta, S., & Boopathi, S. (2023). Integrating Machine Learning and AI for Improved Hydrological Modeling and Water Resource Management. In *Artificial Intelligence Applications in Water Treatment and Water Resource Management* (pp. 46–70). IGI Global. doi:10.4018/978-1-6684-6791-6.ch003

Chapter 8
Fog Computing–Integrated ML–Based Framework and Solutions for Intelligent Systems:
Digital Healthcare Applications

R. Pitchai

iD https://orcid.org/0000-0002-3759-6915
Department of Computer Science and Engineering, B.V. Raju Institute of Technology, India

K. Venkatesh Guru
Department of Computer Science and Engineering, KSR College of Engineering, India

J. Nirmala Gandhi
Department of Computer Science and Engineering, KSR College of Engineering, India

C. R. Komala
Department of Information Science and Engineering, HKBK College of Engineering, India

J. R. Dinesh Kumar
Department of Electronics and Communication Engineering, Sri Krishna College of Engineering and Technology, India

Sampath Boopathi
iD https://orcid.org/0000-0002-2065-6539
Mechanical Engineering, Muthayammal Engineering College, India

ABSTRACT

The integration of fog computing and machine learning (ML) in digital healthcare has revolutionized patient care, operations, and personalized treatment. This chapter explores the potential of fog computing in telemedicine, remote monitoring, and personalized treatment. It highlights its role in addressing data processing challenges, enabling real-time data analytics, and ensuring secure transmission of medical information. Key case studies demonstrate how these integrated solutions are driving innovation in the healthcare industry. The combination of fog computing and ML offers a promising avenue for the future of digital healthcare, focusing on data-driven decision-making and precision medicine.

DOI: 10.4018/979-8-3693-0968-1.ch008

INTRODUCTION

Fog computing is a digital technology that extends cloud computing to tackle challenges in healthcare and other sectors. It involves decentralized data processing and analysis at the network's edge, closer to data sources, rather than distant cloud servers. This solution aligns with the sector's requirements for timely and secure handling of vast amounts of data. Fog computing significantly reduces latency in healthcare, enabling immediate decision-making by professionals and faster responses to patient needs. This is particularly important during emergency situations or real-time monitoring, as delays can be life-threatening. Fog computing is a technology that integrates with IoT devices in healthcare, enabling data processing and analysis closer to the source. This allows healthcare providers to use IoT for monitoring patients, managing equipment, and conducting medical research (Bakhshi & Balador, 2019; Kadu & Singh, 2023). Fog computing also enhances data security and privacy, minimizing the risk of data breaches during data transmission. This ensures the confidentiality and security of patients' personal and medical information.

Fog computing systems are highly adaptable, allowing for the expansion and contraction of computing resources as needed to handle varying workloads in healthcare. This flexibility is crucial for handling data volumes that can fluctuate greatly, from routine monitoring to sudden surges during public health crises. Fog computing offers reduced latency, enhanced IoT support, improved data security and privacy, and adaptable scalability, making it an essential technology for enhancing the efficiency and effectiveness of healthcare services and applications (Yang, Luo, Chu, Zhou, et al., 2020; Yazdani et al., 2023).

Machine learning (ML) techniques are rapidly advancing in healthcare, transforming various domains like diagnostics and personalized treatment. ML algorithms can analyze vast datasets like medical images, pathology slides, and patient records, aiding in early disease detection. For example, in radiology, ML models can detect anomalies in X-rays, MRIs, and CT scans, facilitating quicker and more accurate diagnoses. ML-powered diagnostic systems can also assist in early disease identification, improving patient outcomes like cancer. ML plays a crucial role in predicting patient outcomes and personalizing treatment plans (Maheswari et al., 2023; Ramudu et al., 2023). It analyzes patient data, including genomic information, history, and lifestyle, to develop predictive models. These models help clinicians anticipate disease progression and tailor treatment strategies. Personalized medicine relies on ML to identify effective treatment options, optimize therapies, and minimize adverse effects. ML also supports drug discovery and development by predicting potential candidates and identifying new applications, accelerating the process, reducing costs, and increasing the likelihood of successful outcomes (Maguluri et al., 2023; Syamala et al., 2023).

Machine learning (ML) is increasingly being used in healthcare for remote monitoring and wearable health devices. It allows algorithms to collect and interpret patient data, providing real-time feedback and timely interventions. This empowers patients to actively engage in their healthcare and provides valuable insights for healthcare professionals. ML has the potential to revolutionize patient care and streamline operations, improving healthcare outcomes and patient experiences (Maheswari et al., 2023; Veeranjaneyulu et al., 2023).

The integration of fog computing and machine learning in healthcare architecture has revolutionized the industry by enabling intelligent systems that use real-time data processing for efficient care. The deployment of fog nodes, strategically positioned for data processing closer to the source, reduces latency and improves medical decision-making (Boopathi, 2023b; Ramudu et al., 2023; Subha et al., 2023). These frameworks facilitate seamless data exchange between fog nodes and cloud resources, ensuring timely access to patient care insights. Intelligent healthcare systems, powered by fog computing and machine learning, heavily rely on IoT devices like wearable health monitors and remote sensors. These devices collect and analyze healthcare data in real time, providing immediate feedback to healthcare providers and patients. This interconnected ecosystem enables continuous monitoring of patients' health, offering a holistic view of their well-being, enhancing the overall healthcare experience.

Integrating intelligent systems and real-time data processing in healthcare offers data-driven decision-making. Machine learning algorithms and predictive analytics help identify patterns in patient data, supporting diagnoses, treatment recommendations, and intervention plans. This combination of fog computing and machine learning enhances patient care and optimizes healthcare operations, thereby enhancing the overall quality of care. The convergence of technologies in healthcare is transforming the industry by enabling intelligent systems equipped with IoT devices to support telemedicine, remote patient monitoring, and wearable health devices, enhancing accessibility and patient-centric treatment, redefining healthcare delivery through proactive care, personalized treatment, and early intervention (Hussain & Srimathy, 2023; Maguluri et al., 2023; Ugandar et al., 2023).

The integration of fog computing and machine learning, along with intelligent systems and IoT devices, provides healthcare providers with real-time data processing capabilities, enabling more efficient, effective, and personalized care, ultimately improving patient outcomes and the overall healthcare experience.

Background and Significance

The healthcare industry has undergone significant transformation due to the integration of fog computing and machine learning technologies. Fog computing, an extension of cloud computing, allows data processing and analysis at the network's edge, a crucial aspect in healthcare. Machine learning, with its data-driven capabilities, revolutionizes healthcare applications by enabling predictive analytics, personalization, and diagnostic support. This chapter explores how fog computing and machine learning are poised to reshape digital healthcare (Boopathi, 2023c, 2023b; Reddy et al., 2023; Satav, Hasan, et al., 2024). The integration of fog computing and machine learning in digital healthcare applications can address challenges like increasing healthcare data volume, real-time decision-making, and patient care improvement. By processing data closer to patients, analysing it in real-time, and providing timely insights, this integration can redefine healthcare delivery, making it more efficient, accessible, and patient-centric.

Scope of the Chapter

This chapter explores the application and implications of fog computing and machine learning in digital healthcare, focusing on their integration to create intelligent systems that empower healthcare professionals and benefit patients, with specific areas of focus.

- The fundamentals of fog computing and how they apply to healthcare.
- Machine learning techniques and their applications in healthcare, from diagnostics to personalized treatment.
- Architectural frameworks and real-time data processing capabilities achieved through the integration of fog computing and machine learning.
- The role of intelligent systems, IoT devices, and data-driven decision-making in healthcare.
- Key digital healthcare applications, such as telemedicine, remote patient monitoring, and wearable health devices, are enriched by these integrated technologies.
- Case studies illustrating successful implementations and innovations.
- The critical issue of data security, privacy, ethical considerations, and compliance in healthcare.

FOG COMPUTING IN DIGITAL HEALTHCARE

Fog Computing Fundamentals

Fog computing, an extension of cloud computing, is a crucial technology in the digital healthcare sector. It extends cloud computing principles to the network's

Figure 1. Fog computing in digital healthcare

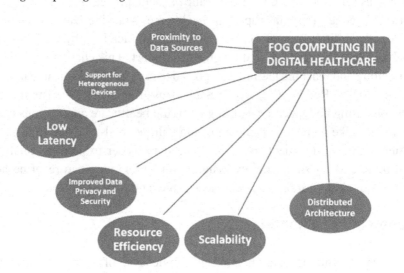

edge, closer to the data source, and has distinct features that differentiate it from traditional cloud computing (Figure 1). This in-depth exploration of fog computing's fundamentals is essential for its advancement (Kaur et al., 2020; Khalid et al., 2019; Nkenyereye et al., 2021; Sun et al., 2019).

- **Proximity to Data Sources**: One of the primary features of fog computing is its physical proximity to the data sources. While cloud computing processes data in centralized data centers, fog computing takes place at the edge of the network, much closer to where data is generated. This proximity reduces data transmission latency, which is crucial for real-time applications such as IoT and critical systems like autonomous vehicles and healthcare devices.
- **Low Latency**: Fog computing is designed to provide low-latency data processing. It offers faster response times, making it suitable for applications that require immediate decision-making, such as industrial automation, augmented reality, and real-time analytics.
- **Distributed Architecture**: Fog computing utilizes a distributed architecture, where processing tasks can be distributed across a network of fog nodes. This architecture ensures that computational resources are available closer to where they are needed, enhancing the efficiency and scalability of the system.
- **Scalability**: Fog computing is highly scalable. Its decentralized approach allows for the easy addition of fog nodes as needed to accommodate increasing workloads. This scalability is essential for handling the growing volume of data generated by IoT devices and other edge devices.

- **Resource Efficiency**: Fog computing optimizes resource utilization by processing data locally or at the network edge. This efficiency minimizes the need for long-distance data transmission and reduces the load on centralized cloud data centers, resulting in cost savings and reduced network congestion.
- **Improved Data Privacy and Security**: By processing data closer to the source, fog computing can enhance data privacy and security. Since sensitive data can remain within a local network, the risk of data breaches during transmission is minimized. This feature is particularly crucial in industries like healthcare, where data confidentiality is paramount.
- **Support for Heterogeneous Devices**: Fog computing can accommodate a wide range of edge devices, including IoT sensors, smartphones, and industrial machinery. It is designed to work seamlessly with different device types and operating systems, making it versatile in various application domains.
- **Local Decision-Making**: Fog computing allows for local decision-making and autonomy, which is valuable in scenarios where immediate actions are necessary. For example, autonomous vehicles can make split-second decisions based on locally processed data.

Fog computing, a technology with advantages like proximity to data sources, low latency, distributed architecture, scalability, resource efficiency, data privacy, security, and device support, is highly valuable for edge computing applications in real-time processing and decision-making industries.

Architectural Components

Fog computing systems comprise several architectural components that work together to enable efficient data processing and analytics at the network's edge (Figure 2). These components are essential for the seamless functioning of fog computing in various applications (Bakhshi & Balador, 2019; Kadu & Singh, 2023; Pareek et al., 2021; Yang, Luo, Chu, & Zhou, 2020).

- **Fog Nodes**: Fog nodes are the foundational components of a fog computing system. They are distributed edge devices or servers located close to data sources, such as IoT devices or sensors. These nodes are responsible for processing, storing, and analyzing data locally. Fog nodes come in various forms, from edge servers to gateway devices, and are equipped with computational resources, including CPUs, GPUs, and memory, to perform data processing tasks.
- **Connectivity**: Connectivity components enable communication between fog nodes, IoT devices, and other parts of the network. This includes both

Figure 2. Fog computing systems: Architectural components

wired and wireless communication technologies such as Ethernet, Wi-Fi, 4G/5G cellular networks, and low-power wide-area networks (LPWAN). Connectivity options must be robust to handle the diverse data sources that interact with fog nodes.

- **Edge Analytics**: Edge analytics software or platforms run on fog nodes to perform real-time data analysis. These components often include machine learning and data analytics algorithms that process and interpret data generated by edge devices. Edge analytics allows for immediate insights and decision-making at the edge, reducing the need to send data to remote cloud servers for processing.
- **Data Storage**: Fog computing systems may have local data storage capabilities to store relevant data for a certain period. This can include structured databases or file systems. Local storage is beneficial for situations where data needs to be retained for further analysis or when network connectivity is intermittent.
- **Security Mechanisms**: Security components, including firewalls, intrusion detection systems, and encryption protocols, are crucial in fog computing systems to protect data and devices at the network edge. Data security is a top priority, especially when processing sensitive healthcare or financial data.
- **Management and Orchestration**: Fog computing systems require management and orchestration components to handle the deployment, configuration, and maintenance of fog nodes. This includes monitoring the health of edge devices, distributing workloads efficiently, and ensuring resource allocation for various applications.

- **IoT Device Management**: IoT device management tools are essential to interact with and manage the diverse IoT devices connected to the fog computing system. This includes device onboarding, firmware updates, and data collection from IoT sensors.
- **Data Ingestion and Pre-processing**: Data ingestion components are responsible for receiving and pre-processing data from edge devices. This may include data cleansing, normalization, and data format conversion to ensure data consistency and compatibility for analytics.
- **Communication Protocols**: Fog computing systems rely on various communication protocols to enable data exchange between devices, fog nodes, and, if necessary, cloud servers. These protocols vary depending on the application and the type of devices in use.
- **Scalability and Load Balancing**: Scalability and load balancing mechanisms are vital for handling varying workloads and the addition of new edge devices. Fog computing systems need to be designed to efficiently distribute processing tasks across fog nodes to maintain optimal performance.

Fog computing systems combine architectural components to enable real-time data processing, analytics, and decision-making at the network's edge, while ensuring data security and efficient resource utilization (Lin et al., 2020; Shahzad et al., 2022). The configuration varies based on application requirements and use case. Fog computing is particularly beneficial in healthcare, addressing challenges from IoT devices and real-time data processing. Use cases and examples of fog computing applications are provided.

Fog Computing for Healthcare Applications

This section discusses the role of fog computing in healthcare, highlighting its importance in modernizing healthcare systems. It discusses the significance of proximity to data sources in healthcare data processing, addresses issues of latency, bandwidth, and network reliability, and showcases how fog computing enhances data processing and analytics for healthcare IoT devices (Figure 3). It also discusses the role of fog nodes and edge computing in healthcare infrastructure. Fog computing

Figure 3. Fog computing for healthcare applications

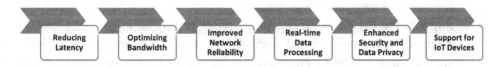

| Reducing Latency | Optimizing Bandwidth | Improved Network Reliability | Real-time Data Processing | Enhanced Security and Data Privacy | Support for IoT Devices |

significantly impacts healthcare operations, patient care, and the overall healthcare landscape (Ijaz et al., 2021; Kaur et al., 2020; Sun et al., 2019).

- **Reducing Latency**: One of the most significant advantages of fog computing in healthcare is its ability to minimize latency. In healthcare, especially during emergencies and real-time patient monitoring, every millisecond counts. Fog nodes, located closer to the data sources, can process data with minimal delay. This reduction in latency ensures that healthcare professionals receive timely information and can make faster, more informed decisions. For example, in telemedicine applications, reduced latency allows for smoother and more interactive remote consultations, improving the overall patient experience.
- **Optimizing Bandwidth**: Fog computing reduces the need for constant data transmission to remote cloud servers. By processing data at the network edge, only relevant information or insights need to be sent to the cloud. This optimization of bandwidth is crucial in healthcare, where large volumes of data are generated, such as medical imaging and patient monitoring. It not only conserves network resources but also prevents network congestion, ensuring that healthcare data transmission remains efficient and uninterrupted (Boopathi, 2022a, 2022b, 2022c, 2023a).
- **Improved Network Reliability**: Fog computing increases network reliability in healthcare by decentralizing data processing. In cases of network disruptions or failures, fog nodes can continue to process and store data locally, ensuring continuity of essential healthcare services. This redundancy is crucial for scenarios like remote patient monitoring, where uninterrupted data collection and real-time alerts are imperative.
- **Real-time Data Processing**: Fog computing enables real-time data processing and analysis at the edge of the network. This capability has far-reaching implications for healthcare, where immediate responses are often required. For example, in intensive care units (ICUs), real-time monitoring and data analytics can trigger alarms and notifications for healthcare providers in case of critical changes in a patient's condition, allowing for immediate intervention.
- **Enhanced Security and Data Privacy**: By processing healthcare data locally at the network edge, fog computing minimizes the risk of data exposure during data transmission to distant cloud servers. This enhanced security and data privacy are critical in healthcare, where patient confidentiality and regulatory compliance are paramount.
- **Support for IoT Devices**: Healthcare relies heavily on IoT devices, such as wearable health monitors and medical sensors. Fog computing is designed to support these devices by providing the necessary edge infrastructure for data

processing (Kavitha et al., 2023; Reddy et al., 2023; Ugandar et al., 2023). This support enables continuous monitoring, data collection, and feedback, enhancing the quality of patient care.

Fog computing enhances healthcare data processing, reduces latency, optimizes bandwidth, improves network reliability, supports real-time data processing, and supports IoT devices, leading to more efficient systems, improved patient care, and increased engagement, ultimately improving health outcomes and a more effective healthcare environment.

Benefits and Challenges

While fog computing offers numerous benefits, it is not without its challenges. In this section, we explore:

- The advantages of fog computing in healthcare, such as reduced latency, improved data privacy, and enhanced scalability.
- The challenges and limitations, including security concerns, resource management, and interoperability issues.
- Strategies for mitigating these challenges and maximizing the potential of fog computing in digital healthcare.

This chapter provides a comprehensive understanding of fog computing's role in healthcare, its benefits and challenges, and its integration with machine learning in digital healthcare applications, laying the groundwork for understanding its future applications.

MACHINE LEARNING IN HEALTHCARE

Machine Learning Techniques

Machine learning is at the heart of healthcare's transformation, and this section provides a comprehensive overview of machine learning techniques (Munawar et al., 2021; Shi et al., 2020; Zhou et al., 2021), including:

- An introduction to the principles of machine learning.
- Classification of machine learning algorithms (supervised, unsupervised, reinforcement learning).
- Deep learning and neural networks.

- Natural language processing (NLP) and its healthcare applications.
- How machine learning models are trained and evaluated.

ML in Diagnostics and Predictive Healthcare

This section explores the use of machine learning in healthcare diagnostics and predictive analytics, highlighting its significant role in transforming the healthcare landscape by enhancing diagnostics and enhancing predictive analytics, marking a new era in healthcare (Figure 4).

Figure 4. ML in diagnostics and predictive healthcare

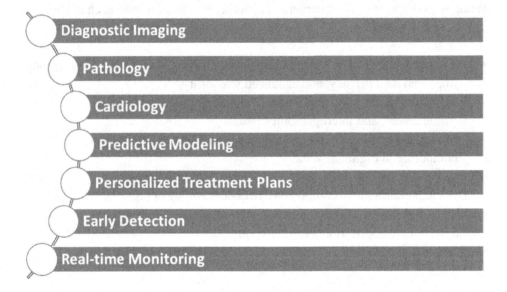

Diagnostic Imaging: ML algorithms are revolutionizing diagnostic imaging across radiology, pathology, and cardiology. In radiology, deep learning models are now capable of accurately detecting anomalies in X-rays, MRIs, and CT scans. These algorithms aid radiologists in identifying and diagnosing diseases such as cancer, fractures, and cardiovascular issues with greater speed and accuracy (Boopathi, Pandey, et al., 2023; Boopathi & Kanike, 2023).

Pathology: ML-driven image analysis in pathology is automating the detection of abnormalities in tissue samples, making it faster and more consistent. Pathologists can leverage these algorithms to improve the accuracy of cancer diagnoses, reduce workload, and enhance patient outcomes.

Cardiology: In cardiology, ML models are used to analyze electrocardiograms (ECGs) and other cardiac data, enabling early detection of heart conditions and predicting the risk of heart disease. These predictive models assist healthcare providers in customizing treatment and preventive measures for patients.

Predictive Modeling: Machine learning excels in predictive modeling for healthcare. It is employed to create models for predicting disease risk, patient outcomes, and healthcare resource utilization. For instance, predictive analytics can identify patients at higher risk of readmission after hospital discharge, enabling targeted interventions and reducing healthcare costs.

Personalized Treatment Plans: ML techniques analyze patient-specific data, such as genomics, patient history, and lifestyle, to create personalized treatment plans. These plans are tailored to the individual patient, ensuring that the most effective treatments and interventions are administered while minimizing side effects. The advent of personalized medicine is paving the way for precision healthcare.

Early Detection: Machine learning algorithms excel at early detection. They can identify subtle patterns and anomalies in patient data, leading to the early diagnosis of diseases like cancer, diabetes, and Alzheimer's. Early detection often results in more successful treatments and improved patient outcomes.

Real-time Monitoring: ML-driven monitoring systems can track patient data in real time, issuing alerts and predictions based on deviations from baseline health parameters. For example, wearable devices and IoT sensors continuously monitor vital signs and notify healthcare providers or patients of potential issues, enabling proactive interventions.

Machine learning in diagnostics and predictive healthcare is revolutionizing the field by improving diagnostic accuracy, predicting patient outcomes, facilitating personalized treatment plans, and enabling early detection. These advancements enable healthcare professionals to make informed decisions, deliver proactive care, and enhance patient well-being.

ML in Personalized Medicine

This section explores the use of machine learning in personalized medicine in healthcare, focusing on its application in tailoring treatments and interventions to individual patients, the role of genomics and patient data, and case studies showcasing ML-driven advancements.

This chapter provides a comprehensive understanding of machine learning techniques, their applications in healthcare diagnostics and predictive analytics, and their role in shaping personalized medicine. It also explores the integration of machine learning with fog computing in digital healthcare applications.

INTEGRATION OF FOG COMPUTING AND MACHINE LEARNING

Synergies and Complementarity

This section delves into the integration of fog computing and machine learning in digital healthcare, highlighting their synergies and complementarity (Agrawal et al., 2024a; Reddy et al., 2023; Satav, Lamani, G, et al., 2024; Venkateswaran, Vidhya, et al., 2023).

The chapter discusses the integration of fog computing and machine learning in healthcare applications, highlighting their complementary nature, edge processing capabilities, and real-time decision support advantages, with case studies illustrating the synergistic benefits.

Architectural Models and Design Principles

This section discusses the importance of robust architectural models and design principles in integrating fog computing and machine learning in healthcare to create intelligent systems (Boopathi, 2023b; Koshariya et al., 2023; Syamala et al., 2023; Zekrifa et al., 2023).

Distributed Architecture: Intelligent healthcare systems are characterized by a distributed architecture that leverages both edge devices and fog nodes. This architecture enables data processing, analysis, and decision-making at the network's edge, reducing latency and enhancing real-time capabilities. Data from various healthcare sources, including wearable devices, medical sensors, and patient records, can be efficiently processed through this distributed model.

Decentralization: A fundamental design principle involves decentralization, ensuring that computational resources are available closer to where they are needed. This principle optimizes the use of fog nodes and edge devices, enhancing the system's responsiveness and minimizing the need to transfer large volumes of data to centralized cloud servers.

Scalability, Fault Tolerance, and Resource Management

Scalability, fault tolerance, and resource management are crucial considerations in integrated fog computing and machine learning systems for healthcare:

Scalability: Scalability is essential in healthcare systems that handle varying workloads and the addition of new edge devices or fog nodes. The architecture must accommodate these changes while maintaining optimal performance. Scalability is particularly important in applications like remote patient monitoring, which can experience fluctuations in data volume.

Fault Tolerance: Healthcare applications cannot afford system failures. Fault tolerance mechanisms are implemented to ensure system resilience. Redundancy in fog nodes and edge devices, along with fault detection and recovery protocols, is necessary to maintain uninterrupted healthcare services.

Resource Management: Efficient resource management is vital for optimal performance. Resource allocation and load balancing mechanisms ensure that computational resources are distributed effectively across the fog nodes, enhancing the system's overall efficiency. These mechanisms also prioritize critical healthcare tasks and ensure that they receive the necessary resources.

Real-World Examples of Architectural Frameworks

Real-world examples of architectural frameworks that optimize healthcare processes serve as practical illustrations of these principles (Boopathi, Khare, et al., 2023; Pramila et al., 2023; Sengeni et al., 2023; Ugandar et al., 2023):

Example 1: **Hospital IoT Integration Framework**: This framework incorporates fog computing and machine learning to process patient data from IoT devices. It efficiently manages patient data, optimizes the use of fog nodes, and ensures real-time analytics for better patient care. The system's scalability accommodates an increasing number of devices as the hospital's IoT infrastructure grows.

Example 2: **Telemedicine Platform**: A telemedicine platform is designed with a distributed architecture that integrates fog computing for real-time patient consultations. It optimizes bandwidth by processing video and audio data at the network edge. The framework's fault tolerance mechanisms ensure that patient consultations continue seamlessly, even in the event of network disruptions.

Example 3: **Mobile Health (mHealth) Application**: An mHealth application integrates fog computing to process data from wearable health devices. The architecture employs scalable edge processing to analyze patient health data, providing real-time feedback and predictive insights. Resource management ensures that computational resources are allocated effectively to support continuous monitoring and early intervention.

Real-world examples demonstrate the use of architectural frameworks incorporating fog computing and machine learning principles in healthcare processes, enhancing efficiency, fault tolerance, and resource management, thereby enhancing responsiveness.

INTELLIGENT SYSTEMS IN HEALTHCARE

IoT Devices and Sensors

This section explores the pivotal role of Internet of Things (IoT) devices and sensors in the development of intelligent healthcare systems (Hussain & Srimathy, 2023; Kavitha et al., 2023; Syamala et al., 2023; Venkateswaran, Kumar, et al., 2023). Smart healthcare environments integrate technology and healthcare infrastructure to improve patient care, streamline operations, and improve outcomes (Figure 5). They utilize digital technology, data analytics, and connectivity to create an efficient, patient-centric healthcare ecosystem, focusing on key aspects such as data analytics and connectivity.

Figure 5. Smart healthcare environments integrate technology and healthcare infrastructure

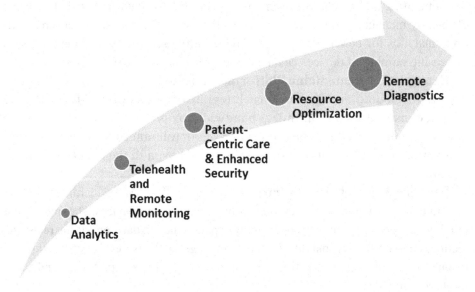

- **Automation**: Smart healthcare environments leverage automation to reduce manual tasks, optimize resource allocation, and enhance efficiency. For example, automated scheduling and appointment systems reduce administrative burdens, while robotic process automation streamlines back-end operations.

- **Internet of Things (IoT)**: IoT devices play a crucial role in smart healthcare environments. These devices, such as wearable health monitors, medical sensors, and connected medical equipment, continuously collect and transmit patient data. This real-time data enables healthcare providers to monitor patients remotely and make timely interventions.

- **Data Integration**: Smart healthcare environments integrate data from various sources, including electronic health records (EHRs), medical devices, and patient-generated data. This holistic view of patient information improves clinical decision-making, aids in the early detection of health issues, and supports personalized treatment plans.

- **Data Analytics**: Advanced analytics and machine learning are employed to derive insights from the vast amount of healthcare data generated. Predictive analytics can identify patient trends, while diagnostic algorithms can aid in the early detection of diseases. Data analytics also assist in resource optimization, helping healthcare facilities allocate staff and equipment more effectively.

- **Telehealth and Remote Monitoring**: Smart healthcare environments enable telehealth and remote monitoring, providing patients with access to healthcare services from the comfort of their homes. Telemedicine appointments, real-time monitoring of vital signs, and remote consultation with healthcare providers are key components of this model.

- **Patient-Centric Care**: The integration of technology allows for more patient-centric care. Patients have greater access to their health information, can actively engage in their care, and receive personalized treatment plans. These environments foster better communication between patients and healthcare providers.

- **Enhanced Security and Privacy**: With the integration of technology, smart healthcare environments prioritize security and privacy. Robust data encryption, access controls, and compliance with healthcare regulations are fundamental to maintaining the confidentiality of patient information.

- **Resource Optimization**: Efficient use of resources is a central focus of smart healthcare environments. By automating processes, optimizing workflows, and employing data-driven decision-making, these environments reduce healthcare costs and improve resource allocation.

- **Remote Diagnostics and Consultation**: Specialists from various locations can remotely diagnose and consult on cases, expanding access to expertise and reducing geographical barriers to quality healthcare.

Smart healthcare environments are transforming healthcare by integrating technology and data analytics to enhance patient care, streamline operations, and improve the overall healthcare experience, utilizing automation, IoT, data integration, and analytics.

Data-driven Decision Making

This section discusses the role of IoT devices and data analytics in enabling data-driven decision-making in modern healthcare. The text emphasizes the significance of data-driven healthcare decision-making, utilizing analytics and machine learning for clinical and operational insights, and discussing real-world examples and ethical considerations in this context.

This chapter provides a comprehensive understanding of how intelligent systems, IoT devices, and data-driven decision-making are transforming the healthcare industry, highlighting key components for developing intelligent healthcare solutions and preparing readers for exploring digital healthcare applications.

DIGITAL HEALTHCARE APPLICATIONS

Telemedicine and Remote Consultation

This section discusses the significance of telemedicine and remote consultation in modern digital healthcare (Jarva et al., 2022; Lupton & Leahy, 2019; Morris et al., 2022). Telemedicine, a digital healthcare solution, facilitates remote consultation, offers benefits and challenges, and has been successfully implemented in healthcare delivery through case studies.

Remote Patient Monitoring

This section explores the transformative role of remote patient monitoring in healthcare by providing real-time, continuous patient data (Boopathi, 2023b; Kavitha et al., 2023; Subha et al., 2023; Ugandar et al., 2023). The text discusses the importance of remote patient monitoring in managing chronic conditions and post-operative care, the role of IoT devices in data collection and transmission, and the significance of data security and privacy considerations.

Personalized Treatment Plans

This section delves into the advancement of personalized treatment plans in precision medicine, highlighting the use of machine learning and data analytics, genomics' role in personalization, real-world healthcare examples, and ethical and regulatory aspects of personalized medicine.

Wearable Health Devices

Wearable health devices are gaining prominence in healthcare, transforming patient and provider management. These devices collect real-time data about an individual's health and lifestyle, and their growing importance can be attributed to several factors (Anitha et al., 2023; Boopathi, Khare, et al., 2023; Reddy et al., 2023; Subha et al., 2023; Ugandar et al., 2023).

Continuous Monitoring: Wearable health devices offer continuous monitoring of vital signs, activity levels, and other health parameters. This continuous data collection provides a more comprehensive view of a patient's health status, enabling early detection of health issues and more proactive intervention.

Remote Patient Monitoring: These devices enable remote patient monitoring, particularly for individuals with chronic conditions. Healthcare providers can track patients' health remotely, reducing the need for frequent in-person visits and allowing for more timely adjustments to treatment plans.

Personalized Treatment Plans: The data collected by wearable devices can be used to create personalized treatment plans. Machine learning algorithms analyze the data to tailor recommendations for exercise, diet, medication, and other interventions to an individual's specific needs.

Patient Engagement: Wearable devices engage patients in their own health management. Patients can track their progress, set health goals, and receive real-time feedback. This engagement fosters a sense of ownership over one's health and motivates individuals to make healthier choices.

Preventive Healthcare: Wearable devices are not only about managing existing conditions but also play a significant role in preventive healthcare. By continuously monitoring health parameters, these devices can alert individuals to potential issues and encourage early lifestyle changes to prevent health problems.

Data-Driven Decision Making: The data generated by wearable devices is invaluable for healthcare providers. It provides a wealth of information for data-driven decision-making, enabling clinicians to make more informed choices regarding patient care, treatment adjustments, and interventions.

Telemedicine: Wearable devices can be integrated with telemedicine platforms, allowing for real-time remote consultations between patients and healthcare providers. These devices can transmit vital signs and other health data to the healthcare team, enhancing telemedicine's effectiveness).

Research and Population Health: Aggregated data from wearable devices can be used for large-scale health research and population health management. Researchers can gain insights into trends and patterns, while public health officials can use this data for early disease surveillance.

The rise of wearable health devices presents challenges such as data security, privacy, accuracy, and interoperability with existing healthcare systems. However, this shift towards patient-centric and data-driven healthcare offers improved health outcomes and cost-effective management. By the end of this chapter, readers will understand digital healthcare applications integrating fog computing and machine learning, intelligent systems, IoT devices, and data-driven decision-making, impacting patient care and healthcare delivery (Satav, Lamani, K. G., et al., 2024).

CASE STUDIES

This section presents case studies showcasing the practical implementation and benefits of fog computing integrated with machine learning in telehealth platforms.

Case Study 1

Real-time Monitoring for Chronic Disease Management: This case study showcases a telehealth platform that uses fog computing to analyze patient data from wearable devices, providing real-time insights and predictive alerts for better chronic disease management (Ramudu et al., 2023).

Chronic diseases, such as diabetes and hypertension, require continuous monitoring and management to prevent complications and improve patient outcomes. This case study examines the implementation of a telehealth platform that utilizes fog computing to analyze patient data from wearable devices, providing real-time insights and predictive alerts to enhance chronic disease management. Managing chronic diseases traditionally involves periodic visits to healthcare facilities, leading to delayed interventions and the possibility of overlooking critical changes in a patient's condition. Remote monitoring through wearable devices can provide a continuous stream of patient data, but analyzing and responding to this data in real-time is a complex task (Agrawal et al., 2024b; Das et al., 2024; Kumar B et al., 2024).

A telehealth platform has been developed to tackle chronic disease management issues, utilizing fog computing for real-time data processing and analysis at the network's edge.

- **Wearable Health Devices**: Patients with chronic diseases are provided with wearable health devices, such as continuous glucose monitors or blood pressure monitors. These devices collect data on vital signs and health parameters.

- **Data Ingestion and Pre-processing**: Data generated by wearable devices are ingested into the telehealth platform, which pre-processes the data. This step includes data cleansing, normalization, and the extraction of relevant health parameters.
- **Fog Nodes**: Fog nodes are strategically placed near patients' homes to serve as edge computing resources. These nodes receive pre-processed data and run machine learning algorithms for real-time analysis.
- **Real-time Analytics**: Fog nodes continuously analyse patient data, looking for deviations from baseline health parameters. Machine learning models identify patterns and trends that may indicate deteriorating health. For example, a sudden increase in blood glucose levels or a significant drop in blood pressure can trigger alerts.
- **Alerting System**: When the machine learning models detect anomalies or trends of concern, the telehealth platform issues real-time alerts. Healthcare providers and patients receive these alerts, enabling immediate intervention. Alerts can be delivered via mobile apps or email notifications.
- **Patient Engagement**: Patients are actively engaged in their healthcare management. They can access their health data through a mobile app, view trends over time, and receive personalized recommendations. This engagement empowers patients to take control of their health.

Benefits and Outcomes

The implementation of a telehealth platform using fog computing has provided numerous advantages (Kumar et al., 2023; Ugandar et al., 2023; Venkateswaran, Kumar, et al., 2023).

- **Early Intervention**: Real-time monitoring and predictive alerts enable early intervention in response to deteriorating health conditions, reducing the risk of complications and hospitalization.
- **Improved Patient Outcomes**: Patients with chronic diseases experience better health outcomes due to timely adjustments in treatment plans and lifestyle modifications.
- **Reduced Healthcare Costs**: Early interventions and fewer hospitalizations result in cost savings for healthcare systems and patients.
- **Enhanced Patient Engagement**: Patients are more engaged in their healthcare management, leading to greater adherence to treatment plans and healthier lifestyle choices.

- **Data for Research**: The aggregated data from this platform contributes to research on chronic disease management and can inform future healthcare practices.

The case study showcases the transformative effect of fog computing in healthcare, especially in chronic disease management, where real-time monitoring and predictive alerts from telehealth platforms improve patient outcomes and reduce healthcare costs.

Case Study 2: *Virtual Consultations Enhanced by Machine Learning*: This case study explores how a telehealth platform integrates machine learning to personalize virtual consultations, optimizing diagnostic accuracy and treatment recommendations.

Case Study 3: *Remote ICU Monitoring*: This case study focuses on a telehealth platform that employs fog computing and machine learning to enable remote monitoring of intensive care unit (ICU) patients. It highlights how real-time data analytics support timely interventions and reduce mortality rates.

Case Study 4: *Telepsychiatry with Predictive Analytics*: In this case study, the use of machine learning algorithms in telepsychiatry is examined. It demonstrates how fog computing enhances predictive analytics for mental health interventions, leading to more effective patient care.

Case studies demonstrate the potential of fog computing and machine learning in telehealth platforms to enhance healthcare accessibility, patient outcomes, and service quality.

DATA SECURITY AND PRIVACY

Healthcare Data Protection

Ensuring the security and privacy of healthcare data is paramount in the digital healthcare landscape (Dhanya et al., 2023; Pramila et al., 2023; Ramudu et al., 2023). This text discusses data protection strategies, patient data security in healthcare, best practices for safeguarding EHRs and other sensitive data, and case studies showcasing successful data protection measures.

Compliance and Regulations

This section discusses the importance of healthcare regulations like HIPAA and GDPR in maintaining data security and privacy. It highlights the role of regulatory compliance in healthcare data protection, challenges and solutions for digital healthcare compliance, and examples of effective healthcare organizations adhering to regulations.

Ethical Considerations

This section discusses the ethical considerations for the responsible use of healthcare data, including data ownership, consent, sharing, AI and machine learning use, case studies highlighting ethical challenges, and strategies for creating an ethical framework for digital healthcare.

This chapter aims to provide readers with a comprehensive understanding of data security and privacy's critical role in digital healthcare, emphasizing the significance of regulatory compliance and ethical considerations in healthcare data management practices.

FUTURE DIRECTIONS AND CHALLENGES

Emerging Trends

The future of digital healthcare is characterized by emerging trends such as artificial intelligence and machine learning, telemedicine expansion, wearable health technology innovations, and data interoperability and sharing, which are expected to significantly change the healthcare landscape.

Challenges and Limitations

Digital healthcare, despite its potential, faces challenges such as data security and privacy issues, interoperability issues, the digital divide, and regulatory and ethical dilemmas in the use of emerging technologies, despite the increasing volume of healthcare data.

Research Opportunities

The evolving landscape of digital healthcare presents numerous research opportunities (Chakraborty et al., 2022; Lupton & Leahy, 2019; Satybaldy et al., 2022; Tebeje & Klein, 2021). This chapter explores potential research areas for improving data security and privacy, advancing machine learning algorithms in healthcare applications, enhancing usability and user experience of digital healthcare platforms, and exploring the social and ethical implications of emerging technologies. It provides a forward-looking view of the future of digital healthcare, highlighting industry trends and challenges, and identifying research opportunities for innovation and improvement.

CONCLUSION

The chapter concludes by summarizing key points, including the integration of fog computing and machine learning in digital healthcare, the role of intelligent systems, the significance of data security and privacy, and their diverse healthcare applications. The chapter discusses the potential benefits of integrating fog computing and machine learning in digital healthcare, highlighting their potential to revolutionize the industry. The goal is to enhance patient care and outcomes through real-time data processing and personalized treatment plans, improve healthcare efficiency through telemedicine and remote monitoring, drive innovation, ensure data security and privacy, and raise ethical considerations in AI and data-driven decision-making in healthcare. The chapter highlights the potential of fog computing and machine learning in transforming the future of digital healthcare by enhancing the delivery, access, and personalized nature of healthcare services. It concludes by highlighting the transformative potential of these technologies in the healthcare industry.

List of Abbreviations

ML - Machine Learning
IoT - Internet of Things
EHRs - Electronic Health Records
mHealth - Mobile Health
ECG - Electrocardiogram
Fog Computing
CT - Computed Tomography
MRI - Magnetic Resonance Imaging
LPWAN - Low-Power Wide-Area Network

REFERENCES

Agrawal, A. V., Shashibhushan, G., Pradeep, S., Padhi, S. N., Sugumar, D., & Boopathi, S. (2024a). Synergizing Artificial Intelligence, 5G, and Cloud Computing for Efficient Energy Conversion Using Agricultural Waste. In Practice, Progress, and Proficiency in Sustainability (pp. 475–497). IGI Global. doi:10.4018/979-8-3693-1186-8.ch026

Agrawal, A. V., Shashibhushan, G., Pradeep, S., Padhi, S. N., Sugumar, D., & Boopathi, S. (2024b). Synergizing Artificial Intelligence, 5G, and Cloud Computing for Efficient Energy Conversion Using Agricultural Waste. In B. K. Mishra (Ed.), Practice, Progress, and Proficiency in Sustainability. IGI Global. doi:10.4018/979-8-3693-1186-8.ch026

Anitha, C., Komala, C., Vivekanand, C. V., Lalitha, S., & Boopathi, S. (2023). Artificial Intelligence driven security model for Internet of Medical Things (IoMT). *IEEE Explore*, 1–7.

Bakhshi, Z., & Balador, A. (2019). An overview on security and privacy challenges and their solutions in fog-based vehicular application. *2019 IEEE 30th International Symposium on Personal, Indoor and Mobile Radio Communications (PIMRC Workshops)*, 1–7.

Boopathi, S. (2022a). An experimental investigation of Quench Polish Quench (QPQ) coating on AISI 4150 steel. *Engineering Research Express*, *4*(4), 045009. doi:10.1088/2631-8695/ac9ddd

Boopathi, S. (2022b). Experimental investigation and multi-objective optimization of cryogenic Friction-stir-welding of AA2014 and AZ31B alloys using MOORA technique. *Materials Today. Communications*, *33*, 104937. doi:10.1016/j.mtcomm.2022.104937

Boopathi, S. (2022c). Performance Improvement of Eco-Friendly Near-Dry wire-Cut Electrical Discharge Machining Process Using Coconut Oil-Mist Dielectric Fluid. *World Scientific: Journal of Advanced Manufacturing Systems.*

Boopathi, S. (2023a). An Investigation on Friction Stir Processing of Aluminum Alloy-Boron Carbide Surface Composite. In *Springer: Advances in Processing of Lightweight Metal Alloys and Composites* (pp. 249–257). Springer. doi:10.1007/978-981-19-7146-4_14

Boopathi, S. (2023b). Internet of Things-Integrated Remote Patient Monitoring System: Healthcare Application. In *Dynamics of Swarm Intelligence Health Analysis for the Next Generation* (pp. 137–161). IGI Global. doi:10.4018/978-1-6684-6894-4.ch008

Boopathi, S. (2023c). Securing Healthcare Systems Integrated With IoT: Fundamentals, Applications, and Future Trends. In Dynamics of Swarm Intelligence Health Analysis for the Next Generation (pp. 186–209). IGI Global.

Boopathi, S., & Kanike, U. K. (2023). Applications of Artificial Intelligent and Machine Learning Techniques in Image Processing. In *Handbook of Research on Thrust Technologies' Effect on Image Processing* (pp. 151–173). IGI Global. doi:10.4018/978-1-6684-8618-4.ch010

Boopathi, S., Khare, R., KG, J. C., Muni, T. V., & Khare, S. (2023). Additive Manufacturing Developments in the Medical Engineering Field. In Development, Properties, and Industrial Applications of 3D Printed Polymer Composites (pp. 86–106). IGI Global.

Boopathi, S., Pandey, B. K., & Pandey, D. (2023). Advances in Artificial Intelligence for Image Processing: Techniques, Applications, and Optimization. In Handbook of Research on Thrust Technologies' Effect on Image Processing (pp. 73–95). IGI Global.

Chakraborty, I., Vigneswara Ilavarasan, P., & Edirippulige, S. (2022). E-Health Startups' Framework for Value Creation and Capture: Some Insights from Systematic Review. *Proceedings of the International Conference on Cognitive and Intelligent Computing: ICCIC 2021, 1*, 141–152. 10.1007/978-981-19-2350-0_13

Das, S., Lekhya, G., Shreya, K., Lydia Shekinah, K., Babu, K. K., & Boopathi, S. (2024). Fostering Sustainability Education Through Cross-Disciplinary Collaborations and Research Partnerships: Interdisciplinary Synergy. In P. Yu, J. Mulli, Z. A. S. Syed, & L. Umme (Eds.), Advances in Higher Education and Professional Development. IGI Global. doi:10.4018/979-8-3693-0487-7.ch003

Dhanya, D., Kumar, S. S., Thilagavathy, A., Prasad, D., & Boopathi, S. (2023). Data Analytics and Artificial Intelligence in the Circular Economy: Case Studies. In Intelligent Engineering Applications and Applied Sciences for Sustainability (pp. 40–58). IGI Global.

Hussain, Z., & Srimathy, G. (2023). *IoT and AI Integration for Enhanced Efficiency and Sustainability*. Academic Press.

Ijaz, M., Li, G., Lin, L., Cheikhrouhou, O., Hamam, H., & Noor, A. (2021). Integration and applications of fog computing and cloud computing based on the internet of things for provision of healthcare services at home. *Electronics (Basel), 10*(9), 1077. doi:10.3390/electronics10091077

Jarva, E., Oikarinen, A., Andersson, J., Tuomikoski, A.-M., Kääriäinen, M., Meriläinen, M., & Mikkonen, K. (2022). Healthcare professionals' perceptions of digital health competence: A qualitative descriptive study. *Nursing Open, 9*(2), 1379–1393. doi:10.1002/nop2.1184 PMID:35094493

Kadu, A., & Singh, M. (2023). Fog-Enabled Framework for Patient Health-Monitoring Systems Using Internet of Things and Wireless Body Area Networks. In *Computational Intelligence: Select Proceedings of InCITe 2022* (pp. 607–616). Springer. doi:10.1007/978-981-19-7346-8_52

Kaur, J., Agrawal, A., & Khan, R. A. (2020). Security issues in fog environment: A systematic literature review. *International Journal of Wireless Information Networks*, *27*(3), 467–483. doi:10.1007/s10776-020-00491-7

Kavitha, C. R., Varalatchoumy, M., Mithuna, H. R., Bharathi, K., Geethalakshmi, N. M., & Boopathi, S. (2023). Energy Monitoring and Control in the Smart Grid: Integrated Intelligent IoT and ANFIS. In M. Arshad (Ed.), Advances in Bioinformatics and Biomedical Engineering. IGI Global., doi:10.4018/978-1-6684-6577-6.ch014

Khalid, T., Khan, A. N., Ali, M., Adeel, A., ur Rehman Khan, A., & Shuja, J. (2019). A fog-based security framework for intelligent traffic light control system. *Multimedia Tools and Applications*, *78*(17), 24595–24615. doi:10.1007/s11042-018-7008-z

Koshariya, A. K., Kalaiyarasi, D., Jovith, A. A., Sivakami, T., Hasan, D. S., & Boopathi, S. (2023). AI-Enabled IoT and WSN-Integrated Smart Agriculture System. In *Artificial Intelligence Tools and Technologies for Smart Farming and Agriculture Practices* (pp. 200–218). IGI Global. doi:10.4018/978-1-6684-8516-3.ch011

Kumar, B. M., Kumar, K. K., Sasikala, P., Sampath, B., Gopi, B., & Sundaram, S. (2024). Sustainable Green Energy Generation From Waste Water: IoT and ML Integration. In B. K. Mishra (Ed.), Practice, Progress, and Proficiency in Sustainability. IGI Global. doi:10.4018/979-8-3693-1186-8.ch024

Kumar, P. R., Meenakshi, S., Shalini, S., Devi, S. R., & Boopathi, S. (2023). Soil Quality Prediction in Context Learning Approaches Using Deep Learning and Blockchain for Smart Agriculture. In R. Kumar, A. B. Abdul Hamid, & N. I. Binti Ya'akub (Eds.), Advances in Computational Intelligence and Robotics. IGI Global. doi:10.4018/978-1-6684-9151-5.ch001

Lin, S.-Y., Du, Y., Ko, P.-C., Wu, T.-J., Ho, P.-T., Sivakumar, V., & Subbareddy, R. (2020). Fog computing based hybrid deep learning framework in effective inspection system for smart manufacturing. *Computer Communications*, *160*, 636–642. doi:10.1016/j.comcom.2020.05.044

Lupton, D., & Leahy, D. (2019). Reimagining digital health education: Reflections on the possibilities of the storyboarding method. *Health Education Journal*, *78*(6), 633–646. doi:10.1177/0017896919841413

Maguluri, L. P., Arularasan, A. N., & Boopathi, S. (2023). Assessing Security Concerns for AI-Based Drones in Smart Cities. In R. Kumar, A. B. Abdul Hamid, & N. I. Binti Ya'akub (Eds.), Advances in Computational Intelligence and Robotics. IGI Global. doi:10.4018/978-1-6684-9151-5.ch002

Maheswari, B. U., Imambi, S. S., Hasan, D., Meenakshi, S., Pratheep, V., & Boopathi, S. (2023). Internet of Things and Machine Learning-Integrated Smart Robotics. In Global Perspectives on Robotics and Autonomous Systems: Development and Applications (pp. 240–258). IGI Global. doi:10.4018/978-1-6684-7791-5.ch010

Morris, B. B., Rossi, B., & Fuemmeler, B. (2022). The role of digital health technology in rural cancer care delivery: A systematic review. *The Journal of Rural Health*, *38*(3), 493–511. doi:10.1111/jrh.12619 PMID:34480506

Munawar, H. S., Hammad, A. W., & Waller, S. T. (2021). A review on flood management technologies related to image processing and machine learning. *Automation in Construction*, *132*, 103916. doi:10.1016/j.autcon.2021.103916

Nkenyereye, L., Islam, S. R., Bilal, M., Abdullah-Al-Wadud, M., Alamri, A., & Nayyar, A. (2021). Secure crowd-sensing protocol for fog-based vehicular cloud. *Future Generation Computer Systems*, *120*, 61–75. doi:10.1016/j.future.2021.02.008

Pareek, K., Tiwari, P. K., & Bhatnagar, V. (2021). Fog computing in healthcare: A review. *IOP Conference Series. Materials Science and Engineering*, *1099*(1), 012025. doi:10.1088/1757-899X/1099/1/012025

Pramila, P., Amudha, S., Saravanan, T., Sankar, S. R., Poongothai, E., & Boopathi, S. (2023). Design and Development of Robots for Medical Assistance: An Architectural Approach. In Contemporary Applications of Data Fusion for Advanced Healthcare Informatics (pp. 260–282). IGI Global.

Ramudu, K., Mohan, V. M., Jyothirmai, D., Prasad, D., Agrawal, R., & Boopathi, S. (2023). Machine Learning and Artificial Intelligence in Disease Prediction: Applications, Challenges, Limitations, Case Studies, and Future Directions. In Contemporary Applications of Data Fusion for Advanced Healthcare Informatics (pp. 297–318). IGI Global.

Reddy, M. A., Gaurav, A., Ushasukhanya, S., Rao, V. C. S., Bhattacharya, S., & Boopathi, S. (2023). Bio-Medical Wastes Handling Strategies During the COVID-19 Pandemic. In Multidisciplinary Approaches to Organizational Governance During Health Crises (pp. 90–111). IGI Global. doi:10.4018/978-1-7998-9213-7.ch006

Satav, S. D., Hasan, D. S., Pitchai, R., Mohanaprakash, T. A., Sultanuddin, S. J., & Boopathi, S. (2024). Next Generation of Internet of Things (NGIoT) in Healthcare Systems. In Practice, Progress, and Proficiency in Sustainability (pp. 307–330). IGI Global. doi:10.4018/979-8-3693-1186-8.ch017

Satav, S. D., Lamani, D. G, H. K., Kumar, N. M. G., Manikandan, S., & Sampath, B. (2024). Energy and Battery Management in the Era of Cloud Computing. In Practice, Progress, and Proficiency in Sustainability (pp. 141–166). IGI Global. doi:10.4018/979-8-3693-1186-8.ch009

Satybaldy, A., Hasselgren, A., & Nowostawski, M. (2022). Decentralized Identity Management for E-Health Applications: State-of-the-Art and Guidance for Future Work. *Blockchain in Healthcare Today*, 5. doi:10.30953/bhty.v5.195 PMID:36779018

Sengeni, D., Padmapriya, G., Imambi, S. S., Suganthi, D., Suri, A., & Boopathi, S. (2023). Biomedical Waste Handling Method Using Artificial Intelligence Techniques. In *Handbook of Research on Safe Disposal Methods of Municipal Solid Wastes for a Sustainable Environment* (pp. 306–323). IGI Global. doi:10.4018/978-1-6684-8117-2.ch022

Shahzad, A., Gherbi, A., & Zhang, K. (2022). Enabling fog–blockchain computing for autonomous-vehicle-parking system: A solution to reinforce iot–cloud platform for future smart parking. *Sensors (Basel)*, *22*(13), 4849. doi:10.3390/s22134849 PMID:35808345

Shi, F., Wang, J., Shi, J., Wu, Z., Wang, Q., Tang, Z., He, K., Shi, Y., & Shen, D. (2020). Review of artificial intelligence techniques in imaging data acquisition, segmentation, and diagnosis for COVID-19. *IEEE Reviews in Biomedical Engineering*, *14*, 4–15. doi:10.1109/RBME.2020.2987975 PMID:32305937

Subha, S., Inbamalar, T., Komala, C., Suresh, L. R., Boopathi, S., & Alaskar, K. (2023). A Remote Health Care Monitoring system using internet of medical things (IoMT). *IEEE Explore*, 1–6.

Sun, G., Sun, S., Sun, J., Yu, H., Du, X., & Guizani, M. (2019). Security and privacy preservation in fog-based crowd sensing on the internet of vehicles. *Journal of Network and Computer Applications*, *134*, 89–99. doi:10.1016/j.jnca.2019.02.018

Syamala, M., Komala, C., Pramila, P., Dash, S., Meenakshi, S., & Boopathi, S. (2023). Machine Learning-Integrated IoT-Based Smart Home Energy Management System. In *Handbook of Research on Deep Learning Techniques for Cloud-Based Industrial IoT* (pp. 219–235). IGI Global. doi:10.4018/978-1-6684-8098-4.ch013

Tebeje, T. H., & Klein, J. (2021). Applications of e-health to support person-centered health care at the time of COVID-19 pandemic. *Telemedicine Journal and e-Health*, *27*(2), 150–158. doi:10.1089/tmj.2020.0201 PMID:32746750

Ugandar, R. E., Rahamathunnisa, U., Sajithra, S., Christiana, M. B. V., Palai, B. K., & Boopathi, S. (2023). Hospital Waste Management Using Internet of Things and Deep Learning: Enhanced Efficiency and Sustainability. In M. Arshad (Ed.), Advances in Bioinformatics and Biomedical Engineering. IGI Global. doi:10.4018/978-1-6684-6577-6.ch015

Veeranjaneyulu, R., Boopathi, S., Narasimharao, J., Gupta, K. K., Reddy, R. V. K., & Ambika, R. (2023). Identification of Heart Diseases using Novel Machine Learning Method. *IEEE- Explore*, 1–6.

Venkateswaran, N., Kumar, S. S., Diwakar, G., Gnanasangeetha, D., & Boopathi, S. (2023). Synthetic Biology for Waste Water to Energy Conversion: IoT and AI Approaches. In M. Arshad (Ed.), Advances in Bioinformatics and Biomedical Engineering. IGI Global. doi:10.4018/978-1-6684-6577-6.ch017

Venkateswaran, N., Vidhya, K., Ayyannan, M., Chavan, S. M., Sekar, K., & Boopathi, S. (2023). A Study on Smart Energy Management Framework Using Cloud Computing. In 5G, Artificial Intelligence, and Next Generation Internet of Things: Digital Innovation for Green and Sustainable Economies (pp. 189–212). IGI Global. doi:10.4018/978-1-6684-8634-4.ch009

Yang, Y., Luo, X., Chu, X., & Zhou, M.-T. (2020). *Fog-enabled intelligent IoT systems*. Springer. doi:10.1007/978-3-030-23185-9

Yang, Y., Luo, X., Chu, X., Zhou, M.-T., Yang, Y., Luo, X., Chu, X., & Zhou, M.-T. (2020). Fog-enabled intelligent transportation system. *Fog-Enabled Intelligent IoT Systems*, 163–184.

Yazdani, A., Dashti, S. F., & Safdari, Y. (2023). A fog-assisted information model based on priority queue and clinical decision support systems. *Health Informatics Journal*, 29(1). doi:10.1177/14604582231152792 PMID:36645733

Zekrifa, D. M. S., Kulkarni, M., Bhagyalakshmi, A., Devireddy, N., Gupta, S., & Boopathi, S. (2023). Integrating Machine Learning and AI for Improved Hydrological Modeling and Water Resource Management. In *Artificial Intelligence Applications in Water Treatment and Water Resource Management* (pp. 46–70). IGI Global. doi:10.4018/978-1-6684-6791-6.ch003

Zhou, S. K., Greenspan, H., Davatzikos, C., Duncan, J. S., Van Ginneken, B., Madabhushi, A., Prince, J. L., Rueckert, D., & Summers, R. M. (2021). A review of deep learning in medical imaging: Imaging traits, technology trends, case studies with progress highlights, and future promises. *Proceedings of the IEEE*, 109(5), 820–838. doi:10.1109/JPROC.2021.3054390 PMID:37786449

Chapter 9

Artificial Intelligence (AI) and Machine Learning (ML) Technology–Driven Structural Systems

Akash Mohanty
ⓘ https://orcid.org/0000-0002-1215-0642
School of Mechanical Engineering, Vellore Institute of Technology, India

G. S. Raghavendra
ⓘ https://orcid.org/0009-0008-9897-2559
Department of Computer Science and Engineering, Koneru Lakshmaiah Education Foundation, India

J. Rajini
ⓘ https://orcid.org/0000-0002-5080-7545
Department of English, Kongu Engineering College, India

B. Sachuthananthan
Department Mechanical Engineering, Sree Vidyanikethan Engineering College, India

E. Afreen Banu
Department of Computing Technologies, Saveetha School of Engineering, Saveetha Institute of Medical and Technical Sciences (SIMATS), India

B. Subhi
MEC Engineering College (Autonomous), India

ABSTRACT

This chapter explores the integration of artificial intelligence (AI) and machine learning (ML) technologies in structural engineering, focusing on their applications in automating design processes, optimizing structural configurations, and assessing performance metrics. It highlights the efficiency of AI-driven algorithms in generating design alternatives, predicting structural behavior, and enhancing sustainability. The chapter also provides a performance comparison framework for evaluating different structural designs, considering safety, cost-effectiveness, and environmental impact. It discusses case studies and practical examples that demonstrate the advantages of AI/ML-driven autonomous design in achieving superior structural performance while minimizing resource utilization. The chapter emphasizes the potential of AI and ML in revolutionizing structural engineering, enabling engineers to create sustainable and high-performing structures, contributing to a more environmentally conscious and economically viable built environment.

DOI: 10.4018/979-8-3693-0968-1.ch009

INTRODUCTION

The field of structural engineering is facing a growing demand for innovative solutions that prioritize sustainability and performance efficiency, as architects face the challenge of optimizing structures for safety and sustainability while adhering to strict budget constraints. The traditional structural design method is time-consuming and heavily reliant on human expertise. Advancements in AI and machine learning have revolutionized this process. This chapter explores the integration of intelligent structural engineering with optimization techniques, performance comparison methodologies, and sustainable design principles, all powered by AI and ML technologies (L. Sun et al., 2020a).

This chapter explores the use of AI and ML in structural engineering, focusing on their automation, optimization, and performance metrics. It also discusses sustainable design principles and their integration with AI and ML to create more environmentally conscious structures. Through case studies and practical examples, it showcases the benefits of AI/ML-driven autonomous design, improving structural performance and resource utilization. The chapter also addresses challenges and ethical considerations associated with AI and ML integration in structural engineering (Möhring et al., 2020).

Artificial intelligence and machine learning are revolutionizing structural engineering by providing new tools and techniques for building design, analysis, and maintenance. AI and ML algorithms can analyze vast datasets, identifying patterns that humans cannot, leading to improved predictive modeling and risk assessment. Engineers can use AI to analyze historical data, such as construction failures and maintenance records, to identify potential issues and recommend design modifications, ultimately improving the safety and longevity of structures (Shea & Smith, 2005).

AI-powered design optimization tools aid engineers in creating efficient and cost-effective structures by suggesting innovative solutions considering parameters like materials, load distribution, and environmental factors, thereby reducing costs and minimizing environmental impact. AI and ML are enhancing real-time monitoring and maintenance of structures, enabling early detection of damage and reducing maintenance costs. This proactive approach ensures building safety and durability. AI-driven simulations, such as complex finite element analysis and computational fluid dynamics, can improve the accuracy and efficiency of structural analysis, enabling more resilient and reliable design of structures under various conditions (Liu et al., 2004). The integration of AI and ML with Building Information Modeling (BIM) enhances collaborative decision-making, improving stakeholder communication, project management, and design, construction, and maintenance outcomes. These tools are becoming indispensable in structural engineering, paving the way for a new era of innovation and efficiency. AI and ML enable structural engineers to create intricate designs that optimize cost, energy efficiency, and material usage. ML algorithms can adapt to local environmental conditions, ensuring structures can withstand earthquakes or extreme weather events. AI can also analyze complex data from sensors in buildings, providing real-time feedback on structural health (Salehi & Burgueño, 2018).

AI and ML are crucial in risk assessment, identifying potential weaknesses in new projects and minimizing structural failures. They also aid in advancing sustainable construction practices by optimizing building designs for energy efficiency and sustainability. AI algorithms can identify renewable energy sources and fine-tune HVAC systems for optimal energy consumption (L. Sun et al., 2020b). ML supports the use of sustainable materials by analyzing their performance and environmental impact. AI and ML are also accelerating innovation in materials science and construction techniques. They can help engineers discover new composite materials with improved strength and durability (Huang & Fu, 2019). Additionally, AI can optimize construction processes, enhancing productivity and reducing waste. By analyzing construction data, AI can identify areas for process scalability, leading to cost savings and more sustainable practices (Pan & Zhang, 2021). AI and ML are increasingly being used in urban infrastructure design and maintenance, enabling predictive maintenance systems for critical components like bridges and tunnels. These smart city initiatives improve traffic flow, manage utilities, and respond to emergencies, ensuring the efficient functioning of urban environments (Guo et al., 2021).

Artificial intelligence and machine learning are revolutionizing structural engineering by improving safety, efficiency, and sustainability. These technologies enable data-driven decisions, optimize designs, and manage structural health, enhancing the built environment's quality and resilience. As AI and ML advance, their applications in structural engineering will become more sophisticated, paving the way for a new era of innovation.

Objectives

- To elucidate the role of AI and ML in enhancing the field of structural engineering.
- To present various optimization techniques that leverage AI/ML for structural design.
- To establish a framework for performance comparison, including safety, cost-effectiveness, and environmental impact assessment.
- To emphasize the importance of sustainability in structural engineering and how AI/ML can contribute to sustainable design.

- To provide real-world case studies demonstrating the practical application of AI/ML-driven autonomous design.
- To discuss the benefits, challenges, and ethical considerations associated with the use of AI and ML in the field.

TYPES OF INTELLIGENT STRUCTURAL ANALYSIS

In the ever-evolving field of structural engineering, the quest for safer, more efficient, and sustainable structures has led to the integration of cutting-edge technologies. Among these, artificial intelligence (AI) and machine learning (ML) have emerged as formidable tools that have the potential to revolutionize the way we analyze, assess, and optimize structures. This chapter is dedicated to exploring the various types of intelligent structural analysis, shedding light on how AI and ML are applied to address diverse challenges across the spectrum of structural engineering (Dolšak & Novak, 2011; Soh & Soh, 1988).

Structural Health Monitoring (SHM): Structural health monitoring is a critical facet of intelligent structural analysis. It involves the continuous assessment of a structure's condition and performance in real-time. AI and ML play a pivotal role in SHM by processing sensor data, identifying anomalies, and predicting potential issues before they escalate. This section delves into the methodologies and technologies used in SHM, showcasing how AI and ML enhance the safety and longevity of structures.

Predictive Analysis and Modeling: Predictive analysis and modeling harness the power of AI and ML to foresee how structures will behave under varying conditions. Engineers can simulate and predict structural responses to environmental factors, loads, and other variables with remarkable precision. This section explores the applications of predictive analysis, including earthquake forecasting, weather impact assessment, and long-term structural performance predictions.

Optimization Techniques: Structural optimization lies at the heart of creating efficient and cost-effective structures. AI-driven optimization techniques, such as genetic algorithms and particle swarm optimization, enable engineers to explore a vast design space to identify optimal configurations. This section delves into the principles of optimization and showcases how AI and ML can lead to resource-efficient and sustainable structural solutions.

Performance Evaluation and Simulation: Performance evaluation and simulation are essential for assessing how structures will fare under various scenarios and loads. AI and ML models facilitate complex simulations, enabling engineers to analyze structural behavior and make informed decisions. This section discusses the role of AI and ML in simulating structural responses to dynamic events, such as wind, traffic, and seismic activity.

Sustainability Assessment: Sustainability assessment has become a paramount concern in structural engineering. AI and ML assist in evaluating the environmental impact, energy efficiency, and carbon footprint of structures. This section explores how these technologies enable engineers to make environmentally conscious decisions, promoting sustainable design practices (Rahamathunnisa et al., 2024; Vijayakumar et al., 2024).

This chapter explores AI and ML-powered structural analysis methods for monitoring structural health, predicting behavior, optimizing designs, evaluating performance, and assessing sustainability, promoting resilient, efficient, and sustainable structures in structural engineering.

INTEGRATING MACHINE LEARNING (ML) INTO VARIOUS TYPES OF STRUCTURAL ANALYSIS

The integration of machine learning in intelligent structural analysis can improve accuracy, efficiency, and adaptability, as illustrated in Figure 1. This section provides an explanation on the integration of machine learning into various types of structural analysis (H. Sun et al., 2021; Westermayr et al., 2021).

Structural Health Monitoring (SHM)

- **Sensor Data Analysis:** ML algorithms can process sensor data, including strain gauges, accelerometers, and temperature sensors, to continuously monitor a structure's health. They can detect anomalies, identify patterns, and predict potential issues, such as cracks or material degradation.

Figure 1. Integrating machine learning (ML) into various types of structural analysis

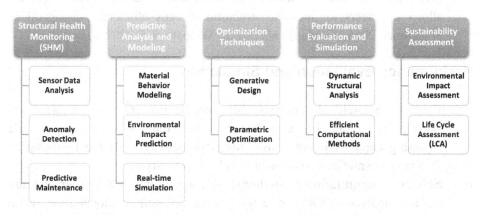

- **Anomaly Detection:** ML models, particularly anomaly detection algorithms like Isolation Forests or One-Class SVMs, can identify deviations from normal structural behavior, signaling the need for inspections or maintenance.
- **Predictive Maintenance:** ML-driven predictive maintenance models can estimate when specific structural components may require maintenance or replacement based on historical data, reducing downtime and repair costs.

Predictive Analysis and Modeling

- **Material Behavior Modeling:** ML can be used to model the behavior of materials under different conditions, improving the accuracy of predictive models for structural responses (Boopathi et al., 2021; Haribalaji et al., 2022; Kannan et al., 2022).
- **Environmental Impact Prediction:** ML algorithms can predict the impact of environmental factors, such as temperature changes or corrosion, on structural performance (Arunprasad & Boopathi, 2019; Boopathi, 2022c; Gowri et al., 2023a).
- **Real-time Simulation:** ML can enable real-time simulations that consider dynamic variables, helping engineers make immediate decisions based on changing conditions.

Optimization Techniques

- **Generative Design:** ML can drive generative design processes, exploring a vast design space to find optimal configurations. Genetic algorithms and neural networks can generate design alternatives that meet specified constraints and objectives.
- **Parametric Optimization:** ML models can optimize design parameters iteratively, considering various constraints and objectives. This approach allows engineers to fine-tune structural designs efficiently (Boopathi & Sivakumar, 2016; Kalidas et al., 2012a; Sampath et al., 2022a).

Performance Evaluation and Simulation

- **Dynamic Structural Analysis:** ML models can improve the accuracy of dynamic structural analysis by accounting for non-linear behavior and capturing complex interactions. This is particularly valuable in scenarios involving seismic analysis or wind load assessments.
- **Efficient Computational Methods:** ML algorithms can accelerate finite element analysis (FEA) simulations, reducing computational time while

maintaining accuracy. Reduced analysis time allows for more extensive parametric studies.

Sustainability Assessment

- **Environmental Impact Assessment:** ML can aid in assessing the environmental protection impact of structural designs by considering factors such as material choices, energy efficiency, and carbon emissions. This information informs sustainable design decisions.
- **Life Cycle Assessment (LCA):** ML can be used to conduct LCA, analyzing the environmental impact of structures over their entire life cycle. ML models can help identify opportunities for reducing environmental footprints.

Machine learning (ML) is being integrated into structural analysis, enhancing accuracy, efficiency, and adaptive decision-making. This approach leads to safer, more efficient, and sustainable structures in the built environment, based on historical and real-time data updates.

INTELLIGENT STRUCTURAL ENGINEERING

The Role of AI and ML in Structural Engineering

The integration of AI and machine learning technologies has revolutionized structural engineering by enabling efficient and effective problem-solving. These advanced computational tools revolutionize the design, analysis, and decision-making processes, enabling structural engineers to tackle complex challenges more efficiently. This section explores the pivotal role of AI and ML in shaping the future of structural engineering (Perry et al., 2022).

- *Enhancing Decision-Making:* AI and ML algorithms assist engineers in making informed decisions by analyzing vast datasets, historical performance data, and real-time information, thereby improving the reliability of structural designs.
- *Design Optimization:* AI-driven optimization algorithms enable the exploration of a multitude of design alternatives, leading to more efficient and cost-effective structural solutions.
- *Predictive Maintenance:* ML models can predict structural deterioration, allowing for proactive maintenance, cost reduction, and improved safety.

Figure 2. Integration of artificial intelligence (AI) in structural engineering

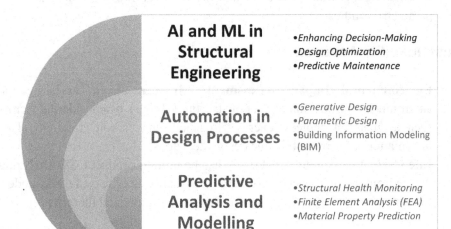

Automation in Design Processes

One of the primary benefits of AI and ML in structural engineering is automation. Automation streamlines the design process, reduces human error, and accelerates project timelines. In this section, we will explore how AI and ML technologies are transforming various aspects of design automation (M. Kumar et al., 2023; Pachiappan et al., 2024; Sathish et al., 2023).

- *Generative Design:* AI-powered generative design tools can autonomously generate numerous design alternatives based on specified criteria, saving engineers valuable time in the conceptual design phase.
- *Parametric Design:* ML algorithms can optimize design parameters iteratively, achieving optimal structural configurations while considering various constraints.
- *BIM Integration:* Building Information Modeling (BIM) platforms leverage AI to enhance collaboration among project stakeholders and provide real-time updates on structural changes.

Predictive Analysis and Modelling

AI and ML excel in predictive analysis and modelling, allowing engineers to anticipate structural behaviour accurately. These technologies enable the creation of robust predictive models that consider various environmental conditions and loads.

- *Structural Health Monitoring:* ML models can predict structural health based on sensor data, enabling early detection of issues and ensuring structural safety.
- *Finite Element Analysis (FEA):* AI-assisted FEA simulations provide more accurate and efficient results, reducing computational time and resources.
- *Material Property Prediction:* ML models can predict material properties and performance, aiding in the selection of the most suitable materials for a project.

In conclusion, AI and ML have become indispensable tools in the field of structural engineering, driving advancements in automation, optimization, and predictive analysis. Engineers can leverage these technologies to create safer, more efficient, and sustainable structures, ultimately shaping the future of the built environment. The next section of this chapter will delve into various optimization techniques enabled by AI and ML in structural engineering (Dhanya et al., 2023; Gunasekaran & Boopathi, 2023a; Vanitha et al., 2023).

OPTIMIZATION TECHNIQUES

Optimization is at the core of structural engineering, aiming to find the best possible solution given a set of constraints and objectives (Figure 3). This section provides an overview of the optimization methods commonly employed in structural engineering

Figure 3. Various optimization applied to solve core of structural engineering problems

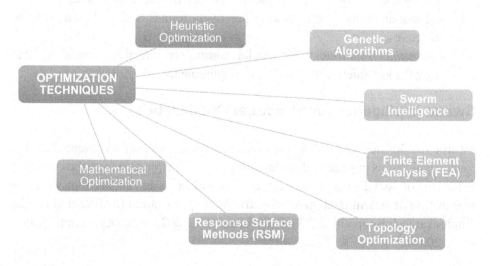

(Boopathi, 2013a; Haribalaji et al., 2021; Kalidas et al., 2012b; Myilsamy & Sampath, 2017; Nishanth et al., 2023; Sampath et al., 2023a).

- *Mathematical Optimization:* This traditional approach relies on mathematical models and techniques such as linear programming, nonlinear programming, and integer programming to optimize structural designs.
- *Heuristic Optimization:* Heuristic methods, unlike mathematical optimization, do not guarantee an optimal solution but are often more suitable for complex problems. They include genetic algorithms, particle swarm optimization, simulated annealing, and more.

Genetic Algorithms in Structural Design

Genetic algorithms (GAs) are a powerful heuristic optimization technique inspired by the principles of natural selection and genetics. In structural engineering, GAs have gained prominence for their ability to search a vast design space efficiently. This subsection explores the application of GAs in structural design optimization (Boopathi et al., 2022; Boopathi & Sivakumar, 2013; Hussain & Srimathy, 2023; Sampath et al., 2022b).

- *Chromosome Representation:* GAs represent structural designs as chromosomes composed of genes encoding design parameters. Operators like mutation and crossover are used to evolve and improve the population of designs.
- *Objective Functions:* GAs utilize objective functions to evaluate the performance of designs, considering factors like structural integrity, cost, and sustainability. The algorithm iteratively refines designs based on these objectives.
- *Constraint Handling:* GAs handle constraints effectively, ensuring that designs meet safety codes and other requirements.

Swarm Intelligence for Structural Optimization

Swarm intelligence is another nature-inspired optimization technique that has found applications in structural engineering. It draws inspiration from the collective behaviour of social organisms, such as ants and bees. In this section, we delve into the use of swarm intelligence for structural optimization (Anitha et al., 2023; Gunasekaran & Boopathi, 2023b; P. R. Kumar et al., 2023; Venkateswaran, Vidhya, et al., 2023).

- *Particle Swarm Optimization (PSO):* PSO is a popular swarm intelligence algorithm. In structural optimization, PSO uses a population of particles that move through the design space, adjusting their positions based on personal best and global best solutions to find optimal designs.
- *Ant Colony Optimization (ACO):* ACO algorithms are inspired by the foraging behaviour of ants. In structural optimization, ACO can be used to find optimal pathways for load distribution in structures, leading to more efficient designs.
- *Benefits:* Swarm intelligence algorithms are well-suited for problems with complex and dynamic design spaces, making them valuable tools in optimizing intricate structural systems.

The other optimization techniques will delve into further details (Gowri et al., 2023b; Kumara et al., 2023; Rahamathunnisa et al., 2023; Samikannu et al., 2022; Vennila et al., 2022a).

Finite Element Analysis (FEA): FEA is a widely used numerical technique for solving complex structural problems. It divides a structure into smaller, finite-sized elements, allowing engineers to analyze stress, deformation, and other behaviors. Optimization in FEA involves adjusting parameters (such as material properties, element sizes, or boundary conditions) to achieve desired structural performance while minimizing weight or cost.

Topology Optimization: Topology optimization is a technique that optimizes material distribution within a given design space to achieve specific objectives, such as minimizing weight while maintaining structural integrity. AI and ML can enhance topology optimization by automating the process of generating and evaluating design alternatives.

Response Surface Methods (RSM): RSM is a statistical technique used to approximate the behavior of a complex system, such as a structural model, with a simpler mathematical model. It is often used in conjunction with optimization algorithms to reduce the computational cost of finding optimal designs (Gowri et al., 2023a; Sampath et al., 2023b; Vennila et al., 2022b).

Simulated Annealing: Simulated annealing is a probabilistic optimization algorithm inspired by the annealing process in metallurgy. It explores the design space by probabilistically accepting or rejecting changes to the design. It can be effective in finding near-optimal solutions for complex structural optimization problems.

Gradient-Based Optimization: Gradient-based optimization methods use gradients (derivatives) of the objective function to guide the search for optimal solutions. These methods, such as gradient descent and conjugate gradient methods, are often used when the objective function is smooth and differentiable.

Multi-Objective Optimization: In structural analysis, it's common to have multiple conflicting objectives, such as minimizing cost and maximizing strength.

Multi-objective optimization techniques aim to find a set of solutions that represent trade-offs between these objectives, known as the Pareto front (Boopathi, 2013b; Gowri et al., 2023a; Paul et al., 2024).

Nonlinear Programming: Nonlinear programming methods are employed when structural analysis problems involve nonlinearities, such as material nonlinearity or geometric nonlinearities. Algorithms like Sequential Quadratic Programming (SQP) can be used to handle such complexities.

Discrete Optimization: In some structural design problems, design variables must take on discrete values, such as selecting standard beam sizes or bolt diameters. Discrete optimization algorithms, like integer programming or genetic algorithms with integer coding, are suited for such cases.

Surrogate-Based Optimization: Surrogate models, often built using machine learning techniques like Gaussian Process Regression, can be used to approximate the objective function. Surrogates enable faster optimization by reducing the number of costly structural simulations.

Reinforcement Learning (RL): RL, a subfield of machine learning, has found applications in structural optimization. RL agents can learn to make design decisions by interacting with a structural model over time, adapting designs based on learned rewards and penalties.

PERFORMANCE COMPARISON FRAMEWORK

Importance of Performance Metrics

In the realm of structural engineering, assessing the performance of different design alternatives is paramount. The selection of the most suitable design must consider various factors, ranging from safety and cost-effectiveness to environmental impact. The creation of a robust performance comparison framework is crucial for engineers to make informed decisions when selecting design alternatives (Hussain & Srimathy, 2023; Jeevanantham et al., 2022; Koshariya et al., 2023).

- *Multifaceted Decision-Making:* Performance metrics allow for a holistic evaluation of structural designs, considering diverse criteria and objectives.
- *Enhanced Sustainability:* A comprehensive framework ensures that sustainability considerations are integrated into the decision-making process, contributing to more environmentally responsible designs.

Safety Assessment

Safety is a fundamental concern in structural engineering. Evaluating the safety of a design alternative involves assessing its ability to withstand loads, adhere to safety codes and regulations, and mitigate risks effectively (Hanumanthakari et al., 2023; Sengeni et al., 2023; Ugandar et al., 2023).

- *Structural Integrity:* Safety assessments involve analyzing the structural integrity of a design, ensuring it can withstand expected loads and conditions without failure.
- *Risk Analysis:* Engineers employ risk analysis techniques to identify potential hazards and vulnerabilities in a design, taking proactive measures to mitigate risks.

Cost-Effectiveness Evaluation

Cost-effectiveness is a critical aspect of any structural engineering project. Evaluating cost-effectiveness involves considering the life cycle costs of a design, including initial construction costs, maintenance expenses, and potential future upgrades or replacements (Babu et al., 2022; Mohanty et al., 2023).

- *Life Cycle Cost Analysis (LCCA):* LCCA helps in determining the most cost-effective design option by considering both short-term and long-term costs.
- *Value Engineering:* Engineers explore design alternatives that maintain or enhance performance while reducing costs, thus achieving optimal cost-effectiveness.

Environmental Impact Assessment

The environmental impact of structural designs has gained significant attention in recent years. An environmental impact assessment evaluates the design's carbon footprint, energy efficiency, and overall contribution to sustainability (Boopathi, 2022d, 2022b; Boopathi, Alqahtani, et al., 2023; Gowri et al., 2023b; Maguluri, Ananth, et al., 2023).

- *Carbon Footprint:* Assessing the carbon emissions associated with a design helps identify opportunities for reducing its environmental impact.
- *Sustainable Materials:* Engineers evaluate the use of sustainable materials, energy-efficient systems, and environmentally friendly construction practices to reduce the environmental footprint of structures.

A well-defined performance comparison framework is crucial for comprehensive structural design evaluation, prioritizing safety, cost-effectiveness, and sustainability. This chapter will explore sustainable design principles and their integration into intelligent structural engineering processes using AI and ML technologies.

SUSTAINABLE DESIGN PRINCIPLES

Sustainable Design in Structural Engineering

Sustainability has become a central focus in the field of structural engineering. Sustainable design principles prioritize creating structures that minimize environmental impact, reduce resource consumption, and promote long-term resilience. This section delves into the integration of sustainability into structural engineering (Kavitha et al., 2023; Srinivas et al., 2023; Venkateswaran, Kumar, et al., 2023).

- *Holistic Approach:* Sustainable design encompasses a holistic approach that considers environmental, economic, and social factors, striving for a balance that benefits both the built and natural environments.
- *Long-Term Perspective:* Sustainable structures are designed with longevity in mind, aiming to minimize the need for repairs and replacements, which can be resource-intensive.

Energy Efficiency Considerations

Energy efficiency is a crucial aspect of sustainable design, particularly as buildings and infrastructure are significant consumers of energy. The implementation of energy-efficient strategies not only reduces operational costs but also mitigates environmental impact (Hussain & Srimathy, 2023; Ingle et al., 2023; Kumara et al., 2023; Syamala et al., 2023).

- *Passive Design:* Passive design strategies optimize a structure's orientation, insulation, and use of natural lighting to minimize the need for heating, cooling, and artificial lighting.
- *Renewable Energy Integration:* Sustainable structures often incorporate renewable energy sources such as solar panels, wind turbines, or geothermal systems to reduce reliance on non-renewable energy sources.
- *Smart Building Systems:* Building management systems and automation can optimize energy consumption by adjusting lighting, HVAC, and other systems based on occupancy and environmental conditions.

Material Selection for Sustainability

The choice of materials used in construction significantly impacts a structure's sustainability. Sustainable material selection aims to minimize resource depletion, reduce waste, and promote eco-friendly production practices (Boopathi, Umareddy, et al., 2023; Boopathi & Davim, 2023b, 2023a; Fowziya et al., 2023).

- *Recycled and Recyclable Materials:* Using recycled and recyclable materials reduces the environmental footprint of a structure and promotes a circular economy.
- *Low-Impact Materials:* Sustainable design often involves selecting materials with a lower environmental impact, such as those with lower embodied energy or emissions during production.
- *Local Sourcing:* Sourcing materials locally reduces transportation-related emissions and supports the local economy.
- *Life Cycle Assessment (LCA):* LCA evaluates the environmental impact of materials from extraction and production to use and disposal, aiding in informed material selection decisions.

Sustainable design principles are crucial for creating environmentally responsible, energy-efficient, and economically viable structures in structural engineering. The integration of AI and ML technologies enhances sustainability considerations in structural design. The next section will explore how AI and ML can be applied to achieve sustainable design goals in autonomous design contexts.

AI AND ML IN SUSTAINABLE AUTONOMOUS DESIGN

Sustainability is a critical consideration in modern structural engineering, and integrating it into AI and ML models is essential for creating truly autonomous, sustainable designs (Figure 4). This section delves into the integration of sustainability into AI and ML models for structural engineering (Boopathi & Kanike, 2023a; Maheswari et al., 2023; Ramudu et al., 2023; Syamala et al., 2023).

Sustainability Metrics

AI and ML models can incorporate sustainability metrics and objectives into the design optimization process. This involves defining specific sustainability goals, such as reducing carbon emissions, minimizing resource use (e.g., materials and energy), or enhancing energy efficiency. The AI-ML system then integrates these objectives

Figure 4. AI and ML in sustainable autonomous design

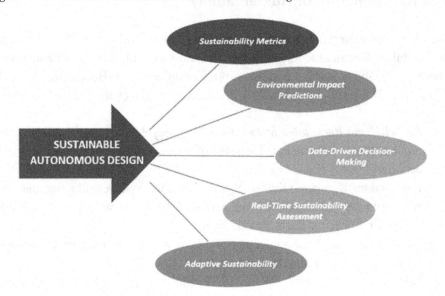

as part of the optimization algorithm. During the design process, the system evaluates design alternatives based on how well they meet these sustainability metrics.

For example, in designing a building, an AI-ML system can consider various factors like the choice of materials, insulation, HVAC systems, and renewable energy sources to optimize the design for reduced energy consumption, lower carbon emissions, and overall sustainability.

Environmental Impact Predictions

ML algorithms can predict the environmental impact of different design alternatives by analyzing historical data and making data-driven projections. For instance, if engineers are considering different materials for a construction project, ML models can estimate the environmental footprint associated with each material choice. This includes factors like embodied carbon, energy use, and water consumption during production and transportation (Boopathi, 2022b; Maguluri, Ananth, et al., 2023; Sampath, 2021; Venkateswaran, Kumar, et al., 2023).

Engineers can make informed decisions by estimating environmental impact, ensuring they choose materials and designs that minimize negative environmental consequences, contributing to an eco-friendlier construction process.

Data-Driven Decision-Making

AI and ML models excel at analyzing vast datasets, which is particularly valuable in assessing sustainability factors. These models can process data related to energy consumption, emissions, resource utilization, and other relevant sustainability indicators. They identify patterns and relationships within the data that may not be apparent through traditional analysis.

Through data-driven insights, engineers gain a deeper understanding of how different design choices impact the environment. They can identify areas for improvement to improve sustainability and make more informed decisions during the design process.

Real-Time Sustainability Assessment

AI-ML systems can be implemented to continuously monitor and assess a structure's sustainability performance during its entire lifecycle. Sensors and IoT devices can collect data on energy usage, structural integrity, and environmental conditions in real time. ML models process this data to provide ongoing assessments of a structure's sustainability (Boopathi, 2022a; Boopathi, Kumar, et al., 2023; Boopathi & Davim, 2023b; Domakonda et al., 2022; Hussain & Srimathy, 2023; Samikannu et al., 2022; Sampath, 2021).

The system detects deviations from sustainability goals or environmental parameters, suggesting adjustments or improvements, such as optimizing HVAC settings or incorporating insulation for thermal efficiency, ensuring structures remain sustainable as conditions change over time.

Adaptive Sustainability

AI and ML models can adapt designs in real time to environmental conditions or sustainability goals, such as adjusting heating and cooling settings if a building's energy usage exceeds predefined thresholds. Integrating sustainability into AI-ML models allows engineers to achieve sustainability objectives autonomously and adaptively. This section explores case studies and practical examples of AI and ML-driven autonomous design, achieving superior structural performance while minimizing resource utilization and promoting sustainability (Boopathi, 2024; Boopathi & Kanike, 2023b; Verma et al., 2024).

CASE STUDIES

Case Study 1: The AI-Optimized Skyscraper

In a major metropolitan area, a project aimed to design a high-rise skyscraper that would maximize usable space, energy efficiency, and environmental sustainability. AI-driven generative design algorithms were employed to explore thousands of design possibilities, considering factors such as structural stability, wind load resistance, and natural lighting.

The AI model generated designs that optimized the building's shape and layout to minimize energy consumption for heating, cooling, and lighting. Moreover, the model considered sustainable materials with low embodied energy and carbon emissions. The final design reduced the building's carbon footprint by 30% compared to traditional designs while providing an additional 10% of usable space.

Case Study 2: Rehabilitation of an Aging Bridge

Engineers used machine learning (ML) algorithms to assess an aging bridge's structural health, identifying areas of deterioration and stress concentration. AI-ML models predicted future structural weaknesses based on historical data and environmental conditions. The system recommended targeted repairs and retrofitting, resulting in a 20% cost savings compared to traditional methods. The bridge now has improved structural integrity and a longer lifespan.

Case Study 3: Sustainable Transportation Infrastructure

A government agency responsible for transportation infrastructure sought to reduce the carbon footprint of its projects. AI-ML models were used to analyze traffic patterns, vehicle emissions, and environmental data to optimize the design of road networks and public transit systems (Boopathi, 2024; Maguluri, Arularasan, et al., 2023).

The AI-ML system recommended strategies such as traffic flow optimization, the integration of electric vehicle charging stations, and the use of eco-friendly road materials. As a result, the agency reduced emissions by 15%, enhanced traffic flow, and promoted sustainable transportation options.

These case studies demonstrate the practical application of AI and ML-driven autonomous design in structural engineering. By leveraging these technologies, engineers can optimize designs, reduce resource consumption, and promote sustainability, contributing to a more environmentally conscious and economically viable built environment.

BENEFITS AND CHALLENGES

Advantages of AI-ML in Structural Engineering

The integration of AI and machine learning technologies in structural engineering offers numerous advantages (Liu et al., 2004; Möhring et al., 2020; Shea & Smith, 2005).

- *Efficiency and Speed:* AI and ML enable the automation of design processes, reducing the time required to explore design alternatives, conduct simulations, and analyze data.
- *Optimization:* These technologies excel at optimization, allowing engineers to find more efficient and cost-effective structural solutions in complex design spaces.
- *Predictive Analysis:* ML models can accurately predict structural behavior, helping engineers identify potential issues early in the design phase.
- *Sustainability:* AI-ML models can integrate sustainability considerations seamlessly into designs, promoting eco-friendly and energy-efficient solutions.
- *Cost Savings:* AI-ML-driven designs often lead to cost savings in terms of material usage, construction, and maintenance.
- *Enhanced Safety:* AI can assist in structural health monitoring, identifying safety concerns and structural issues that might be missed in traditional inspections.

Challenges and Ethical Considerations

AI and ML offer significant advantages in structural engineering, but they also present challenges and ethical issues (Liu et al., 2004; H. Sun et al., 2021).

- *Data Quality and Bias:* The effectiveness of AI-ML models heavily depends on the quality and representativeness of training data. Biased or incomplete data can lead to biased outcomes.
- *Complexity:* Implementing AI and ML in structural engineering requires expertise in both engineering and data science, which may pose a barrier for some professionals.
- *Privacy and Security:* The use of AI in structural health monitoring raises privacy and security concerns, as it involves collecting and analyzing data from sensors and IoT devices.

- *Ethical Decision-Making:* Autonomous AI-ML systems may raise ethical questions, particularly when it comes to decisions that impact safety, the environment, or societal well-being.
- *Regulatory Compliance:* Compliance with existing regulations and standards can be challenging when implementing AI-ML in engineering, especially in highly regulated industries.
- *Interpretability:* Some AI-ML models are complex and not easily interpretable, making it difficult for engineers to understand and trust their recommendations.

AI and ML in structural engineering necessitates meticulous planning, ethical frameworks, and continuous monitoring to ensure responsible and effective use, balancing benefits with challenges and ethical considerations.

FUTURE TRENDS AND DIRECTIONS

Emerging Technologies

Emerging technologies are expected to significantly advance the field of structural engineering (Huang & Fu, 2019; Pan & Zhang, 2021; L. Sun et al., 2020b).

- **Digital Twins:** The development of digital twins, virtual replicas of physical structures, will continue to gain traction. These digital replicas allow real-time monitoring, analysis, and predictive maintenance of structures.
- **Quantum Computing:** Quantum computing holds promise for solving complex structural engineering problems at unprecedented speeds, revolutionizing optimization, and simulation processes.
- **Nanotechnology:** Nanomaterials and nanosensors will enable the creation of stronger, more resilient, and self-monitoring structural components.
- **3D Printing:** Advancements in 3D printing technologies will expand the possibilities for rapid prototyping and on-site construction, reducing material waste.
- **Smart Materials:** The integration of smart materials that can adapt to changing conditions will enhance structural performance and safety.

Future Research Avenues

The future of structural engineering is predicted to be shaped by various promising research avenues as it continues to evolve.

- **Resilience and Disaster Preparedness:** Research on designing structures to withstand natural disasters, such as earthquakes and hurricanes, will remain a critical focus.
- **Sustainable Materials:** Exploring and developing sustainable materials with low environmental impact will be a priority for achieving more eco-friendly structures.
- **AI and Ethics:** Research into ethical guidelines and frameworks for the responsible use of AI and ML in structural engineering will gain importance.
- **Human-AI Collaboration:** Investigating how engineers can effectively collaborate with AI systems to enhance decision-making and design processes will be a prominent area of study.
- **Autonomous Construction:** Research on fully autonomous construction processes, including robotic assembly and 3D printing, will advance the field of construction.
- **Climate Change Adaptation:** Addressing the impact of climate change on structural design and developing adaptive solutions will be a growing concern.
- **Biologically Inspired Design:** Exploring biological systems for inspiration in structural design, such as mimicking the strength and efficiency of natural materials, will gain attention.

Structural engineering is expected to evolve in response to technological advancements, sustainability, and the need for more resilient structures, with researchers and professionals playing a crucial role in driving these innovations.

CONCLUSION

This chapter delves into the transformative role of AI and ML in structural engineering, highlighting their significant role in design, optimization, and evaluation of structures.

- The pivotal role of AI and ML in automating design processes, predicting structural behavior, and optimizing configurations.
- The application of AI-ML in developing a performance comparison framework, allowing engineers to evaluate safety, cost-effectiveness, and environmental impact comprehensively.
- The integration of sustainability principles into AI-ML models, enabling the creation of sustainable, energy-efficient, and environmentally responsible designs.

- Real-world case studies that demonstrate how AI-ML-driven autonomous design has been applied to achieve superior structural performance while minimizing resource utilization and promoting sustainability.
- The numerous benefits of AI-ML in structural engineering, such as efficiency gains, cost savings, and enhanced safety, as well as the challenges and ethical considerations that come with their implementation.
- Future trends and research directions, including emerging technologies like digital twins and quantum computing, and research avenues such as climate change adaptation and human-AI collaboration.

AI and ML are revolutionizing structural engineering, enabling more resilient, sustainable, and efficient structures. However, responsible and ethical use is crucial for long-term success and positive impact on the built environment.

LIST OF ABBREVIATIONS

AI - Artificial Intelligence
ML - Machine Learning
GA - Genetic Algorithm
PSO - Particle Swarm Optimization
ACO - Ant Colony Optimization
BIM - Building Information Modeling
LCCA - Life Cycle Cost Analysis
IoT - Internet of Things
LCA - Life Cycle Assessment

REFERENCES

Anitha, C., Komala, C., Vivekanand, C. V., Lalitha, S., & Boopathi, S. (2023). Artificial Intelligence driven security model for Internet of Medical Things (IoMT). *IEEE Explore*, 1–7.

Arunprasad, R., & Boopathi, S. (2019). Chapter-4 Alternate Refrigerants for Minimization Environmental Impacts: A Review. In Advances in Engineering Technology (p. 75). AkiNik Publications.

Babu, B. S., Kamalakannan, J., Meenatchi, N., Karthik, S., & Boopathi, S. (2022). Economic impacts and reliability evaluation of battery by adopting Electric Vehicle. *IEEE Explore*, 1–6.

Boopathi, S. (2013). *Experimental study and multi-objective optimization of near-dry wire-cut electrical discharge machining process* [PhD Thesis]. http://hdl.handle.net/10603/16933

Boopathi, S. (2022a). An extensive review on sustainable developments of dry and near-dry electrical discharge machining processes. *ASME: Journal of Manufacturing Science and Engineering, 144*(5), 050801–1.

Boopathi, S. (2022b). An investigation on gas emission concentration and relative emission rate of the near-dry wire-cut electrical discharge machining process. *Environmental Science and Pollution Research International, 29*(57), 86237–86246. doi:10.1007/s11356-021-17658-1 PMID:34837614

Boopathi, S. (2022c). Cryogenically treated and untreated stainless steel grade 317 in sustainable wire electrical discharge machining process: A comparative study. *Springer :Environmental Science and Pollution Research*, 1–10.

Boopathi, S. (2024). Advancements in Machine Learning and AI for Intelligent Systems in Drone Applications for Smart City Developments. In *Futuristic e-Governance Security With Deep Learning Applications* (pp. 15–45). IGI Global. doi:10.4018/978-1-6684-9596-4.ch002

Boopathi, S., Alqahtani, A. S., Mubarakali, A., & Panchatcharam, P. (2023). Sustainable developments in near-dry electrical discharge machining process using sunflower oil-mist dielectric fluid. *Environmental Science and Pollution Research International*, 1–20. doi:10.1007/s11356-023-27494-0 PMID:37199846

Boopathi, S., Balasubramani, V., Kumar, R. S., & Singh, G. R. (2021). The influence of human hair on kenaf and Grewia fiber-based hybrid natural composite material: An experimental study. *Functional Composites and Structures, 3*(4), 045011. doi:10.1088/2631-6331/ac3afc

Boopathi, S., & Davim, J. P. (2023a). Applications of Nanoparticles in Various Manufacturing Processes. In *Sustainable Utilization of Nanoparticles and Nanofluids in Engineering Applications* (pp. 1–31). IGI Global. doi:10.4018/978-1-6684-9135-5.ch001

Boopathi, S., & Davim, J. P. (2023b). *Sustainable Utilization of Nanoparticles and Nanofluids in Engineering Applications*. IGI Global. doi:10.4018/978-1-6684-9135-5

Boopathi, S., & Kanike, U. K. (2023). Applications of Artificial Intelligent and Machine Learning Techniques in Image Processing. In *Handbook of Research on Thrust Technologies' Effect on Image Processing* (pp. 151–173). IGI Global. doi:10.4018/978-1-6684-8618-4.ch010

Boopathi, S., Kumar, P. K. S., Meena, R. S., Sudhakar, M., & Associates. (2023). Sustainable Developments of Modern Soil-Less Agro-Cultivation Systems: Aquaponic Culture. In Human Agro-Energy Optimization for Business and Industry (pp. 69–87). IGI Global.

Boopathi, S., & Sivakumar, K. (2013). Experimental investigation and parameter optimization of near-dry wire-cut electrical discharge machining using multi-objective evolutionary algorithm. *International Journal of Advanced Manufacturing Technology*, *67*(9–12), 2639–2655. doi:10.1007/s00170-012-4680-4

Boopathi, S., & Sivakumar, K. (2016). Optimal parameter prediction of oxygen-mist near-dry wire-cut EDM. *Inderscience: International Journal of Manufacturing Technology and Management*, *30*(3–4), 164–178. doi:10.1504/IJMTM.2016.077812

Boopathi, S., Sureshkumar, M., & Sathiskumar, S. (2022). Parametric Optimization of LPG Refrigeration System Using Artificial Bee Colony Algorithm. *International Conference on Recent Advances in Mechanical Engineering Research and Development*, 97–105.

Boopathi, S., Umareddy, M., & Elangovan, M. (2023). Applications of Nano-Cutting Fluids in Advanced Machining Processes. In *Sustainable Utilization of Nanoparticles and Nanofluids in Engineering Applications* (pp. 211–234). IGI Global. doi:10.4018/978-1-6684-9135-5.ch009

Dhanya, D., Kumar, S. S., Thilagavathy, A., Prasad, D., & Boopathi, S. (2023). Data Analytics and Artificial Intelligence in the Circular Economy: Case Studies. In Intelligent Engineering Applications and Applied Sciences for Sustainability (pp. 40–58). IGI Global.

Dolšak, B., & Novak, M. (2011). Intelligent decision support for structural design analysis. *Advanced Engineering Informatics*, *25*(2), 330–340. doi:10.1016/j.aei.2010.11.001

Domakonda, V. K., Farooq, S., Chinthamreddy, S., Puviarasi, R., Sudhakar, M., & Boopathi, S. (2022). Sustainable Developments of Hybrid Floating Solar Power Plants: Photovoltaic System. In Human Agro-Energy Optimization for Business and Industry (pp. 148–167). IGI Global.

Fowziya, S., Sivaranjani, S., Devi, N. L., Boopathi, S., Thakur, S., & Sailaja, J. M. (2023). Influences of nano-green lubricants in the friction-stir process of TiAlN coated alloys. *Materials Today: Proceedings*. Advance online publication. doi:10.1016/j.matpr.2023.06.446

Gowri, N. V., Dwivedi, J. N., Krishnaveni, K., Boopathi, S., Palaniappan, M., & Medikondu, N. R. (2023a). Experimental investigation and multi-objective optimization of eco-friendly near-dry electrical discharge machining of shape memory alloy using Cu/SiC/Gr composite electrode. *Environmental Science and Pollution Research International, 30*(49), 1–19. doi:10.1007/s11356-023-26983-6 PMID:37126160

Gowri, N. V., Dwivedi, J. N., Krishnaveni, K., Boopathi, S., Palaniappan, M., & Medikondu, N. R. (2023b). Experimental investigation and multi-objective optimization of eco-friendly near-dry electrical discharge machining of shape memory alloy using Cu/SiC/Gr composite electrode. *Environmental Science and Pollution Research International, 30*(49), 1–19. doi:10.1007/s11356-023-26983-6 PMID:37126160

Gunasekaran, K., & Boopathi, S. (2023). Artificial Intelligence in Water Treatments and Water Resource Assessments. In *Artificial Intelligence Applications in Water Treatment and Water Resource Management* (pp. 71–98). IGI Global. doi:10.4018/978-1-6684-6791-6.ch004

Guo, K., Yang, Z., Yu, C.-H., & Buehler, M. J. (2021). Artificial intelligence and machine learning in design of mechanical materials. *Materials Horizons, 8*(4), 1153–1172. doi:10.1039/D0MH01451F PMID:34821909

Hanumanthakari, S., Gift, M. M., Kanimozhi, K., Bhavani, M. D., Bamane, K. D., & Boopathi, S. (2023). Biomining Method to Extract Metal Components Using Computer-Printed Circuit Board E-Waste. In *Handbook of Research on Safe Disposal Methods of Municipal Solid Wastes for a Sustainable Environment* (pp. 123–141). IGI Global. doi:10.4018/978-1-6684-8117-2.ch010

Haribalaji, V., Boopathi, S., & Asif, M. M. (2021). Optimization of friction stir welding process to join dissimilar AA2014 and AA7075 aluminum alloys. *Materials Today: Proceedings, 50*, 2227–2234. doi:10.1016/j.matpr.2021.09.499

Haribalaji, V., Boopathi, S., Asif, M. M., Yuvaraj, T., Velmurugan, D., Lewise, K. A. S., Sudhagar, S., & Suresh, P. (2022). Influences of Mg-Cr filler materials in Friction Stir Process of Aluminium-based dissimilar alloys. *Materials Today: Proceedings, 66*(3), 948–954. doi:10.1016/j.matpr.2022.04.668

Huang, Y., & Fu, J. (2019). Review on application of artificial intelligence in civil engineering. *Computer Modeling in Engineering & Sciences, 121*(3), 845–875. doi:10.32604/cmes.2019.07653

Hussain, Z., & Srimathy, G. (2023). *IoT and AI Integration for Enhanced Efficiency and Sustainability*. Academic Press.

Ingle, R. B., Senthil, T. S., Swathi, S., Muralidharan, N., Mahendran, G., & Boopathi, S. (2023). Sustainability and Optimization of Green and Lean Manufacturing Processes Using Machine Learning Techniques. IGI Global. doi:10.4018/978-1-6684-8238-4.ch012

Jeevanantham, Y. A., Saravanan, A., Vanitha, V., Boopathi, S., & Kumar, D. P. (2022). Implementation of Internet-of Things (IoT) in Soil Irrigation System. *IEEE Explore*, 1–5.

Kalidas, R., Boopathi, S., Sivakumar, K., & Mohankumar, P. (2012). Optimization of Machining Parameters of WEDM Process Based On the Taguchi Method. *IJEST, 6*(1).

Kannan, E., Trabelsi, Y., Boopathi, S., & Alagesan, S. (2022). Influences of cryogenically treated work material on near-dry wire-cut electrical discharge machining process. *Surface Topography: Metrology and Properties, 10*(1), 015027. doi:10.1088/2051-672X/ac53e1

Kavitha, C. R., Varalatchoumy, M., Mithuna, H. R., Bharathi, K., Geethalakshmi, N. M., & Boopathi, S. (2023). Energy Monitoring and Control in the Smart Grid: Integrated Intelligent IoT and ANFIS. In M. Arshad (Ed.), Advances in Bioinformatics and Biomedical Engineering. IGI Global. doi:10.4018/978-1-6684-6577-6.ch014

Koshariya, A. K., Kalaiyarasi, D., Jovith, A. A., Sivakami, T., Hasan, D. S., & Boopathi, S. (2023). AI-Enabled IoT and WSN-Integrated Smart Agriculture System. In *Artificial Intelligence Tools and Technologies for Smart Farming and Agriculture Practices* (pp. 200–218). IGI Global. doi:10.4018/978-1-6684-8516-3.ch011

Kumar, M., Kumar, K., Sasikala, P., Sampath, B., Gopi, B., & Sundaram, S. (2023). Sustainable Green Energy Generation From Waste Water: IoT and ML Integration. In Sustainable Science and Intelligent Technologies for Societal Development (pp. 440–463). IGI Global.

Kumar, P. R., Meenakshi, S., Shalini, S., Devi, S. R., & Boopathi, S. (2023). Soil Quality Prediction in Context Learning Approaches Using Deep Learning and Blockchain for Smart Agriculture. In R. Kumar, A. B. Abdul Hamid, & N. I. Binti Ya'akub (Eds.), Advances in Computational Intelligence and Robotics. IGI Global. doi:10.4018/978-1-6684-9151-5.ch001

Kumara, V., Mohanaprakash, T., Fairooz, S., Jamal, K., Babu, T., & Sampath, B. (2023). Experimental Study on a Reliable Smart Hydroponics System. In *Human Agro-Energy Optimization for Business and Industry* (pp. 27–45). IGI Global. doi:10.4018/978-1-6684-4118-3.ch002

Liu, S., Tomizuka, M., & Ulsoy, A. (2004). Challenges and opportunities in the engineering of intelligent systems. *Proc. of the 4th International Workshop on Structural Control,* 295–300.

Maguluri, L. P., Ananth, J., Hariram, S., Geetha, C., Bhaskar, A., & Boopathi, S. (2023). Smart Vehicle-Emissions Monitoring System Using Internet of Things (IoT). In Handbook of Research on Safe Disposal Methods of Municipal Solid Wastes for a Sustainable Environment (pp. 191–211). IGI Global.

Maguluri, L. P., Arularasan, A., & Boopathi, S. (2023). Assessing Security Concerns for AI-Based Drones in Smart Cities. In Effective AI, Blockchain, and E-Governance Applications for Knowledge Discovery and Management (pp. 27–47). IGI Global. doi:10.4018/978-1-6684-9151-5.ch002

Maheswari, B. U., Imambi, S. S., Hasan, D., Meenakshi, S., Pratheep, V., & Boopathi, S. (2023). Internet of Things and Machine Learning-Integrated Smart Robotics. In Global Perspectives on Robotics and Autonomous Systems: Development and Applications (pp. 240–258). IGI Global. doi:10.4018/978-1-6684-7791-5.ch010

Mohanty, A., Venkateswaran, N., Ranjit, P., Tripathi, M. A., & Boopathi, S. (2023). Innovative Strategy for Profitable Automobile Industries: Working Capital Management. In Handbook of Research on Designing Sustainable Supply Chains to Achieve a Circular Economy (pp. 412–428). IGI Global.

Möhring, H.-C., Müller, M., Krieger, J., Multhoff, J., Plagge, C., de Wit, J., & Misch, S. (2020). Intelligent lightweight structures for hybrid machine tools. *Production Engineering, 14*(5-6), 583–600. doi:10.1007/s11740-020-00988-3

Myilsamy, S., & Sampath, B. (2017). Grey Relational Optimization of Powder Mixed Near-Dry Wire Cut Electrical Discharge Machining of Inconel 718 Alloy. *Asian Journal of Research in Social Sciences and Humanities, 7*(3), 18–25. doi:10.5958/2249-7315.2017.00157.5

Nishanth, J., Deshmukh, M. A., Kushwah, R., Kushwaha, K. K., Balaji, S., & Sampath, B. (2023). Particle Swarm Optimization of Hybrid Renewable Energy Systems. In *Intelligent Engineering Applications and Applied Sciences for Sustainability* (pp. 291–308). IGI Global. doi:10.4018/979-8-3693-0044-2.ch016

Pachiappan, K., Anitha, K., Pitchai, R., Sangeetha, S., Satyanarayana, T., & Boopathi, S. (2024). Intelligent Machines, IoT, and AI in Revolutionizing Agriculture for Water Processing. In *Handbook of Research on AI and ML for Intelligent Machines and Systems* (pp. 374–399). IGI Global.

Pan, Y., & Zhang, L. (2021). Roles of artificial intelligence in construction engineering and management: A critical review and future trends. *Automation in Construction, 122*, 103517. doi:10.1016/j.autcon.2020.103517

Paul, A., Thilagham, K., KG, J., Reddy, P. R., Sathyamurthy, R., & Boopathi, S. (2024). Multi-criteria Optimization on Friction Stir Welding of Aluminum Composite (AA5052-H32/B4C) using Titanium Nitride Coated Tool. Engineering Research Express.

Perry, B. J., Guo, Y., & Mahmoud, H. N. (2022). Automated site-specific assessment of steel structures through integrating machine learning and fracture mechanics. *Automation in Construction, 133*, 104022. doi:10.1016/j.autcon.2021.104022

Rahamathunnisa, U., Sudhakar, K., Murugan, T. K., Thivaharan, S., Rajkumar, M., & Boopathi, S. (2023). Cloud Computing Principles for Optimizing Robot Task Offloading Processes. In *AI-Enabled Social Robotics in Human Care Services* (pp. 188–211). IGI Global. doi:10.4018/978-1-6684-8171-4.ch007

Rahamathunnisa, U., Sudhakar, K., Padhi, S., Bhattacharya, S., Shashibhushan, G., & Boopathi, S. (2024). Sustainable Energy Generation From Waste Water: IoT Integrated Technologies. In Adoption and Use of Technology Tools and Services by Economically Disadvantaged Communities: Implications for Growth and Sustainability (pp. 225–256). IGI Global.

Ramudu, K., Mohan, V. M., Jyothirmai, D., Prasad, D., Agrawal, R., & Boopathi, S. (2023). Machine Learning and Artificial Intelligence in Disease Prediction: Applications, Challenges, Limitations, Case Studies, and Future Directions. In Contemporary Applications of Data Fusion for Advanced Healthcare Informatics (pp. 297–318). IGI Global.

Salehi, H., & Burgueño, R. (2018). Emerging artificial intelligence methods in structural engineering. *Engineering Structures, 171*, 170–189. doi:10.1016/j.engstruct.2018.05.084

Samikannu, R., Koshariya, A. K., Poornima, E., Ramesh, S., Kumar, A., & Boopathi, S. (2022). Sustainable Development in Modern Aquaponics Cultivation Systems Using IoT Technologies. In *Human Agro-Energy Optimization for Business and Industry* (pp. 105–127). IGI Global.

Sampath, B. (2021). *Sustainable Eco-Friendly Wire-Cut Electrical Discharge Machining: Gas Emission Analysis*. Academic Press.

Sampath, B., Pandian, M., Deepa, D., & Subbiah, R. (2022). Operating parameters prediction of liquefied petroleum gas refrigerator using simulated annealing algorithm. *AIP Conference Proceedings, 2460*(1), 070003. doi:10.1063/5.0095601

Sampath, B., Sasikumar, C., & Myilsamy, S. (2023). Application of TOPSIS Optimization Technique in the Micro-Machining Process. In IGI: Trends, Paradigms, and Advances in Mechatronics Engineering (pp. 162–187). IGI Global.

Sathish, T., Sunagar, P., Singh, V., Boopathi, S., Al-Enizi, A. M., Pandit, B., Gupta, M., & Sehgal, S. S. (2023). Characteristics estimation of natural fibre reinforced plastic composites using deep multi-layer perceptron (MLP) technique. *Chemosphere, 337*, 139346. doi:10.1016/j.chemosphere.2023.139346 PMID:37379988

Sengeni, D., Padmapriya, G., Imambi, S. S., Suganthi, D., Suri, A., & Boopathi, S. (2023). Biomedical Waste Handling Method Using Artificial Intelligence Techniques. In *Handbook of Research on Safe Disposal Methods of Municipal Solid Wastes for a Sustainable Environment* (pp. 306–323). IGI Global. doi:10.4018/978-1-6684-8117-2.ch022

Shea, K., & Smith, I. (2005). Intelligent structures: A new direction in structural control. *Artificial Intelligence in Structural Engineering: Information Technology for Design, Collaboration, Maintenance, and Monitoring*, 398–410.

Soh, C.-K., & Soh, A.-K. (1988). Example of intelligent structural design system. *Journal of Computing in Civil Engineering, 2*(4), 329–345. doi:10.1061/(ASCE)0887-3801(1988)2:4(329)

Srinivas, B., Maguluri, L. P., Naidu, K. V., Reddy, L. C. S., Deivakani, M., & Boopathi, S. (2023). Architecture and Framework for Interfacing Cloud-Enabled Robots. In *Handbook of Research on Data Science and Cybersecurity Innovations in Industry 4.0 Technologies* (pp. 542–560). IGI Global. doi:10.4018/978-1-6684-8145-5.ch027

Sun, H., Burton, H. V., & Huang, H. (2021). Machine learning applications for building structural design and performance assessment: State-of-the-art review. *Journal of Building Engineering, 33*, 101816. doi:10.1016/j.jobe.2020.101816

Sun, L., Shang, Z., Xia, Y., Bhowmick, S., & Nagarajaiah, S. (2020). Review of bridge structural health monitoring aided by big data and artificial intelligence: From condition assessment to damage detection. *Journal of Structural Engineering, 146*(5), 04020073. doi:10.1061/(ASCE)ST.1943-541X.0002535

Syamala, M., Komala, C., Pramila, P., Dash, S., Meenakshi, S., & Boopathi, S. (2023). Machine Learning-Integrated IoT-Based Smart Home Energy Management System. In *Handbook of Research on Deep Learning Techniques for Cloud-Based Industrial IoT* (pp. 219–235). IGI Global. doi:10.4018/978-1-6684-8098-4.ch013

Ugandar, R. E., Rahamathunnisa, U., Sajithra, S., Christiana, M. B. V., Palai, B. K., & Boopathi, S. (2023). Hospital Waste Management Using Internet of Things and Deep Learning: Enhanced Efficiency and Sustainability. In M. Arshad (Ed.), Advances in Bioinformatics and Biomedical Engineering. IGI Global. doi:10.4018/978-1-6684-6577-6.ch015

Vanitha, S., Radhika, K., & Boopathi, S. (2023). Artificial Intelligence Techniques in Water Purification and Utilization. In *Human Agro-Energy Optimization for Business and Industry* (pp. 202–218). IGI Global. doi:10.4018/978-1-6684-4118-3.ch010

Venkateswaran, N., Kumar, S. S., Diwakar, G., Gnanasangeetha, D., & Boopathi, S. (2023). Synthetic Biology for Waste Water to Energy Conversion: IoT and AI Approaches. In M. Arshad (Ed.), Advances in Bioinformatics and Biomedical Engineering. IGI Global. doi:10.4018/978-1-6684-6577-6.ch017

Venkateswaran, N., Vidhya, K., Ayyannan, M., Chavan, S. M., Sekar, K., & Boopathi, S. (2023). A Study on Smart Energy Management Framework Using Cloud Computing. In 5G, Artificial Intelligence, and Next Generation Internet of Things: Digital Innovation for Green and Sustainable Economies (pp. 189–212). IGI Global. doi:10.4018/978-1-6684-8634-4.ch009

Vennila, T., Karuna, M., Srivastava, B. K., Venugopal, J., Surakasi, R., & Sampath, B. (2022). New Strategies in Treatment and Enzymatic Processes: Ethanol Production From Sugarcane Bagasse. In Human Agro-Energy Optimization for Business and Industry (pp. 219–240). IGI Global.

Verma, R., Christiana, M. B. V., Maheswari, M., Srinivasan, V., Patro, P., Dari, S. S., & Boopathi, S. (2024). Intelligent Physarum Solver for Profit Maximization in Oligopolistic Supply Chain Networks. In *AI and Machine Learning Impacts in Intelligent Supply Chain* (pp. 156–179). IGI Global. doi:10.4018/979-8-3693-1347-3.ch011

Vijayakumar, G. N. S., Domakonda, V. K., Farooq, S., Kumar, B. S., Pradeep, N., & Boopathi, S. (2024). Sustainable Developments in Nano-Fluid Synthesis for Various Industrial Applications. In Adoption and Use of Technology Tools and Services by Economically Disadvantaged Communities: Implications for Growth and Sustainability (pp. 48–81). IGI Global.

Westermayr, J., Gastegger, M., Schütt, K. T., & Maurer, R. J. (2021). Perspective on integrating machine learning into computational chemistry and materials science. *The Journal of Chemical Physics*, *154*(23), 230903. doi:10.1063/5.0047760 PMID:34241249

Chapter 10
Additive Manufacturing and 3D Printing Innovations:
Revolutionizing Industry 5.0

M. D. Mohan Gift
https://orcid.org/0000-0003-4939-8809
Department of Mechanical Engineering,
Panimalar Engineering College, India

K. Alagarraja
Department of Mechanical Engineering,
New Prince Shri Bhavani College of
Engineering and Technology, India

T. S. Senthil
Department of Marine Engineering, Noorul
Islam Centre for Higher Education, India

P. Jayaseelan
Department of Mechanical Engineering,
Achariya College of Engineering and
Technology, India

Dler Salih Hasan
https://orcid.org/0009-0008-3212-5509
Department of Computer Science and
Information Technology, College of
Science, University of Salahaddin, Iraq

Sampath Boopathi
https://orcid.org/0000-0002-2065-6539
Mechanical Engineering, Muthammal
Engineering College, India

ABSTRACT

Additive manufacturing (AM), commonly known as 3D printing, has emerged as a transformative technology with profound implications for multiple industries. The convergence of AM with Industry 4.0 principles and advanced technologies has given rise to Industry 5.0, a new era of manufacturing characterized by enhanced integration and digitalization. This chapter explores the dynamic landscape of AM within the context of Industry 5.0, highlighting research trends, innovations, and challenges. Key developments include materials advancements, multi-material printing, digital twins, bioprinting, AI-driven design, and sustainability initiatives. Industry 5.0's impact is felt globally, with applications spanning aerospace, healthcare, fashion, and beyond. Collaboration between academia and industry, regulatory frameworks, and the pursuit of sustainable practices are driving forces shaping the future of AM in Industry 5.0.

DOI: 10.4018/979-8-3693-0968-1.ch010

INTRODUCTION

Industry 5.0 is the latest phase of industrial production, combining human expertise and advanced technologies. It builds on the foundations of Industry 4.0, which introduced automation, connectivity, and data-driven decision-making. However, Industry 5.0 emphasizes the importance of human expertise, creativity, and collaboration in smart factories and production environments (Jeyaraman et al., 2022). Industry 5.0's transformative potential lies in the integration of additive manufacturing and 3D printing technologies, which have transformed the way we design, create, and distribute products across various industries from prototyping tools to full-fledged production processes (George & George, 2023).

This chapter explores the relationship between Industry 5.0 and additive manufacturing/3D printing innovations, examining their historical development, fundamental principles, and integration with the broader framework. It also examines recent advancements, applications across sectors, and real-world case studies showcasing their tangible benefits (Zhang et al., 2019). The text provides a comprehensive overview of the challenges and opportunities in the rapidly evolving world of additive manufacturing and 3D printing, highlighting regulatory considerations, sustainability concerns, and emerging trends, aiming to shape Industry 5.0 and guide a more agile, sustainable, and customized industrial production future (Maddikunta et al., 2022). Industry 5.0, a new paradigm emerging from the convergence of Industry 4.0 and additive manufacturing, is focusing on the integration of advanced technologies like IoT, AI, and robotics to transform manufacturing processes. This era is driving significant advancements and discoveries in additive manufacturing research and innovation (Tiwari et al., 2022):

Researchers are exploring new materials for Advanced Manufacturing (AM), including alloys, ceramics, composites, and sustainable biopolymers, which offer enhanced properties like strength, thermal resistance, and environmental sustainability. Multi-material and multi-process printing innovations are expanding AM possibilities, enabling the creation of complex components with varying properties (Al-Emran & Al-Sharafi, 2022). Digital twin technology is being integrated into additive manufacturing (AM) processes for real-time monitoring, optimization, and predictive maintenance. Bioprinting is being used for transplantation, drug testing, and regenerative medicine. Artificial intelligence and machine learning algorithms are being used for design optimization, part consolidation, and generative design, enhancing product performance and reducing material usage (Raphey et al., 2019).

The integration of robotics and automation in additive manufacturing (AM) is enhancing efficiency, reducing labor costs, and improving repeatability. Sustainable practices aim to minimize waste, reduce energy consumption, and develop eco-friendly materials. Recycling solutions for 3D printing materials are also being explored (Al-

Emran & Al-Sharafi, 2022; M. Sharma et al., 2022). Additive Manufacturing (AM) allows for cost-effective, customized product production, with industry-academia collaborations and international research initiatives promoting innovation. Efforts are underway to establish regulatory frameworks and industry standards for 3D-printed products, particularly in critical sectors like healthcare and aerospace, ensuring safety and quality(Boopathi, Khare, et al., 2023a; Boopathi & Kumar, 2024; Palaniappan et al., 2023a; Senthil et al., 2023a).

Global Impact: Additive manufacturing is significantly influencing global development and resilience through applications in space exploration, disaster relief, and localized manufacturing hubs.

In Industry 5.0, additive manufacturing is a key technological innovation, offering solutions to complex challenges across industries. Researchers, industry leaders, and policymakers are working together to maximize AM's potential, drive progress in materials science, design optimization, and sustainable manufacturing practices (Daminabo et al., 2020). The integration of additive manufacturing and 3D printing in Industry 5.0 is a groundbreaking advancement that combines advanced technologies and human expertise, transforming the way we conceptualize, design, and produce physical objects (Daminabo et al., 2020; Vafadar et al., 2021):

- **Customization and Personalization:** Additive manufacturing and 3D printing enable highly customized products, enabling Industry 5.0 consumers to have products tailored to their unique preferences and needs, a level previously challenging in traditional manufacturing (Al-Emran & Al-Sharafi, 2022; Daminabo et al., 2020; M. Sharma et al., 2022; Tiwari et al., 2022).
- **On-Demand Production:** Technologies in Industry 5.0 promote on-demand manufacturing, reducing mass production and large inventories, promoting flexible, responsive, and sustainable processes.
- **Design Freedom:** Additive manufacturing and 3D printing provide designers with unprecedented freedom to create intricate, complex geometries, fostering innovation and pushing the boundaries of product design by overcoming previously impossible or costly production methods.
- **Reduced Waste:** Traditional subtractive manufacturing generates significant waste, while additive manufacturing is more efficient and aligns with Industry 5.0's sustainability goals of reducing environmental impact.
- **Supply Chain Optimization:** Industry 5.0 encourages smart supply chains and logistics, with additive manufacturing promoting distributed manufacturing facilities and reducing reliance on centralized factories, resulting in more resilient and efficient supply chains(Mohanty, Venkateswaran, et al., 2023a; Verma et al., 2024).

- **Human-Machine Collaboration:** In Industry 5.0, humans work alongside intelligent machines, leveraging the strengths of both. In the realm of additive manufacturing and 3D printing, humans bring design creativity and problem-solving skills, while machines execute precise and repetitive tasks, ensuring high-quality production(Revathi et al., 2024).

- **Innovations in Materials:** Additive manufacturing is driving innovations in materials science. Industry 5.0 benefits from the development of new materials that are lightweight, durable, and tailored to specific applications, such as aerospace, healthcare, and automotive(Boopathi, 2024b; Haribalaji et al., 2014a).

- **Regulatory Challenges:** As these technologies evolve, they raise questions about regulatory frameworks and quality assurance. Industry 5.0 calls for adaptive regulatory approaches that ensure product safety and quality while accommodating the unique aspects of additive manufacturing.

- **Education and Skills Development:** Industry 5.0 necessitates a workforce equipped with the skills to harness additive manufacturing and 3D printing effectively. Training and education programs become critical in preparing individuals for roles in this innovative field.

- **Global Impact:** Additive manufacturing has the potential to democratize production on a global scale. In Industry 5.0, this can lead to a more equitable distribution of manufacturing capabilities and economic opportunities across regions.

Additive manufacturing and 3D printing are key to Industry 5.0, fostering innovation, sustainability, and improved collaboration between humans and machines. As these technologies evolve, they will revolutionize the way we design, create, and deliver products in the future industrial landscape.

SIGNIFICANCE OF ADDITIVE MANUFACTURING AND 3D PRINTING

Additive manufacturing and 3D printing are crucial technologies in modern industry, revolutionizing product design, prototype, and manufacturing, impacting various sectors. The significant factors are included their wide-ranging implications (Jihong et al., 2021; Zhang et al., 2019):

- **Customization and Personalization:** Additive manufacturing and 3D printing enable the creation of highly customized and personalized products. This is particularly significant in industries such as healthcare (custom implants and prosthetics), fashion (bespoke clothing and accessories), and automotive (customized vehicle parts).

- **Reduced Costs:** These technologies can significantly reduce production costs, especially for complex and low-volume parts. Traditional manufacturing methods often involve costly tooling and machining processes, while additive manufacturing builds objects layer by layer, minimizing waste and setup costs.

- **Rapid Prototyping:** Additive manufacturing and 3D printing have become indispensable tools for rapid prototyping. Engineers and designers can quickly iterate and test their designs, leading to faster product development cycles and reduced time-to-market.

- **Complex Geometries:** Unlike traditional manufacturing methods, which are limited by subtractive processes, additive manufacturing can create intricate and complex geometries. This allows for the development of innovative designs that were previously impossible to manufacture.

- **Supply Chain Resilience:** These technologies enable distributed manufacturing, reducing reliance on centralized factories and long supply chains. This can enhance supply chain resilience and reduce the risk of disruptions, as parts can be produced locally as needed.

- **Sustainability:** Additive manufacturing produces less waste material compared to subtractive manufacturing, aligning with sustainability goals. Additionally, it allows for lightweight designs, which can lead to energy savings, particularly in industries like aerospace and automotive.

- **Medical Advancements:** In healthcare, additive manufacturing has led to significant advancements, including the production of patient-specific implants, prosthetics, and medical instruments. It has also enabled the creation of anatomical models for surgical planning and education(Boopathi, Khare, et al., 2023b; Palaniappan et al., 2023b; Senthil et al., 2023b).

- **Aerospace Innovation:** The aerospace industry has adopted additive manufacturing for producing lightweight, complex, and high-performance components. This has resulted in fuel-efficient aircraft and reduced emissions.

- **Art and Design:** Additive manufacturing has found its place in art and design, allowing artists and creators to produce intricate sculptures, jewelry, and architectural models with precision.

- **Education and Skills Development:** The widespread adoption of additive manufacturing and 3D printing has created opportunities for education and skills development. This technology is being integrated into curricula to prepare the workforce of the future.

- **Small-Batch and On-Demand Production:** These technologies make it economically viable to produce small batches of products and even facilitate on-demand production. This reduces inventory costs and minimizes the risk of overproduction.

• **Innovation Ecosystem:** The growth of additive manufacturing has spawned an innovation ecosystem, including startups, research institutions, and open-source communities, driving continuous advancements and collaborative research.

Additive manufacturing and 3D printing have become transformative forces across industries, disrupting traditional manufacturing processes, fostering innovation, enhancing customization, and contributing to sustainability goals. They have reshaped the way we think about design and production in the modern era.

FUNDAMENTALS OF ADDITIVE MANUFACTURING

Additive manufacturing, also known as 3D printing, is a revolutionary technology that creates three-dimensional objects layer by layer. This section delves into its historical development, principles, technologies, materials, and processes that underpin its significance and versatility (Boopathi & Kumar, 2024).

Historical Development

Additive manufacturing has its roots in rapid prototyping techniques developed in the 1980s. The journey from prototyping to a full-fledged manufacturing technology has been marked by several key milestones (Boopathi, Khare, et al., 2023b; Mohanty, Jothi, et al., 2023):

• **1980s**: The concept of layer-by-layer additive fabrication techniques emerges, primarily for rapid prototyping in engineering and design.
• **1990s**: Stereolithography (SLA), fused deposition modeling (FDM), and selective laser sintering (SLS) technologies are commercialized.
• **2000s**: Advancements in materials and processes expand the applications of additive manufacturing, with aerospace and medical industries leading the way.
• **2010s**: Widespread adoption in various industries, including automotive, healthcare, and consumer goods. Innovations in metal 3D printing technologies open new possibilities.

Principles and Technologies

At its core, additive manufacturing follows these fundamental principles (Deepak Kumar et al., 2021; Kantaros et al., 2023; Kuang et al., 2019):

- **Layer-by-Layer Building:** Objects are constructed layer by layer, with each layer representing a cross-sectional slice of the final design. This approach contrasts with subtractive manufacturing, where material is removed from a solid block.
- **Digital Design and Data:** AM relies on digital 3D models, typically created using computer-aided design (CAD) software. These models are sliced into thin horizontal layers, and the printer follows these instructions to build the object.
- **Material Deposition:** Additive manufacturing employs various techniques for material deposition. These may include extrusion (FDM), photo-polymerization (SLA), sintering (SLS), or jetting (PolyJet), among others.
- **Support Structures:** Complex geometries may require temporary support structures during printing, which are removed in post-processing.

Technologies in additive manufacturing include:

- **Fused Deposition Modeling (FDM):** FDM uses a heated nozzle to extrude thermoplastic material layer by layer. It's widely used for desktop 3D printers.
- **Stereolithography (SLA):** SLA utilizes a UV laser to solidify a liquid resin layer by layer. It's known for high precision and surface finish.
- **Selective Laser Sintering (SLS):** SLS employs a laser to selectively sinter powdered material, often plastics or metals, into a solid form.
- **Binder Jetting:** In binder jetting, a liquid binder is selectively deposited onto a powder bed, solidifying the material layer by layer.
- **Metal 3D Printing:** This category encompasses technologies like selective laser melting (SLM) and electron beam melting (EBM), which print metal parts by fusing metal powder layer by layer.

Materials and Processes

The materials used in additive manufacturing vary widely and include plastics, metals, ceramics, composites, and even biological materials. Each material has specific properties and is processed using different techniques (Haribalaji, Boopathi, Asif, Jeyakumar, et al., 2022; Haribalaji, Boopathi, Asif, Yuvaraj, et al., 2022; Haribalaji, Venkatesan, et al., 2022).

The processes involved in AM include:

- **Layer Deposition:** Material is added layer by layer according to the 3D model.

- **Support Structure Generation:** For overhangs and complex geometries, temporary support structures may be generated to prevent material from sagging or collapsing during printing.
- **Post-Processing:** After printing, objects often require post-processing steps like cleaning, curing, heat treatment, or machining to achieve the desired finish and properties.

The foundations of additive manufacturing are rooted in a rich history, layer-by-layer construction principles, and diverse technologies, materials, and processes. Understanding these is crucial for fully utilizing the potential of additive manufacturing across various industries.

3D PRINTING IN INDUSTRY 5.0

Industry 5.0 is a significant shift in manufacturing, focusing on human-machine collaboration and the integration of advanced technologies, as depicted in Figure 1. 3D printing, also known as additive manufacturing, is crucial in transforming industrial processes and achieving Industry 5.0 goals. It aligns with and enhances the principles of Industry 5.0 (Javaid & Haleem, 2019a; Kumari et al., 2022; Moroni et al., 2022):

Figure 1. 3D printing versus Industry 5.0

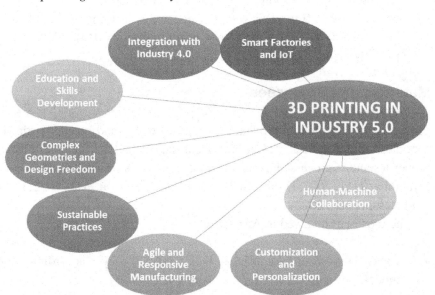

Integration with Industry 4.0: Industry 5.0 utilizes 3D printing as a critical enabler, offering on-demand, decentralized manufacturing capabilities. Smart factories integrate 3D printers into their production lines, enabling rapid customization and localized production, building on the foundations of Industry 4.0.

Smart Factories and IoT: In Industry 5.0, 3D printers are integrated into IoT-enabled smart factories. This integration enables real-time monitoring, data collection, and adaptive manufacturing, optimizing processes and reducing downtime. Smart 3D printers can communicate with other machines and systems, making production more responsive to changing demands (Karthik et al., 2023a; Koshariya et al., 2023; Maguluri et al., 2023; Syamala et al., 2023).

Human-Machine Collaboration: Industry 5.0 emphasizes collaboration between human workers and machines. 3D printing empowers workers to become digital craftsmen, using their creativity and expertise to design and oversee the manufacturing process. Humans play a vital role in design, quality control, and post-processing, ensuring that 3D-printed parts meet the highest standards (Myilsamy & Sampath, 2017; Vennila et al., 2022).

Customization and Personalization: One of the hallmarks of Industry 5.0 is the ability to produce highly customized and personalized products. 3D printing excels in this regard, allowing for the cost-effective production of unique items tailored to individual preferences. Industries such as healthcare leverage 3D printing to create patient-specific implants, prosthetics, and medical devices.

Agile and Responsive Manufacturing: Industry 5.0 necessitates agile manufacturing processes that can adapt to market changes. 3D printing facilitates rapid prototyping and production of small-batch items, reducing lead times and inventory costs, and enhancing supply chains' resilience by strategically distributing 3D printing facilities.

Sustainable Practices: Industry 5.0 prioritizes sustainability, and 3D printing's minimal waste and energy-efficient processes can reduce environmental impact. Its lightweight designs can also lead to energy savings in transportation industries.

Complex Geometries and Design Freedom: 3D printing allows for the production of complex and intricate geometries that were previously challenging or impossible to achieve. This design freedom fosters innovation and product optimization. Industries such as aerospace benefit from lightweight, structurally efficient components created through 3D printing.

Education and Skills Development: Industry 5.0 requires a skilled workforce capable of leveraging advanced technologies. 3D printing is integrated into educational programs, ensuring that future professionals are well-equipped to work in this evolving landscape. In summary, 3D printing is a cornerstone technology in Industry 5.0, where human expertise and collaboration with advanced machines take center stage (Agrawal et al., 2023; Durairaj et al., 2023a). The technology's capabilities in customization, agility, sustainability, and innovation align with the objectives of the transformative industrial era, revolutionizing product design, production, and interaction.

INNOVATIONS IN ADDITIVE MANUFACTURING

Advanced additive manufacturing techniques utilize advanced technologies, materials, and methods to expand the capabilities of 3D printing as illustrated in Figure 2. Advancements in additive manufacturing processes have expanded application areas, improved quality, and increased efficiency, with advanced techniques and materials and methods being utilized (Dass james & Boopathi, 2016; Haribalaji et al., 2014b; Mohanty, Venkateswaran, et al., 2023b). Advanced additive manufacturing techniques and materials are revolutionizing various industries, driving innovation, customization, and efficiency in manufacturing processes, making it an increasingly integral part of modern industry, thereby expanding the possibilities of 3D printing.

Multi-Material 3D Printing

Materials and Methods: Combining different materials within a single print job is a significant advancement. This is achieved through techniques like multi-nozzle

Figure 2. Innovations in additive manufacturing

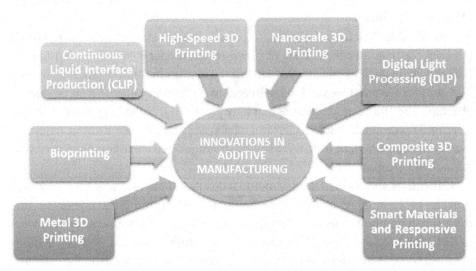

extrusion or multi-jet printing (Moroni et al., 2022; Osouli-Bostanabad et al., 2022; Tibbits, 2014).

- *Applications:* It allows for the creation of complex, multi-functional objects with varying properties within a single build.

Metal 3D Printing

- *Materials and Methods:* Various metal additive manufacturing methods have emerged, such as Selective Laser Melting (SLM) and Electron Beam Melting (EBM). These methods involve the selective melting of metal powders layer by layer.
- *Applications:* Metal 3D printing is used in aerospace, automotive, and healthcare for producing high-strength, lightweight, and complex metal parts.

Bioprinting

Materials and Methods: Bioprinting utilizes bioinks composed of living cells and biocompatible materials. These bioinks are deposited layer by layer to create functional tissues and organs (Deepak Kumar et al., 2021; Kuang et al., 2019).

- *Applications:* Bioprinting has immense potential in regenerative medicine, tissue engineering, and drug testing.

Continuous Liquid Interface Production (CLIP)

- *Materials and Methods:* CLIP is a photopolymerization technique that uses continuous liquid interface production to create objects at impressive speeds by harnessing light and oxygen to control the polymerization process.
- *Applications:* CLIP is used for high-speed, high-quality 3D printing of parts with engineering-grade materials.

High-Speed 3D Printing

- *Materials and Methods:* Advanced printers and techniques have been developed to significantly increase printing speed while maintaining quality. This includes methods like volumetric 3D printing and simultaneous multi-material deposition.
- *Applications:* High-speed 3D printing is crucial for rapid prototyping and manufacturing applications with tight deadlines.

Nanoscale 3D Printing

Materials and Methods: Nanoscale 3D printing involves techniques like two-photon polymerization and focused electron beam-induced deposition (FEBID) for creating structures at the nanometer scale.

- *Applications:* It's used in microelectronics, optics, and the development of nanoscale devices.

Digital Light Processing (DLP)

- *Materials and Methods:* DLP uses a digital light projector to cure photosensitive resin layer by layer.
- *Applications:* DLP is known for its high-speed, high-resolution capabilities and is used in industries requiring intricate details, such as jewelry and dental prosthetics.

Composite 3D Printing

- *Materials and Methods:* Composite 3D printing combines multiple materials, often reinforcing a polymer matrix with fibers or other materials for improved strength and stiffness.
- *Applications:* It's employed in industries requiring lightweight, strong, and durable components, such as automotive and aerospace.

Smart Materials and Responsive Printing

- *Materials and Methods:* Advanced materials can change properties in response to external stimuli like heat, light, or magnetic fields. Responsive printing techniques use these materials for specific applications.
- *Applications:* Responsive materials are utilized in fields like soft robotics, sensors, and adaptive structures.

MATERIALS ADVANCEMENTS

The development of new materials, improvements in existing ones, and tailoring materials for specific industries and use cases have significantly expanded the capabilities and applications of 3D printing technologies, as highlighted in Figure 3. Advancements in materials drive innovation in additive manufacturing, enabling

Figure 3. Materials advancements in additive manufacturing

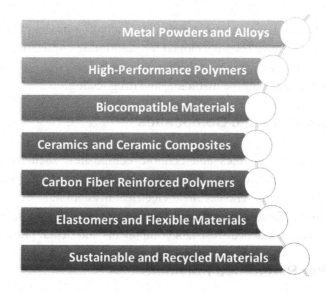

the production of complex, high-performance, and customized parts across various industries. As research and development continue, 3D printing technologies are expected to continue expanding (Liu et al., 2021; Shahrubudin et al., 2019):

Metal Powders and Alloys

- *Advancements:* The development of a wide range of metal powders and alloys, including titanium, aluminum, nickel-based superalloys, and copper, has enabled the production of high-strength, lightweight, and complex metal components.
- *Applications:* Metal additive manufacturing is used in aerospace, automotive, and healthcare for producing parts with exceptional mechanical properties and intricate designs.

High-Performance Polymers

- *Advancements:* Enhanced polymer materials, such as PEEK (Polyether Ether Ketone), ULTEM, and PAEK, offer improved temperature resistance, chemical resistance, and mechanical properties.
- *Applications:* These materials are used in aerospace, automotive, and medical industries for producing functional end-use parts.

Biocompatible Materials

- *Advancements:* Biocompatible materials, including biodegradable polymers and hydrogels, have been developed for bioprinting applications.
- *Applications:* Bioprinting with biocompatible materials is used in tissue engineering, regenerative medicine, and drug testing.

Ceramics and Ceramic Composites

- *Advancements:* Ceramics and ceramic composites, such as alumina and zirconia, have been optimized for additive manufacturing, providing high-temperature stability and excellent electrical insulation.
- *Applications:* These materials find use in aerospace, electronics, and healthcare for applications like heat-resistant components and dental prosthetics.

Carbon Fiber Reinforced Polymers

- *Advancements:* Carbon fiber reinforced polymers (CFRPs) combine the lightweight properties of polymers with the strength of carbon fibers, offering improved mechanical properties.
- *Applications:* CFRPs are used in aerospace, automotive, and sporting goods for producing lightweight, high-strength components.

Elastomers and Flexible Materials

- *Advancements:* Developments in flexible materials, including thermoplastic elastomers (TPEs) and silicone-based materials, have expanded the possibilities for creating soft and flexible parts.
- *Applications:* These materials are used in industries like robotics, healthcare, and consumer goods for producing soft grips, gaskets, and wearable devices.

Sustainable and Recycled Materials

- *Advancements:* The drive towards sustainability has led to the development of recycled and bio-based materials that are eco-friendly and reduce the environmental footprint of 3D printing.
- *Applications:* These materials are used in various industries to promote environmentally conscious manufacturing practices.

Smart and Functional Materials

- *Advancements:* Materials with added functionalities, such as shape memory polymers, conductive inks, and thermochromic materials, enable the creation of smart and responsive 3D-printed objects.
- *Applications:* Smart materials find use in electronics, aerospace, and automotive industries for applications like sensors and adaptive structures.

Nanocomposites

- *Advancements:* Nanocomposite materials incorporate nanoparticles into a polymer matrix, enhancing mechanical, thermal, and electrical properties.
- *Applications:* Nanocomposites are used in aerospace, electronics, and automotive industries for lightweight, high-performance components.

Design Optimization and Simulation

Design optimization and simulation are crucial in additive manufacturing (3D printing) to enhance the efficiency, functionality, and quality of printed objects, thereby maximizing the full potential of 3D printing technologies (Fan et al., 2020; Hao & Lin, 2020). This summary provides an overview of design optimization and simulation in the context of additive manufacturing.

Design Optimization

Design optimization in additive manufacturing involves creating 3D models that are tailored to take full advantage of the capabilities of 3D printing technologies (Boopathi, 2013, 2022b; Nishanth et al., 2023). This process aims to improve the final product's performance, reduce material usage, and minimize production time. Key aspects of design optimization include:

- **Topology Optimization:** This technique involves using specialized software to generate designs that minimize material usage while maintaining structural integrity. It often results in complex, organic-looking structures that are lighter and more efficient than traditionally designed parts.
- **Lattice Structures:** Designers use lattice structures to reduce material consumption while maintaining strength. These lattice patterns are designed to distribute loads effectively and can be customized for specific applications.
- **Generative Design:** Generative design software uses algorithms to explore numerous design variations and find the most efficient and structurally sound

solutions. It often considers factors like weight, stress, and manufacturing constraints.

- **Light weighting:** Light weighting is the process of designing parts to be as light as possible without compromising their functionality. It is crucial in industries like aerospace and automotive, where weight reduction can lead to fuel savings and improved performance.
- **Customization:** Additive manufacturing allows for easy customization of products. Design optimization can ensure that each customized item meets the specific needs of the end-user, such as personalized medical implants or ergonomic tools.
- **Complex Geometries:** Additive manufacturing enables the creation of complex shapes and internal structures that were previously impossible to manufacture. Design optimization exploits these capabilities to improve product performance and functionality.

Simulation

Simulation is a crucial step in additive manufacturing, involving virtual testing and analysis of 3D designs before production. It helps identify potential issues, validate designs, and optimize printing parameters. These iterative processes often involve multiple refinements, resulting in more efficient, functional, and reliable 3D-printed objects by designers and engineers.

a. **Stress Analysis:** Simulations can predict how a 3D-printed object will respond to different loads and forces. This helps ensure that parts are structurally sound and meet safety standards.

b. **Thermal Analysis:** Understanding how heat is distributed during the printing process is critical for avoiding warping, distortion, and other defects. Thermal simulations help optimize print parameters and prevent overheating.

c. **Fluid Flow Analysis:** In some cases, 3D printing involves the deposition of materials in a liquid or paste form. Fluid flow simulations ensure that the material is accurately deposited and that the final product meets dimensional accuracy requirements.

d. **Support Structure Analysis:** Simulations can assess the effectiveness of support structures in 3D printing. They help determine where supports are needed, how they should be designed, and how they can be removed efficiently after printing.

e. **Printability Analysis:** Before printing, simulations can predict how well a design will work with specific 3D printing technologies, helping designers make informed choices about the printing process and materials.

f.   **Material Behavior:** Understanding how materials behave during printing and post-processing is crucial. Material simulations can predict factors like shrinkage, distortion, and residual stresses, helping ensure the final product's dimensional accuracy.

AM APPLICATIONS ACROSS INDUSTRIES

Additive manufacturing (3D printing) revolutionizes product design, prototype, and manufacturing across various industries, with notable applications in various sectors. These applications demonstrate the versatility of 3D printing across a multitude of industries, enabling innovation, customization, and cost-effective production across diverse sectors (Figure 4). As the technology continues to advance, its impact on various industries is expected to grow, leading to new and exciting possibilities (Javaid & Haleem, 2019b; Ntouanoglou et al., 2018):

Figure 4. AM applications across industries

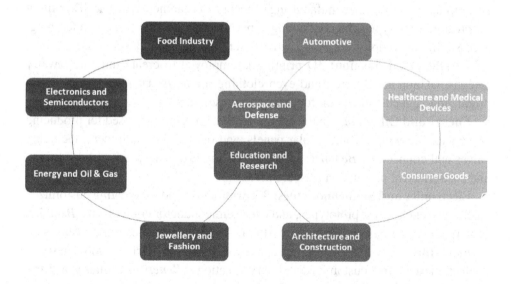

Aerospace and Défense: Aerospace companies use 3D printing for producing lightweight, complex components like aircraft engine parts, brackets, and interior components. In defines, it's used for creating customized military equipment and drones. *Benefits:* Weight reduction, fuel efficiency, cost savings, and rapid prototyping.

Automotive: Automotive manufacturers utilize 3D printing for prototyping, creating concept models, and manufacturing vehicle components like engine parts, customized interiors, and even entire vehicles. *Benefits:* Reduced lead times, lightweight components, improved fuel efficiency, and cost-effective customization (Mohanty, Venkateswaran, et al., 2023a; Ravisankar et al., 2023).

Healthcare and Medical Devices: Medical applications include 3D-printed prosthetics, orthodontic devices, dental implants, anatomical models for surgical planning, and even tissue engineering for bioprinting organs. *Benefits:* Customization, patient-specific solutions, reduced surgery time, and improved patient outcomes (Boopathi, 2023a; Karthik et al., 2023a; Pramila et al., 2023; Ramudu et al., 2023).

Consumer Goods: 3D printing is used to create customized consumer products like fashion accessories, footwear, home decor, and electronics cases. *Benefits:* Personalization, rapid prototyping, and reduced waste.

Architecture and Construction: Architects and builders use 3D printing for creating detailed architectural models, scale prototypes of buildings, and even large-scale construction components. *Benefits:* Enhanced design visualization, reduced labor costs, and the ability to create complex structures (Karthik et al., 2023b).

Education and Research: 3D printing is used in educational settings to teach design, engineering, and manufacturing concepts. Researchers leverage 3D printing for creating prototypes and conducting experiments. *Benefits:* Hands-on learning, accessibility to complex concepts, and efficient research and development.

Jewellery and Fashion: 3D printing is employed to create intricate jewelry designs, fashion accessories, and even clothing. *Benefits:* Unique designs, rapid production, and customization for individual customers.

Energy and Oil & Gas: In the energy sector, 3D printing is used for producing components in wind turbines, solar panels, and oil and gas equipment, including valves and connectors. *Benefits:* Improved energy efficiency, reduced downtime, and cost-effective production of spare parts.

Electronics and Semiconductors: 3D printing is used for creating customized electronics enclosures, prototypes, and even semiconductor components. *Benefits:* Rapid prototyping, design flexibility, and the ability to integrate electronics seamlessly.

Food Industry: 3D printing is employed to create intricate food designs, confectioneries, and customized culinary creations. *Benefits:* Culinary artistry, precise portion control, and innovative presentation.

Education and Training: - 3D printing is used in educational institutions for teaching STEM subjects, allowing students to design and create 3D-printed projects. Hands-on learning, fostering creativity, and preparing students for careers in technology and engineering (Das et al., 2024; Durairaj et al., 2023b; D. M. Sharma et al., 2024).

3D printing has significantly impacted healthcare and biomedical research, with applications in patient diagnosis and treatment. It has the potential to enhance patient care, reduce healthcare costs, and drive medical innovation. As technology advances, it is expected to play a significant role in shaping the future of healthcare and biomedicine.

Patient-Specific Implants and Prosthetics: 3D printing allows for the creation of patient-specific implants, such as cranial implants, hip and knee replacements, and dental implants. These implants are tailored to match the patient's anatomy precisely, resulting in better fit and improved long-term outcomes.

Customized Surgical Instruments: Surgeons can benefit from 3D-printed surgical instruments designed for specific procedures. These instruments can be customized to match the patient's unique anatomy or the surgeon's preferences, enhancing surgical precision.

Anatomical Models for Surgical Planning: 3D printing is used to create anatomical models that replicate a patient's specific anatomy. Surgeons can use these models for preoperative planning, helping them understand complex cases and practice procedures before entering the operating room.

Bioprinting and Tissue Engineering: Bioprinting combines living cells with biomaterials to create 3D-printed tissues and organs. This technology holds great promise for regenerative medicine, enabling the production of replacement organs and tissues for transplantation (Boopathi & Kumar, 2024; Ugandar et al., 2023; Venkateswaran et al., 2023).

Dental Applications: 3D printing is widely used in dentistry for producing dental crowns, bridges, aligners, and dentures. It enables quicker and more accurate dental restorations and orthodontic treatments.

Pharmaceuticals and Drug Delivery: 3D printing is used to create personalized drug formulations and dosage forms. It allows for precise control over drug release rates, which can be tailored to individual patient needs.

Orthopedics and Orthotics: Custom orthotic insoles, braces, and orthopedic devices are designed and manufactured using 3D printing technology. These devices offer enhanced comfort and support for patients with musculoskeletal conditions.

Medical Models for Education: Medical schools and healthcare institutions use 3D-printed anatomical models to enhance medical education. These models provide students with a hands-on learning experience, allowing them to practice surgical techniques and understand complex anatomy(Anitha et al., 2023; Boopathi, Khare, et al., 2023a; Sengeni et al., 2023; Subha et al., 2023).

Surgical Guides and Templates: Surgeons use 3D-printed guides and templates during procedures, ensuring precise incisions and implant placements. These guides enhance surgical accuracy and reduce operating time.

Biological and Drug Testing Models: 3D-printed tissue and organ models serve as platforms for drug testing and disease modeling. Researchers can study the effects of drugs on realistic tissue structures, leading to more accurate results.

Prosthetic Limbs: Customized 3D-printed prosthetic limbs are more affordable and accessible than traditional prosthetics. They can be designed to meet the unique needs and preferences of individual amputees.

Surgical Training and Simulation: Surgeons use 3D-printed anatomical models and surgical simulators for training and skill development. These tools help improve surgical techniques and reduce the learning curve.

Point-of-Care Manufacturing: Hospitals and clinics are adopting 3D printing for on-demand production of medical devices, enabling rapid response to emergencies and reducing reliance on external suppliers.

CASE STUDIES

These case studies illustrate the diverse applications and benefits of 3D printing across various industries, including aerospace, healthcare, automotive, fashion, education, manufacturing, and energy (Chiu, 2020; Gentry, 2021; Kermanidis, 2020). As technology continues to advance, 3D printing is likely to play an even more significant role in reshaping traditional processes and driving innovation.

Aerospace - GE Aviation's LEAP Fuel Nozzles: Aviation utilized 3D printing to produce complex fuel nozzles for their LEAP engines. These nozzles are essential for fuel efficiency and engine performance. The design complexity made traditional manufacturing methods costly and inefficient. 3D printing allowed for the creation of a single, intricately designed part that reduced weight, improved fuel efficiency, and lowered production costs (Yengst, 2010).

Healthcare - 3D-Printed Titanium Jaw Implant: A patient in the Netherlands received a 3D-printed titanium jaw implant after a severe infection. Surgeons used CT scans to create a customized implant that perfectly matched the patient's jaw structure. This not only saved the patient's life but also restored their ability to speak and eat normally (Boopathi, 2023b; Durairaj et al., 2023b).

Automotive - Local Motors' 3D-Printed Car: Local Motors produced the world's first 3D-printed car called the "Strati." This electric vehicle was created in just 44 hours using a large-scale 3D printer. The design was highly customizable, and the project showcased the potential for rapid, on-demand vehicle manufacturing.

Architecture - MX3D's 3D-Printed Bridge in Amsterdam: MX3D, a Dutch robotics company, used large-scale 3D printing robots to create a pedestrian bridge in Amsterdam. The robots autonomously printed the steel structure layer by layer, resulting in an innovative and visually stunning bridge.

Fashion - 3D-Printed Clothing by Iris van Herpen: Renowned fashion designer Iris van Herpen incorporates 3D printing into her couture creations. She combines traditional textile materials with 3D-printed elements to design avant-garde fashion pieces, blurring the lines between fashion and technology.

Education - The University of Michigan's Human Organ Models: The University of Michigan uses 3D printing to create highly detailed, anatomically accurate human organ models. These models serve as educational tools for medical students and help enhance their understanding of complex human anatomy.

Manufacturing - BMW's 3D-Printed Water Pump Wheel: BMW has employed 3D printing to produce water pump wheels for their vehicles. The 3D-printed aluminum wheels are lighter and more efficient than traditionally manufactured versions. This demonstrates how 3D printing can improve performance and reduce production costs in manufacturing.

Consumer Goods - Adidas Future craft 4D Shoes: Adidas introduced Future craft 4D shoes featuring midsoles 3D-printed using digital light synthesis technology. These shoes offer superior cushioning and support tailored to individual athletes, showcasing the potential for customization in the consumer goods industry (Revathi et al., 2024; Suresh et al., 2024).

Energy - Siemens' 3D-Printed Gas Turbine Blades: Siemens successfully used 3D printing to manufacture gas turbine blades for power generation. These blades are subject to extreme temperatures and stresses and require intricate internal cooling channels. 3D printing enabled the creation of complex geometries that improve performance and energy efficiency.

CHALLENGES AND FUTURE DIRECTIONS

The future of additive manufacturing is promising, with continuous advancements and innovations aiming to overcome challenges and unlock new possibilities across industries. As 3D printing technologies mature, their integration will accelerate (Fan et al., 2020; Hao & Lin, 2020; Liu et al., 2021; Shahrubudin et al., 2019).

Challenges

- **Material Limitations:** While there have been significant advancements in 3D printing materials, there are still limitations in terms of material diversity, especially for high-performance applications. Developing materials with improved properties, such as higher strength and thermal resistance, remains a challenge (Kavitha et al., 2023; Murali et al., 2023; Suresh et al., 2024).

- **Speed and Scalability:** 3D printing can be slow, especially for large or complex parts. Improving print speeds while maintaining quality is a challenge. Scaling up 3D printing for mass production also presents scalability challenges.

- **Post-Processing:** Post-processing steps like cleaning, curing, and support structure removal can be labor-intensive and time-consuming. Streamlining post-processing is essential for efficient production

- **Quality Assurance:** Ensuring consistent quality across 3D-printed parts is critical, particularly in industries like aerospace and healthcare. Developing robust quality control processes and standards is an ongoing challenge.

- **Intellectual Property and Security:** The digital nature of 3D printing raises concerns about intellectual property theft and unauthorized replication of patented designs. Protecting digital files and regulating the industry to prevent counterfeiting are challenges.

- **Regulatory Compliance:** The regulatory landscape for 3D-printed medical devices and aerospace components is still evolving. Ensuring compliance with safety and quality standards is a challenge for manufacturers.

- **Cost and Material Waste:** 3D printing can be expensive, especially for industrial-grade equipment and materials. Reducing costs and minimizing material waste are ongoing challenges.

- **Environmental Impact:** Sustainable 3D printing materials and practices are essential to reduce the environmental footprint of the technology. Developing eco-friendly materials and recycling solutions is a challenge (Boopathi, 2022a; Boopathi, Alqahtani, et al., 2023; Gowri et al., 2023).

Future Directions

- **Advanced Materials:** Continued research and development in materials science will lead to the creation of novel materials with improved properties, including greater strength, durability, and thermal resistance (Suresh et al., 2024).

- **Multi-Material Printing:** Advancements in multi-material and multi-color 3D printing will enable more complex and functional parts and products.

- **Speed and Automation:** Future directions include improving print speeds through innovations like volumetric 3D printing and increasing automation in post-processing steps.

- **Digital Twins:** The integration of 3D printing with digital twin technology will enable real-time monitoring and optimization of the printing process, enhancing quality control.

- **Bioprinting and Organ Manufacturing:** Bioprinting will continue to advance, leading to the production of functional organs and tissues for transplantation and drug testing.
- **On-Demand and Distributed Manufacturing:** 3D printing hubs and micro-factories will emerge, allowing for localized and on-demand production, reducing transportation costs and emissions.
- **AI and Machine Learning:** These technologies will be applied to optimize 3D printing processes, including design optimization, quality control, and predictive maintenance (Boopathi, 2024a; Boopathi & Kanike, 2023; Zekrifa et al., 2023).
- **Sustainability:** Sustainable 3D printing practices will gain prominence, with a focus on recycling, reduced energy consumption, and environmentally friendly materials (Boopathi & Davim, 2023a, 2023b; Rahamathunnisa et al., 2024; Vijayakumar et al., 2024).
- **Regulatory Frameworks:** Robust regulatory frameworks will be established to ensure the safety and quality of 3D-printed products, especially in critical industries like healthcare and aerospace.
- **Education and Workforce Development:** As 3D printing becomes more widespread, education and workforce development programs will play a crucial role in training skilled professionals and fostering innovation.
- **Global Collaboration:** International collaboration and standardization efforts will help harmonize 3D printing practices and regulations across borders.
- **Space Exploration:** 3D printing will continue to play a vital role in space exploration, with the potential to manufacture tools, parts, and even habitats on other celestial bodies.

CONCLUSION

3D printing, a transformative technology, has transformed various industries through remarkable advancements, innovative applications, and evolving challenges. It has evolved from a prototyping tool to a mainstream manufacturing method, highlighting its wide-ranging implications.

3D printing is a versatile technology that allows for the creation of intricate, highly customized designs, enabling applications in industries like aerospace, healthcare, fashion, and education. This technology has opened new innovation frontiers, enabling engineers to create functional prototypes and push boundaries of design freedom.

Additive manufacturing offers efficiency, waste reduction, and sustainability benefits by enabling on-demand production. However, it faces challenges like material limitations, speed constraints, quality control, regulatory compliance, and intellectual property concerns, despite its potential to improve sustainability and reduce waste.

3D printing is a rapidly evolving technology that has revolutionized various industries, including the biomedical sector. Its advancements in materials, such as strength, heat resistance, and biocompatibility, have significantly improved patient care and medical research. Future directions in additive manufacturing include exploring advanced materials, multi-material printing, automation, digital twins, and sustainable practices. 3D printing's global impact extends to space exploration, disaster relief, and local manufacturing hubs, democratizing production and empowering communities.

Education and workforce development are crucial for the next generation of professionals to fully utilize 3D printing's potential for innovation. This technology has revolutionized product design, production, and industry transformation, enhanced sustainability and improving global quality of life. As additive manufacturing evolves, its impact will likely become even more profound, reshaping our understanding of manufacturing and innovation in the future.

ABBREVIATIONS

AM - Additive Manufacturing
3D Printing - Three-Dimensional Printing
R&D - Research and Development
IoT - Internet of Things
DLP - Digital Light Processing
CFRPs - Carbon Fiber Reinforced Polymers
TPEs - Thermoplastic Elastomers
STEM - Science, Technology, Engineering, and Mathematics
AI - Artificial Intelligence
IP - Intellectual Property
FDA - Food and Drug Administration
CNC - Computer Numerical Control
CLIP - Continuous Liquid Interface Production

REFERENCES

Agrawal, A. V., Pitchai, R., Senthamaraikannan, C., Balaji, N. A., Sajithra, S., & Boopathi, S. (2023). Digital Education System During the COVID-19 Pandemic. In Using Assistive Technology for Inclusive Learning in K-12 Classrooms (pp. 104–126). IGI Global. doi:10.4018/978-1-6684-6424-3.ch005

Al-Emran, M., & Al-Sharafi, M. A. (2022). Revolutionizing education with industry 5.0: Challenges and future research agendas. *International Journal of Information Technology : an Official Journal of Bharati Vidyapeeth's Institute of Computer Applications and Management, 6*(3), 1–5.

Anitha, C., Komala, C., Vivekanand, C. V., Lalitha, S., & Boopathi, S. (2023). Artificial Intelligence driven security model for Internet of Medical Things (IoMT). *IEEE Explore*, 1–7.

Boopathi, S. (2013). *Experimental study and multi-objective optimization of near-dry wire-cut electrical discharge machining process* [PhD Thesis]. http://hdl.handle.net/10603/16933

Boopathi, S. (2022a). An investigation on gas emission concentration and relative emission rate of the near-dry wire-cut electrical discharge machining process. *Environmental Science and Pollution Research International, 29*(57), 86237–86246. doi:10.1007/s11356-021-17658-1 PMID:34837614

Boopathi, S. (2022b). Experimental investigation and multi-objective optimization of cryogenic Friction-stir-welding of AA2014 and AZ31B alloys using MOORA technique. *Materials Today. Communications, 33*, 104937. doi:10.1016/j.mtcomm.2022.104937

Boopathi, S. (2023). Securing Healthcare Systems Integrated With IoT: Fundamentals, Applications, and Future Trends. In Dynamics of Swarm Intelligence Health Analysis for the Next Generation (pp. 186–209). IGI Global.

Boopathi, S. (2024a). Advancements in Machine Learning and AI for Intelligent Systems in Drone Applications for Smart City Developments. In *Futuristic e-Governance Security With Deep Learning Applications* (pp. 15–45). IGI Global. doi:10.4018/978-1-6684-9596-4.ch002

Boopathi, S. (2024b). Balancing Innovation and Security in the Cloud: Navigating the Risks and Rewards of the Digital Age. In Improving Security, Privacy, and Trust in Cloud Computing (pp. 164–193). IGI Global.

Boopathi, S., Alqahtani, A. S., Mubarakali, A., & Panchatcharam, P. (2023). Sustainable developments in near-dry electrical discharge machining process using sunflower oil-mist dielectric fluid. *Environmental Science and Pollution Research International*, 1–20. doi:10.1007/s11356-023-27494-0 PMID:37199846

Boopathi, S., & Davim, J. P. (2023a). Applications of Nanoparticles in Various Manufacturing Processes. In *Sustainable Utilization of Nanoparticles and Nanofluids in Engineering Applications* (pp. 1–31). IGI Global. doi:10.4018/978-1-6684-9135-5.ch001

Boopathi, S., & Davim, J. P. (2023b). *Sustainable Utilization of Nanoparticles and Nanofluids in Engineering Applications*. IGI Global. doi:10.4018/978-1-6684-9135-5

Boopathi, S., & Kanike, U. K. (2023). Applications of Artificial Intelligent and Machine Learning Techniques in Image Processing. In *Handbook of Research on Thrust Technologies' Effect on Image Processing* (pp. 151–173). IGI Global. doi:10.4018/978-1-6684-8618-4.ch010

Boopathi, S., Khare, R., KG, J. C., Muni, T. V., & Khare, S. (2023). Additive Manufacturing Developments in the Medical Engineering Field. In Development, Properties, and Industrial Applications of 3D Printed Polymer Composites (pp. 86–106). IGI Global.

Boopathi, S., & Kumar, P. (2024). Advanced bioprinting processes using additive manufacturing technologies: Revolutionizing tissue engineering. *3D Printing Technologies: Digital Manufacturing, Artificial Intelligence, Industry 4.0*, 95.

Chiu, B. W. (2020). *Additive manufacturing applications and implementation in aerospace* [PhD Thesis]. Massachusetts Institute of Technology.

Daminabo, S. C., Goel, S., Grammatikos, S. A., Nezhad, H. Y., & Thakur, V. K. (2020). Fused deposition modeling-based additive manufacturing (3D printing): Techniques for polymer material systems. *Materials Today. Chemistry, 16*, 100248. doi:10.1016/j.mtchem.2020.100248

Das, S., Lekhya, G., Shreya, K., Shekinah, K. L., Babu, K. K., & Boopathi, S. (2024). Fostering Sustainability Education Through Cross-Disciplinary Collaborations and Research Partnerships: Interdisciplinary Synergy. In Facilitating Global Collaboration and Knowledge Sharing in Higher Education With Generative AI (pp. 60–88). IGI Global.

Dass James, A., & Boopathi, S. (2016). Experimental Study of Eco-friendly Wire-Cut Electrical Discharge Machining Processes. *International Journal of Innovative Research in Science, Engineering and Technology, 5*.

Deepak Kumar, S., Dewangan, S., Jha, S. K., Parida, S. K., & Behera, A. (2021). 3D and 4D Printing in Industry 4.0: Trends, Challenges, and Opportunities. *Next Generation Materials and Processing Technologies: Select Proceedings of RDMPMC 2020*, 579–587.

Durairaj, M., Jayakumar, S., Karpagavalli, V., Maheswari, B. U., Boopathi, S., & ... (2023). Utilization of Digital Tools in the Indian Higher Education System During Health Crises. In *Multidisciplinary Approaches to Organizational Governance During Health Crises* (pp. 1–21). IGI Global. doi:10.4018/978-1-7998-9213-7.ch001

Fan, D., Li, Y., Wang, X., Zhu, T., Wang, Q., Cai, H., Li, W., Tian, Y., & Liu, Z. (2020). Progressive 3D printing technology and its application in medical materials. *Frontiers in Pharmacology*, *11*, 122. doi:10.3389/fphar.2020.00122 PMID:32265689

Gentry, G. (2021). *Proposed International Space Station Life Support Hardware Changes for a Lunar/Mars Surface Human Habitat Common Cabin Air Assembly Case Study*. Academic Press.

George, A. S., & George, A. H. (2023). Revolutionizing Manufacturing: Exploring the Promises and Challenges of Industry 5.0. *Partners Universal International Innovation Journal*, *1*(2), 22–38.

Gowri, N. V., Dwivedi, J. N., Krishnaveni, K., Boopathi, S., Palaniappan, M., & Medikondu, N. R. (2023). Experimental investigation and multi-objective optimization of eco-friendly near-dry electrical discharge machining of shape memory alloy using Cu/SiC/Gr composite electrode. *Environmental Science and Pollution Research International*, *30*(49), 1–19. doi:10.1007/s11356-023-26983-6 PMID:37126160

Hao, B., & Lin, G. (2020). 3D printing technology and its application in industrial manufacturing. *IOP Conference Series. Materials Science and Engineering*, *782*(2), 022065. doi:10.1088/1757-899X/782/2/022065

Haribalaji, V., Boopathi, S., Asif, M. M., Jeyakumar, M., Subbiah, R., & Lewise, K. A. S. (2022). Influences of Friction stir tool parameters for joining two similar AZ61A alloy plates. *Materials Today: Proceedings*, *50*(5), 2547–2553. doi:10.1016/j.matpr.2021.12.074

Haribalaji, V., Boopathi, S., Asif, M. M., Yuvaraj, T., Velmurugan, D., Lewise, K. A. S., Sudhagar, S., & Suresh, P. (2022). Influences of Mg-Cr filler materials in Friction Stir Process of Aluminium-based dissimilar alloys. *Materials Today: Proceedings*, *66*(3), 948–954. doi:10.1016/j.matpr.2022.04.668

Haribalaji, V., Boopathi, S., & Balamurugan, S. (2014). Effect of Welding Processes on Mechanical and Metallurgical Properties of High Strength Low Alloy (HSLA) Steel Joints. *International Journal of Innovation and Scientific Research*, *12*(1), 170–179.

Haribalaji, V., Venkatesan, G., Pandian, M., Subbiah, R., & Boopathi, S. (2022). Investigation on corrosion and tensile Characteristics: Friction stir welding of AA7075 and AA2014. *Materials Today: Proceedings, 66*(3), 743–748. doi:10.1016/j.matpr.2022.04.037

Javaid, M., & Haleem, A. (2019). 4D printing applications in medical field: A brief review. *Clinical Epidemiology and Global Health, 7*(3), 317–321. doi:10.1016/j.cegh.2018.09.007

Jeyaraman, M., Nallakumarasamy, A., & Jeyaraman, N. (2022). Industry 5.0 in orthopaedics. *Indian Journal of Orthopaedics, 56*(10), 1694–1702. doi:10.1007/s43465-022-00712-6 PMID:36187596

Jihong, Z., Han, Z., Chuang, W., Lu, Z., Shangqin, Y., & Zhang, W. (2021). A review of topology optimization for additive manufacturing: Status and challenges. *Chinese Journal of Aeronautics, 34*(1), 91–110. doi:10.1016/j.cja.2020.09.020

Kantaros, A., Ganetsos, T., & Piromalis, D. (2023). 3D and 4D Printing as Integrated Manufacturing Methods of Industry 4.0. *Kantaros, A., Ganetsos, T. & Piromalis, D.(2023). 3D and 4D Printing as Integrated Manufacturing Methods of Industry, 4, 12–22.*

Karthik, S., Hemalatha, R., Aruna, R., Deivakani, M., Reddy, R. V. K., & Boopathi, S. (2023). Study on Healthcare Security System-Integrated Internet of Things (IoT). In Perspectives and Considerations on the Evolution of Smart Systems (pp. 342–362). IGI Global.

Kavitha, C., Malini, P. G., Kantumuchu, V. C., Kumar, N. M., Verma, A., & Boopathi, S. (2023). An experimental study on the hardness and wear rate of carbonitride coated stainless steel. *Materials Today: Proceedings, 74*, 595–601. doi:10.1016/j.matpr.2022.09.524

Kermanidis, A. T. (2020). Aircraft aluminum alloys: Applications and future trends. *Revolutionizing Aircraft Materials and Processes*, 21–55.

Koshariya, A. K., Kalaiyarasi, D., Jovith, A. A., Sivakami, T., Hasan, D. S., & Boopathi, S. (2023). AI-Enabled IoT and WSN-Integrated Smart Agriculture System. In *Artificial Intelligence Tools and Technologies for Smart Farming and Agriculture Practices* (pp. 200–218). IGI Global. doi:10.4018/978-1-6684-8516-3.ch011

Kuang, X., Roach, D. J., Wu, J., Hamel, C. M., Ding, Z., Wang, T., Dunn, M. L., & Qi, H. J. (2019). Advances in 4D printing: Materials and applications. *Advanced Functional Materials, 29*(2), 1805290. doi:10.1002/adfm.201805290

Kumari, G., Abhishek, K., Singh, S., Hussain, A., Altamimi, M. A., Madhyastha, H., Webster, T. J., & Dev, A. (2022). A voyage from 3D to 4D printing in nanomedicine and healthcare: Part II. *Nanomedicine (London)*, *17*(4), 255–270. doi:10.2217/nnm-2021-0454 PMID:35109687

Liu, C., Xu, N., Zong, Q., Yu, J., & Zhang, P. (2021). Hydrogel prepared by 3D printing technology and its applications in the medical field. *Colloid and Interface Science Communications*, *44*, 100498. doi:10.1016/j.colcom.2021.100498

Maddikunta, P. K. R., Pham, Q.-V., Prabadevi, B., Deepa, N., Dev, K., Gadekallu, T. R., Ruby, R., & Liyanage, M. (2022). Industry 5.0: A survey on enabling technologies and potential applications. *Journal of Industrial Information Integration*, *26*, 100257. doi:10.1016/j.jii.2021.100257

Maguluri, L. P., Ananth, J., Hariram, S., Geetha, C., Bhaskar, A., & Boopathi, S. (2023). Smart Vehicle-Emissions Monitoring System Using Internet of Things (IoT). In Handbook of Research on Safe Disposal Methods of Municipal Solid Wastes for a Sustainable Environment (pp. 191–211). IGI Global.

Mohanty, A., Jothi, B., Jeyasudha, J., Ranjit, P., Isaac, J. S., & Boopathi, S. (2023). Additive Manufacturing Using Robotic Programming. In *AI-Enabled Social Robotics in Human Care Services* (pp. 259–282). IGI Global. doi:10.4018/978-1-6684-8171-4.ch010

Mohanty, A., Venkateswaran, N., Ranjit, P., Tripathi, M. A., & Boopathi, S. (2023). Innovative Strategy for Profitable Automobile Industries: Working Capital Management. In Handbook of Research on Designing Sustainable Supply Chains to Achieve a Circular Economy (pp. 412–428). IGI Global.

Moroni, S., Casettari, L., & Lamprou, D. A. (2022). 3D and 4D Printing in the Fight against Breast Cancer. *Biosensors (Basel)*, *12*(8), 568. doi:10.3390/bios12080568 PMID:35892465

Murali, B., Padhi, S., Patil, C. K., Kumar, P. S., Santhanakrishnan, M., & Boopathi, S. (2023). Investigation on hardness and tensile strength of friction stir processing of Al6061/TiN surface composite. *Materials Today: Proceedings*.

Myilsamy, S., & Sampath, B. (2017). Grey Relational Optimization of Powder Mixed Near-Dry Wire Cut Electrical Discharge Machining of Inconel 718 Alloy. *Asian Journal of Research in Social Sciences and Humanities*, *7*(3), 18–25. doi:10.5958/2249-7315.2017.00157.5

Nishanth, J., Deshmukh, M. A., Kushwah, R., Kushwaha, K. K., Balaji, S., & Sampath, B. (2023). Particle Swarm Optimization of Hybrid Renewable Energy Systems. In *Intelligent Engineering Applications and Applied Sciences for Sustainability* (pp. 291–308). IGI Global. doi:10.4018/979-8-3693-0044-2.ch016

Ntouanoglou, K., Stavropoulos, P., & Mourtzis, D. (2018). 4D printing prospects for the aerospace industry: A critical review. *Procedia Manufacturing*, *18*, 120–129. doi:10.1016/j.promfg.2018.11.016

Osouli-Bostanabad, K., Masalehdan, T., Kapsa, R. M., Quigley, A., Lalatsa, A., Bruggeman, K. F., Franks, S. J., Williams, R. J., & Nisbet, D. R. (2022). Traction of 3D and 4D Printing in the Healthcare Industry: From Drug Delivery and Analysis to Regenerative Medicine. *ACS Biomaterials Science & Engineering*, *8*(7), 2764–2797. doi:10.1021/acsbiomaterials.2c00094 PMID:35696306

Palaniappan, M., Tirlangi, S., Mohamed, M. J. S., Moorthy, R. S., Valeti, S. V., & Boopathi, S. (2023). Fused Deposition Modelling of Polylactic Acid (PLA)-Based Polymer Composites: A Case Study. In Development, Properties, and Industrial Applications of 3D Printed Polymer Composites (pp. 66–85). IGI Global.

Pramila, P., Amudha, S., Saravanan, T., Sankar, S. R., Poongothai, E., & Boopathi, S. (2023). Design and Development of Robots for Medical Assistance: An Architectural Approach. In Contemporary Applications of Data Fusion for Advanced Healthcare Informatics (pp. 260–282). IGI Global.

Rahamathunnisa, U., Sudhakar, K., Padhi, S., Bhattacharya, S., Shashibhushan, G., & Boopathi, S. (2024). Sustainable Energy Generation From Waste Water: IoT Integrated Technologies. In Adoption and Use of Technology Tools and Services by Economically Disadvantaged Communities: Implications for Growth and Sustainability (pp. 225–256). IGI Global.

Ramudu, K., Mohan, V. M., Jyothirmai, D., Prasad, D., Agrawal, R., & Boopathi, S. (2023). Machine Learning and Artificial Intelligence in Disease Prediction: Applications, Challenges, Limitations, Case Studies, and Future Directions. In Contemporary Applications of Data Fusion for Advanced Healthcare Informatics (pp. 297–318). IGI Global.

Raphey, V., Henna, T., Nivitha, K., Mufeedha, P., Sabu, C., & Pramod, K. (2019). Advanced biomedical applications of carbon nanotube. *Materials Science and Engineering C*, *100*, 616–630. doi:10.1016/j.msec.2019.03.043 PMID:30948098

Ravisankar, A., Sampath, B., & Asif, M. M. (2023). Economic Studies on Automobile Management: Working Capital and Investment Analysis. In Multidisciplinary Approaches to Organizational Governance During Health Crises (pp. 169–198). IGI Global.

Revathi, S., Babu, M., Rajkumar, N., Meti, V. K. V., Kandavalli, S. R., & Boopathi, S. (2024). Unleashing the Future Potential of 4D Printing: Exploring Applications in Wearable Technology, Robotics, Energy, Transportation, and Fashion. In Human-Centered Approaches in Industry 5.0: Human-Machine Interaction, Virtual Reality Training, and Customer Sentiment Analysis (pp. 131–153). IGI Global.

Sengeni, D., Padmapriya, G., Imambi, S. S., Suganthi, D., Suri, A., & Boopathi, S. (2023). Biomedical waste handling method using artificial intelligence techniques. In *Handbook of Research on Safe Disposal Methods of Municipal Solid Wastes for a Sustainable Environment* (pp. 306–323). IGI Global. doi:10.4018/978-1-6684-8117-2.ch022

Senthil, T., Puviyarasan, M., Babu, S. R., Surakasi, R., & Sampath, B. (2023). Industrial Robot-Integrated Fused Deposition Modelling for the 3D Printing Process. In Development, Properties, and Industrial Applications of 3D Printed Polymer Composites (pp. 188–210). IGI Global.

Shahrubudin, N., Lee, T. C., & Ramlan, R. (2019). An overview on 3D printing technology: Technological, materials, and applications. *Procedia Manufacturing, 35*, 1286–1296. doi:10.1016/j.promfg.2019.06.089

Sharma, D. M., Ramana, K. V., Jothilakshmi, R., Verma, R., Maheswari, B. U., & Boopathi, S. (2024). Integrating Generative AI Into K-12 Curriculums and Pedagogies in India: Opportunities and Challenges. *Facilitating Global Collaboration and Knowledge Sharing in Higher Education With Generative AI*, 133–161.

Sharma, M., Sehrawat, R., Luthra, S., Daim, T., & Bakry, D. (2022). Moving towards industry 5.0 in the pharmaceutical manufacturing sector: Challenges and solutions for Germany. *IEEE Transactions on Engineering Management*.

Subha, S., Inbamalar, T., Komala, C., Suresh, L. R., Boopathi, S., & Alaskar, K. (2023). A Remote Health Care Monitoring system using internet of medical things (IoMT). *IEEE Explore*, 1–6.

Suresh, S., Natarajan, E., Boopathi, S., & Kumar, P. (2024). Processing of smart materials by additive manufacturing and 4D printing. In A. Kumar, P. Kumar, N. Sharma, & A. K. Srivastava (Eds.), *Digital Manufacturing, Artificial Intelligence, Industry 4.0* (pp. 181–196). De Gruyter. doi:10.1515/9783111215112-008

Syamala, M., Komala, C., Pramila, P., Dash, S., Meenakshi, S., & Boopathi, S. (2023). Machine Learning-Integrated IoT-Based Smart Home Energy Management System. In *Handbook of Research on Deep Learning Techniques for Cloud-Based Industrial IoT* (pp. 219–235). IGI Global. doi:10.4018/978-1-6684-8098-4.ch013

Tibbits, S. (2014). 4D printing: Multi-material shape change. *Architectural Design*, *84*(1), 116–121. doi:10.1002/ad.1710

Tiwari, S., Bahuguna, P. C., & Walker, J. (2022). Industry 5.0: A macroperspective approach. In Handbook of Research on Innovative Management Using AI in Industry 5.0 (pp. 59–73). IGI Global.

Ugandar, R., Rahamathunnisa, U., Sajithra, S., Christiana, M. B. V., Palai, B. K., & Boopathi, S. (2023). Hospital Waste Management Using Internet of Things and Deep Learning: Enhanced Efficiency and Sustainability. In Applications of Synthetic Biology in Health, Energy, and Environment (pp. 317–343). IGI Global.

Vafadar, A., Guzzomi, F., Rassau, A., & Hayward, K. (2021). Advances in metal additive manufacturing: A review of common processes, industrial applications, and current challenges. *Applied Sciences (Basel, Switzerland)*, *11*(3), 1213. doi:10.3390/app11031213

Venkateswaran, N., Kumar, S. S., Diwakar, G., Gnanasangeetha, D., & Boopathi, S. (2023). Synthetic Biology for Waste Water to Energy Conversion: IoT and AI Approaches. *Applications of Synthetic Biology in Health. Energy & Environment*, 360–384.

Vennila, T., Karuna, M., Srivastava, B. K., Venugopal, J., Surakasi, R., & Sampath, B. (2022). New Strategies in Treatment and Enzymatic Processes: Ethanol Production From Sugarcane Bagasse. In Human Agro-Energy Optimization for Business and Industry (pp. 219–240). IGI Global.

Verma, R., Christiana, M. B. V., Maheswari, M., Srinivasan, V., Patro, P., Dari, S. S., & Boopathi, S. (2024). Intelligent Physarum Solver for Profit Maximization in Oligopolistic Supply Chain Networks. In *AI and Machine Learning Impacts in Intelligent Supply Chain* (pp. 156–179). IGI Global. doi:10.4018/979-8-3693-1347-3.ch011

Vijayakumar, G. N. S., Domakonda, V. K., Farooq, S., Kumar, B. S., Pradeep, N., & Boopathi, S. (2024). Sustainable Developments in Nano-Fluid Synthesis for Various Industrial Applications. In Adoption and Use of Technology Tools and Services by Economically Disadvantaged Communities: Implications for Growth and Sustainability (pp. 48–81). IGI Global.

Yengst, W. (2010). *Lightning Bolts: First Maneuvering Reentry Vehicles*. Tate Publishing.

Zekrifa, D. M. S., Kulkarni, M., Bhagyalakshmi, A., Devireddy, N., Gupta, S., & Boopathi, S. (2023). Integrating Machine Learning and AI for Improved Hydrological Modeling and Water Resource Management. In *Artificial Intelligence Applications in Water Treatment and Water Resource Management* (pp. 46–70). IGI Global. doi:10.4018/978-1-6684-6791-6.ch003

Zhang, J., Wang, J., Dong, S., Yu, X., & Han, B. (2019). A review of the current progress and application of 3D printed concrete. *Composites. Part A, Applied Science and Manufacturing, 125*, 105533. doi:10.1016/j.compositesa.2019.105533

Chapter 11
Smart Grid Fault Detection and Classification Framework Utilizing AIoT in India

Sandhya Avasthi

iD https://orcid.org/0000-0003-3828-0813
ABES Engineering College, Ghaziabad, India

Tanushree Sanwal

iD https://orcid.org/0000-0002-5703-1700
KIET Group of Institutions, Delhi, India

Shikha Verma
ABES Engineering College, Ghaziabad, India

ABSTRACT

The energy sector is facing obstacles such as increased consumption, efficiency, and losses affecting mainly developing countries. One of the major challenges is unauthorized power connections due to which a significant portion of consumed energy is not billed, causing business loss. The misuse of energy indirectly increases the amount of CO_2 emissions because unauthorized users utilize energy irresponsibly. As the third-largest producer and consumer of electricity in the world, India is facing a variety of power-related issues such as distribution losses, electricity fraud, and environmental issues. The artificial internet of things (AIoT) is proving beneficial in energy use optimization, fault detection, and identification. The technological issues and solutions are discussed for fault detection and classification in a smart grid. A case study is provided as a first step towards automated fault detection in smart grids. This chapter aims to identify factors that could assist India in developing its smart infrastructure and evaluate the numerous components of the smart grid.

DOI: 10.4018/979-8-3693-0968-1.ch011

1. INTRODUCTION

AI is capable of reducing energy waste, minimizing energy prices, and facilitating and accelerating the global implementation of renewable energy sources. AI can also improve the design, operation, and control of power systems. Thus, AI technologies are inextricably related to the capacity to provide development-critical, affordable, and clean energy. The power sector has a promising future due to the creation of AI-powered smart grids and electrical networks enabling communication between consumers and utility companies. The information layer of Smart Grids establishes communication, observes rapid changes in energy usage, and handles emergencies efficiently by utilizing modern technology such as AIoT. The use of Smart meters along with sensors makes it possible to collect and store data and supports the different functions of the information layer. In the rapidly evolving world of the Internet of Things, which connects and exchanges data across a vast network of devices or "things," organizations flourish via the use of analytics. AI is a critical sort of analytics for any organization that wants to maximize the value of IoT since it can make snap decisions, find significant insights, and "learn" from massive amounts of IoT data at the same time. In this article, we'll look at how IoT analytics, also known as the "Artificial Intelligence of Things" or AIoT, helps businesses in a variety of industries, such as manufacturing, retail, energy, smart cities, healthcare, and more, provide new value to their customers. These industries include and are not limited to manufacturing, retail, energy, smart cities, and healthcare.

Smart devices connected to the Internet contribute to collective intelligence with the help of Artificial Intelligence when applied to data from a network. Utility companies and the manufacturing sector can benefit by detecting underperforming assets and can use AI to predict maintenance requirements (Abdalla et al. 2021, Franki & Majnarić 2023, Lyu & Liu, 2021). In addition, AI AI-powered system will guide when to shut the system so that hazardous failure situations can be avoided. A variety of sensors and equipment cannot rely on cloud-based information or instructions. Sometimes it is just not necessary. It makes sense to analyze as close to the unit as feasible for monitoring, diagnosing, and taking action on certain pieces of equipment, such as home automation systems. Transferring locally gathered and used data to a distant data center causes unnecessary network traffic, slowed decision-making, and battery drain in mobile devices. Analytics has moved from traditional data centers to devices on the edge — the "things" — or additional processing resources close to the edge and cloud — the fog — due to the exponential growth of IoT devices and related data volumes as well as the necessity for low latency. Fog computing, a notion that is still in its infancy, shifts networking, security, and networking tasks from a centralized cloud to distributed clouds that are closer to IoT devices and services. Fog computing, also referred to as "fogging," enables local data processing. A centralized data center only receives notifications, exceptions, and outcomes. performance improvement while bandwidth reduction.

Energy sustainability and environmental protection are currently major global issues as a result of the multiple effects of climate change and the increasing energy demand. Cities and countries use more electricity as a result of their increased technological sophistication, and it may become hard to maintain without outside help. The transition to environmentally friendly technology, including distributed generation and microgrids, has prompted the development of the smart grid (Şerban & Lytras, 2020, Khosrojerdi et al., 2021). This document offers an overview of the Smart Grid, including its main functions and traits. The basics of the Smart Grid and related technologies are covered. Additionally, it covers the research processes, challenges, and issues (Dhanabalan & Sathish, 2018). It demonstrates how the current power grid has changed as a result of these technologies and how it has continued to develop while improving its ability to balance supply and demand. Furthermore, highlighted are the deployment and use of the Smart Grid in various areas. Initiatives for the Smart Grid are made easier in all countries by concrete energy rules (Yousuf et al.,2020, Kannan & Madhumita 2020). The practices of Smart Grid in numerous fields are noteworthy because they don't necessarily show competitiveness. Instead, they show a global society with common goals and lessons.

There are a growing number of high-performance IoT devices and environments with tens of thousands of connection points on the network. The perfect storm has arrived. Due to declining hardware costs, it is now possible to put sensors and connections in nearly anything. Analytics, light-speed communications, and computer advancements have enabled the development of AI-driven intelligence wherever it is necessary, including at the network's edge. Together, these technologies are ushering in a new era in which the Internet of Things is only the state of things and the phrase is rendered redundant, similar to the World Wide Web or "internet-connected," which are no longer required.

1.1 Power Crisis in India

For the continuous progress of people and to improve their development, development seeks to eradicate poverty and increase access to basic requirements, one of the key factors is energy. Communities are surrounded by the institutions, laws, and policies of the state; they do not exist in a vacuum. Thus, it is our job to provide an energy strategy that will assist us in achieving our objectives. Industrialization and population growth have increased India's energy needs. By 2040, India's primary energy consumption will climb from 6% to 11% (BP Publishers, 2019). In November 2021, India had 150.54 GW of renewable energy capacity, with solar at 48.55 GW, wind at 40.03 GW, small hydro at 4.83 GW, biomass at 10.62 GW, and large hydro at 46.51 GW (MNRE, 2021). The NITI Aayog (2015) expects India to generate 175 GW of renewable energy by 2022 and 500 GW by 2030. This goal intends to reconstruct the energy system to integrate renewable energy sources and accelerate the green energy transition due to global warming and fossil fuel depletion. India's power system has high transmission and distribution losses due to operational inefficiencies (Jadhav & Dharme, 2012, Sharma et al., 2017, Avasthi et al, 2023).

Predictive maintenance can reduce capital expenditures associated with equipment maintenance in the renewable energy sector. By anticipating asset breakdowns, energy companies can reduce unplanned downtime and associated costs. They can help reduce asset repair costs by responding to data-driven maintenance schedules.

1.2 Toward a Smart Power Sector

The integration of renewable energy sources and the optimization of energy usage considerably aids climate change mitigation and sustainable energy transitions. The Internet of Things (IoT) and other modern technologies can considerably assist the energy business in a variety of ways, including energy production, transmission, distribution, and consumption. Energy consumption can be made less detrimental to the environment by utilizing the Internet of Things, more renewable energy can be produced, and energy efficiency can be raised (Rahman, et al., 2013). The present literature on the use of IoT in energy systems in general, and smart grids in particular, is reviewed in this paper. In addition, we explore the enabling technologies of the Internet of Things, such as cloud computing and other data analysis platforms. Furthermore, we look at the problems of integrating IoT in the energy sector, such as privacy and security, as well as potential solutions like blockchain technology (Chakraborty et al., 2017, Zanella et al., 2014). This survey provides an overview of the importance of IoT in energy system optimization to energy policymakers, energy economists, and managers (Avasthi et al., 2023, Yan et al., 2014).

The rising need for energy can be traced back to urbanization, better living standards, and technological advancements. Thus, if nothing was done, the amount of energy required to power homes and businesses would grow to unsustainable proportions. The natural ecology and the worldwide supply of renewable energy are in a dangerous spot right now. Urban areas are responsible for between 75% and 80% of global energy use and emissions. During the day, power is often distributed via a centralized grid. often just called "the grid" when discussing electricity. Despite technological developments, the fundamental structure, dynamics, and underpinnings of the world's electric grids have remained unchanged since the invention of electricity. Traditional power networks focus on the production, delivery, and control of electrical energy.

1.3 Data Analytics for Fault Detection in Smart Grid

Generally, any Smart Grid can face challenges such as fault, which is a condition where a certain component in the electric grid is not working properly. The fault is usually associated with abnormal electric current such as a short circuit, a fault occurs due to excessive operating power. Smart Grids are an interconnected electric network of end-users that integrates actions and behaviors. Business scenarios previously discussed involve both discrete data (like customer profiles and past purchase history) and continuously changing and moving data (like a driver's geolocation or the temperature inside a data center) (Jadhav & Dharme, 2012). Analytics must be used in a variety of ways and for a variety of reasons in light of this fact. To draw value from the linked environment, the AIoT system must first have access to a range of data to recognize what is significant as it occurs (Chakraborty et al., 2017). It must then derive insights from the data in a rich context. Finally, it must produce results quickly, whether to notify a device operator, extend an offer, or modify how a device performs. Figure 1 depicts various dimensions of analytics and their interactions.

The smart grid is a multi-stakeholder, intricate system. It is vital to comprehend the needs and viewpoints of various stakeholders while implementing novel technologies and formulating fresh rules. The smart grid is also a consumer-driven technology, meaning that advancements in technology are determined by human demands and habits. The power grid these days has installed IoT sensors for real-time monitoring of the power grid. In addition, the organization wants to utilize the sensors' data by integrating AI with smart grids. The purpose is to reduce the operating cost of maintaining units and losses in the distribution of energy. AIoT architecture powered through edge computing supports connections, management of terminals, data privacy, data analysis, fault prediction, and classification of faults.

The main contribution of this chapter is listed as follows.

i.   The chapter provides concepts of Smart Grid and its architecture
ii.   The chapter provides an analysis of the various components of smart grid technology and its development prospects.
iii. The chapter describes the smart grid fault detection and classification framework.
iv.   Issues and challenges in the development and maintenance of smart grid in India are discussed.

2. AIOT APPLICATIONS IN THE ENERGY SECTOR

Past researches show various application domains that utilize AIoT technologies (Avasthi et al., 2022, Shi et al., 2020, Samantaray, 2014). Some of the applications

Figure 1. Three dimensions of analysis and their interaction

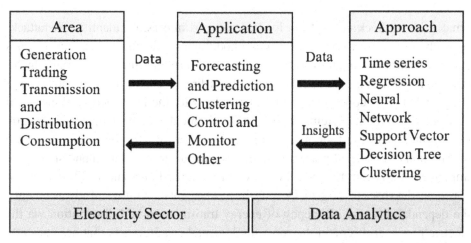

include smart cities, smart healthcare (Avasthi et al., 2022), smart homes (Chauhan et al., 2021), smart agriculture, and smart industry. Additionally, there has been a rapid development of Internet of Things applications that are centered on particular things, such as the Internet of Vehicles (IoV) and the Internet of Video Things (IoVT). The key technology used in AIoT is artificial intelligence, hardware accelerators, and 5G networks. 5G (fifth generation networks) delivers fast speed which is faster than 4G/LTE for advanced data analytics needed for fast transmission over the cloud.

The use of Artificial Intelligence in smart grids for security purposes is beneficial too. A Deep learning solution based on a Deep Belief network can detect false data injection attacks quickly and with good accuracy. Another useful solution is a cloud-centric system for theft detection that detects abnormal behavior in smart grids.

3. SMART POWER SECTOR SOLUTIONS

Smart grids and smart meters are two examples of the technology employed by smart energy solutions for the collection of relevant data. This information pertains to the flow of electricity and may range from equipment performance to end-user energy consumption. By analyzing this data, an energy provider may make prudent judgments to govern power flow in all three verticals of generation of power, transmission, and distribution. The Internet of Things is crucial for ensuring that electricity flows through each of these three processes. It helps power companies to regulate the flow of electricity even during peak demand and reduce waste.

3.1 Smart Grid and Role of AIoT

Smart grids can track and schedule loads, detect grid failures, and identify cyberattacks by applying the latest AIoT tools and methodologies. The power distribution poles classification and estimate of any damage are done through Unmanned aerial vehicles (UAVs) which are part of a cellular network and directly connected to a control center (Beg, 2016). This concept began to take shape with the introduction of electrical network distribution systems. Different requirements, such as those for control, monitoring, tariffs, and services, were required over time for the transmission and distribution of electrical power. Typically, smart meter installation and smart grid implementation occur together. They were used in the 1970s and 1980s to transmit consumer data back to the grid. Despite the most recent technological advancements, the dependability and efficiency of energy transmission and distribution via the electric power grid remain the most fundamental requirements that are currently being met.

A Smart Grid is an electricity network that can intelligently integrate the actions of all users connected to it – generators, consumers and those that do both to efficiently deliver sustainable, economical and secure electricity supplies. (Shahzad, 2020)

To distribute electricity to users, a grid or network of electrical cables is required. The term "Smart Grid" may apply to this network if its control and monitoring mechanisms are automated and it is intelligent. A "smart grid" is a technical term for conventional networks that combines current, automated technologies to boost their sustainability and dependability. In the past, grids were just used to transfer and distribute electricity, but today's smart grid can interact, store data, and even make decisions based on the circumstances. Therefore, a smart grid is an intelligent network of electricity that integrates the actions of all stakeholders—generators, consumers, and one who does both—to supply electricity with efficiency, sustainability, economy, and security, according to the Strategic Deployment Document for Europe's Electricity Networks of the Future. Thus, Smart Grid technology will not be the only one used.

Knowledge illustration and causal relationship development are also studied for power grid breakdown diagnosis and effect cause analysis (Aboumalik et al., 2019). Transfer learning and deep reinforcement learning methods for load monitoring and electric car charging scheduling are given (Wang, 2015, Avasthi et al., 2022). A distributed deep reinforcement learning method is useful in safeguarding and maintaining the privacy of households while managing load schedules. This method is based on the idea of federated learning implemented using action networks at distributed households and the critic network belongs to an aggregator from a third party(Jenkins, 2015). The security issue of cyberattacks on smart grids has received substantial attention. Recently, a semi-supervised deep learning system based on generative adversarial networks and autoencoders was suggested, and it is capable of identifying attacks in smart grids that use bogus data injection.

3.2 Smart Meter

Utility companies all around the world are currently in the process of putting in place expansive networks of advanced metering infrastructure (AMI), sometimes known as smart meters (Hosseini et al., 2020, Chen et al., 2016). But are utilities truly optimizing their use of both their investment and all of this data to its full potential? The continuous and real-time analysis of meter data to continue providing utilities with important answers to their operational and business-related questions is the key to realizing the full potential of smart meters and the smart grid. This analysis is the key to realizing the full potential of smart meters and the smart grid. Take, for example:

- Which customers have the most potential to help manage peak demand using our time-of-use pricing or demand response programs?
- To effectively plan for power generation and negotiate the most affordable contracts for wholesale market electricity, how can we make sure that our estimations of load and peak demand are as accurate as possible?
- To construct larger transformers or switch meters to transformers that are not running at capacity, how can we shift the load off of these transformers temporarily?
- Is the rollout of our smart meters proceeding on time and with minimal equipment or installation issues? How well does our network of smart meters perform over time?
- Is it possible to use new ways to save energy or lower reactive power on a large scale? For example, could conservation voltage reduction programs be used to save energy or lower reactive power?
- What proactive maintenance strategies can we implement to replace our current reactive maintenance approach and focus our meager field personnel on the equipment that is most likely to malfunction?

Understanding and engaging customers through AMI analytics- With the use of AMI analytics, utilities can enhance several client programs, including demand response, energy efficiency, and time-of-use pricing, which have advantages for both the business and its clients (Liu et al., 2016). Some common activities are program design, identifying participants, helping customers to make choices, evaluation, and reporting incidents. In the program planning step, the right mix of customer-facing measures and rewards is chosen. Based on their real energy data, online calculators can tell each customer if they could save money or get other benefits from joining a program or switching to a time-of-use rate. The different programs that people are using are looked at every so often to see if they're meeting their goals.

Optimizing and improving the energy market- The energy industry and its structure have a significant impact on the financial landscape. Utilities that possess the capability to accurately predict their power requirements generally enjoy the advantage of negotiating more cost-effective long-term contracts when procuring wholesale power (Liu et al., 2016). Additionally, they avoid significantly more expensive last-minute power purchases on the secondary market. This results in cost savings for regulated distribution utilities, which may be transferred to consumers, or potentially even profits for shareholders. The utilization of AMI analytics facilitates more precise prediction of system capacity and peak demand, leading to more informed procurement decisions. Through the use of analytics, utilities can determine when and how system peaks occur, as well as divide system loads into significant customer and regional peaks. By utilizing such real-time and detailed data, utility companies can observe the evolution of consumer behavior regarding device and energy consumption (Chen et al., 2016).

3.3 Fault Detection and Classification

Smart Grid (SG) defect detection is a crucial research topic that is gaining attention from both the academic world and business. Identifying problems or potential failures on the smart grid involves sensing and assessing variations in electrical power (such as current and voltage), environmental, and equipment characteristics. System status awareness, system maintenance, and system functioning depend on autonomous smart grid fault detection. Continuous monitoring and fault detection are imperative steps for maintaining quality of service (QoS) in different SG applications. Power transmission, distribution, and consumption all necessitate the implementation of autonomous smart grid fault detection (Raza et al., 2022). The faults that can be found at different layers of SG systems can be faults due to Physical devices/component *failures, communication faults,* and *software/hardware* level faults (Vyas et al., 2019). There are two primary categories for faults: balanced faults and unbalanced faults. In general, unbalanced faults occur frequently which are divided into series and shunt faults. Shunt faults can easily be detected by observing an increase or decrease in voltage and frequency. The common problems related to energy distribution and management are discussed as follows.

- **Power Transmission**: As the size, complexity, and intelligence of UHV AC and DC transfer systems have grown, the way the power grid works has changed in big ways. On the one hand, things like changing regional climate and a complicated operating environment can affect UHV power transmission. At the same time, it is important to keep an eye on how the power grid is running. On the other hand, AC and DC are closely connected to UHV power grid transfer and reception, which can easily make global security risks worse. So, finding bugs and early warnings of cross-regional risks in real-time at the network level is very important for helping to plan operations (Li et al., 2023).

- **Power Distribution:** More and more distributed generators, devices that charge electric cars, devices that store energy, and microgrids are connected to the distribution network as the penetration rate rises. Large power changes and voltage over-limits are likely to happen because of the random nature of green energy sources and loads, as well as the spread multi-agent control. This makes it hard to run the distribution network. On the other hand, the tie switch-based method of network reconfiguration has limits on its response time, working life, and inrush current. This means that it won't be able to meet the needs of future users who need high reliability (Sidhu and Xu, 2010).

- **Power Consumption:** Low-voltage power grids are very complicated in how they are put together. During operation, electrical faults like leaky faults, short circuit faults, overload faults, and high contact resistance often happen, making it hard for users to do the things they need to do every day. The only way to make sure that the collection system works well and that different rating signs get better is to get better at running and maintaining it.

The data-driven method uses different machine learning algorithms to classify faults and perform better than conventional methods. Some Data-driven methods for fault detection are Artificial Neural networks, Fuzzy logic, Support Vector Machines and Genetic Algorithms.

4. AIOT TECHNIQUES FOR SMART GRID FAULT DETECTION

The electricity demand is growing due to the smart city and Industry 4.0 application development. For getting insights on usage and optimizing performance Fault analysis and detection have become an essential task. This is the basic measure that can be taken to detect, locate, classify, and clear faults in the power system for proper functioning without interruptions. The recent technology being used in Smart Grid fault detection is shown in Figure 2.

Figure 2. Technology used in fault detection in smart grid

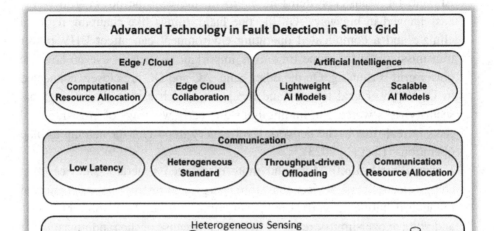

(a) **Advanced Sensing and Communication**: The smart grid is continually developing, and fault detection technology is changing with it. Together with the standard current and voltage transformers, the grid system also includes a range of sensing devices, such as phasor measuring units, smart meters, vibration, acoustic, and environmental sensors, in addition to visible and infrared cameras. One of the imperative steps in SG system is the transfer of sensor data generated in real-time to cloud storage/server or edge devices for processing further and to perform analysis. The connections to edge devices and cloud servers are generally low latency connections so improvement is essential. The different communication standards such as Ethernet, optical fiber, LTE, WiFi, Zigbee are utilized in the smart (Xiong et al., 2020). 5G technology helps in real-time identification of faults in the distribution network (Chang et al., 2019). 5G features like Ultra Reliable Low-Latency Communications provide high data rates and support multiplexing. Massive Machine Type

Communications (mMTC) enables connectivity for IoT devices and supports low latency and highly reliable communication between connecting nodes.

(b) **Machine Learning Methods**: With continued advancement, advanced artificial intelligence (AI) technology will no longer require manual control throughout the process as it enters the stage of autonomous learning based on huge data. This is especially clear in the process of detecting faults in power systems. Conventional power systems have a complicated internal network with incredibly laborious linkages. Using conventional manual troubleshooting techniques will be exceedingly challenging and error-prone if the power system breaks while the system is in use. As artificial intelligence (AI) becomes more widely used, machine learning algorithms can be used to deeply integrate, analyze, and extract mapping relationships from the massive amounts of online and offline multi-source heterogeneous power system data. This allows for the quick, accurate, and efficient detection of most power system faults as well as their intelligent handling. Different models work well with different kinds of data, and deep learning can combine heterogeneous data from several sources, which increases efficiency and guarantees the power grid's safe and dependable functioning.

(c) **Edge Computing and Cloud-Edge Collaboration**: Even though AI and computing technologies are getting better, there is still a need for quick access to the computing power that is needed. This is because the number of smart devices is growing and machine learning algorithms are becoming more complicated. Communication and cloud computing make it possible for cloud servers to store and handle huge amounts of data. Cloud computing systems, on the other hand, have problems with network lag and high dynamic jitter, which makes it harder to meet the strict delay requirements for fault detection in smart grid [43-44].

5. POWER MANAGEMENT THROUGH AIOT: CASE STUDY INDIA

Indian government's efforts to increase metering because of the growing popularity of smart meters on a worldwide scale is worth appreciable. The budget for the Financial Year 2022 included £29 billion ($39 billion) for smart metering as part of the Smart Metering National Initiative; over the following five years, 250 million conventional electricity meters will be replaced with smart meters. Governments are in charge of providing water, and each state uses its system to obtain and distribute it (Shankar & Singh, 2022). For instance, Maharashtra is at the forefront with more than 500,000 smart water meters installed in the state's two largest cities, Pune and Nagpur. The city of Jaipur will continue to use the current meters even though Rajasthan has allocated over \$53 million to replace all current meters in the city of Jaipur over the next three years.

In terms of gas distribution, pipeline natural gas (PNG) and compressed natural gas (CNG) are new to the country, with only 4 - 5% of the population receiving supply. The Ministry of Petroleum and Natural Gas in India is working hard to accelerate the adoption of gas as the primary fuel for consumers in the home, cars, and businesses. Key figures include 50-55 million new PNG connections over the next six years, as well as 6.6 million PNG connections today (Sinha et al., 2011). Even though smart metering initiatives to reduce customer attrition and increase efficiency are already underway, water utility metering is a zero-tech industry, with manual meters and readings and pipeline gas being a recent phenomenon (Vyas et al., 2019, Kumar et al., 2023). These utilities, however, are set to grow exponentially as a result of government mandates. For example, domestic gas supply will shift away from LPG, and cities must provide at least 200 liters of water per person per day. The Indian government's aim of lowering transmission and distribution losses depends on the Internet of Things (IoT). This relates to the statewide deployment of smart meters under state supervision. One important requirement is that all meters bought under the initiative have to be produced locally, with at least 50% of the value added happening in India. As of March 2022, 15 million meters had been bought; to meet government commitments, an additional 235 million must be purchased by 2025.3.

5.1 IoT as Part of the Ecosystem

When it comes to smart metering in India and other developing nations, the business model and the entire customer solution are the most innovative aspects. The managed services or hybrid CAPEX/OPEX models that utilities pursue depend on the country in which they operate. The ecosystem contains essential elements such as IoT networks and device-manufacturing companies. This implies that IoT companies should exert significant pressure to overhaul the entire utility, as opposed to simply connecting the meter to the cloud. Collaboration is required to develop an end-to-end solution involving the utility, device makers, software suppliers, billing platforms, ERP systems, and customer support. For example, we partner with Raychem, a large industrial group that makes gas meters and has the greatest number of gas meters in use in India (Salkuti, 2020).

5.2 AIoT Architecture

AIoT architecture shows the design that identifies each layer as having a distinct task to accomplish is commonly done layer by layer (Li et al., 2018). More pertinent to IoT applications and energy system regulations compliance is the four-layered approach. The 4 layers are the physical layer, communication network layer, cyber layer, and application layer. The cyber layer uses cloud-based processing applications and distributed systems to optimize computing. The layer of application known as the management layer is used in analyzing concerns from economic, social, and environmental viewpoints from collected data about market regulation, incentive measures, and pricing. Figure 3 describes different components in layers and protocols that can be used in energy distribution networks.

Figure 3. The architecture of energy distribution networks

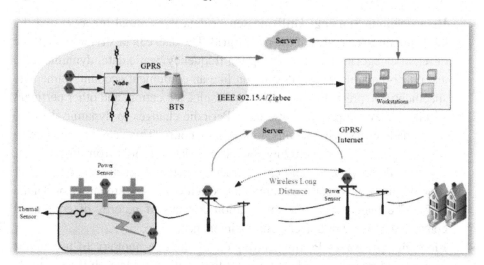

6. CHALLENGES IN SENSOR DATA PROCESSING

The primary challenges in smart grid fault detection and classification are discussed here.

- **Lack of theoretical background-** The decision maker's lack of knowledge of the technology is one factor contributing to the sluggish adoption of AI in the sector of energy. Many organizations just lack the technical knowledge to understand how incorporating AI might improve their operations. Conservative stakeholders would rather take the risk of trying something new than deviate from tried-and-true tactics and resources. As more sectors, including education, healthcare, finance, and transportation, embrace AI's promise, decision-makers in the energy industry are focused on it (Rahman et al., 2013).

- **Lack of practical expertise**- AI is still a young technology, with few professionals who have mastered it. There are many experts with wide theoretical knowledge of the issue. However, finding experts who can create robust AI-powered software with practical applications is very challenging. Furthermore, the sector of energy is notoriously conservative. Energy companies gather and handle data, but it can be challenging to digitize that data using state-of-the-art technology. There are risks associated with data loss, improper modification, system failure, and unauthorized access. Due to the high cost of error in the energy sector, many businesses are reluctant to explore new approaches that they are inexperienced with (Lyu et al., 2021, Butt et al., 2021).

- **Heterogenous Sensing**- Utilizing sensor data is essential for assessing the hardware infrastructures of the power grid. The data can be divided into three different categories based on sampling frequency: static data, dynamic data, and quasi-dynamic data. Information like an equipment account, nameplate specifications, pre-commissioning test results, a location, and other pertinent specifics are examples of static data. Periodic changes to dynamic data are often made every few seconds, minutes, or hours. This category includes a variety of data types, including operational data, records from inspections, real-time detection data, and environmental meteorological data. Regular or sporadic updates to quasi-dynamic data often occur on a monthly or annual basis. The majority of this information consists of records of equipment concealed risks, fault defects, and maintenance.

- **Financial pressure-** Putting cutting-edge smart technology to use in the energy field might be the best thing to do, but it's not cheap. It takes a lot of time and money to find an expert software services provider, make software that fits your needs, and keep an eye on it while you make changes and manage it. Before energy companies can get the most out of AI, machine learning, and deep learning, they need to be ready to spend a lot of money and risk a lot to replace their old systems.

- **Abnormality in power equipment-** The reason for power equipment failure is mainly abnormalities that generally pre-occur, also known as incipient faults that last for a short period and then recur. The characteristics of such faults are uncertainty and random arcs, which last between quarter to four cycles making it difficult for analysts to work on it for any analysis purpose. The majority of conventional techniques for detecting early-stage faults first analyze the waveform's properties before classifying the fault. AI techniques enable speedy defect detection and simple response to waveform characteristic changes. On the other hand, incipient defects are extremely brief and rarely arise. When they do, the fault recorder won't be able to capture the signals and the protection mechanisms installed in the power system might not function. As a result, insufficient training data are available to build a reliable AI model.

- **Edge computing with resource limitations-** The advantage of edge computing is due to the processing that takes place on communicating nodes which saves time. Edge computing powered with artificial algorithms also known as edge intelligence is capable of analysing data on a device locally. Most edge devices have limited resources that limit the accuracy of detecting data locally. Therefore large models that depend on billions of parameters implementation and deployment becomes difficult and sometimes impossible.

7. CONCLUSION

The fundamental technologies employed in the smart grid encompass sensing, communication, optimization, and data analysis, serving diverse objectives. The power sector can enhance its value by integrating smart devices, advanced user interfaces, cloud computing, big data, and services. The smart devices or objects of AIoT are wi-fi chipsets, and sensors such as accelerometers. The power network in question facilitates bidirectional transmission of electricity and data utilizing digital communication technologies, hence enabling the detection, response, and proactive management of fluctuations in consumption and various concerns. The primary emphasis of this chapter is to provide the use of Artificial Intelligence, and sensor data processing for fault detection and a brief discussion of challenges that exist in this research area.

REFERENCES

Abdalla, A. N., Nazir, M. S., Tao, H., Cao, S., Ji, R., Jiang, M., & Yao, L. (2021). Integration of energy storage system and renewable energy sources based on artificial intelligence: An overview. *Journal of Energy Storage, 40*, 102811. doi:10.1016/j. est.2021.102811

Aboumalik, M., Brak, M. E., & Essaaidi, M. (2019). Moving toward a smarter power grid: A proposed strategy for strengthen smart grid roadmaps through a case study. *Int. J. Smart Grid Clean Energy*, 131-139.

Avasthi, S., Chauhan, R., & Acharjya, D. P. (2021). Techniques, applications, and issues in mining large-scale text databases. *Advances in Information Communication Technology and Computing Proceedings of AICTC, 2019*, 385–396.

Avasthi, S., Chauhan, R., & Acharjya, D. P. (2021). Processing large text corpus using N-gram language modeling and smoothing. In *Proceedings of the Second International Conference on Information Management and Machine Intelligence: ICIMMI 2020* (pp. 21-32). Springer Singapore. 10.1007/978-981-15-9689-6_3

Avasthi, S., Chauhan, R., & Acharjya, D. P. (2022). Significance of Preprocessing Techniques on Text Classification Over Hindi and English Short Texts. In *Applications of Artificial Intelligence and Machine Learning: Select Proceedings of ICAAAIML 2021* (pp. 743-751). Singapore: Springer Nature Singapore. 10.1007/978-981-19-4831-2_61

Avasthi, S., Chauhan, R., & Acharjya, D. P. (2023). Extracting information and inferences from a large text corpus. *International Journal of Information Technology : an Official Journal of Bharati Vidyapeeth's Institute of Computer Applications and Management, 15*(1), 435–445. doi:10.1007/s41870-022-01123-4 PMID:36440061

Avasthi, S., Sanwal, T., Sareen, P., & Tripathi, S. L. (2022). Augmenting Mental Healthcare With Artificial Intelligence, Machine Learning, and Challenges in Telemedicine. In Handbook of Research on Lifestyle Sustainability and Management Solutions Using AI, Big Data Analytics, and Visualization (pp. 75-90). IGI Global.

Avasthi, S., Sanwal, T., Sharma, S., & Roy, S. (2023). VANETs and the Use of IoT: Approaches, Applications, and Challenges. *Revolutionizing Industrial Automation Through the Convergence of Artificial Intelligence and the Internet of Things*, 1-23.

Beg, F. (2016). An auxiliary study of the smart grid deployment in India. Philosophy and key drivers. *International Journal of Smart Grid and Green Communications, 1*(1), 38–49. doi:10.1504/IJSGGC.2016.077288

Butt, O. M., Zulqarnain, M., & Butt, T. M. (2021). Recent advancement in smart grid technology: Future prospects in the electrical power network. *Ain Shams Engineering Journal, 12*(1), 687–695. doi:10.1016/j.asej.2020.05.004

Chakraborty, S., Chowdhury, A., & Chakraborty, S. (2017). Smart Grids & smart grid technologies in India. *International Research Journal of Engineering and Technology, 4*(1), 1536–1541.

Chang, G. W., Hong, Y.-H., & Li, G.-Y. (2019). A hybrid intelligent approach for classification of incipient faults in transmission network. *IEEE Transactions on Power Delivery, 34*(4), 1785–1794. doi:10.1109/TPWRD.2019.2924840

Chauhan, R., Avasthi, S., Alankar, B., & Kaur, H. (2021). Smart IoT Systems: Data Analytics, Secure Smart Home, and Challenges. In Transforming the Internet of Things for Next-Generation Smart Systems (pp. 100-119). IGI Global.

Chen, K., Hu, J., & He, J. (2016). Detection and classification of transmission line faults based on unsupervised feature learning and convolutional sparse autoencoder. *IEEE Transactions on Smart Grid, 9*(3), 1748–1758. doi:10.1109/TSG.2016.2598881

Dhanabalan, T., & Sathish, A. (2018). Transforming Indian industries through artificial intelligence and robotics in industry 4.0. *International Journal of Mechanical Engineering and Technology, 9*(10), 835–845.

Franki, V., Majnarić, D., & Višković, A. (2023). A Comprehensive Review of Artificial Intelligence (AI) Companies in the Power Sector. *Energies, 16*(3), 1077. doi:10.3390/en16031077

Hosseini, M. M., Umunnakwe, A., Parvania, M., & Tasdizen, T. (2020). Intelligent damage classification and estimation in power distribution poles using unmanned aerial vehicles and convolutional neural networks. *IEEE Transactions on Smart Grid, 11*(4), 3325–3333. doi:10.1109/TSG.2020.2970156

Jadhav, G. N., & Dharme, A. A. (2012, March). Technical challenges for development of smart grid in India. In *IEEE-International Conference On Advances In Engineering, Science And Management (ICAESM-2012)* (pp. 784-788). IEEE.

Jenkins, N., Long, C., & Wu, J. (2015). An overview of the smart grid in Great Britain. *Engineering (Beijing), 1*(4), 413–421. doi:10.15302/J-ENG-2015112

Kannan, R. R., & Madhumita, G. (2020). Smart grid—introduction, advantages and implementation status in India with a focus on Tamil Nadu: A systematic review. *Int. J. Adv. Sci. Technol, 29*, 1146–1156.

Khosrojerdi, F., Akhigbe, O., Gagnon, S., Ramirez, A., & Richards, G. (2021). Integrating artificial intelligence and analytics in smart grids: A systematic literature review. *International Journal of Energy Sector Management, 16*(2), 318–338.

Kumar, R., Badwal, L., Avasthi, S., & Prakash, A. (2023, January). A Secure Decentralized E-Voting with Blockchain & Smart Contracts. In *2023 13th International Conference on Cloud Computing, Data Science & Engineering (Confluence)* (pp. 419-424). IEEE. 10.1109/Confluence56041.2023.10048871

Li, L., Ota, K., & Dong, M. (2018). Deep learning for smart industry: Efficient manufacture inspection system with fog computing. *IEEE Transactions on Industrial Informatics, 14*(10), 4665–4673. doi:10.1109/TII.2018.2842821

Li, Q., Deng, Y., Liu, X., Sun, W., Li, W., Li, J., & Liu, Z. (2023). *Autonomous smart grid fault detection*. IEEE Communications Standards Magazine. doi:10.1109/MCOMSTD.0001.2200019

Lyu, W., & Liu, J. (2021). Artificial Intelligence and emerging digital technologies in the energy sector. *Applied Energy*, *303*, 117615. doi:10.1016/j.apenergy.2021.117615

Mahdavinejad, M. S., Rezvan, M., Barekatain, M., Adibi, P., Barnaghi, P., & Sheth, A. P. (2018). Machine learning for internet of things data analysis: A survey. *Digital Communications and Networks*, *4*(3), 161–175. doi:10.1016/j.dcan.2017.10.002

Mohammadi, M., Al-Fuqaha, A., Sorour, S., & Guizani, M. (2018). Deep learning for iot big data and streaming analytics: A survey. *IEEE Communications Surveys and Tutorials*, *20*(4), 2923–2960. doi:10.1109/COMST.2018.2844341

Ota, K., Dao, M. S., Mezaris, V., & Natale, F. G. D. (2017). Deep learning for mobile multimedia: A survey. *ACM Transactions on Multimedia Computing Communications and Applications*, *13*(3s, no. 3s), 1–22. doi:10.1145/3092831

Perera, C., Zaslavsky, A., Christen, P., & Georgakopoulos, D. (2013). Context aware computing for the internet of things: A survey. *IEEE Communications Surveys and Tutorials*, *16*(1), 414–454. doi:10.1109/SURV.2013.042313.00197

Rahman, M. G., Chowdhury, M. F. B. R., Al Mamun, M. A., Hasan, M. R., & Mahfuz, S. (2013). Summary of smart grid: Benefits and issues. *International Journal of Scientific and Engineering Research*, *4*(3), 1–5.

Raza, M. A., Aman, M. M., Abro, A. G., Tunio, M. A., Khatri, K. L., & Shahid, M. (2022). Challenges and potentials of implementing a smart grid for Pakistan's electric network. *Energy Strategy Reviews*, *43*, 100941. doi:10.1016/j.esr.2022.100941

Salkuti, S. R. (2020). Challenges, issues and opportunities for the development of smart grid. *Iranian Journal of Electrical and Computer Engineering*, *10*(2), 1179–1186. doi:10.11591/ijece.v10i2.pp1179-1186

Samantaray, S. R. (2014). Smart grid initiatives in India. *Electric Power Components and Systems*, *42*(3-4), 262–266. doi:10.1080/15325008.2013.867555

Şerban, A. C., & Lytras, M. D. (2020). Artificial intelligence for smart renewable energy sector in europe—Smart energy infrastructures for next generation smart cities. *IEEE Access : Practical Innovations, Open Solutions*, *8*, 77364–77377. doi:10.1109/ACCESS.2020.2990123

Shahzad, U. (2020). Significance of smart grids in electric power systems: A brief overview. *Journal of Electrical Engineering, Electronics. Control and Computer Science*, *6*(1), 7–12.

Shankar, R., & Singh, S. (2022). Development of smart grid for the power sector in India. *Cleaner Energy Systems*, *2*, 100011. doi:10.1016/j.cles.2022.100011

Sharma, A., Saxena, B. K., & Rao, K. V. S. (2017, April). Comparison of smart grid development in five developed countries with focus on smart grid implementations in India. In *2017 International Conference on Circuit, Power and Computing Technologies (ICCPCT)* (pp. 1-6). IEEE. 10.1109/ICCPCT.2017.8074195

Shi, Z., Yao, W., Li, Z., Zeng, L., Zhao, Y., Zhang, R., Tang, Y., & Wen, J. (2020). Artificial intelligence techniques for stability analysis and control in smart grids: Methodologies, applications, challenges and future directions. *Applied Energy, 278,* 115733. doi:10.1016/j.apenergy.2020.115733

Sidhu, T. S., & Xu, Z. (2010). Detection of incipient faults in distribution underground cables. *IEEE Transactions on Power Delivery, 25*(3), 1363–1371. doi:10.1109/TPWRD.2010.2041373

Sinha, A., Neogi, S., Lahiri, R. N., Chowdhury, S., Chowdhury, S. P., & Chakraborty, N. (2011, July). *Smart grid initiative for power distribution utility in India. In 2011 IEEE Power and Energy Society General Meeting.* IEEE.

Tsai, C.-W., Lai, C.-F., Chiang, M.-C., & Yang, L. T. (2013). Data mining for internet of things: A survey. *IEEE Communications Surveys and Tutorials, 16*(1), 77–97. doi:10.1109/SURV.2013.103013.00206

Vyas, D. G., Trivedi, N., Pandya, V., Bhatt, P., & Pujara, A. (2019, December). Future challenges and issues in evolution of the smart grid and recommended possible solutions. In *2019 IEEE 16th India council international conference (INDICON)* (pp. 1-4). IEEE. 10.1109/INDICON47234.2019.9029044

Wang, L., Chen, Q., Gao, Z., Niu, L., Zhao, Y., Ma, Z., & Wu, D. (2015). Knowledge representation and general petri net models for power grid fault diagnosis. *IET Generation, Transmission & Distribution, 9*(9), 866–873. doi:10.1049/iet-gtd.2014.0659

Xiong, Liu, Fang, Dai, Luo, & Jiang. (2020). Incipient fault identification in power distribution systems via human-level concept learning. *IEEE Transactions on Smart Grid.*

Yan, Z., Zhang, P., & Vasilakos, A. V. (2014). A survey on trust management for internet of things. *Journal of Network and Computer Applications, 42,* 120–134. doi:10.1016/j.jnca.2014.01.014

Yousuf, H., Zainal, A. Y., Alshurideh, M., & Salloum, S. A. (2020). Artificial intelligence models in power system analysis. In *Artificial intelligence for sustainable development: Theory, practice and future applications* (pp. 231–242). Springer International Publishing.

Zanella, A., Bui, N., Castellani, A., Vangelista, L., & Zorzi, M. (2014). Internet of things for smart cities. *IEEE Internet of Things Journal*, *1*(1), 22–32. doi:10.1109/JIOT.2014.2306328

Compilation of References

Abba Ari, A. A., Ngangmo, O. K., Titouna, C., Thiare, O., Mohamadou, A., & Gueroui, A. M. (2024). Enabling privacy and security in Cloud of Things: Architecture, applications, security & privacy challenges. *Applied Computing and Informatics*, 20(1/2), 119–141. doi:10.1016/j.aci.2019.11.005

Abbasian Dehkordi, S., Farajzadeh, K., Rezazadeh, J., Farahbakhsh, R., Sandrasegaran, K., & Abbasian Dehkordi, M. (2020). A survey on data aggregation techniques in IoT sensor networks. *Wireless Networks*, 26(2), 1243–1263. doi:10.1007/s11276-019-02142-z

Abdalla, A. N., Nazir, M. S., Tao, H., Cao, S., Ji, R., Jiang, M., & Yao, L. (2021). Integration of energy storage system and renewable energy sources based on artificial intelligence: An overview. *Journal of Energy Storage*, 40, 102811. doi:10.1016/j.est.2021.102811

Abidin, S., & Raghunath, M. P. (2022). Identification of Disease Based on Symptoms by Employing ML. *2022 International Conference on Inventive Computation Technologies (ICICT)*, 1357–62. 10.1109/ICICT54344.2022.9850480

Aboumalik, M., Brak, M. E., & Essaaidi, M. (2019). Moving toward a smarter power grid: A proposed strategy for strengthen smart grid roadmaps through a case study. *Int. J. Smart Grid Clean Energy*, 131-139.

Adadi, A., & Berrada, M. (2018). Peeking inside the black-box: A survey on explainable artificial intelligence (XAI). *IEEE Access : Practical Innovations, Open Solutions*, 6, 52138–52160. doi:10.1109/ACCESS.2018.2870052

Agrawal, A. V., Pitchai, R., Senthamaraikannan, C., Balaji, N. A., Sajithra, S., & Boopathi, S. (2023). Digital Education System During the COVID-19 Pandemic. In Using Assistive Technology for Inclusive Learning in K-12 Classrooms (pp. 104–126). IGI Global. doi:10.4018/978-1-6684-6424-3.ch005

Agrawal, A. V., Shashibhushan, G., Pradeep, S., Padhi, S., Sugumar, D., & Boopathi, S. (2023). Synergizing Artificial Intelligence, 5G, and Cloud Computing for Efficient Energy Conversion Using Agricultural Waste. In Sustainable Science and Intelligent Technologies for Societal Development (pp. 475–497). IGI Global.

Agrawal, A. V., Magulur, L. P., Priya, S. G., Kaur, A., Singh, G., & Boopathi, S. (2023). Smart Precision Agriculture Using IoT and WSN. In *Handbook of Research on Data Science and Cybersecurity Innovations in Industry 4.0 Technologies* (pp. 524–541). IGI Global. doi:10.4018/978-1-6684-8145-5.ch026

Agrawal, A. V., Shashibhushan, G., Pradeep, S., Padhi, S. N., Sugumar, D., & Boopathi, S. (2024a). Synergizing Artificial Intelligence, 5G, and Cloud Computing for Efficient Energy Conversion Using Agricultural Waste. In B. K. Mishra (Ed.), Practice, Progress, and Proficiency in Sustainability. IGI Global. doi:10.4018/979-8-3693-1186-8.ch026

Ahmadi, S. A. A. (2019). Relationship between emotional intelligence and psychological well being. In *Relationship Between Emotional Intelligence and Psychological Well Being*. Academic Press.

Ahmadi-Assalemi, G., Al-Khateeb, H., Maple, C., Epiphaniou, G., Alhaboby, Z. A., Alkaabi, S., & Alhaboby, D. (2020). Digital twins for precision healthcare. *Cyber Defence in the Age of AI, Smart Societies and Augmented Humanity*, 133–158.

Ahmed, M., & Zubair, S. (2022). Explainable artificial intelligence in sustainable smart healthcare. In Explainable Artificial Intelligence for Cyber Security: Next Generation Artificial Intelligence (pp. 265–280). Springer. doi:10.1007/978-3-030-96630-0_12

Aithal, P. (2023). Advances and New Research Opportunities in Quantum Computing Technology by Integrating it with Other ICCT Underlying Technologies. *International Journal of Case Studies in Business IT and Education*, 7(3), 314–358.

Akanksha, K. R., & Vyas, N. (2023). Deep Learning-Based Automatic Face Expression Recognition Framework. *2023 International Conference on Circuit Power and Computing Technologies (ICCPCT)*, 1291–1296. 10.1109/ICCPCT58313.2023.10245885

Akrami, N. E., Hanine, M., Flores, E. S., Aray, D. G., & Ashraf, I. (2023). Unleashing the Potential of Blockchain and Machine Learning: Insights and Emerging Trends from Bibliometric Analysis. *IEEE Access : Practical Innovations, Open Solutions*, 11, 78879–78903. doi:10.1109/ACCESS.2023.3298371

Akyildiz, I. F., & Vuran, M. C. (2010). *Wireless sensor networks*. John Wiley & Sons. doi:10.1002/9780470515181

Al Sadawi, A., Hassan, M. S., & Ndiaye, M. (2021). A survey on integrating blockchain with IoT to enhance performance and eliminate challenges. *IEEE Access : Practical Innovations, Open Solutions*, 9, 54478–54497. doi:10.1109/ACCESS.2021.3070555

Alam, F., Mehmood, R., Katib, I., Albogami, N. N., & Albeshri, A. (2017). Data fusion and IoT for smart ubiquitous environments: A survey. *IEEE Access : Practical Innovations, Open Solutions*, 5, 9533–9554. doi:10.1109/ACCESS.2017.2697839

Alamri, A., Ansari, W. S., Hassan, M. M., Hossain, M. S., Alelaiwi, A., & Hossain, M. A. (2013). A Survey on Sensor-Cloud: Architecture, Applications, and Approaches. *International Journal of Distributed Sensor Networks*, 9(2), 917923. doi:10.1155/2013/917923

Albataineh, H., & Nijim, M. (2021). Enhancing the cybersecurity education curricula through quantum computation. *Advances in Security, Networks, and Internet of Things: Proceedings from SAM'20, ICWN'20, ICOMP'20, and ESCS'20*, 223–231.

Al-Emran, M., & Al-Sharafi, M. A. (2022). Revolutionizing education with industry 5.0: Challenges and future research agendas. *International Journal of Information Technology : an Official Journal of Bharati Vidyapeeth's Institute of Computer Applications and Management*, 6(3), 1–5.

Al-Garadi, M. A., Mohamed, A., Al-Ali, A. K., Du, X., Ali, I., & Guizani, M. (2020). A Survey of Machine and Deep Learning Methods for Internet of Things (IoT) Security. *IEEE Communications Surveys and Tutorials*, 22(3), 1646–1685. doi:10.1109/COMST.2020.2988293

Ali, G., Dida, M. A., & Sam, A. E. (2021). A Secure and Efficient Multi-Factor Authentication Algorithm for Mobile Money Applications. *Future Internet*, 13(12), 299. doi:10.3390/fi13120299

Ali, S., Yue, T., & Abreu, R. (2022). When software engineering meets quantum computing. *Communications of the ACM*, 65(4), 84–88. doi:10.1145/3512340

Al-Shareeda, M. A., Anbar, M., Manickam, S., & Hasbullah, I. H. (2020). Review of Prevention Schemes for Man-in-the-Middle (MITM) Attack in Vehicular Ad Hoc Networks. *International Journal of Engineering and Management Research*, 10(3), 10. doi:10.31033/ijemr.10.3.23

Al-Shareeda, M. A., & Manickam, S. (2022). Man-in-the-Middle Attacks in Mobile Ad Hoc Networks (MANETs): Analysis and Evaluation. *Symmetry*, 14(8), 1543. doi:10.3390/sym14081543

Altaş, H., Dalkiliç, G., & Çabuk, U. C. (2022). Data Immutability and Event Management via Blockchain in the Internet of Things. *Turkish Journal of Electrical Engineering and Computer Sciences*, 30(2), 451–468. doi:10.3906/elk-2103-105

Altinkaya, E., Polat, K., & Barakli, B. (2020). Detection of Alzheimer's disease and dementia states based on deep learning from MRI images: A comprehensive review. *Journal of the Institute of Electronics and Computer*, 1(1), 39–53.

Ambika, P. (2020). Machine Learning and Deep Learning Algorithms on the Industrial Internet of Things (IIoT). *Advances in Computers*, 117(1), 321–338. doi:10.1016/bs.adcom.2019.10.007

Andoni, M., Robu, V., Flynn, D., Abram, S., Geach, D., Jenkins, D., McCallum, P., & Peacock, A. (2019). Blockchain Technology in the Energy Sector: A Systematic Review of Challenges and Opportunities. *Renewable & Sustainable Energy Reviews*, 100, 143–174. doi:10.1016/j.rser.2018.10.014

Andreas, A., Mavromoustakis, C. X., Mastorakis, G., Batalla, J. M., Sahalos, J. N., Pallis, E., & Markakis, E. (2021). Robust encryption to enhance IoT confidentiality for healthcare ecosystems. *2021 IEEE 26th International Workshop on Computer Aided Modeling and Design of Communication Links and Networks (CAMAD)*, 1–6.

Angelini, M., Blasilli, G., Lenti, S., & Santucci, G. (2023). A Visual Analytics Conceptual Framework for Explorable and Steerable Partial Dependence Analysis. *IEEE Transactions on Visualization and Computer Graphics*. PMID:37027262

Anitha, C., Komala, C., Vivekanand, C. V., Lalitha, S., & Boopathi, S. (2023). Artificial Intelligence driven security model for Internet of Medical Things (IoMT). *IEEE Explore*, 1–7.

Ante, L. (2021). Smart contracts on the blockchain–A bibliometric analysis and review. *Telematics and Informatics*, *57*, 101519.

Antoniadi, A. M., Galvin, M., Heverin, M., Hardiman, O., & Mooney, C. (2021). Prediction of caregiver quality of life in amyotrophic lateral sclerosis using explainable machine learning. *Scientific Reports*, *11*(1), 12237. doi:10.1038/s41598-021-91632-2 PMID:34112871

Apostolakis, K. C., Dimitriou, N., Margetis, G., Ntoa, S., Tzovaras, D., & Stephanidis, C. (2021). DARLENE–Improving Situational Awareness of European Law Enforcement Agents through a Combination of Augmented Reality and Artificial Intelligence Solutions. *Open Research Europe*, 1. PMID:37645167

Arrieta, A. B., Díaz-Rodríguez, N., Del Ser, J., Bennetot, A., Tabik, S., Barbado, A., García, S., Gil-López, S., Molina, D., & Benjamins, R. (2020). Explainable Artificial Intelligence (XAI): Concepts, taxonomies, opportunities and challenges toward responsible AI. *Information Fusion*, *58*, 82–115. doi:10.1016/j.inffus.2019.12.012

Arunprasad, R., & Boopathi, S. (2019). Chapter-4 Alternate Refrigerants for Minimization Environmental Impacts: A Review. In Advances in Engineering Technology (p. 75). AkiNik Publications.

Ateniese, G., Pietro, R. D., Mancini, L., & Tsudik, G. (2008). Scalable and efficient provable data possession. *IACR Cryptol. ePrint Arch.* doi:10.1145/1460877.1460889

Avasthi, S., Chauhan, R., & Acharjya, D. P. (2021). Processing large text corpus using N-gram language modeling and smoothing. In *Proceedings of the Second International Conference on Information Management and Machine Intelligence: ICIMMI 2020* (pp. 21-32). Springer Singapore. 10.1007/978-981-15-9689-6_3

Avasthi, S., Chauhan, R., & Acharjya, D. P. (2022). Significance of Preprocessing Techniques on Text Classification Over Hindi and English Short Texts. In *Applications of Artificial Intelligence and Machine Learning: Select Proceedings of ICAAAIML 2021* (pp. 743-751). Singapore: Springer Nature Singapore. 10.1007/978-981-19-4831-2_61

Avasthi, S., Sanwal, T., Sareen, P., & Tripathi, S. L. (2022). Augmenting Mental Healthcare With Artificial Intelligence, Machine Learning, and Challenges in Telemedicine. In Handbook of Research on Lifestyle Sustainability and Management Solutions Using AI, Big Data Analytics, and Visualization (pp. 75-90). IGI Global.

Avasthi, S., Sanwal, T., Sharma, S., & Roy, S. (2023). VANETs and the Use of IoT: Approaches, Applications, and Challenges. *Revolutionizing Industrial Automation Through the Convergence of Artificial Intelligence and the Internet of Things*, 1-23.

Avasthi, S., Chauhan, R., & Acharjya, D. P. (2021). Techniques, applications, and issues in mining large-scale text databases. *Advances in Information Communication Technology and Computing Proceedings of AICTC, 2019*, 385–396.

Avasthi, S., Chauhan, R., & Acharjya, D. P. (2023). Extracting information and inferences from a large text corpus. *International Journal of Information Technology : an Official Journal of Bharati Vidyapeeth's Institute of Computer Applications and Management, 15*(1), 435–445. doi:10.1007/s41870-022-01123-4 PMID:36440061

Azbeg, K., Ouchetto, O., & Andaloussi, S. J. (2022a). BlockMedCare: A healthcare system based on IoT, Blockchain, and IPFS for data management security. *Egyptian Informatics Journal, 23*(2), 329–343. doi:10.1016/j.eij.2022.02.004

B, M. K., K, K. K., Sasikala, P., Sampath, B., Gopi, B., & Sundaram, S. (2024). Sustainable Green Energy Generation From Waste Water. In *Practice, Progress, and Proficiency in Sustainability* (pp. 440–463). IGI Global. doi:10.4018/979-8-3693-1186-8.ch024

Babu, B. S., Kamalakannan, J., Meenatchi, N., Karthik, S., & Boopathi, S. (2022). Economic impacts and reliability evaluation of battery by adopting Electric Vehicle. *IEEE Explore*, 1–6.

Bakhshi, Z., & Balador, A. (2019). An overview on security and privacy challenges and their solutions in fog-based vehicular application. *2019 IEEE 30th International Symposium on Personal, Indoor and Mobile Radio Communications (PIMRC Workshops)*, 1–7.

Banerjee, A. (2019). Blockchain with IoT: Applications and use cases for a new supply chain paradigm driving efficiency and cost. In *Advances in Computers* (Vol. 115, pp. 259–292). Elsevier. https://www.sciencedirect.com/science/article/pii/S0065245819300336

Bayley, J., & Phipps, D. (2019). Extending the concept of research impact literacy: Levels of literacy, institutional role and ethical considerations. *Emerald Open Research, 1*(3), 14. doi:10.1108/EOR-03-2023-0005

Beg, F. (2016). An auxiliary study of the smart grid deployment in India. Philosophy and key drivers. *International Journal of Smart Grid and Green Communications, 1*(1), 38–49. doi:10.1504/IJSGGC.2016.077288

Bellavista, P., Cardone, G., Corradi, A., & Foschini, L. (2013). Convergence of MANET and WSN in IoT urban scenarios. *IEEE Sensors Journal, 13*(10), 3558–3567. doi:10.1109/JSEN.2013.2272099

Benbya, H., Davenport, T. H., & Pachidi, S. (2020). Artificial intelligence in organizations: Current state and future opportunities. *MIS Quarterly Executive, 19*(4).

Bender, A., Groll, A., & Scheipl, F. (2018). A generalized additive model approach to time-to-event analysis. *Statistical Modelling, 18*(3–4), 299–321. doi:10.1177/1471082X17748083

Bhakta, I., Phadikar, S., & Majumder, K. (2019). State-of-the-art technologies in precision agriculture: A systematic review. *Journal of the Science of Food and Agriculture, 99*(11), 4878–4888. doi:10.1002/jsfa.9693 PMID:30883757

Bhaskar, P., Tiwari, C. K., & Joshi, A. (2020). Blockchain in education management: Present and future applications. *Interactive Technology and Smart Education*, *18*(1), 1–17. doi:10.1108/ITSE-07-2020-0102

Bhatia, M., & Sood, S. K. (2020). Quantum computing-inspired network optimization for IoT applications. *IEEE Internet of Things Journal*, *7*(6), 5590–5598. doi:10.1109/JIOT.2020.2979887

Bien, J., & Tibshirani, R. J. (2011). Sparse estimation of a covariance matrix. *Biometrika*, *98*(4), 807–820. doi:10.1093/biomet/asr054 PMID:23049130

Bjørnsen, H. N., Espnes, G. A., Eilertsen, M.-E. B., Ringdal, R., & Moksnes, U. K. (2019). The relationship between positive mental health literacy and mental well-being among adolescents: Implications for school health services. *The Journal of School Nursing: the Official Publication of the National Association of School Nurses*, *35*(2), 107–116. doi:10.1177/1059840517732125 PMID:28950750

Blinowski, G. J., & Piotrowski, P. (2020). CVE Based Classification of Vulnerable IoT Systems. *Theory and Applications of Dependable Computer Systems: Proceedings of the Fifteenth International Conference on Dependability of Computer Systems DepCoS-RELCOMEX, June 29–July 3, 2020, Brunów, Poland*, *15*, 82–93. 10.1007/978-3-030-48256-5_9

Boopathi, S. (2013). *Experimental study and multi-objective optimization of near-dry wire-cut electrical discharge machining process* [PhD Thesis]. http://hdl.handle.net/10603/16933

Boopathi, S. (2022b). Cryogenically treated and untreated stainless steel grade 317 in sustainable wire electrical discharge machining process: A comparative study. *Springer :Environmental Science and Pollution Research*, 1–10.

Boopathi, S. (2022c). Cryogenically treated and untreated stainless steel grade 317 in sustainable wire electrical discharge machining process: A comparative study. *Springer :Environmental Science and Pollution Research*, 1–10.

Boopathi, S. (2022c). Performance Improvement of Eco-Friendly Near-Dry wire-Cut Electrical Discharge Machining Process Using Coconut Oil-Mist Dielectric Fluid. *World Scientific: Journal of Advanced Manufacturing Systems*.

Boopathi, S. (2023). Securing Healthcare Systems Integrated With IoT: Fundamentals, Applications, and Future Trends. In Dynamics of Swarm Intelligence Health Analysis for the Next Generation (pp. 186–209). IGI Global.

Boopathi, S. (2023b). Securing Healthcare Systems Integrated With IoT: Fundamentals, Applications, and Future Trends. In Dynamics of Swarm Intelligence Health Analysis for the Next Generation (pp. 186–209). IGI Global.

Boopathi, S. (2023c). Securing Healthcare Systems Integrated With IoT: Fundamentals, Applications, and Future Trends. In Dynamics of Swarm Intelligence Health Analysis for the Next Generation (pp. 186–209). IGI Global.

Boopathi, S. (2024b). Balancing Innovation and Security in the Cloud: Navigating the Risks and Rewards of the Digital Age. In Improving Security, Privacy, and Trust in Cloud Computing (pp. 164–193). IGI Global.

Boopathi, S. (2024b). Energy Cascade Conversion System and Energy-Efficient Infrastructure. In Sustainable Development in AI, Blockchain, and E-Governance Applications (pp. 47–71). IGI Global.

Boopathi, S. (2024c). Sustainable Development Using IoT and AI Techniques for Water Utilization in Agriculture. In Sustainable Development in AI, Blockchain, and E-Governance Applications (pp. 204–228). IGI Global.

Boopathi, S., & Kumar, P. (2024). Advanced bioprinting processes using additive manufacturing technologies: Revolutionizing tissue engineering. *3D Printing Technologies: Digital Manufacturing, Artificial Intelligence, Industry 4.0, 95.*

Boopathi, S., Arigela, S. H., Raman, R., Indhumathi, C., Kavitha, V., & Bhatt, B. C. (2022). Prominent Rule Control-based Internet of Things: Poultry Farm Management System. *IEEE Explore,* 1–6.

Boopathi, S., Khare, R., KG, J. C., Muni, T. V., & Khare, S. (2023). Additive Manufacturing Developments in the Medical Engineering Field. In Development, Properties, and Industrial Applications of 3D Printed Polymer Composites (pp. 86–106). IGI Global.

Boopathi, S., Kumar, P. K. S., Meena, R. S., & Sudhakar, M. (2023). Sustainable Developments of Modern Soil-Less Agro-Cultivation Systems: Aquaponic Culture. In Human Agro-Energy Optimization for Business and Industry (pp. 69–87). IGI Global.

Boopathi, S., Kumar, P. K. S., Meena, R. S., Sudhakar, M., & Associates. (2023). Sustainable Developments of Modern Soil-Less Agro-Cultivation Systems: Aquaponic Culture. In Human Agro-Energy Optimization for Business and Industry (pp. 69–87). IGI Global.

Boopathi, S., Pandey, B. K., & Pandey, D. (2023). Advances in Artificial Intelligence for Image Processing: Techniques, Applications, and Optimization. In Handbook of Research on Thrust Technologies' Effect on Image Processing (pp. 73–95). IGI Global.

Boopathi, S., Siva Kumar, P. K., Meena, R. S. J., S. I., P., S. K., & Sudhakar, M. (2023). Sustainable Developments of Modern Soil-Less Agro-Cultivation Systems: Aquaponic Culture. In P. Vasant, R. Rodríguez-Aguilar, I. Litvinchev, & J. A. Marmolejo-Saucedo (Eds.), Advances in Environmental Engineering and Green Technologies (pp. 69–87). IGI Global. doi:10.4018/978-1-6684-4118-3.ch004

Boopathi, S. (2022a). An experimental investigation of Quench Polish Quench (QPQ) coating on AISI 4150 steel. *Engineering Research Express, 4*(4), 045009. doi:10.1088/2631-8695/ac9ddd

Boopathi, S. (2022a). An extensive review on sustainable developments of dry and near-dry electrical discharge machining processes. *ASME: Journal of Manufacturing Science and Engineering, 144*(5), 050801–1.

Boopathi, S. (2022a). An investigation on gas emission concentration and relative emission rate of the near-dry wire-cut electrical discharge machining process. *Environmental Science and Pollution Research International, 29*(57), 86237–86246. doi:10.1007/s11356-021-17658-1 PMID:34837614

Boopathi, S. (2022c). Experimental investigation and multi-objective optimization of cryogenic Friction-stir-welding of AA2014 and AZ31B alloys using MOORA technique. *Materials Today. Communications, 33,* 104937. doi:10.1016/j.mtcomm.2022.104937

Boopathi, S. (2023). Securing Healthcare Systems Integrated With IoT: Fundamentals, Applications, and Future Trends. In A. Suresh Kumar, U. Kose, S. Sharma, & S. Jerald Nirmal Kumar (Eds.), Advances in Healthcare Information Systems and Administration. IGI Global. doi:10.4018/978-1-6684-6894-4.ch010

Boopathi, S. (2023a). An Investigation on Friction Stir Processing of Aluminum Alloy-Boron Carbide Surface Composite. In *Springer: Advances in Processing of Lightweight Metal Alloys and Composites* (pp. 249–257). Springer. doi:10.1007/978-981-19-7146-4_14

Boopathi, S. (2023a). Internet of Things-Integrated Remote Patient Monitoring System: Healthcare Application. In *Dynamics of Swarm Intelligence Health Analysis for the Next Generation* (pp. 137–161). IGI Global. doi:10.4018/978-1-6684-6894-4.ch008

Boopathi, S. (2024a). Advancements in Machine Learning and AI for Intelligent Systems in Drone Applications for Smart City Developments. In *Futuristic e-Governance Security With Deep Learning Applications* (pp. 15–45). IGI Global. doi:10.4018/978-1-6684-9596-4.ch002

Boopathi, S., Alqahtani, A. S., Mubarakali, A., & Panchatcharam, P. (2023). Sustainable developments in near-dry electrical discharge machining process using sunflower oil-mist dielectric fluid. *Environmental Science and Pollution Research International,* 1–20. doi:10.1007/s11356-023-27494-0 PMID:37199846

Boopathi, S., Balasubramani, V., Kumar, R. S., & Singh, G. R. (2021). The influence of human hair on kenaf and Grewia fiber-based hybrid natural composite material: An experimental study. *Functional Composites and Structures, 3*(4), 045011. doi:10.1088/2631-6331/ac3afc

Boopathi, S., & Davim, J. P. (2023a). Applications of Nanoparticles in Various Manufacturing Processes. In *Sustainable Utilization of Nanoparticles and Nanofluids in Engineering Applications* (pp. 1–31). IGI Global. doi:10.4018/978-1-6684-9135-5.ch001

Boopathi, S., & Davim, J. P. (2023b). *Sustainable Utilization of Nanoparticles and Nanofluids in Engineering Applications.* IGI Global. doi:10.4018/978-1-6684-9135-5

Boopathi, S., & Kanike, U. K. (2023). Applications of Artificial Intelligent and Machine Learning Techniques in Image Processing. In *Handbook of Research on Thrust Technologies' Effect on Image Processing* (pp. 151–173). IGI Global. doi:10.4018/978-1-6684-8618-4.ch010

Boopathi, S., & Khang, A. (2023). AI-Integrated Technology for a Secure and Ethical Healthcare Ecosystem. In *AI and IoT-Based Technologies for Precision Medicine* (pp. 36–59). IGI Global. doi:10.4018/979-8-3693-0876-9.ch003

Boopathi, S., & Sivakumar, K. (2013). Experimental investigation and parameter optimization of near-dry wire-cut electrical discharge machining using multi-objective evolutionary algorithm. *International Journal of Advanced Manufacturing Technology, 67*(9–12), 2639–2655. doi:10.1007/s00170-012-4680-4

Boopathi, S., & Sivakumar, K. (2016). Optimal parameter prediction of oxygen-mist near-dry wire-cut EDM. *Inderscience: International Journal of Manufacturing Technology and Management, 30*(3–4), 164–178. doi:10.1504/IJMTM.2016.077812

Boopathi, S., Sureshkumar, M., & Sathiskumar, S. (2022). Parametric Optimization of LPG Refrigeration System Using Artificial Bee Colony Algorithm. *International Conference on Recent Advances in Mechanical Engineering Research and Development*, 97–105.

Boopathi, S., Umareddy, M., & Elangovan, M. (2023). Applications of Nano-Cutting Fluids in Advanced Machining Processes. In *Sustainable Utilization of Nanoparticles and Nanofluids in Engineering Applications* (pp. 211–234). IGI Global. doi:10.4018/978-1-6684-9135-5.ch009

Botta, A., De Donato, W., Persico, V., & Pescapé, A. (2016). Integration of cloud computing and internet of things: A survey. *Future Generation Computer Systems, 56*, 684–700. doi:10.1016/j.future.2015.09.021

Bumblauskas, D., Mann, A., Dugan, B., & Rittmer, J. (2020). A blockchain use case in food distribution: Do you know where your food has been? *International Journal of Information Management, 52*, 102008. doi:10.1016/j.ijinfomgt.2019.09.004

Butt, O. M., Zulqarnain, M., & Butt, T. M. (2021). Recent advancement in smart grid technology: Future prospects in the electrical power network. *Ain Shams Engineering Journal, 12*(1), 687–695. doi:10.1016/j.asej.2020.05.004

Cabrera-Gutiérrez, A. J., Castillo, E., Escobar-Molero, A., Alvarez-Bermejo, J. A., Morales, D. P., & Parrilla, L. (2022). Integration of Hardware Security Modules and Permissioned Blockchain in Industrial Iot Networks. *IEEE Access: Practical Innovations, Open Solutions, 10*, 114331–114345. doi:10.1109/ACCESS.2022.3217815

Casalicchio, G., Molnar, C., & Bischl, B. (2019). Visualizing the feature importance for black box models. *Machine Learning and Knowledge Discovery in Databases: European Conference, ECML PKDD 2018, Dublin, Ireland, September 10–14, 2018. Proceedings, 18*(Part I), 655–670.

Chaddad, A., Peng, J., Xu, J., & Bouridane, A. (2023). Survey of explainable AI techniques in healthcare. *Sensors (Basel), 23*(2), 634. doi:10.3390/s23020634 PMID:36679430

Chakraborty, I., Vigneswara Ilavarasan, P., & Edirippulige, S. (2022). E-Health Startups' Framework for Value Creation and Capture: Some Insights from Systematic Review. *Proceedings of the International Conference on Cognitive and Intelligent Computing: ICCIC 2021, 1*, 141–152. 10.1007/978-981-19-2350-0_13

Chakraborty, S., Chowdhury, A., & Chakraborty, S. (2017). Smart Grids & smart grid technologies in India. *International Research Journal of Engineering and Technology, 4*(1), 1536–1541.

Chang, G. W., Hong, Y.-H., & Li, G.-Y. (2019). A hybrid intelligent approach for classification of incipient faults in transmission network. *IEEE Transactions on Power Delivery, 34*(4), 1785–1794. doi:10.1109/TPWRD.2019.2924840

Chan, H. H. S., Meister, R., Jones, T., Tew, D. P., & Benjamin, S. C. (2023). Grid-based methods for chemistry simulations on a quantum computer. *Science Advances, 9*(9), eabo7484. doi:10.1126/sciadv.abo7484 PMID:36857445

Chauhan, R., Avasthi, S., Alankar, B., & Kaur, H. (2021). Smart IoT Systems: Data Analytics, Secure Smart Home, and Challenges. In Transforming the Internet of Things for Next-Generation Smart Systems (pp. 100-119). IGI Global.

Chawla, C. (2020). Trust in blockchains: Algorithmic and organizational. *Journal of Business Venturing Insights, 14*, e00203.

Chen, F., Huo, Y., Zhu, J., & Fan, D. (2020). A Review on the Study on MQTT Security Challenge. *2020 IEEE International Conference on Smart Cloud (SmartCloud)*, 128–33. 10.1109/SmartCloud49737.2020.00032

Cheng, L., & Yu, T. (2019). A new generation of AI: A review and perspective on machine learning technologies applied to smart energy and electric power systems. *International Journal of Energy Research, 43*(6), 1928–1973. doi:10.1002/er.4333

Cheng, M., Zhang, Y., Xie, Y., Pan, Y., Li, X., Liu, W., Yu, C., Zhang, D., Xing, Y., Huang, X., Wang, F., You, C., Zou, Y., Liu, Y., Liang, F., Zhu, H., Tang, C., Deng, H., Zou, X., & Li, M. (2023). Computer-Aided Autism Spectrum Disorder Diagnosis With Behavior Signal Processing. *IEEE Transactions on Affective Computing, 14*(4), 2982–3000. doi:10.1109/TAFFC.2023.3238712

Chen, K., Hu, J., & He, J. (2016). Detection and classification of transmission line faults based on unsupervised feature learning and convolutional sparse autoencoder. *IEEE Transactions on Smart Grid, 9*(3), 1748–1758. doi:10.1109/TSG.2016.2598881

Chen, R. J., Wang, J. J., Williamson, D. F. K., Chen, T. Y., Lipkova, J., Lu, M. Y., Sahai, S., & Mahmood, F. (2023). Algorithmic fairness in artificial intelligence for medicine and healthcare. *Nature Biomedical Engineering, 7*(6), 719–742. doi:10.1038/s41551-023-01056-8 PMID:37380750

Chinu & Bansal, U. (2023). Explainable AI: To Reveal the Logic of Black-Box Models. *New Generation Computing*, 1–35.

Chiu, B. W. (2020). *Additive manufacturing applications and implementation in aerospace* [PhD Thesis]. Massachusetts Institute of Technology.

Chong, C-Y., & Kumar, S. (2003). Sensor networks: Evolution, opportunities, and challenges. *Proceedings of the IEEE, 91*(8), 1247–1256.

Ciravegna, G., Barbiero, P., Giannini, F., Gori, M., Lió, P., Maggini, M., & Melacci, S. (2023). Logic explained networks. *Artificial Intelligence, 314*, 103822. doi:10.1016/j.artint.2022.103822

Cisternas, I., Velásquez, I., Caro, A., & Rodríguez, A. (2020). Systematic literature review of implementations of precision agriculture. *Computers and Electronics in Agriculture, 176*, 105626. doi:10.1016/j.compag.2020.105626

Cliff, A., Romero, J., Kainer, D., Walker, A., Furches, A., & Jacobson, D. (2019). A high-performance computing implementation of iterative random forest for the creation of predictive expression networks. *Genes, 10*(12), 996. doi:10.3390/genes10120996 PMID:31810264

Core, M. G., Lane, H. C., Van Lent, M., Gomboc, D., Solomon, S., & Rosenberg, M. (2006). Building explainable artificial intelligence systems. AAAI, 1766–1773.

Cruz, J. P., Kaji, Y., & Yanai, N. (2018). RBAC-SC: Role-Based Access Control Using Smart Contract. *IEEE Access : Practical Innovations, Open Solutions, 6*, 12240–12251. doi:10.1109/ACCESS.2018.2812844

Dalal, A., Bagherimehrab, M., & Sanders, B. C. (2021). Quantum-assisted support vector regression for detecting facial landmarks. *arXiv Preprint arXiv:2111.09304.*

Daminabo, S. C., Goel, S., Grammatikos, S. A., Nezhad, H. Y., & Thakur, V. K. (2020). Fused deposition modeling-based additive manufacturing (3D printing): Techniques for polymer material systems. *Materials Today. Chemistry, 16*, 100248. doi:10.1016/j.mtchem.2020.100248

Dang, L. M., Piran, M. J., Han, D., Min, K., & Moon, H. (2019). A Survey on Internet of Things and Cloud Computing for Healthcare. *Electronics (Basel), 8*(7), 768. doi:10.3390/electronics8070768

Dartmann, G., Song, H., & Schmeink, A. (2019). *Big Data Analytics for Cyber-Physical Systems: Machine Learning for the Internet of Things.* Elsevier.

Das, S., Lekhya, G., Shreya, K., Shekinah, K. L., Babu, K. K., & Boopathi, S. (2024). Fostering Sustainability Education Through Cross-Disciplinary Collaborations and Research Partnerships: Interdisciplinary Synergy. In Facilitating Global Collaboration and Knowledge Sharing in Higher Education With Generative AI (pp. 60–88). IGI Global.

Das, P., Ramapraba, P., Seethalakshmi, K., Mary, M. A., Karthick, S., & Sampath, B. (2024). Sustainable Advanced Techniques for Enhancing the Image Process. In *Fostering Cross-Industry Sustainability With Intelligent Technologies* (pp. 350–374). IGI Global.

Dass James, A., & Boopathi, S. (2016). Experimental Study of Eco-friendly Wire-Cut Electrical Discharge Machining Processes. *International Journal of Innovative Research in Science, Engineering and Technology, 5*.

Das, S., Lekhya, G., Shreya, K., Lydia Shekinah, K., Babu, K. K., & Boopathi, S. (2024). Fostering Sustainability Education Through Cross-Disciplinary Collaborations and Research Partnerships: Interdisciplinary Synergy. In P. Yu, J. Mulli, Z. A. S. Syed, & L. Umme (Eds.), Advances in Higher Education and Professional Development. IGI Global. doi:10.4018/979-8-3693-0487-7.ch003

de Lima Marquezino, F., Portugal, R., & Lavor, C. (2019). *A primer on quantum computing.* Springer. doi:10.1007/978-3-030-19066-8 de Morais, C. M., Sadok, D., & Kelner, J. (2019). An IoT sensor and scenario survey for data researchers. *Journal of the Brazilian Computer Society*, 25(1), 1–17. doi:10.1186/s13173-019-0085-7

Dedeoglu, V., Jurdak, R., Putra, G. D., Dorri, A., & Kanhere, S. S. (2019). A trust architecture for blockchain in IoT. *Proceedings of the 16th EAI International Conference on Mobile and Ubiquitous Systems: Computing, Networking and Services*, 190–199. 10.1145/3360774.3360822

Deepak Kumar, S., Dewangan, S., Jha, S. K., Parida, S. K., & Behera, A. (2021). 3D and 4D Printing in Industry 4.0: Trends, Challenges, and Opportunities. *Next Generation Materials and Processing Technologies: Select Proceedings of RDMPMC 2020*, 579–587.

Dhanabalan, T., & Sathish, A. (2018). Transforming Indian industries through artificial intelligence and robotics in industry 4.0. *International Journal of Mechanical Engineering and Technology*, 9(10), 835–845.

Dhanya, D., Kumar, S. S., Thilagavathy, A., Prasad, D., & Boopathi, S. (2023). Data Analytics and Artificial Intelligence in the Circular Economy: Case Studies. In Intelligent Engineering Applications and Applied Sciences for Sustainability (pp. 40–58). IGI Global.

Di Fabio, A., & Saklofske, D. H. (2021). The relationship of compassion and self-compassion with personality and emotional intelligence. *Personality and Individual Differences*, 169, 110109. doi:10.1016/j.paid.2020.110109 PMID:32394994

Di Martino, F., & Delmastro, F. (2023). Explainable AI for clinical and remote health applications: A survey on tabular and time series data. *Artificial Intelligence Review*, 56(6), 5261–5315. doi:10.1007/s10462-022-10304-3 PMID:36320613

Djourova, N. P., Rodríguez Molina, I., Tordera Santamatilde, N., & Abate, G. (2020). Self-efficacy and resilience: Mediating mechanisms in the relationship between the transformational leadership dimensions and well-being. *Journal of Leadership & Organizational Studies*, 27(3), 256–270. doi:10.1177/1548051819849002

Dolšak, B., & Novak, M. (2011). Intelligent decision support for structural design analysis. *Advanced Engineering Informatics*, 25(2), 330–340. doi:10.1016/j.aei.2010.11.001

Domakonda, V. K., Farooq, S., Chinthamreddy, S., Puviarasi, R., Sudhakar, M., & Boopathi, S. (2022). Sustainable Developments of Hybrid Floating Solar Power Plants: Photovoltaic System. In Human Agro-Energy Optimization for Business and Industry (pp. 148–167). IGI Global.

Domakonda, V. K., Farooq, S., Chinthamreddy, S., Puviarasi, R., Sudhakar, M., & Boopathi, S. (2022a). Sustainable Developments of Hybrid Floating Solar Power Plants: Photovoltaic System. In Human Agro-Energy Optimization for Business and Industry (pp. 148–167). IGI Global.

Domakonda, V. K., Farooq, S., Chinthamreddy, S., Puviarasi, R., Sudhakar, M., & Boopathi, S. (2022b). Sustainable Developments of Hybrid Floating Solar Power Plants: Photovoltaic System. In Human Agro-Energy Optimization for Business and Industry (pp. 148–167). IGI Global.

Domakonda, V. K., Farooq, S., Chinthamreddy, S., Puviarasi, R., Sudhakar, M., & Boopathi, S. (2023). Sustainable Developments of Hybrid Floating Solar Power Plants: Photovoltaic System. In P. Vasant, R. Rodríguez-Aguilar, I. Litvinchev, & J. A. Marmolejo-Saucedo (Eds.), Advances in Environmental Engineering and Green Technologies. IGI Global. doi:10.4018/978-1-6684-4118-3.ch008

Dougherty, N. (2017). The Altruistic Self. *Dialogue & Nexus*, *4*(1), 5.

Doukas, C., & Maglogiannis, I. (2011). Managing Wearable Sensor Data through Cloud Computing. *2011 IEEE Third International Conference on Cloud Computing Technology and Science*, 440–445. 10.1109/CloudCom.2011.65

Dsouli, O., Khan, N., Kakabadse, N. K., & Skouloudis, A. (2018). Mitigating the Davos dilemma: Towards a global self-sustainability index. *International Journal of Sustainable Development and World Ecology*, *25*(1), 81–98. doi:10.1080/13504509.2016.1278565

Duckworth, C., Chmiel, F. P., Burns, D. K., Zlatev, Z. D., White, N. M., Daniels, T. W. V., Kiuber, M., & Boniface, M. J. (2021). Using explainable machine learning to characterise data drift and detect emergent health risks for emergency department admissions during COVID-19. *Scientific Reports*, *11*(1), 23017. doi:10.1038/s41598-021-02481-y PMID:34837021

Durairaj, M., Jayakumar, S., Karpagavalli, V., Maheswari, B. U., Boopathi, S., & ... (2023). Utilization of Digital Tools in the Indian Higher Education System During Health Crises. In *Multidisciplinary Approaches to Organizational Governance During Health Crises* (pp. 1–21). IGI Global. doi:10.4018/978-1-7998-9213-7.ch001

Eceiza, M., Flores, J. L., & Iturbe, M. (2021). Fuzzing the Internet of Things: A Review on the Techniques and Challenges for Efficient Vulnerability Discovery in Embedded Systems. *IEEE Internet of Things Journal*, *8*(13), 10390–10411. doi:10.1109/JIOT.2021.3056179

EliotD. L. B. (2021). The Need For Explainable AI (XAI) Is Especially Crucial In The Law. *Available at* SSRN 3975778. doi:10.2139/ssrn.3975778

Erevelles, S., Bordia, K., Whelan, B., Canter, J. R., & Guimont-Blackburn, E. (2022). Blockchain and the transformation of customer co-creation. *Journal of Indian Business Research*, *14*(2), 88–107. doi:10.1108/JIBR-03-2021-0085

Ezzat, D., Hassanien, A. E., & Ella, H. A. (2021). An optimized deep learning architecture for the diagnosis of COVID-19 disease based on gravitational search optimization. *Applied Soft Computing*, *98*, 106742. doi:10.1016/j.asoc.2020.106742 PMID:32982615

Fan, D., Li, Y., Wang, X., Zhu, T., Wang, Q., Cai, H., Li, W., Tian, Y., & Liu, Z. (2020). Progressive 3D printing technology and its application in medical materials. *Frontiers in Pharmacology*, *11*, 122. doi:10.3389/fphar.2020.00122 PMID:32265689

Farooq, M. S., Khan, M., & Abid, A. (2020). A framework to make charity collection transparent and auditable using blockchain technology. *Computers & Electrical Engineering*, *83*, 106588. doi:10.1016/j.compeleceng.2020.106588

Feng, Zhu, Han, Zhou, Wen, & Xiang. (2022). Detecting Vulnerability on IoT Device Firmware: A Survey. *IEEE/CAA Journal of Automatica Sinica, 10*(1), 25–41.

Fisher, A., Rudin, C., & Dominici, F. (2019). All Models are Wrong, but Many are Useful: Learning a Variable's Importance by Studying an Entire Class of Prediction Models Simultaneously. *Journal of Machine Learning Research, 20*(177), 1–81. PMID:34335110

Fowziya, S., Sivaranjani, S., Devi, N. L., Boopathi, S., Thakur, S., & Sailaja, J. M. (2023). Influences of nano-green lubricants in the friction-stir process of TiAlN coated alloys. *Materials Today: Proceedings*. Advance online publication. doi:10.1016/j.matpr.2023.06.446

Franki, V., Majnarić, D., & Višković, A. (2023). A Comprehensive Review of Artificial Intelligence (AI) Companies in the Power Sector. *Energies, 16*(3), 1077. doi:10.3390/en16031077

Ganapathy, A. (2021). Quantum computing in high frequency trading and fraud detection. *Engineering International, 9*(2), 61–72. doi:10.18034/ei.v9i2.549

Garg, P., Gupta, B., Chauhan, A. K., Sivarajah, U., Gupta, S., & Modgil, S. (2021). Measuring the perceived benefits of implementing blockchain technology in the banking sector. *Technological Forecasting and Social Change, 163*, 120407.

Garvin, M. R., & Prates, E., Pavicic, M., Jones, P., Amos, B. K., Geiger, A., Shah, M. B., Streich, J., Felipe Machado Gazolla, J. G., & Kainer, D. (2020). Potentially adaptive SARS-CoV-2 mutations discovered with novel spatiotemporal and explainable AI models. *Genome Biology, 21*, 1–26. doi:10.1186/s13059-020-02191-0 PMID:33357233

Gaynor, M., Moulton, S., Welsh, M., LaCombe, E., Rowan, A., & Wynne, J. (2004). Integrating wireless sensor networks with the grid. *IEEE Internet Computing, 8*(4), 32–39. doi:10.1109/MIC.2004.18

Gentry, G. (2021). *Proposed International Space Station Life Support Hardware Changes for a Lunar/Mars Surface Human Habitat Common Cabin Air Assembly Case Study*. Academic Press.

George, A. S., & George, A. H. (2023). Revolutionizing Manufacturing: Exploring the Promises and Challenges of Industry 5.0. *Partners Universal International Innovation Journal, 1*(2), 22–38.

Gill, S. S. (2021). A manifesto for modern fog and edge computing: Vision, new paradigms, opportunities, and future directions. In Operationalizing Multi-Cloud Environments: Technologies, Tools and Use Cases (pp. 237–253). Springer.

Gill, S. S., Kumar, A., Singh, H., Singh, M., Kaur, K., Usman, M., & Buyya, R. (2022). Quantum computing: A taxonomy, systematic review and future directions. *Software, Practice & Experience, 52*(1), 66–114. doi:10.1002/spe.3039

Glaser, F., Hawlitschek, F., & Notheisen, B. (2019). Blockchain as a Platform. In H. Treiblmaier & R. Beck (Eds.), *Business Transformation through Blockchain* (pp. 121–143). Springer International Publishing. doi:10.1007/978-3-319-98911-2_4

Glazebrook, P. (2012). *The agrarian vision: Sustainability and environmental ethics.* Taylor & Francis.

Gnanaprakasam, C., Vankara, J., Sastry, A. S., Prajval, V., Gireesh, N., & Boopathi, S. (2023). Long-Range and Low-Power Automated Soil Irrigation System Using Internet of Things: An Experimental Study. In Contemporary Developments in Agricultural Cyber-Physical Systems (pp. 87–104). IGI Global.

Gnanaprakasam, C., Vankara, J., Sastry, A. S., Prajval, V., Gireesh, N., & Boopathi, S. (2023). Long-Range and Low-Power Automated Soil Irrigation System Using Internet of Things: An Experimental Study. In G. S. Karthick (Ed.), Advances in Environmental Engineering and Green Technologies. IGI Global. doi:10.4018/978-1-6684-7879-0.ch005

Gopinath, M., & Sethuraman, S. C. (2023). A comprehensive survey on deep learning based malware detection techniques. *Computer Science Review, 47,* 100529. doi:10.1016/j.cosrev.2022.100529

Górski, Ł., & Ramakrishna, S. (2021). Explainable artificial intelligence, lawyer's perspective. *Proceedings of the Eighteenth International Conference on Artificial Intelligence and Law,* 60–68.

Gowri, N. V., Dwivedi, J. N., Krishnaveni, K., Boopathi, S., Palaniappan, M., & Medikondu, N. R. (2023). Experimental investigation and multi-objective optimization of eco-friendly near-dry electrical discharge machining of shape memory alloy using Cu/SiC/Gr composite electrode. *Environmental Science and Pollution Research International, 30*(49), 1–19. doi:10.1007/s11356-023-26983-6 PMID:37126160

Graziani, M., Andrearczyk, V., Marchand-Maillet, S., & Müller, H. (2020). Concept attribution: Explaining CNN decisions to physicians. *Computers in Biology and Medicine, 123,* 103865. doi:10.1016/j.compbiomed.2020.103865 PMID:32658785

Guangzhong, L. (2020). Application of IoT and Countermeasure in Agriculture of Shandong Province, China. *Internet of Things and Cloud Computing, 8*(1), 8. doi:10.11648/j.iotcc.20200801.12

Gunasekaran, K., & Boopathi, S. (2023). Artificial Intelligence in Water Treatments and Water Resource Assessments. In *Artificial Intelligence Applications in Water Treatment and Water Resource Management* (pp. 71–98). IGI Global. doi:10.4018/978-1-6684-6791-6.ch004

Guo, K., Yang, Z., Yu, C.-H., & Buehler, M. J. (2021). Artificial intelligence and machine learning in design of mechanical materials. *Materials Horizons, 8*(4), 1153–1172. doi:10.1039/D0MH01451F PMID:34821909

Gupta, B. B., & Dahiya, A. (2021). *Distributed Denial of Service (DDoS) Attacks: Classification, Attacks, Challenges and Countermeasures.* CRC Press. doi:10.1201/9781003107354

Haddaji, A., Ayed, S., & Fourati, L. C. (2022). Artificial Intelligence Techniques to Mitigate Cyber-Attacks within Vehicular Networks: Survey. *Computers & Electrical Engineering, 104,* 108460. doi:10.1016/j.compeleceng.2022.108460

Hamon, R., Junklewitz, H., Sanchez, I., Malgieri, G., & De Hert, P. (2022). Bridging the gap between AI and explainability in the GDPR: Towards trustworthiness-by-design in automated decision-making. *IEEE Computational Intelligence Magazine, 17*(1), 72–85. doi:10.1109/MCI.2021.3129960

Han, G., Tu, J., Liu, L., Martínez-García, M., & Choi, C. (2021). An intelligent signal processing data denoising method for control systems protection in the industrial Internet of Things. *IEEE Transactions on Industrial Informatics, 18*(4), 2684–2692. doi:10.1109/TII.2021.3096970

Hanumanthakari, S., Gift, M. M., Kanimozhi, K., Bhavani, M. D., Bamane, K. D., & Boopathi, S. (2023). Biomining Method to Extract Metal Components Using Computer-Printed Circuit Board E-Waste. In *Handbook of Research on Safe Disposal Methods of Municipal Solid Wastes for a Sustainable Environment* (pp. 123–141). IGI Global. doi:10.4018/978-1-6684-8117-2.ch010

Hao, B., & Lin, G. (2020). 3D printing technology and its application in industrial manufacturing. *IOP Conference Series. Materials Science and Engineering, 782*(2), 022065. doi:10.1088/1757-899X/782/2/022065

Haq, A. U., Ping Li, J., Khan, G. A., Khan, J., Ishrat, M., Guru, A., & Agbley, B. L. Y. (2022). Community Detection Approach Via Graph Regularized Non-Negative Matrix Factorization. *2022 19th International Computer Conference on Wavelet Active Media Technology and Information Processing, ICCWAMTIP 2022*. 10.1109/ICCWAMTIP56608.2022.10016496

Haribalaji, V., Boopathi, S., & Asif, M. M. (2021). Optimization of friction stir welding process to join dissimilar AA2014 and AA7075 aluminum alloys. *Materials Today: Proceedings, 50*, 2227–2234. doi:10.1016/j.matpr.2021.09.499

Haribalaji, V., Boopathi, S., Asif, M. M., Jeyakumar, M., Subbiah, R., & Lewise, K. A. S. (2022). Influences of Friction stir tool parameters for joining two similar AZ61A alloy plates. *Materials Today: Proceedings, 50*(5), 2547–2553. doi:10.1016/j.matpr.2021.12.074

Haribalaji, V., Boopathi, S., Asif, M. M., Yuvaraj, T., Velmurugan, D., Lewise, K. A. S., Sudhagar, S., & Suresh, P. (2022). Influences of Mg-Cr filler materials in Friction Stir Process of Aluminium-based dissimilar alloys. *Materials Today: Proceedings, 66*(3), 948–954. doi:10.1016/j.matpr.2022.04.668

Haribalaji, V., Boopathi, S., & Balamurugan, S. (2014). Effect of Welding Processes on Mechanical and Metallurgical Properties of High Strength Low Alloy (HSLA) Steel Joints. *International Journal of Innovation and Scientific Research, 12*(1), 170–179.

Haribalaji, V., Venkatesan, G., Pandian, M., Subbiah, R., & Boopathi, S. (2022). Investigation on corrosion and tensile Characteristics: Friction stir welding of AA7075 and AA2014. *Materials Today: Proceedings, 66*(3), 743–748. doi:10.1016/j.matpr.2022.04.037

Hassanalieragh, M., Page, A., Soyata, T., Sharma, G., Aktas, M., Mateos, G., Kantarci, B., & Andreescu, S. (2015). Health monitoring and management using Internet-of-Things (IoT) sensing with cloud-based processing: Opportunities and challenges. *2015 IEEE International Conference on Services Computing*, 285–292. 10.1109/SCC.2015.47

Hellfeldt, K., López-Romero, L., & Andershed, H. (2020). Cyberbullying and psychological well-being in young adolescence: The potential protective mediation effects of social support from family, friends, and teachers. *International Journal of Environmental Research and Public Health, 17*(1), 45. doi:10.3390/ijerph17010045 PMID:31861641

Holzinger, A., Malle, B., Saranti, A., & Pfeifer, B. (2021). Towards multi-modal causability with graph neural networks enabling information fusion for explainable AI. *Information Fusion, 71,* 28–37. doi:10.1016/j.inffus.2021.01.008

Hosseini, M. M., Umunnakwe, A., Parvania, M., & Tasdizen, T. (2020). Intelligent damage classification and estimation in power distribution poles using unmanned aerial vehicles and convolutional neural networks. *IEEE Transactions on Smart Grid, 11*(4), 3325–3333. doi:10.1109/TSG.2020.2970156

Huang, Y., & Fu, J. (2019). Review on application of artificial intelligence in civil engineering. *Computer Modeling in Engineering & Sciences, 121*(3), 845–875. doi:10.32604/cmes.2019.07653

Humayun, M., Jhanjhi, N. Z., Alsayat, A., & Ponnusamy, V. (2021). Internet of Things and Ransomware: Evolution, Mitigation and Prevention. *Egyptian Informatics Journal, 22*(1), 105–117. doi:10.1016/j.eij.2020.05.003

Hussain, Z., & Srimathy, G. (2023). *IoT and AI Integration for Enhanced Efficiency and Sustainability.* Academic Press.

Hussain, Z., Babe, M., Saravanan, S., Srimathy, G., Roopa, H., & Boopathi, S. (2023). Optimizing Biomass-to-Biofuel Conversion: IoT and AI Integration for Enhanced Efficiency and Sustainability. In Circular Economy Implementation for Sustainability in the Built Environment (pp. 191–214). IGI Global.

Hussain, R. I., Bashir, S., & Hussain, S. (2020). Financial sustainability and corporate social responsibility under mediating effect of operational self-sustainability. *Frontiers in Psychology, 11,* 550029. doi:10.3389/fpsyg.2020.550029 PMID:33424672

Ijaz, M., Li, G., Lin, L., Cheikhrouhou, O., Hamam, H., & Noor, A. (2021). Integration and applications of fog computing and cloud computing based on the internet of things for provision of healthcare services at home. *Electronics (Basel), 10*(9), 1077. doi:10.3390/electronics10091077

Ikemura, T., Wada, K., Wada, Y., Iwasaki, Y., & Abe, T. (2020). Unsupervised explainable AI for simultaneous molecular evolutionary study of forty thousand SARS-CoV-2 genomes. Biorxiv, 2010–2020. doi:10.1101/2020.10.11.335406

Ingle, R. B., Swathi, S., Mahendran, G., Senthil, T., Muralidharan, N., & Boopathi, S. (2023). Sustainability and Optimization of Green and Lean Manufacturing Processes Using Machine Learning Techniques. In *Circular Economy Implementation for Sustainability in the Built Environment* (pp. 261–285). IGI Global. doi:10.4018/978-1-6684-8238-4.ch012

Jadhav, G. N., & Dharme, A. A. (2012, March). Technical challenges for development of smart grid in India. In *IEEE-International Conference On Advances In Engineering, Science And Management (ICAESM-2012)* (pp. 784-788). IEEE.

Jaouhari, S. E., & Bouvet, E. (2022). Secure Firmware Over-The-Air Updates for IoT: Survey, Challenges, and Discussions. *Internet of Things : Engineering Cyber Physical Human Systems, 18*, 100508. doi:10.1016/j.iot.2022.100508

Jarva, E., Oikarinen, A., Andersson, J., Tuomikoski, A.-M., Kääriäinen, M., Meriläinen, M., & Mikkonen, K. (2022). Healthcare professionals' perceptions of digital health competence: A qualitative descriptive study. *Nursing Open, 9*(2), 1379–1393. doi:10.1002/nop2.1184 PMID:35094493

Jasim, A. D. (2022). A Survey of Intrusion Detection Using Deep Learning in Internet of Things. *Iraqi Journal For Computer Science and Mathematics, 3*(1), 83–93.

Jatothu, R., & Lal, J. D. (2022). End-to-End Latency Analysis for Data Transmission via Optimum Path Allocation in Industrial Sensor Networks. *Wireless Communications and Mobile Computing.*

Javaid, M., & Haleem, A. (2019). 4D printing applications in medical field: A brief review. *Clinical Epidemiology and Global Health, 7*(3), 317–321. doi:10.1016/j.cegh.2018.09.007

Jeevanantham, Y. A., Saravanan, A., Vanitha, V., Boopathi, S., & Kumar, D. P. (2022). Implementation of Internet-of Things (IoT) in Soil Irrigation System. *IEEE Explore*, 1–5.

Jenkins, N., Long, C., & Wu, J. (2015). An overview of the smart grid in Great Britain. *Engineering (Beijing), 1*(4), 413–421. doi:10.15302/J-ENG-2015112

Jeyaraman, M., Nallakumarasamy, A., & Jeyaraman, N. (2022). Industry 5.0 in orthopaedics. *Indian Journal of Orthopaedics, 56*(10), 1694–1702. doi:10.1007/s43465-022-00712-6 PMID:36187596

Jha, S. K., Pinsonneault, A., & Dubé, L. (2016). The evolution of an ict platform-enabled ecosystem for poverty alleviation. *Management Information Systems Quarterly, 40*(2), 431–446. doi:10.25300/MISQ/2016/40.2.08

Jiang, Y., Wang, C., Wang, Y., & Gao, L. (2019). A cross-chain solution to integrating multiple blockchains for IoT data management. *Sensors (Basel), 19*(9), 2042. doi:10.3390/s19092042 PMID:31052380

Jihong, Z., Han, Z., Chuang, W., Lu, Z., Shangqin, Y., & Zhang, W. (2021). A review of topology optimization for additive manufacturing: Status and challenges. *Chinese Journal of Aeronautics, 34*(1), 91–110. doi:10.1016/j.cja.2020.09.020

Jo, J., Cho, J., & Moon, J. (2023). A Malware Detection and Extraction Method for the Related Information Using the ViT Attention Mechanism on Android Operating System. *Applied Sciences (Basel, Switzerland), 13*(11), 6839. doi:10.3390/app13116839

Jurcut, A., Niculcea, T., Ranaweera, P., & Le-Khac, N.-A. (2020). Security Considerations for Internet of Things: A Survey. *SN Computer Science, 1*(4), 1–19. doi:10.1007/s42979-020-00201-3

Kadu, A., & Singh, M. (2023). Fog-Enabled Framework for Patient Health-Monitoring Systems Using Internet of Things and Wireless Body Area Networks. In *Computational Intelligence: Select Proceedings of InCITe 2022* (pp. 607–616). Springer. doi:10.1007/978-981-19-7346-8_52

Kalidas, R., Boopathi, S., Sivakumar, K., & Mohankumar, P. (2012). Optimization of Machining Parameters of WEDM Process Based On the Taguchi Method. *IJEST, 6*(1).

Kangra, K., & Singh, J. (2022). Explainable Artificial Intelligence: Concepts and Current Progression. In Explainable Edge AI: A Futuristic Computing Perspective (pp. 1–17). Springer.

Kannan, E., Trabelsi, Y., Boopathi, S., & Alagesan, S. (2022). Influences of cryogenically treated work material on near-dry wire-cut electrical discharge machining process. *Surface Topography : Metrology and Properties, 10*(1), 015027. doi:10.1088/2051-672X/ac53e1

Kannan, R. R., & Madhumita, G. (2020). Smart grid—introduction, advantages and implementation status in India with a focus on Tamil Nadu: A systematic review. *Int. J. Adv. Sci. Technol, 29*, 1146–1156.

Kantaros, A., Ganetsos, T., & Piromalis, D. (2023). 3D and 4D Printing as Integrated Manufacturing Methods of Industry 4.0. *Kantaros, A., Ganetsos, T. & Piromalis, D.(2023). 3D and 4D Printing as Integrated Manufacturing Methods of Industry, 4*, 12–22.

Karthik, S., Hemalatha, R., Aruna, R., Deivakani, M., Reddy, R. V. K., & Boopathi, S. (2023). Study on Healthcare Security System-Integrated Internet of Things (IoT). In Perspectives and Considerations on the Evolution of Smart Systems (pp. 342–362). IGI Global.

Kaur, J., Agrawal, A., & Khan, R. A. (2020). Security issues in fog environment: A systematic literature review. *International Journal of Wireless Information Networks, 27*(3), 467–483. doi:10.1007/s10776-020-00491-7

Kavitha, C. R., Varalatchoumy, M., Mithuna, H. R., Bharathi, K., Geethalakshmi, N. M., & Boopathi, S. (2023). Energy Monitoring and Control in the Smart Grid: Integrated Intelligent IoT and ANFIS. In M. Arshad (Ed.), Advances in Bioinformatics and Biomedical Engineering. IGI Global. doi:10.4018/978-1-6684-6577-6.ch014

Kavitha, C., Malini, P. G., Kantumuchu, V. C., Kumar, N. M., Verma, A., & Boopathi, S. (2023). An experimental study on the hardness and wear rate of carbonitride coated stainless steel. *Materials Today: Proceedings, 74*, 595–601. doi:10.1016/j.matpr.2022.09.524

Kermanidis, A. T. (2020). Aircraft aluminum alloys: Applications and future trends. *Revolutionizing Aircraft Materials and Processes*, 21–55.

Keshk, M., Koroniotis, N., Pham, N., Moustafa, N., Turnbull, B., & Zomaya, A. Y. (2023). An explainable deep learning-enabled intrusion detection framework in IoT networks. *Information Sciences, 639*, 119000. doi:10.1016/j.ins.2023.119000

Khalid, T., Khan, A. N., Ali, M., Adeel, A., ur Rehman Khan, A., & Shuja, J. (2019). A fog-based security framework for intelligent traffic light control system. *Multimedia Tools and Applications, 78*(17), 24595–24615. doi:10.1007/s11042-018-7008-z

Khan, W., Bitm, L., & Awasthi, M. S. (n.d.). *MATLAB based implementation and comparative analysis of de-blocking algorithms.* Academic Press.

Khan, A. S., Balan, K., Javed, Y., Tarmizi, S., & Abdullah, J. (2019). Secure trust-based blockchain architecture to prevent attacks in VANET. *Sensors (Basel)*, *19*(22), 4954. doi:10.3390/s19224954 PMID:31739437

Khan, A., Ahmad, A., Ahmed, M., Sessa, J., & Anisetti, M. (2022). Authorization Schemes for Internet of Things: Requirements, Weaknesses, Future Challenges and Trends. *Complex & Intelligent Systems*, *8*(5), 3919–3941. doi:10.1007/s40747-022-00765-y

Khan, D., Jung, L. T., & Hashmani, M. A. (2021). Systematic literature review of challenges in blockchain scalability. *Applied Sciences (Basel, Switzerland)*, *11*(20), 9372. doi:10.3390/app11209372

Khan, M. A., Khan, G. A., Khan, J., Anwar, T., Ashraf, Z., Atoum, I., Ahmad, N., Shahid, M., Ishrat, M., & Alghamdi, A. A. (2023). Adaptive Weighted Low-Rank Sparse Representation for Multi-View Clustering. *IEEE Access : Practical Innovations, Open Solutions*, *11*, 60681–60692. doi:10.1109/ACCESS.2023.3285662

Khan, T. M., & Robles-Kelly, A. (2020). Machine learning: Quantum vs classical. *IEEE Access : Practical Innovations, Open Solutions*, *8*, 219275–219294. doi:10.1109/ACCESS.2020.3041719

Khan, W., Ansari, H., & Shaikh, A. A. (2015). Log files utility for software maintenance. *International Journal of Advanced Research in Computer Engineering and Technology*, *4*(9).

Khan, W., & Haroon, M. (2022a). A Pilot Study and Survey on Methods for Anomaly Detection in Online Social Networks. *Human-Centric Smart Computing Proceedings of ICHCSC*, *2022*, 119–128.

Khan, W., & Haroon, M. (2022b). An efficient framework for anomaly detection in attributed social networks. *International Journal of Information Technology : an Official Journal of Bharati Vidyapeeth's Institute of Computer Applications and Management*, *14*(6), 3069–3076. Advance online publication. doi:10.1007/s41870-022-01044-2

Khan, W., & Haroon, M. (2022c). An unsupervised deep learning ensemble model for anomaly detection in static attributed social networks. *International Journal of Cognitive Computing in Engineering*, *3*, 153–160. doi:10.1016/j.ijcce.2022.08.002

Khan, W., Haroon, M., Khan, A. N., Hasan, M. K., Khan, A., Mokhtar, U. A., & Islam, S. (2022). DVAEGMM: Dual Variational Autoencoder With Gaussian Mixture Model for Anomaly Detection on Attributed Networks. *IEEE Access : Practical Innovations, Open Solutions*, *10*, 91160–91176. doi:10.1109/ACCESS.2022.3201332

Khan, W., Ishrat, M., Haleem, M., Khan, A. N., Hasan, M. K., & Farooqui, N. A. (2023). *An Extensive Study and Review on Dark Web Threats and Detection Techniques.* doi:10.4018/978-1-6684-8133-2.ch011

Khare, S., & Totaro, M. (2019). Big data in IoT. *2019 10th International Conference on Computing, Communication and Networking Technologies (ICCCNT)*, 1–7.

Khosrojerdi, F., Akhigbe, O., Gagnon, S., Ramirez, A., & Richards, G. (2021). Integrating artificial intelligence and analytics in smart grids: A systematic literature review. *International Journal of Energy Sector Management, 16*(2), 318–338.

Kim, B., Wattenberg, M., Gilmer, J., Cai, C., Wexler, J., & Viegas, F. (2018). Interpretability beyond feature attribution: Quantitative testing with concept activation vectors (tcav). *International Conference on Machine Learning*, 2668–2677.

Kirubakaran, A. P., & Midhunchakkaravarthy, J. (2023). A Hybrid Application of Quantum Computing Methodologies to AI Techniques for Paddy Crop Leaf Disease Identification. In *Integrating Blockchain and Artificial Intelligence for Industry 4.0 Innovations* (pp. 69–83). Springer.

Klerkx, L., Jakku, E., & Labarthe, P. (2019). A review of social science on digital agriculture, smart farming and agriculture 4.0: New contributions and a future research agenda. *NJAS Wageningen Journal of Life Sciences, 90*(1), 100315. doi:10.1016/j.njas.2019.100315

Koshariya, A. K., Kalaiyarasi, D., Jovith, A. A., Sivakami, T., Hasan, D. S., & Boopathi, S. (2023). AI-Enabled IoT and WSN-Integrated Smart Agriculture System. In *Artificial Intelligence Tools and Technologies for Smart Farming and Agriculture Practices* (pp. 200–218). IGI Global. doi:10.4018/978-1-6684-8516-3.ch011

Koshariya, A. K., Khatoon, S., Marathe, A. M., Suba, G. M., Baral, D., & Boopathi, S. (2023). Agricultural Waste Management Systems Using Artificial Intelligence Techniques. In *AI-Enabled Social Robotics in Human Care Services* (pp. 236–258). IGI Global. doi:10.4018/978-1-6684-8171-4.ch009

Krishnamurthi, R., Kumar, A., Gopinathan, D., Nayyar, A., & Qureshi, B. (2020). An overview of IoT sensor data processing, fusion, and analysis techniques. *Sensors (Basel), 20*(21), 6076. doi:10.3390/s20216076 PMID:33114594

Kronlid, D. O., & Öhman, J. (2013). An environmental ethical conceptual framework for research on sustainability and environmental education. *Environmental Education Research, 19*(1), 21–44. doi:10.1080/13504622.2012.687043

Kuang, X., Roach, D. J., Wu, J., Hamel, C. M., Ding, Z., Wang, T., Dunn, M. L., & Qi, H. J. (2019). Advances in 4D printing: Materials and applications. *Advanced Functional Materials, 29*(2), 1805290. doi:10.1002/adfm.201805290

Kumar, M., Kumar, K., Sasikala, P., Sampath, B., Gopi, B., & Sundaram, S. (2023). Sustainable Green Energy Generation From Waste Water: IoT and ML Integration. In Sustainable Science and Intelligent Technologies for Societal Development (pp. 440–463). IGI Global.

Kumar, P., Sampath, B., Kumar, S., Babu, B. H., & Ahalya, N. (2023). Hydroponics, Aeroponics, and Aquaponics Technologies in Modern Agricultural Cultivation. In IGI: Trends, Paradigms, and Advances in Mechatronics Engineering (pp. 223–241). IGI Global.

Kumar, R., Badwal, L., Avasthi, S., & Prakash, A. (2023, January). A Secure Decentralized E-Voting with Blockchain & Smart Contracts. In *2023 13th International Conference on Cloud Computing, Data Science & Engineering (Confluence)* (pp. 419-424). IEEE. 10.1109/Confluence56041.2023.10048871

Kumara, V., Mohanaprakash, T., Fairooz, S., Jamal, K., Babu, T., & Sampath, B. (2023). Experimental Study on a Reliable Smart Hydroponics System. In *Human Agro-Energy Optimization for Business and Industry* (pp. 27–45). IGI Global. doi:10.4018/978-1-6684-4118-3.ch002

Kumari, G., Abhishek, K., Singh, S., Hussain, A., Altamimi, M. A., Madhyastha, H., Webster, T. J., & Dev, A. (2022). A voyage from 3D to 4D printing in nanomedicine and healthcare: Part II. *Nanomedicine (London)*, *17*(4), 255–270. doi:10.2217/nnm-2021-0454 PMID:35109687

Kumar, P. R., Meenakshi, S., Shalini, S., Devi, S. R., & Boopathi, S. (2023). Soil Quality Prediction in Context Learning Approaches Using Deep Learning and Blockchain for Smart Agriculture. In R. Kumar, A. B. Abdul Hamid, & N. I. Binti Ya'akub (Eds.), Advances in Computational Intelligence and Robotics. IGI Global. doi:10.4018/978-1-6684-9151-5.ch001

Landaluce, H., Arjona, L., Perallos, A., Falcone, F., Angulo, I., & Muralter, F. (2020). A Review of IoT Sensing Applications and Challenges Using RFID and Wireless Sensor Networks. *Sensors (Basel)*, *20*(9), 2495. doi:10.3390/s20092495 PMID:32354063

Lao, L., Li, Z., Hou, S., Xiao, B., Guo, S., & Yang, Y. (2021). A Survey of IoT Applications in Blockchain Systems: Architecture, Consensus, and Traffic Modeling. *ACM Computing Surveys*, *53*(1), 1–32. doi:10.1145/3372136

Lebovitz, S., Lifshitz-Assaf, H., & Levina, N. (2022). To engage or not to engage with AI for critical judgments: How professionals deal with opacity when using AI for medical diagnosis. *Organization Science*, *33*(1), 126–148. doi:10.1287/orsc.2021.1549

Lei, J., G'Sell, M., Rinaldo, A., Tibshirani, R. J., & Wasserman, L. (2018). Distribution-free predictive inference for regression. *Journal of the American Statistical Association*, *113*(523), 1094–1111. doi:10.1080/01621459.2017.1307116

Letham, B., Rudin, C., McCormick, T. H., & Madigan, D. (2015). *Interpretable classifiers using rules and bayesian analysis: Building a better stroke prediction model*. Academic Press.

Liang, H., Zhu, L., Yu, F. R., & Wang, X. (2022). A Cross-Layer Defense Method for Blockchain Empowered CBTC Systems against Data Tampering Attacks. *IEEE Transactions on Intelligent Transportation Systems*, *24*(1), 501–515. doi:10.1109/TITS.2022.3211020

Li, L., Ota, K., & Dong, M. (2018). Deep learning for smart industry: Efficient manufacture inspection system with fog computing. *IEEE Transactions on Industrial Informatics*, *14*(10), 4665–4673. doi:10.1109/TII.2018.2842821

Lin, S.-Y., Du, Y., Ko, P.-C., Wu, T.-J., Ho, P.-T., Sivakumar, V., & Subbareddy, R. (2020). Fog computing based hybrid deep learning framework in effective inspection system for smart manufacturing. *Computer Communications*, *160*, 636–642. doi:10.1016/j.comcom.2020.05.044

Li, Q., Deng, Y., Liu, X., Sun, W., Li, W., Li, J., & Liu, Z. (2023). *Autonomous smart grid fault detection.* IEEE Communications Standards Magazine. doi:10.1109/MCOMSTD.0001.2200019

Lisboa, P. J. G., Saralajew, S., Vellido, A., Fernández-Domenech, R., & Villmann, T. (2023). The coming of age of interpretable and explainable machine learning models. *Neurocomputing, 535,* 25–39. doi:10.1016/j.neucom.2023.02.040

Liu, C., Xu, N., Zong, Q., Yu, J., & Zhang, P. (2021). Hydrogel prepared by 3D printing technology and its applications in the medical field. *Colloid and Interface Science Communications, 44,* 100498. doi:10.1016/j.colcom.2021.100498

Liu, S., Tomizuka, M., & Ulsoy, A. (2004). Challenges and opportunities in the engineering of intelligent systems. *Proc. of the 4th International Workshop on Structural Control,* 295–300.

Li, W., Tug, S., Meng, W., & Wang, Y. (2019). Designing Collaborative Blockchained Signature-Based Intrusion Detection in IoT Environments. *Future Generation Computer Systems, 96,* 481–489. doi:10.1016/j.future.2019.02.064

Loh, H. W., Ooi, C. P., Seoni, S., Barua, P. D., Molinari, F., & Acharya, U. R. (2022). Application of explainable artificial intelligence for healthcare: A systematic review of the last decade (2011–2022). *Computer Methods and Programs in Biomedicine, 226,* 107161. doi:10.1016/j. cmpb.2022.107161 PMID:36228495

Lorente, M. P. S., Lopez, E. M., Florez, L. A., Espino, A. L., Martínez, J. A. I., & de Miguel, A. S. (2021). Explaining deep learning-based driver models. *Applied Sciences (Basel, Switzerland), 11*(8), 3321. doi:10.3390/app11083321

Lowenberg-DeBoer, J., & Erickson, B. (2019). Setting the record straight on precision agriculture adoption. *Agronomy Journal, 111*(4), 1552–1569. doi:10.2134/agronj2018.12.0779

Lu, Y. (2019). The blockchain: State-of-the-art and research challenges. *Journal of Industrial Information Integration, 15,* 80–90.

Lupton, D., & Leahy, D. (2019). Reimagining digital health education: Reflections on the possibilities of the storyboarding method. *Health Education Journal, 78*(6), 633–646. doi:10.1177/0017896919841413

Lyu, W., & Liu, J. (2021). Artificial Intelligence and emerging digital technologies in the energy sector. *Applied Energy, 303,* 117615. doi:10.1016/j.apenergy.2021.117615

Maddikunta, P. K. R., Pham, Q.-V., Prabadevi, B., Deepa, N., Dev, K., Gadekallu, T. R., Ruby, R., & Liyanage, M. (2022). Industry 5.0: A survey on enabling technologies and potential applications. *Journal of Industrial Information Integration, 26,* 100257. doi:10.1016/j.jii.2021.100257

Maguluri, L. P., Ananth, J., Hariram, S., Geetha, C., Bhaskar, A., & Boopathi, S. (2023). Smart Vehicle-Emissions Monitoring System Using Internet of Things (IoT). In Handbook of Research on Safe Disposal Methods of Municipal Solid Wastes for a Sustainable Environment (pp. 191–211). IGI Global.

Maguluri, L. P., Arularasan, A. N., & Boopathi, S. (2023). Assessing Security Concerns for AI-Based Drones in Smart Cities. In R. Kumar, A. B. Abdul Hamid, & N. I. Binti Ya'akub (Eds.), Advances in Computational Intelligence and Robotics. IGI Global. doi:10.4018/978-1-6684-9151-5.ch002

Mahdavinejad, M. S., Rezvan, M., Barekatain, M., Adibi, P., Barnaghi, P., & Sheth, A. P. (2018). Machine learning for internet of things data analysis: A survey. *Digital Communications and Networks*, *4*(3), 161–175. doi:10.1016/j.dcan.2017.10.002

Maheswari, B. U., Imambi, S. S., Hasan, D., Meenakshi, S., Pratheep, V., & Boopathi, S. (2023). Internet of Things and Machine Learning-Integrated Smart Robotics. In Global Perspectives on Robotics and Autonomous Systems: Development and Applications (pp. 240–258). IGI Global. doi:10.4018/978-1-6684-7791-5.ch010

Mankodiya, H., Jadav, D., Gupta, R., Tanwar, S., Hong, W.-C., & Sharma, R. (2022). Od-xai: Explainable ai-based semantic object detection for autonomous vehicles. *Applied Sciences (Basel, Switzerland)*, *12*(11), 5310. doi:10.3390/app12115310

Mardaoui, D., & Garreau, D. (2021). An analysis of lime for text data. *International Conference on Artificial Intelligence and Statistics*, 3493–3501.

Markkandeyan, & Shivani Gupta, Narayanan, Reddy, Al-Khasawneh, Ishrat, & Kiran. (2023). Deep Learning Based Semantic Segmentation Approach for Automatic Detection of Brain Tumor. *International Journal of Computers, Communications & Control*, *18*(4). Advance online publication. doi:10.15837/ijccc.2023.4.5186

Meena, P., Pal, M. B., Jain, P. K., & Pamula, R. (2022). 6G Communication Networks: Introduction, Vision, Challenges, and Future Directions. *Wireless Personal Communications*, *125*(2), 1097–1123. doi:10.1007/s11277-022-09590-5

Mekonnen, Y., Namuduri, S., Burton, L., Sarwat, A., & Bhansali, S. (2019). Machine learning techniques in wireless sensor network based precision agriculture. *Journal of the Electrochemical Society*, *167*(3), 037522. doi:10.1149/2.0222003JES

Menon, S., & Jain, K. (2021). Blockchain technology for transparency in agri-food supply chain: Use cases, limitations, and future directions. *IEEE Transactions on Engineering Management*. https://ieeexplore.ieee.org/abstract/document/9578927/

Meyer, B., Zill, A., Dilba, D., Gerlach, R., & Schumann, S. (2021). Employee psychological well-being during the COVID-19 pandemic in Germany: A longitudinal study of demands, resources, and exhaustion. *International Journal of Psychology*, *56*(4), 532–550. doi:10.1002/ijop.12743 PMID:33615477

Mitra, Mohanty, Corcoran, & Kougianos. (2021). IFace: A Deepfake Resilient Digital Identification Framework for Smart Cities. *2021 IEEE International Symposium on Smart Electronic Systems (ISES)*, 361–66. 10.1109/iSES52644.2021.00090

Mittelstadt, B., Russell, C., & Wachter, S. (2019). Explaining explanations in AI. *Proceedings of the Conference on Fairness, Accountability, and Transparency*, 279–288. 10.1145/3287560.3287574

Mohammadi, M., Al-Fuqaha, A., Sorour, S., & Guizani, M. (2018). Deep learning for iot big data and streaming analytics: A survey. *IEEE Communications Surveys and Tutorials*, *20*(4), 2923–2960. doi:10.1109/COMST.2018.2844341

Mohanty, A., Venkateswaran, N., Ranjit, P., Tripathi, M. A., & Boopathi, S. (2023). Innovative Strategy for Profitable Automobile Industries: Working Capital Management. In Handbook of Research on Designing Sustainable Supply Chains to Achieve a Circular Economy (pp. 412–428). IGI Global.

Mohanty, A., Jothi, B., Jeyasudha, J., Ranjit, P., Isaac, J. S., & Boopathi, S. (2023). Additive Manufacturing Using Robotic Programming. In *AI-Enabled Social Robotics in Human Care Services* (pp. 259–282). IGI Global. doi:10.4018/978-1-6684-8171-4.ch010

Möhring, H.-C., Müller, M., Krieger, J., Multhoff, J., Plagge, C., de Wit, J., & Misch, S. (2020). Intelligent lightweight structures for hybrid machine tools. *Production Engineering*, *14*(5-6), 583–600. doi:10.1007/s11740-020-00988-3

Moquin, Kim, Blair, Farnell, Di, & Mantooth. (2019). Enhanced Uptime and Firmware Cybersecurity for Grid-Connected Power Electronics. 2019 IEEE CyberPELS (CyberPELS), 1–6.

Moroni, S., Casettari, L., & Lamprou, D. A. (2022). 3D and 4D Printing in the Fight against Breast Cancer. *Biosensors (Basel)*, *12*(8), 568. doi:10.3390/bios12080568 PMID:35892465

Morris, B. B., Rossi, B., & Fuemmeler, B. (2022). The role of digital health technology in rural cancer care delivery: A systematic review. *The Journal of Rural Health*, *38*(3), 493–511. doi:10.1111/jrh.12619 PMID:34480506

Mukherjee, S., Gupta, S., Rawlley, O., & Jain, S. (2022). Leveraging Big Data Analytics in 5G-enabled IoT and Industrial IoT for the Development of Sustainable Smart Cities. *Transactions on Emerging Telecommunications Technologies*, *33*(12), e4618. doi:10.1002/ett.4618

Munawar, H. S., Hammad, A. W., & Waller, S. T. (2021). A review on flood management technologies related to image processing and machine learning. *Automation in Construction*, *132*, 103916. doi:10.1016/j.autcon.2021.103916

Murali, B., Padhi, S., Patil, C. K., Kumar, P. S., Santhanakrishnan, M., & Boopathi, S. (2023). Investigation on hardness and tensile strength of friction stir processing of Al6061/TiN surface composite. *Materials Today: Proceedings*.

Myilsamy, S., & Sampath, B. (2017). Grey Relational Optimization of Powder Mixed Near-Dry Wire Cut Electrical Discharge Machining of Inconel 718 Alloy. *Asian Journal of Research in Social Sciences and Humanities*, *7*(3), 18–25. doi:10.5958/2249-7315.2017.00157.5

Nagpure, S., & Kurkure, S. (2017). Vulnerability Assessment and Penetration Testing of Web Application. *2017 International Conference on Computing, Communication, Control and Automation (ICCUBEA)*, 1–6. 10.1109/ICCUBEA.2017.8463920

Nazari Jahantigh, M., Masoud Rahmani, A., Jafari Navimirour, N., & Rezaee, A. (2020). Integration of Internet of Things and cloud computing: A systematic survey. *IET Communications*, *14*(2), 165–176. doi:10.1049/iet-com.2019.0537

Nishanth, J., Deshmukh, M. A., Kushwah, R., Kushwaha, K. K., Balaji, S., & Sampath, B. (2023). Particle Swarm Optimization of Hybrid Renewable Energy Systems. In *Intelligent Engineering Applications and Applied Sciences for Sustainability* (pp. 291–308). IGI Global. doi:10.4018/979-8-3693-0044-2.ch016

Nkenyereye, L., Islam, S. R., Bilal, M., Abdullah-Al-Wadud, M., Alamri, A., & Nayyar, A. (2021). Secure crowd-sensing protocol for fog-based vehicular cloud. *Future Generation Computer Systems*, *120*, 61–75. doi:10.1016/j.future.2021.02.008

Ntouanoglou, K., Stavropoulos, P., & Mourtzis, D. (2018). 4D printing prospects for the aerospace industry: A critical review. *Procedia Manufacturing*, *18*, 120–129. doi:10.1016/j.promfg.2018.11.016

Öhman, J. (2016). New ethical challenges within environmental and sustainability education. *Environmental Education Research*, *22*(6), 765–770. doi:10.1080/13504622.2016.1165800

Osouli-Bostanabad, K., Masalehdan, T., Kapsa, R. M., Quigley, A., Lalatsa, A., Bruggeman, K. F., Franks, S. J., Williams, R. J., & Nisbet, D. R. (2022). Traction of 3D and 4D Printing in the Healthcare Industry: From Drug Delivery and Analysis to Regenerative Medicine. *ACS Biomaterials Science & Engineering*, *8*(7), 2764–2797. doi:10.1021/acsbiomaterials.2c00094 PMID:35696306

Ota, K., Dao, M. S., Mezaris, V., & Natale, F. G. D. (2017). Deep learning for mobile multimedia: A survey. *ACM Transactions on Multimedia Computing Communications and Applications*, *13*(3s, no. 3s), 1–22. doi:10.1145/3092831

Oz, H., Aris, A., Levi, A., & Selcuk Uluagac, A. (2022). A Survey on Ransomware: Evolution, Taxonomy, and Defense Solutions. *ACM Computing Surveys*, *54*(11s), 1–37. doi:10.1145/3514229

Pachiappan, K., Anitha, K., Pitchai, R., Sangeetha, S., Satyanarayana, T. V. V., & Boopathi, S. (2023). Intelligent Machines, IoT, and AI in Revolutionizing Agriculture for Water Processing. In B. B. Gupta & F. Colace (Eds.), Advances in Computational Intelligence and Robotics. IGI Global. doi:10.4018/978-1-6684-9999-3.ch015

Pachiappan, K., Anitha, K., Pitchai, R., Sangeetha, S., Satyanarayana, T., & Boopathi, S. (2024). Intelligent Machines, IoT, and AI in Revolutionizing Agriculture for Water Processing. In *Handbook of Research on AI and ML for Intelligent Machines and Systems* (pp. 374–399). IGI Global.

Palaniappan, M., Tirlangi, S., Mohamed, M. J. S., Moorthy, R. S., Valeti, S. V., & Boopathi, S. (2023). Fused Deposition Modelling of Polylactic Acid (PLA)-Based Polymer Composites: A Case Study. In Development, Properties, and Industrial Applications of 3D Printed Polymer Composites (pp. 66–85). IGI Global.

Palatnik de Sousa, I., Maria Bernardes Rebuzzi Vellasco, M., & Costa da Silva, E. (2019). Local interpretable model-agnostic explanations for classification of lymph node metastases. *Sensors (Basel)*, *19*(13), 2969. doi:10.3390/s19132969 PMID:31284419

Pan, Y., & Zhang, L. (2021). Roles of artificial intelligence in construction engineering and management: A critical review and future trends. *Automation in Construction*, *122*, 103517. doi:10.1016/j.autcon.2020.103517

Pareek, K., Tiwari, P. K., & Bhatnagar, V. (2021). Fog computing in healthcare: A review. *IOP Conference Series. Materials Science and Engineering*, *1099*(1), 012025. doi:10.1088/1757-899X/1099/1/012025

Pastor-Escuredo, D., Treleaven, P., & Vinuesa, R. (2022). An Ethical Framework for Artificial Intelligence and Sustainable Cities. *AI*, *3*(4), 961–974. doi:10.3390/ai3040057

Paul, A., Thilagham, K. KG, J., Reddy, P. R., Sathyamurthy, R., & Boopathi, S. (2024). Multi-criteria Optimization on Friction Stir Welding of Aluminum Composite (AA5052-H32/B4C) using Titanium Nitride Coated Tool. Engineering Research Express.

Paul, A., Thilagham, K., KG, J., Reddy, P. R., Sathyamurthy, R., & Boopathi, S. (2024). Multi-criteria Optimization on Friction Stir Welding of Aluminum Composite (AA5052-H32/B4C) using Titanium Nitride Coated Tool. Engineering Research Express.

Perera, C., Zaslavsky, A., Christen, P., & Georgakopoulos, D. (2013). Context aware computing for the internet of things: A survey. *IEEE Communications Surveys and Tutorials*, *16*(1), 414–454. doi:10.1109/SURV.2013.042313.00197

Perry, B. J., Guo, Y., & Mahmoud, H. N. (2022). Automated site-specific assessment of steel structures through integrating machine learning and fracture mechanics. *Automation in Construction*, *133*, 104022. doi:10.1016/j.autcon.2021.104022

Perwej, Y., Haq, K., Parwej, F., Mumdouh, M., & Hassan, M. (2019). The Internet of Things (IoT) and its application domains. *International Journal of Computer Applications*, *975*(8887), 182. doi:10.5120/ijca2019918763

Polychronou, N. F., & Thevenon, P.-H. (2021). Securing Iot/Iiot from Software Attacks Targeting Hardware Vulnerabilities. *2021 19th IEEE International New Circuits and Systems Conference (NEWCAS)*, 1–4.

Polychronou, N.-F., Thevenon, P.-H., Puys, M., & Beroulle, V. (2021). A Comprehensive Survey of Attacks without Physical Access Targeting Hardware Vulnerabilities in IoT/IIoT Devices, and Their Detection Mechanisms. *ACM Transactions on Design Automation of Electronic Systems*, *27*(1), 1–35. doi:10.1145/3471936

Prado, E. B., Moral, R. A., & Parnell, A. C. (2021). Bayesian additive regression trees with model trees. *Statistics and Computing*, *31*(3), 1–13. doi:10.1007/s11222-021-09997-3

Pramila, P., Amudha, S., Saravanan, T., Sankar, S. R., Poongothai, E., & Boopathi, S. (2023). Design and Development of Robots for Medical Assistance: An Architectural Approach. In *Contemporary Applications of Data Fusion for Advanced Healthcare Informatics* (pp. 260–282). IGI Global.

Pramod, A., Naicker, H. S., & Tyagi, A. K. (2021). Machine learning and deep learning: Open issues and future research directions for the next 10 years. *Computational Analysis and Deep Learning for Medical Care: Principles, Methods, and Applications*, 463–490.

Preuer, K., Renz, P., Unterthiner, T., Hochreiter, S., & Klambauer, G. (2018). Fréchet ChemNet distance: A metric for generative models for molecules in drug discovery. *Journal of Chemical Information and Modeling*, *58*(9), 1736–1741. doi:10.1021/acs.jcim.8b00234 PMID:30118593

Price, O. M., Ville, S., Heffernan, E., Gibbons, B., & Johnsson, M. (2020). Finding convergence: Economic perspectives and the economic practices of an Australian ecovillage. *Environmental Innovation and Societal Transitions*, *34*, 209–220. doi:10.1016/j.eist.2019.12.007

Punugoti, R., Duggar, R., Dhargalkar, R. R., & Bhati, N. (2023). Intelligent Healthcare: Using NLP and ML to Power Chatbots for Improved Assistance. *2023 International Conference on IoT, Communication and Automation Technology (ICICAT)*, 1–6. 10.1109/ICICAT57735.2023.10263708

Punugoti, R., Dutt, V., Anand, A., & Bhati, N. (2023). Exploring the Impact of Edge Intelligence and IoT on Healthcare: A Comprehensive Survey. *2023 International Conference on Sustainable Computing and Smart Systems (ICSCSS)*, 1108–1114. 10.1109/ICSCSS57650.2023.10169733

Punugoti, R., Dutt, V., Kumar, A., & Bhati, N. (2023). Boosting the Accuracy of Cardiovascular Disease Prediction Through SMOTE. *2023 International Conference on IoT, Communication and Automation Technology (ICICAT)*, 1-6. 10.1109/ICICAT57735.2023.10263703

Punugoti, R., Vyas, N., Siddiqui, A. T., & Basit, A. (2023). The Convergence of Cutting-Edge Technologies: Leveraging AI and Edge Computing to Transform the Internet of Medical Things (IoMT). *4th International Conference on Electronics and Sustainable Communication Systems (ICESC)*, 600–606. 10.1109/ICESC57686.2023.10193047

Puppala, H., Peddinti, P. R., Tamvada, J. P., Ahuja, J., & Kim, B. (2023). Barriers to the adoption of new technologies in rural areas: The case of unmanned aerial vehicles for precision agriculture in India. *Technology in Society*, *74*, 102335. doi:10.1016/j.techsoc.2023.102335

Puri, M., & Gochhait, S. (2023). Data Security in Healthcare: Enhancing the Safety of Data with CyberSecurity. *2023 8th International Conference on Communication and Electronics Systems (ICCES)*, 1779–1783.

Rahamathunnisa, U., Sudhakar, K., Padhi, S., Bhattacharya, S., Shashibhushan, G., & Boopathi, S. (2024). Sustainable Energy Generation From Waste Water: IoT Integrated Technologies. In *Adoption and Use of Technology Tools and Services by Economically Disadvantaged Communities: Implications for Growth and Sustainability* (pp. 225–256). IGI Global.

Rahamathunnisa, U., Sudhakar, K., Murugan, T. K., Thivaharan, S., Rajkumar, M., & Boopathi, S. (2023). Cloud Computing Principles for Optimizing Robot Task Offloading Processes. In *AI-Enabled Social Robotics in Human Care Services* (pp. 188–211). IGI Global. doi:10.4018/978-1-6684-8171-4.ch007

Rahamathunnisa, U., Sudhakar, K., Padhi, S. N., Bhattacharya, S., Shashibhushan, G., & Boopathi, S. (2023). Sustainable Energy Generation From Waste Water: IoT Integrated Technologies. In A. S. Etim (Ed.), Advances in Human and Social Aspects of Technology. IGI Global. doi:10.4018/978-1-6684-5347-6.ch010

Rahman, M. G., Chowdhury, M. F. B. R., Al Mamun, M. A., Hasan, M. R., & Mahfuz, S. (2013). Summary of smart grid: Benefits and issues. *International Journal of Scientific and Engineering Research, 4*(3), 1–5.

Rains, T. (2020). *Cybersecurity Threats, Malware Trends, and Strategies: Learn to Mitigate Exploits, Malware, Phishing, and Other Social Engineering Attacks.* Packt Publishing Ltd.

Ramudu, K., Mohan, V. M., Jyothirmai, D., Prasad, D., Agrawal, R., & Boopathi, S. (2023). Machine Learning and Artificial Intelligence in Disease Prediction: Applications, Challenges, Limitations, Case Studies, and Future Directions. In Contemporary Applications of Data Fusion for Advanced Healthcare Informatics (pp. 297–318). IGI Global.

Raphey, V., Henna, T., Nivitha, K., Mufeedha, P., Sabu, C., & Pramod, K. (2019). Advanced biomedical applications of carbon nanotube. *Materials Science and Engineering C, 100*, 616–630. doi:10.1016/j.msec.2019.03.043 PMID:30948098

Rasmussen, E. E., Punyanunt-Carter, N., LaFreniere, J. R., Norman, M. S., & Kimball, T. G. (2020a). The serially mediated relationship between emerging adults' social media use and mental well-being. *Computers in Human Behavior, 102*, 206–213. doi:10.1016/j.chb.2019.08.019

Rasool, M., & Khan, W. (2015). Big data: Study in structured and unstructured data. *HCTL Open International Journal of Technology Innovations and Research, 14*, 1–6.

Ravisankar, A., Sampath, B., & Asif, M. M. (2023). Economic Studies on Automobile Management: Working Capital and Investment Analysis. In Multidisciplinary Approaches to Organizational Governance During Health Crises (pp. 169–198). IGI Global.

Rayhan, A. (2023). *AI and the environment: toward sustainable development and conservation.* Academic Press.

Raza, M. A., Aman, M. M., Abro, A. G., Tunio, M. A., Khatri, K. L., & Shahid, M. (2022). Challenges and potentials of implementing a smart grid for Pakistan's electric network. *Energy Strategy Reviews, 43*, 100941. doi:10.1016/j.esr.2022.100941

Rebecca, B., Kumar, K. P. M., Padmini, S., Srivastava, B. K., Halder, S., & Boopathi, S. (2024). Convergence of Data Science-AI-Green Chemistry-Affordable Medicine: Transforming Drug Discovery. In *Handbook of Research on AI and ML for Intelligent Machines and Systems* (pp. 348–373). IGI Global.

Reda, H. T., Anwar, A., & Mahmood, A. (2022). Comprehensive Survey and Taxonomies of False Data Injection Attacks in Smart Grids: Attack Models, Targets, and Impacts. *Renewable & Sustainable Energy Reviews*, *163*, 112423. doi:10.1016/j.rser.2022.112423

Reddy, M. A., Gaurav, A., Ushasukhanya, S., Rao, V. C. S., Bhattacharya, S., & Boopathi, S. (2023). Bio-Medical Wastes Handling Strategies During the COVID-19 Pandemic. In Multidisciplinary Approaches to Organizational Governance During Health Crises (pp. 90–111). IGI Global. doi:10.4018/978-1-7998-9213-7.ch006

Reddy, M. A., Reddy, B. M., Mukund, C., Venneti, K., Preethi, D., & Boopathi, S. (2023). Social Health Protection During the COVID-Pandemic Using IoT. In *The COVID-19 Pandemic and the Digitalization of Diplomacy* (pp. 204–235). IGI Global. doi:10.4018/978-1-7998-8394-4.ch009

Revathi, S., Babu, M., Rajkumar, N., Meti, V. K. V., Kandavalli, S. R., & Boopathi, S. (2024). Unleashing the Future Potential of 4D Printing: Exploring Applications in Wearable Technology, Robotics, Energy, Transportation, and Fashion. In Human-Centered Approaches in Industry 5.0: Human-Machine Interaction, Virtual Reality Training, and Customer Sentiment Analysis (pp. 131–153). IGI Global.

Ribeiro, M. T., Singh, S., & Guestrin, C. (2016). "Why should i trust you?" Explaining the predictions of any classifier. *Proceedings of the 22nd ACM SIGKDD International Conference on Knowledge Discovery and Data Mining*, 1135–1144. 10.1145/2939672.2939778

Ribeiro, M. T., Singh, S., & Guestrin, C. (2018). Anchors: High-precision model-agnostic explanations. *Proceedings of the AAAI Conference on Artificial Intelligence*, *32*(1). Advance online publication. doi:10.1609/aaai.v32i1.11491

Rui, Z., & Lu, Y. (2021). Stakeholder pressure, corporate environmental ethics and green innovation. *Asian Journal of Technology Innovation*, *29*(1), 70–86. doi:10.1080/19761597.2020.1783563

S., P. K., Sampath, B., R., S. K., Babu, B. H., & N., A. (2022). Hydroponics, Aeroponics, and Aquaponics Technologies in Modern Agricultural Cultivation: In M. A. Mellal (Ed.), *Advances in Mechatronics and Mechanical Engineering* (pp. 223–241). IGI Global. doi:10.4018/978-1-6684-5887-7.ch012

Saleh, A., Zulkifley, M. A., Harun, H. H., Gaudreault, F., Davison, I., & Spraggon, M. (2024). Forest fire surveillance systems: A review of deep learning methods. *Heliyon*, *10*(1), e23127. doi:10.1016/j.heliyon.2023.e23127 PMID:38163175

Salehi, H., & Burgueño, R. (2018). Emerging artificial intelligence methods in structural engineering. *Engineering Structures*, *171*, 170–189. doi:10.1016/j.engstruct.2018.05.084

Salkuti, S. R. (2020). Challenges, issues and opportunities for the development of smart grid. *Iranian Journal of Electrical and Computer Engineering*, *10*(2), 1179–1186. doi:10.11591/ijece.v10i2.pp1179-1186

Salomon, D. (2003). *Data privacy and security: Encryption and information hiding*. Springer Science & Business Media. doi:10.1007/978-0-387-21707-9

Samantaray, S. R. (2014). Smart grid initiatives in India. *Electric Power Components and Systems*, *42*(3-4), 262–266. doi:10.1080/15325008.2013.867555

Samara, M. A., Bennis, I., Abouaissa, A., & Lorenz, P. (2022). A survey of outlier detection techniques in IoT: Review and classification. *Journal of Sensor and Actuator Networks*, *11*(1), 4. doi:10.3390/jsan11010004

Samikannu, R., Koshariya, A. K., Poornima, E., Ramesh, S., Kumar, A., & Boopathi, S. (2022). Sustainable Development in Modern Aquaponics Cultivation Systems Using IoT Technologies. In *Human Agro-Energy Optimization for Business and Industry* (pp. 105–127). IGI Global.

Samikannu, R., Koshariya, A. K., Poornima, E., Ramesh, S., Kumar, A., & Boopathi, S. (2023). Sustainable Development in Modern Aquaponics Cultivation Systems Using IoT Technologies. In P. Vasant, R. Rodríguez-Aguilar, I. Litvinchev, & J. A. Marmolejo-Saucedo (Eds.), Advances in Environmental Engineering and Green Technologies. IGI Global. doi:10.4018/978-1-6684-4118-3.ch006

Sampath, B. (2021). *Sustainable Eco-Friendly Wire-Cut Electrical Discharge Machining: Gas Emission Analysis*. Academic Press.

Sampath, B., Sasikumar, C., & Myilsamy, S. (2023). Application of TOPSIS Optimization Technique in the Micro-Machining Process. In IGI: Trends, Paradigms, and Advances in Mechatronics Engineering (pp. 162–187). IGI Global.

Sampath, B., Pandian, M., Deepa, D., & Subbiah, R. (2022). Operating parameters prediction of liquefied petroleum gas refrigerator using simulated annealing algorithm. *AIP Conference Proceedings*, *2460*(1), 070003. doi:10.1063/5.0095601

Sankar, K. M., Booba, B., & Boopathi, S. (2023). Smart Agriculture Irrigation Monitoring System Using Internet of Things. In *Contemporary Developments in Agricultural Cyber-Physical Systems* (pp. 105–121). IGI Global. doi:10.4018/978-1-6684-7879-0.ch006

Sasirekha, S., Priya, A., Anita, T., & Sherubha, P. (2020). Data processing and management in IoT and wireless sensor network. *Journal of Physics: Conference Series*, *1712*(1), 012002. doi:10.1088/1742-6596/1712/1/012002

Satav, S. D., Lamani, D. G, H. K., Kumar, N. M. G., Manikandan, S., & Sampath, B. (2024). Energy and Battery Management in the Era of Cloud Computing. In Practice, Progress, and Proficiency in Sustainability (pp. 141–166). IGI Global. doi:10.4018/979-8-3693-1186-8.ch009

Satav, S. D., Hasan, D. S., Pitchai, R., Mohanaprakash, T. A., Sultanuddin, S. J., & Boopathi, S. (2024). Next Generation of Internet of Things (NGIoT) in Healthcare Systems. In B. K. Mishra (Ed.), Practice, Progress, and Proficiency in Sustainability. IGI Global. doi:10.4018/979-8-3693-1186-8.ch017

Sathish, T., Sunagar, P., Singh, V., Boopathi, S., Al-Enizi, A. M., Pandit, B., Gupta, M., & Sehgal, S. S. (2023). Characteristics estimation of natural fibre reinforced plastic composites using deep multi-layer perceptron (MLP) technique. *Chemosphere*, *337*, 139346. doi:10.1016/j. chemosphere.2023.139346 PMID:37379988

Satybaldy, A., Hasselgren, A., & Nowostawski, M. (2022). Decentralized Identity Management for E-Health Applications: State-of-the-Art and Guidance for Future Work. *Blockchain in Healthcare Today*, 5. doi:10.30953/bhty.v5.195 PMID:36779018

Selvaraju, R. R., Cogswell, M., Das, A., Vedantam, R., Parikh, D., & Batra, D. (2017). Grad-cam: Visual explanations from deep networks via gradient-based localization. *Proceedings of the IEEE International Conference on Computer Vision*, 618–626. 10.1109/ICCV.2017.74

Sengeni, D., Padmapriya, G., Imambi, S. S., Suganthi, D., Suri, A., & Boopathi, S. (2023). Biomedical Waste Handling Method Using Artificial Intelligence Techniques. In *Handbook of Research on Safe Disposal Methods of Municipal Solid Wastes for a Sustainable Environment* (pp. 306–323). IGI Global. doi:10.4018/978-1-6684-8117-2.ch022

Senthil, T., Puviyarasan, M., Babu, S. R., Surakasi, R., & Sampath, B. (2023). Industrial Robot-Integrated Fused Deposition Modelling for the 3D Printing Process. In Development, Properties, and Industrial Applications of 3D Printed Polymer Composites (pp. 188–210). IGI Global.

Şerban, A. C., & Lytras, M. D. (2020). Artificial intelligence for smart renewable energy sector in europe—Smart energy infrastructures for next generation smart cities. *IEEE Access : Practical Innovations, Open Solutions*, 8, 77364–77377. doi:10.1109/ACCESS.2020.2990123

Shafiei, A., Tatar, A., Rayhani, M., Kairat, M., & Askarova, I. (2022). Artificial neural network, support vector machine, decision tree, random forest, and committee machine intelligent system help to improve performance prediction of low salinity water injection in carbonate oil reservoirs. *Journal of Petroleum Science Engineering*, *219*, 111046. doi:10.1016/j.petrol.2022.111046

Shafi, U., Mumtaz, R., García-Nieto, J., Hassan, S. A., Zaidi, S. A. R., & Iqbal, N. (2019). Precision agriculture techniques and practices: From considerations to applications. *Sensors (Basel)*, *19*(17), 3796. doi:10.3390/s19173796 PMID:31480709

Shahrubudin, N., Lee, T. C., & Ramlan, R. (2019). An overview on 3D printing technology: Technological, materials, and applications. *Procedia Manufacturing*, *35*, 1286–1296. doi:10.1016/j. promfg.2019.06.089

Shahzad, A., Gherbi, A., & Zhang, K. (2022). Enabling fog–blockchain computing for autonomous-vehicle-parking system: A solution to reinforce iot–cloud platform for future smart parking. *Sensors (Basel)*, *22*(13), 4849. doi:10.3390/s22134849 PMID:35808345

Shahzad, U. (2020). Significance of smart grids in electric power systems: A brief overview. *Journal of Electrical Engineering, Electronics. Control and Computer Science*, *6*(1), 7–12.

Shankar, R., & Singh, S. (2022). Development of smart grid for the power sector in India. *Cleaner Energy Systems*, *2*, 100011. doi:10.1016/j.cles.2022.100011

Sharma, D. M., Ramana, K. V., Jothilakshmi, R., Verma, R., Maheswari, B. U., & Boopathi, S. (2024). Integrating Generative AI Into K-12 Curriculums and Pedagogies in India: Opportunities and Challenges. *Facilitating Global Collaboration and Knowledge Sharing in Higher Education With Generative AI*, 133–161.

Sharma, A., Jain, A., Gupta, P., & Chowdary, V. (2020). Machine learning applications for precision agriculture: A comprehensive review. *IEEE Access : Practical Innovations, Open Solutions*, 9, 4843–4873. doi:10.1109/ACCESS.2020.3048415

Sharma, A., Saxena, B. K., & Rao, K. V. S. (2017, April). Comparison of smart grid development in five developed countries with focus on smart grid implementations in India. In *2017 International Conference on Circuit, Power and Computing Technologies (ICCPCT)* (pp. 1-6). IEEE. 10.1109/ICCPCT.2017.8074195

Sharma, B., & Vyas, N. (2023). Healthcare in the Aftermath of COVID-19: Charting a Course for the Future. *2023 International Conference on Circuit Power and Computing Technologies (ICCPCT)*, 1280–1285. 10.1109/ICCPCT58313.2023.10244828

Sharma, M., Sehrawat, R., Luthra, S., Daim, T., & Bakry, D. (2022). Moving towards industry 5.0 in the pharmaceutical manufacturing sector: Challenges and solutions for Germany. *IEEE Transactions on Engineering Management*.

Shea, K., & Smith, I. (2005). Intelligent structures: A new direction in structural control. *Artificial Intelligence in Structural Engineering: Information Technology for Design, Collaboration, Maintenance, and Monitoring*, 398–410.

Sheth, H., & Dattani, J. (2019). Overview of blockchain technology. *Asian Journal For Convergence In Technology (AJCT)*. http://asianssr.org/index.php/ajct/article/view/728

Shi, F., Wang, J., Shi, J., Wu, Z., Wang, Q., Tang, Z., He, K., Shi, Y., & Shen, D. (2020). Review of artificial intelligence techniques in imaging data acquisition, segmentation, and diagnosis for COVID-19. *IEEE Reviews in Biomedical Engineering*, 14, 4–15. doi:10.1109/RBME.2020.2987975 PMID:32305937

Shin, D. (2021). The effects of explainability and causability on perception, trust, and acceptance: Implications for explainable AI. *International Journal of Human-Computer Studies*, 146, 102551. doi:10.1016/j.ijhcs.2020.102551

Shi, Z., Yao, W., Li, Z., Zeng, L., Zhao, Y., Zhang, R., Tang, Y., & Wen, J. (2020). Artificial intelligence techniques for stability analysis and control in smart grids: Methodologies, applications, challenges and future directions. *Applied Energy*, 278, 115733. doi:10.1016/j.apenergy.2020.115733

Sidhu, T. S., & Xu, Z. (2010). Detection of incipient faults in distribution underground cables. *IEEE Transactions on Power Delivery*, 25(3), 1363–1371. doi:10.1109/TPWRD.2010.2041373

Singh, A., Sengupta, S., & Lakshminarayanan, V. (2020). Explainable deep learning models in medical image analysis. *Journal of Imaging*, *6*(6), 52. doi:10.3390/jimaging6060052 PMID:34460598

Singh, R. K., Aernouts, M., De Meyer, M., Weyn, M., & Berkvens, R. (2020). Leveraging LoRaWAN technology for precision agriculture in greenhouses. *Sensors (Basel)*, *20*(7), 1827. doi:10.3390/s20071827 PMID:32218353

Singh, R. K., & Khan, A. (2023). A Comparative Study of Quantum and Classical Deep Learning for Intelligent Agriculture. *Journal of Information and Computational Science*, 13.

Sinha, A., Neogi, S., Lahiri, R. N., Chowdhury, S., Chowdhury, S. P., & Chakraborty, N. (2011, July). *Smart grid initiative for power distribution utility in India. In 2011 IEEE Power and Energy Society General Meeting*. IEEE.

Sivamohan, S., & Sridhar, S. S. (2023). An optimized model for network intrusion detection systems in industry 4.0 using XAI based Bi-LSTM framework. *Neural Computing & Applications*, *35*(15), 11459–11475. doi:10.1007/s00521-023-08319-0 PMID:37155462

Soh, C.-K., & Soh, A.-K. (1988). Example of intelligent structural design system. *Journal of Computing in Civil Engineering*, *2*(4), 329–345. doi:10.1061/(ASCE)0887-3801(1988)2:4(329)

Speith, T. (2022). A review of taxonomies of explainable artificial intelligence (XAI) methods. *Proceedings of the 2022 ACM Conference on Fairness, Accountability, and Transparency*, 2239–2250. 10.1145/3531146.3534639

Sridevi, Sameera, Garapati, Krishnamadhuri, & Bethu. (2022). IoT Based Application Designing of Deep Fake Test for Face Animation. *Proceedings of the 2022 6th International Conference on Cloud and Big Data Computing*, 24–30. 10.1145/3555962.3555967

Srinivas, B., Maguluri, L. P., Naidu, K. V., Reddy, L. C. S., Deivakani, M., & Boopathi, S. (2023). Architecture and Framework for Interfacing Cloud-Enabled Robots. In *Handbook of Research on Data Science and Cybersecurity Innovations in Industry 4.0 Technologies* (pp. 542–560). IGI Global. doi:10.4018/978-1-6684-8145-5.ch027

Srivastava, A., Gupta, S., Quamara, M., Chaudhary, P., & Aski, V. J. (2020). Future IoT-enabled Threats and Vulnerabilities: State of the Art, Challenges, and Future Prospects. *International Journal of Communication Systems*, *33*(12), e4443. doi:10.1002/dac.4443

Subha, S., Inbamalar, T., Komala, C., Suresh, L. R., Boopathi, S., & Alaskar, K. (2023). A Remote Health Care Monitoring system using internet of medical things (IoMT). *IEEE Explore*, 1–6.

Sudmann, A. (2019). The Democratization of Artificial Intelligence: Net Politics in the Era of Learning Algorithms. Transcript Verlag.

Sun, Z., Luo, X., & Zhang, Y. (2023). Panda: Security analysis of Algorand smart contracts. *32nd USENIX Security Symposium (USENIX Security 23)*, 1811–1828. https://www.usenix.org/conference/usenixsecurity23/presentation/sun

Sundaramoorthy, K., Singh, A., Sumathy, G., Maheshwari, A., Arunarani, A., & Boopathi, S. (2024). A Study on AI and Blockchain-Powered Smart Parking Models for Urban Mobility. In *Handbook of Research on AI and ML for Intelligent Machines and Systems* (pp. 223–250). IGI Global.

Sun, G., Sun, S., Sun, J., Yu, H., Du, X., & Guizani, M. (2019). Security and privacy preservation in fog-based crowd sensing on the internet of vehicles. *Journal of Network and Computer Applications*, *134*, 89–99. doi:10.1016/j.jnca.2019.02.018

Sun, H., Burton, H. V., & Huang, H. (2021). Machine learning applications for building structural design and performance assessment: State-of-the-art review. *Journal of Building Engineering*, *33*, 101816. doi:10.1016/j.jobe.2020.101816

Sun, L., Shang, Z., Xia, Y., Bhowmick, S., & Nagarajaiah, S. (2020). Review of bridge structural health monitoring aided by big data and artificial intelligence: From condition assessment to damage detection. *Journal of Structural Engineering*, *146*(5), 04020073. doi:10.1061/(ASCE)ST.1943-541X.0002535

Suresh, S., Natarajan, E., Boopathi, S., & Kumar, P. (2024). Processing of smart materials by additive manufacturing and 4D printing. In A. Kumar, P. Kumar, N. Sharma, & A. K. Srivastava (Eds.), *Digital Manufacturing, Artificial Intelligence, Industry 4.0* (pp. 181–196). De Gruyter. doi:10.1515/9783111215112-008

Swamy, S. N., & Kota, S. R. (2020). An Empirical Study on System Level Aspects of Internet of Things (IoT). *IEEE Access : Practical Innovations, Open Solutions*, *8*, 188082–188134. doi:10.1109/ACCESS.2020.3029847

Syamala, M. C. R., K., Pramila, P. V., Dash, S., Meenakshi, S., & Boopathi, S. (2023). Machine Learning-Integrated IoT-Based Smart Home Energy Management System. In P. Swarnalatha & S. Prabu (Eds.), Advances in Computational Intelligence and Robotics (pp. 219–235). IGI Global. doi:10.4018/978-1-6684-8098-4.ch013

Tang, S., Shelden, D. R., Eastman, C. M., Pishdad-Bozorgi, P., & Gao, X. (2019). A review of building information modeling (BIM) and the Internet of Things (IoT) devices integration: Present status and future trends. *Automation in Construction*, *101*, 127–139. doi:10.1016/j.autcon.2019.01.020

Tan, S., Caruana, R., Hooker, G., & Lou, Y. (2018). Distill-and-compare: Auditing black-box models using transparent model distillation. *Proceedings of the 2018 AAAI/ACM Conference on AI, Ethics, and Society*, 303–310. 10.1145/3278721.3278725

Tariq, N., Khan, F. A., & Asim, M. (2021). Security Challenges and Requirements for Smart Internet of Things Applications: A Comprehensive Analysis. *Procedia Computer Science*, *191*, 425–430. doi:10.1016/j.procs.2021.07.053

Tebeje, T. H., & Klein, J. (2021). Applications of e-health to support person-centered health care at the time of COVID-19 pandemic. *Telemedicine Journal and e-Health*, *27*(2), 150–158. doi:10.1089/tmj.2020.0201 PMID:32746750

Tennyson, R. D. (2013). Artificial intelligence and computer-based learning. *Instructional Technology: Foundations*, 319.

Tharini, V. J., & Vijayarani, S. (2020). IoT in healthcare: Ecosystem, pillars, design challenges, applications, vulnerabilities, privacy, and security concerns. In *Incorporating the Internet of Things in healthcare applications and wearable devices* (pp. 1–22). IGI Global. doi:10.4018/978-1-7998-1090-2.ch001

Tibbits, S. (2014). 4D printing: Multi-material shape change. *Architectural Design*, *84*(1), 116–121. doi:10.1002/ad.1710

Tien, J. M. (2017). Internet of things, real-time decision making, and artificial intelligence. *Annals of Data Science*, *4*(2), 149–178. doi:10.1007/s40745-017-0112-5

Tijan, E., Aksentijević, S., Ivanić, K., & Jardas, M. (2019). Blockchain technology implementation in logistics. *Sustainability (Basel)*, *11*(4), 1185. doi:10.3390/su11041185

Tiwari, S., Bahuguna, P. C., & Walker, J. (2022). Industry 5.0: A macroperspective approach. In Handbook of Research on Innovative Management Using AI in Industry 5.0 (pp. 59–73). IGI Global.

Tjoa, E., & Guan, C. (2020). A survey on explainable artificial intelligence (xai): Toward medical xai. *IEEE Transactions on Neural Networks and Learning Systems*, *32*(11), 4793–4813. doi:10.1109/TNNLS.2020.3027314 PMID:33079674

Torky, M., & Hassanein, A. E. (2020). Integrating blockchain and the internet of things in precision agriculture: Analysis, opportunities, and challenges. *Computers and Electronics in Agriculture*, *178*, 105476. doi:10.1016/j.compag.2020.105476

Torres, N., Pinto, P., & Lopes, S. I. (2021). Security Vulnerabilities in LPWANs—An Attack Vector Analysis for the IoT Ecosystem. *Applied Sciences (Basel, Switzerland)*, *11*(7), 3176. doi:10.3390/app11073176

Tsai, C.-W., Lai, C.-F., Chiang, M.-C., & Yang, L. T. (2013). Data mining for internet of things: A survey. *IEEE Communications Surveys and Tutorials*, *16*(1), 77–97. doi:10.1109/SURV.2013.103013.00206

Tsouros, D. C., Bibi, S., & Sarigiannidis, P. G. (2019). A review on UAV-based applications for precision agriculture. *Information (Basel)*, *10*(11), 349. doi:10.3390/info10110349

Tufail, S., Parvez, I., Batool, S., & Sarwat, A. (2021). A Survey on Cybersecurity Challenges, Detection, and Mitigation Techniques for the Smart Grid. *Energies*, *14*(18), 5894. doi:10.3390/en14185894

Ucci, D., Aniello, L., & Baldoni, R. (2019). Survey of machine learning techniques for malware analysis. *Computers & Security*, *81*, 123–147. doi:10.1016/j.cose.2018.11.001

Ugandar, R., Rahamathunnisa, U., Sajithra, S., Christiana, M. B. V., Palai, B. K., & Boopathi, S. (2023). Hospital Waste Management Using Internet of Things and Deep Learning: Enhanced Efficiency and Sustainability. In Applications of Synthetic Biology in Health, Energy, and Environment (pp. 317–343). IGI Global.

Ugandar, R. E., Rahamathunnisa, U., Sajithra, S., Christiana, M. B. V., Palai, B. K., & Boopathi, S. (2023). Hospital Waste Management Using Internet of Things and Deep Learning: Enhanced Efficiency and Sustainability. In M. Arshad (Ed.), Advances in Bioinformatics and Biomedical Engineering. IGI Global. doi:10.4018/978-1-6684-6577-6.ch015

Ullah, H., Nair, N. G., Moore, A., Nugent, C., Muschamp, P., & Cuevas, M. (2019). 5G communication: An overview of vehicle-to-everything, drones, and healthcare use-cases. *IEEE Access : Practical Innovations, Open Solutions, 7*, 37251–37268. doi:10.1109/ACCESS.2019.2905347

Ullah, I., Ahmad, S., Mehmood, F., & Kim, D. (2019). Cloud based IoT network virtualization for supporting dynamic connectivity among connected devices. *Electronics (Basel), 8*(7), 742. doi:10.3390/electronics8070742

Vafadar, A., Guzzomi, F., Rassau, A., & Hayward, K. (2021). Advances in metal additive manufacturing: A review of common processes, industrial applications, and current challenges. *Applied Sciences (Basel, Switzerland), 11*(3), 1213. doi:10.3390/app11031213

Vanitha, S., Radhika, K., & Boopathi, S. (2023). Artificial Intelligence Techniques in Water Purification and Utilization. In *Human Agro-Energy Optimization for Business and Industry* (pp. 202–218). IGI Global. doi:10.4018/978-1-6684-4118-3.ch010

Varam, D., Mitra, R., Mkadmi, M., Riyas, R., Abuhani, D. A., Dhou, S., & Alzaatreh, A. (2023). Wireless Capsule Endoscopy image classification: An Explainable AI approach. *IEEE Access : Practical Innovations, Open Solutions, 11*, 105262–105280. doi:10.1109/ACCESS.2023.3319068

Veeranjaneyulu, R., Boopathi, S., Narasimharao, J., Gupta, K. K., Reddy, R. V. K., & Ambika, R. (2023). Identification of Heart Diseases using Novel Machine Learning Method. *IEEE-Explore*, 1–6.

Vellido, A. (2020). The importance of interpretability and visualization in machine learning for applications in medicine and health care. *Neural Computing & Applications, 32*(24), 18069–18083. doi:10.1007/s00521-019-04051-w

Venkateswaran, N., Vidhya, K., Ayyannan, M., Chavan, S. M., Sekar, K., & Boopathi, S. (2023). A Study on Smart Energy Management Framework Using Cloud Computing. In 5G, Artificial Intelligence, and Next Generation Internet of Things: Digital Innovation for Green and Sustainable Economies (pp. 189–212). IGI Global. doi:10.4018/978-1-6684-8634-4.ch009

Venkateswaran, N., Kumar, S. S., Diwakar, G., Gnanasangeetha, D., & Boopathi, S. (2023). Synthetic Biology for Waste Water to Energy Conversion: IoT and AI Approaches. *Applications of Synthetic Biology in Health. Energy & Environment*, 360–384.

Venkateswaran, N., Kumar, S. S., Diwakar, G., Gnanasangeetha, D., & Boopathi, S. (2023). Synthetic Biology for Waste Water to Energy Conversion: IoT and AI Approaches. In M. Arshad (Ed.), Advances in Bioinformatics and Biomedical Engineering. IGI Global. doi:10.4018/978-1-6684-6577-6.ch017

Vennila, T., Karuna, M., Srivastava, B. K., Venugopal, J., Surakasi, R., & Sampath, B. (2022). New Strategies in Treatment and Enzymatic Processes: Ethanol Production From Sugarcane Bagasse. In Human Agro-Energy Optimization for Business and Industry (pp. 219–240). IGI Global.

Verginadis, Y., Michalas, A., Gouvas, P., Schiefer, G., Hübsch, G., & Paraskakis, I. (2017). Paasword: A holistic data privacy and security by design framework for cloud services. *Journal of Grid Computing*, *15*(2), 219–234. doi:10.1007/s10723-017-9394-2

Verma, P., Sood, S. K., & Kalra, S. (2018). Cloud-centric IoT based student healthcare monitoring framework. *Journal of Ambient Intelligence and Humanized Computing*, *9*(5), 1293–1309. doi:10.1007/s12652-017-0520-6

Verma, R., Christiana, M. B. V., Maheswari, M., Srinivasan, V., Patro, P., Dari, S. S., & Boopathi, S. (2024). Intelligent Physarum Solver for Profit Maximization in Oligopolistic Supply Chain Networks. In *AI and Machine Learning Impacts in Intelligent Supply Chain* (pp. 156–179). IGI Global. doi:10.4018/979-8-3693-1347-3.ch011

Vijayakumar, G. N. S., Domakonda, V. K., Farooq, S., Kumar, B. S., Pradeep, N., & Boopathi, S. (2024). Sustainable Developments in Nano-Fluid Synthesis for Various Industrial Applications. In Adoption and Use of Technology Tools and Services by Economically Disadvantaged Communities: Implications for Growth and Sustainability (pp. 48–81). IGI Global.

Vijayakumar, G. N. S., Domakonda, V. K., Farooq, S., Kumar, B. S., Pradeep, N., & Boopathi, S. (2023). Sustainable Developments in Nano-Fluid Synthesis for Various Industrial Applications. In A. S. Etim (Ed.), Advances in Human and Social Aspects of Technology. IGI Global. doi:10.4018/978-1-6684-5347-6.ch003

Vyas, D. G., Trivedi, N., Pandya, V., Bhatt, P., & Pujara, A. (2019, December). Future challenges and issues in evolution of the smart grid and recommended possible solutions. In *2019 IEEE 16th India council international conference (INDICON)* (pp. 1-4). IEEE. 10.1109/INDICON47234.2019.9029044

Wang, L., Chen, Q., Gao, Z., Niu, L., Zhao, Y., Ma, Z., & Wu, D. (2015). Knowledge representation and general petri net models for power grid fault diagnosis. *IET Generation, Transmission & Distribution*, *9*(9), 866–873. doi:10.1049/iet-gtd.2014.0659

Wei, Q., & Zhang, F. (2019). Mining New Scientific Research Ideas from Quantum Computers and Quantum Communications. *2019 14th International Conference on Computer Science & Education (ICCSE)*, 1069–1074.

Welchowski, T., Maloney, K. O., Mitchell, R., & Schmid, M. (2022). Techniques to Improve Ecological Interpretability of Black-Box Machine Learning Models: Case Study on Biological Health of Streams in the United States with Gradient Boosted Trees. *Journal of Agricultural Biological & Environmental Statistics, 27*(1), 175–197. doi:10.1007/s13253-021-00479-7 PMID:37608853

Westermayr, J., Gastegger, M., Schütt, K. T., & Maurer, R. J. (2021). Perspective on integrating machine learning into computational chemistry and materials science. *The Journal of Chemical Physics, 154*(23), 230903. doi:10.1063/5.0047760 PMID:34241249

Xie, G., Liu, Y., Xin, G., & Yang, Q. (2021). Blockchain-Based Cloud Data Integrity Verification Scheme with High Efficiency. *Security and Communication Networks, 2021*, 1–15. doi:10.1155/2021/9921209

Xiong, Liu, Fang, Dai, Luo, & Jiang. (2020). Incipient fault identification in power distribution systems via human-level concept learning. *IEEE Transactions on Smart Grid.*

Xu, K., Ba, J., Kiros, R., Cho, K., Courville, A., Salakhudinov, R., Zemel, R., & Bengio, Y. (2015). Show, attend and tell: Neural image caption generation with visual attention. *International Conference on Machine Learning*, 2048–2057.

Xu, X., Weber, I., & Staples, M. (2019). *Architecture for Blockchain Applications*. Springer International Publishing. doi:10.1007/978-3-030-03035-3

Yadav, C. S., Singh, J., Yadav, A., Pattanayak, H. S., Kumar, R., Khan, A. A., Haq, M. A., Alhussen, A., & Alharby, S. (2022). Malware Analysis in Iot & Android Systems with Defensive Mechanism. *Electronics (Basel), 11*(15), 2354. doi:10.3390/electronics11152354

Yang, W., Wei, Y., Wei, H., Chen, Y., Huang, G., Li, X., Li, R., Yao, N., Wang, X., & Gu, X. (2023). Survey on Explainable AI: From Approaches, Limitations and Applications Aspects. *Human-Centric Intelligent Systems*, 1–28.

Yang, Y., Luo, X., Chu, X., Zhou, M.-T., Yang, Y., Luo, X., Chu, X., & Zhou, M.-T. (2020). Fog-enabled intelligent transportation system. *Fog-Enabled Intelligent IoT Systems*, 163–184.

Yang, G., Ye, Q., & Xia, J. (2022). Unbox the black-box for the medical explainable AI via multi-modal and multi-centre data fusion: A mini-review, two showcases and beyond. *Information Fusion, 77*, 29–52. doi:10.1016/j.inffus.2021.07.016 PMID:34980946

Yang, X., Shu, L., Liu, Y., Hancke, G. P., Ferrag, M. A., & Huang, K. (2022). Physical Security and Safety of Iot Equipment: A Survey of Recent Advances and Opportunities. *IEEE Transactions on Industrial Informatics, 18*(7), 4319–4330. doi:10.1109/TII.2022.3141408

Yang, Y., Luo, X., Chu, X., & Zhou, M.-T. (2020). *Fog-enabled intelligent IoT systems*. Springer. doi:10.1007/978-3-030-23185-9

Yan, Z., Zhang, P., & Vasilakos, A. V. (2014). A survey on trust management for internet of things. *Journal of Network and Computer Applications, 42*, 120–134. doi:10.1016/j.jnca.2014.01.014

Yazdani, A., Dashti, S. F., & Safdari, Y. (2023). A fog-assisted information model based on priority queue and clinical decision support systems. *Health Informatics Journal, 29*(1). doi:10.1177/14604582231152792 PMID:36645733

Yengst, W. (2010). *Lightning Bolts: First Maneuvering Reentry Vehicles*. Tate Publishing.

Younas, M. I., Iqbal, M. J., Aziz, A., & Sodhro, A. H. (2023). Toward QoS Monitoring in IoT Edge Devices Driven Healthcare—A Systematic Literature Review. *Sensors (Basel), 23*(21), 8885. doi:10.3390/s23218885 PMID:37960584

Yousuf, H., Zainal, A. Y., Alshurideh, M., & Salloum, S. A. (2020). Artificial intelligence models in power system analysis. In *Artificial intelligence for sustainable development: Theory, practice and future applications* (pp. 231–242). Springer International Publishing.

Yuan, J., Barr, B., Overton, K., & Bertini, E. (2022). Visual exploration of machine learning model behavior with hierarchical surrogate rule sets. *IEEE Transactions on Visualization and Computer Graphics*. PMID:36327192

Zaabar, B., Cheikhrouhou, O., Jamil, F., Ammi, M., & Abid, M. (2021). HealthBlock: A secure blockchain-based healthcare data management system. *Computer Networks, 200*, 108500. doi:10.1016/j.comnet.2021.108500

Zanella, A., Bui, N., Castellani, A., Vangelista, L., & Zorzi, M. (2014). Internet of things for smart cities. *IEEE Internet of Things Journal, 1*(1), 22–32. doi:10.1109/JIOT.2014.2306328

Zekrifa, D. M. S., Kulkarni, M., Bhagyalakshmi, A., Devireddy, N., Gupta, S., & Boopathi, S. (2023). Integrating Machine Learning and AI for Improved Hydrological Modeling and Water Resource Management. In *Artificial Intelligence Applications in Water Treatment and Water Resource Management* (pp. 46–70). IGI Global. doi:10.4018/978-1-6684-6791-6.ch003

Zeng, X., Hu, Y., Shu, L., Li, J., Duan, H., Shu, Q., & Li, H. (2021). Explainable machine-learning predictions for complications after pediatric congenital heart surgery. *Scientific Reports, 11*(1), 17244. doi:10.1038/s41598-021-96721-w PMID:34446783

Zhang, J., Wang, J., Dong, S., Yu, X., & Han, B. (2019). A review of the current progress and application of 3D printed concrete. *Composites. Part A, Applied Science and Manufacturing, 125*, 105533. doi:10.1016/j.compositesa.2019.105533

Zhang, L., Wang, Y., Li, F., Hu, Y., & Au, M. H. (2019). A game-theoretic method based on Q-learning to invalidate criminal intelligent contracts. *Information Sciences, 498*, 144–153. doi:10.1016/j.ins.2019.05.061

Zheng, X., Lu, J., Sun, S., & Kiritsis, D. (2020). Decentralized Industrial IoT Data Management Based on Blockchain and IPFS. In B. Lalic, V. Majstorovic, U. Marjanovic, G. Von Cieminski, & D. Romero (Eds.), *Advances in Production Management Systems. Towards Smart and Digital Manufacturing* (Vol. 592, pp. 222–229). Springer International Publishing. doi:10.1007/978-3-030-57997-5_26

Zhou, B., Sun, Y., Bau, D., & Torralba, A. (2018). Interpretable basis decomposition for visual explanation. *Proceedings of the European Conference on Computer Vision (ECCV)*, 119–134.

Zhou, S. K., Greenspan, H., Davatzikos, C., Duncan, J. S., Van Ginneken, B., Madabhushi, A., Prince, J. L., Rueckert, D., & Summers, R. M. (2021). A review of deep learning in medical imaging: Imaging traits, technology trends, case studies with progress highlights, and future promises. *Proceedings of the IEEE, 109*(5), 820–838. doi:10.1109/JPROC.2021.3054390 PMID:37786449

About the Contributors

Shanu Sharma is an Assistant Professor in the Department of Computer Science & Engineering, ABES Engineering College, Ghaziabad (Affiliated to A.K.T University, Lucknow). She has a PhD from Amity University Uttar Pradesh and M.Tech (Intelligent Systems) from IIIT Allahabad. She has 13+ years of teaching and research experience and taught various courses at the graduate and under graduate level such as Image Processing, Data Mining, Machine Learning, Data Science, Data Structures, Analysis and Design of Algorithms, and Compiler Design. Her research areas include Cognitive Computing, Computer Vision, Pattern Recognition, and Machine Learning. She has published 40+ research papers in renowned Conferences and Journals and is currently associated with various reputed International Conferences and journals as a Reviewer. She has edited various special issues in Scopus indexed journals published by IGI Global, and Bentham Science. She has edited five books with renowned publishers such as Springer, IGI, CRC Press, and River Publishers. She is a senior member of IEEE and also an active member of other professional societies like ACM, Soft Computing Research Society (SCRS), EUSFLAT, and IAENG.

Ayushi Prakash is a Professor in the Department of Computer Science and Engineering at Ajay Kumar Garg Engineering College Ghaziabad, Dr. A.P.J. Abdul Kalam Technical University Uttar Pradesh, She received a B.Tech. degree from Dr. R.M.L Awadh University, and an M.Tech. from the AKTU State University of Uttar Pradesh at Lucknow. She received her Ph.D. in Computer Science and Engineering from Dr. K. N. Modi University. From 2010 to 2024, she also has a continuous contribution in the Training & Placement Department in Dr. A.P.J. Abdul Kalam Technical University Uttar Pradesh. Her research interests span both Information retrieval and AI ML . Much of her work has been on improving the understanding and performance of search engine optimization, mainly through the application of data mining, statistics, and performance evaluation. Dr. Prakash is co-editor of3 upcoming book. Prof. Prakash, professional member of IEEE, professional lifetime member of Indgiants Association of Educators & Professional Trainers. She is the founding Chair & trustee of Prayatna Fikar Kal ki NGO. Wipro Certified Faculty for training program. She has received many best paper awards in international conferences. She has contributed to many International Conferences as an organizer, advisor, session chair, and reviewer. She has more than 40 research papers in renowned national and international journals and conferences and published many patents, chapters and research articles.

Vijayan Sugumaran is Professor of Management Information Systems and Chair of the Department of Decision and Information Sciences at Oakland University, Rochester, Michigan, USA. He received his Ph.D in Information Technology from George Mason University, Fairfax, USA. His research interests are in the areas of Big Data Analytics, Ontologies and Semantic Web, Intelligent Agent and Multi-Agent Systems, and Component Based Development. He has published over 200 peer-reviewed articles in Journals, Conferences, and Books. He has edited twelve books and serves on the Editorial Board of eight journals. He has published in top-tier journals such as Information Systems Research, ACM Trans on Database Systems, IEEE Trans on Engineering Management, Communications of the ACM, and IEEE Software. He is the editor-in-chief of the International Journal of Intelligent Information Technologies. He is the Chair of the Intelligent Agent and Multi-Agent Systems mini-track for Americas Conference on Information Systems (AMCIS 1999 - 2019). He has served as the program co-chair for the International Conference on Applications of Natural Language to Information Systems (NLDB 2008, 2013, 2016, and 2019).

* * *

Sandhya Avasthi is an Assistant Professor in Computer Science and Engineering Department at ABES Engineering College (Dr Abdul Kalam Technical University), Ghaziabad, India. She completed her PhD in the area of Machine Learning and Information Extraction. She did her M.Tech in Computer Science and Engineering from UP Technical University, Lucknow and B.E. in Computer Science and Engineering from Dr BR Ambedkar University, Agra. She has more than 18 years of teaching experience and is an active researcher in the field of machine learning and data mining. Her research interests include Natural Language Processing, Information Extraction, Information Retrieval, Data Science and Business Intelligence. She has published numerous research articles in refereed international journals, conference proceedings and book chapters. She is also contributing as reviewer in Springer, IEEE conferences, Hindawi, and Aging International Journal. She is associated as senior member IEEE, ACM and is continuously involved in different professional activities along with academic work.

Sampath Boopathi is an accomplished individual with a strong academic background and extensive research experience. He completed his undergraduate studies in Mechanical Engineering and pursued his postgraduate studies in the field of Computer-Aided Design. Dr. Boopathi obtained his Ph.D. from Anna University, focusing his research on Manufacturing and optimization. Throughout his career, Dr. Boopathi has made significant contributions to the field of engineering. He has authored and published over 180 research articles in internationally peer-reviewed journals, highlighting his expertise and dedication to advancing knowledge in his area of specialization. His research output demonstrates his commitment to conducting rigorous and impactful research. In addition to his research publications, Dr. Boopathi has also been granted one patent and has three published patents to his name. This indicates his innovative thinking and ability to develop practical solutions to real-world engineering challenges. With 17 years of academic and research experience, Dr. Boopathi has enriched the engineering community through his teaching and mentorship roles. He has served in various engineering colleges in Tamilnadu, India, where he has imparted knowledge, guided students, and contributed to the overall academic development of the institutions. Dr. Sampath Boopathi's diverse background, ranging from mechanical engineering to computer-aided design, along with his specialization in manufacturing and optimization, positions him as a valuable asset in the field of engineering. His research contributions, patents, and extensive teaching experience exemplify his expertise and dedication to advancing engineering knowledge and fostering innovation.

Mohammad Husain is holding Ph.D. Degree from Integral University, Lucknow, India in Computer Science & Engineering. He did his M.Tech. from UP Technical University, Lucknow, and a Bachelor of Engineering in Computer Science & Engineering from Amravati University in 1990. He has about 33 Years of Professional experience in the field of IT & Academics. Currently, he is working with the Islamic University of Madinah, Kingdom of Saudi Arabia in the Faculty of Computer and Information Systems. He also has industrial exposure and experience in Software Design and Development. He has published about 159 papers in different National/International Journals/proceedings. Dr. Husain has guided 14 Ph.D. and 11 M.Tech. Students. He has authored a book on the Principles of Programming Languages and contributed a book chapter in Advances in Computer Vision and Information Technology. He has given many lectures on the Gyan Vani Channel of IGNOU on All India Radio, Lucknow, India. He is also an active member of various International Journals, Committees, and Societies.

Mohamad Ishrat with a 20+ International and National academic career in Computer Science and Engineering, holds a Doctorate and Master's degree, showcasing his expertise. He is currently an Associate Professor at KL University (NAAC A++), India. Previously, he has authored many research articles Patents, Book chapters in the fields of Machine Learning, Data Mining, Deep Learning, and Future Networks etc. He has extensive teaching and research experience at various universities, including King Abdul Aziz University, Jeddah, KSA, University of Technology & Applied Science, Oman, and Integral University, Lucknow, India.

Wasim Khan with over 17 years in academia, is a seasoned expert in Computer Science Engineering. His educational journey, which includes a B.Tech., MTech., and a Ph.D., underscores a deep commitment to his field. He has made significant academic contributions, evidenced by numerous patents and a vast array of publications, including conference papers and book chapters. He is currently an Assistant Professor with KL University (NAAC A++ University), India. His research interests include machine learning, deep learning, social network analysis, anomaly detection, and network intrusion detection.

Sureshkumar Myilsamy completed his undergraduate in Mechanical Engineering and postgraduate in the field of Engineering Design. He completed his Ph.D. from Anna University, Chennai, Tamil Nādu, India.

Tanushree Sanwal is an Assistant Professor at the KIET School of Management at the KIET Group of Institutions in Delhi-NCR, Ghaziabad, and is a well-known teacher, and trainer in the education system. She had an illustrious career that spanned more than fifteen years in teaching and handling various administrative and academic positions. She has published numerous articles and papers in journals. She has extensive experience in teaching and writing in a variety of management disciplines. She also presented several research papers at national, international, and IEEE conferences. Ms. Sanwal has contributed chapters in different books published by Springer, and IGI Global. She has conducted and attended various workshops, FDPs and MDPs. Her research interests include social intelligence, human development, organizational behavior, and human resource management.

Narayan Vyas is an accomplished principal research consultant at AVN Innovations, where he is actively involved in research and development. He is also a Technical Trainer at Chandigarh University. He qualified for the NTA UGC NET & JRF in his first attempt, showcasing his academic excellence. He has extensive knowledge of the Internet of Things and Mobile Application Development and has provided training to students worldwide. He has published many articles in reputed, peer-reviewed national and international Scopus journals and conferences. Additionally, he has served as a keynote speaker and resource person for several workshops and webinars conducted in India. His research areas include the Internet of Things, Machine Learning, Deep Learning, and Computer Vision, Bioinformatics. He recently presented one article at the 2023 7th International Conference on Computing Methodologies and Communication (ICCMC) in the IEEE EXPLORE Digital Library [SCOPUS] and two articles at the 2023 International Conference on Artificial Intelligence and Smart Communication (AISC) in the IEEE EXPLORE Digital Library [SCOPUS]. He also works on various book projects with reputed publishers like IGI-Global, and De Gruyter.

Index

3D Printing 135, 244-245, 255-278, 280-281, 283, 285

A

Additive Manufacturing 135, 220, 255-262, 264-271, 275, 277-278, 280, 282-283, 285-286
AI-Driven Design 255
AIoT 289, 292-294, 297, 299-300, 303
Artificial Intelligence 49, 52-54, 79-83, 90-91, 98-105, 107-108, 111, 117, 120, 133, 135-140, 155, 157, 162-163, 165, 168, 173, 191-195, 217-228, 232, 246, 248-250, 252-254, 256, 278-280, 282, 284-285, 287-289, 293, 299, 303-308
Automated Machinery 141-142, 145, 147, 149, 158-160, 162

B

Big Data 22, 24-29, 45-46, 51-52, 54, 56, 104, 179, 253, 303-304, 306
Bioprinting 135, 255-256, 265, 268, 272-273, 277, 280
Black-Box Models 100, 105
Blockchain 26, 49, 52-53, 55, 59-77, 134, 157, 166, 168, 173, 194, 221, 223, 250-251, 291, 305
Blockchain Technology 49, 53, 58-60, 62-64, 66-70, 72-73, 75-76, 157, 291

C

Case Studies 26-27, 38, 58-59, 71, 73, 95-96, 135, 138, 169-171, 186-187, 190-192, 196, 199, 207-208, 212, 214, 216-217, 220, 222, 224-226, 228, 241-242, 246, 248, 252, 256, 274, 284
Climate Modeling 175, 184-185
Cloud Computing 1-2, 5, 7, 17, 21-22, 133, 140, 163, 191, 197, 199-200, 218, 220, 223-224, 252, 254, 279, 291, 299, 303, 305
Crop Optimization 169, 184, 190
Cybersecurity 39, 56-57, 89-90, 119, 138, 156, 160, 163, 191, 195, 253

D

Data Analysis 8, 10-11, 13-14, 24-29, 45, 51-52, 143, 156, 171, 173, 185, 202, 229, 291-292, 303, 306
Data Fusion 1, 8-9, 12-13, 20-21, 106, 138, 222, 252, 284
Data Migration 69-70
Data Privacy 48, 72, 108, 110, 117-119, 126, 139-141, 160-162, 171, 188-190, 201, 204-205, 292
Deep Learning 13-14, 22, 52-55, 79-80, 82, 90-94, 98-99, 101-102, 104-105, 134, 166, 168, 194-195, 205-206, 221, 223-224, 247, 250, 253-254, 279, 286, 293, 295, 299, 302, 305-306
Digital Twins 133, 244, 246, 255, 276, 278
DNS Spoofing 28
DoS 24, 26-27, 51, 90

E

Ecological Responsibility 107, 111, 115, 132
Edge Computing 24, 26, 50, 52, 64, 76, 157, 193, 201, 203, 215, 292, 299, 303

Environmental Sustainability 127, 129-130, 143, 152, 162, 169, 173, 176, 180, 182-185, 190, 242, 256

Ethical Considerations 81, 107, 110, 113-116, 118-120, 124, 127, 130, 132-133, 141, 143, 160-162, 171, 189, 199, 212, 217-218, 226, 228, 243-244, 246

Explainable AI 78, 82, 84, 88, 90, 94-96, 100-101, 105-106

F

Fairness 80, 96, 98, 100, 103, 105, 107, 117, 122, 124-127, 129-130, 132

Fault Detection 209, 288, 292, 296-299, 301, 303, 305

G

Global Food Security 169, 189-190

GPS Technology 141-142, 147, 149, 159-160, 162

H

Healthcare IoT Devices 203

I

Inclusivity 107, 122-124, 130-132, 161

Industry 5.0 139, 255-258, 262-263, 279, 281-283, 285-286

Intelligent Structural Engineering 225-226, 231, 238

Intelligent Systems 55, 106, 134, 196, 198-199, 208, 210, 212, 214, 218, 247, 251, 279

Internet of Things (IoT) 1, 23, 27-28, 37-39, 41, 45, 47-49, 52, 58-59, 67-68, 70, 75-76, 79, 137, 143, 154, 210-211, 251, 282-283, 291, 300

Interpretability 77, 82, 84-86, 94, 97, 103, 106, 244

IoT Sensor Data Management 58, 62-63, 68, 70, 73

IoT Sensors 4, 8-9, 46, 64-65, 67, 71, 141, 143-147, 150, 154-155, 158, 162, 201, 203, 207, 292

IoT Sensory 24-29, 45, 51-52

M

Machine Learning 11, 13, 32, 49, 52-54, 77-79, 81-82, 84-85, 98-101, 103-106, 108-112, 134, 138, 140, 155, 157, 162, 166-168, 179, 185-186, 193-199, 202, 205-209, 211-219, 222, 224-229, 231, 236, 242-243, 246-247, 249-250, 252-254, 256, 277, 279-280, 284, 286-287, 297, 299, 302, 304, 306

Materials Advancements 255, 266-267

MitM 24, 26, 28, 51, 53

Multi-Material Printing 255, 276, 278

O

Optimization Techniques 73, 226-228, 230, 233, 235-236

P

Performance Comparison 225-227, 236, 238, 245

Precision Agriculture 108-109, 112, 141-149, 151-153, 155-164, 166-173, 176, 178, 182, 185, 187, 190-191

Precision Medicine 134, 196, 212

R

RBAC 31, 36, 41-42

Real-Time Data Processing 18, 198-199, 203-205, 214, 218

Reskilling 119-122, 132

Resource Efficiency 109, 145, 154, 159, 173, 185, 187, 190, 201

Resource Optimization 141, 151, 153, 162, 179, 211

Responsible AI Development 107, 126-127, 132

S

Security 2, 7, 10, 18-20, 24-55, 57-64, 66,

69-70, 73-74, 76, 89-90, 99, 105, 117-121, 133-134, 137-141, 143, 156, 160, 162, 166, 169, 171-172, 174, 176, 179, 181-182, 188-191, 197, 199, 201-205, 211-212, 214, 216-219, 221, 223, 243, 246-247, 251, 276, 279, 282, 289, 291, 293-295, 297

Sensors 1-10, 12-19, 21-23, 25-26, 46, 58-59, 64-65, 67, 70-71, 75, 100, 104, 112, 118, 141-152, 154-155, 158-160, 162, 167, 173, 176, 178, 181-182, 185-186, 198, 201, 203-204, 207-208, 210-211, 223, 227, 229, 241, 243, 266, 269, 289-290, 292, 298, 303

Smart Grid 57, 165, 221, 250, 288, 290, 292, 294-299, 301, 303-307

Smart Meter 288, 294-295

Stakeholder Engagement 107, 127, 129-130, 132

Surrogate Models 86, 236

Sustainability 76, 107-109, 112-115, 117, 123, 126-132, 135-138, 140, 142-143, 145, 147, 151-152, 155, 161-163, 165, 167-169, 171-173, 176, 179-180, 183-185, 187-188, 190-193, 218, 220-227, 229, 231, 234, 236-243, 245-246, 248-252, 254-260, 263-264, 268, 277-278, 280, 284, 286, 290, 294, 304

Sustainable Employment 107, 120, 122, 132

T

Traditional Industries 107, 119-120, 132

Trustworthy AI 78

U

Upskilling 107, 119-122, 132

W

Weather Modeling 169, 171

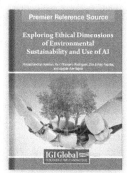

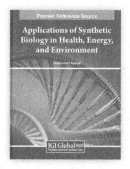

  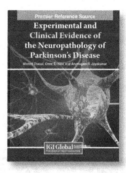